It has been truly wonderful to work with you. See you around the Point! — Judy

ADAM —
We will truly miss you around here. I can only imagine what our graphics would have been good w/c!! Be sure to stop by and give advice!
Mike Pater

Good Luck
Big Guy!
We'll miss you
Love, ka

Best of luck
to you Adam
— Michael A.

CONGRATS!
GOOD LUCK W/ YOUR
FUTURE ENDEAVORS!
—SHAWN B—

Good Luck! You're a great designer w/ many strong talents. One of the few who seems to understand the implications of creativity & the computer. — Eric

Adam —
Best of luck
to ya! I'll
miss ya.
Kathleen

ARCHITECTURE TODAY

JAMES STEELE

"NOT TO BE CONFUSED WITH "JSA TODAY" DON'T BE A STRANGER! —TODD

GOOD LUCK ADAM DEFINITELY KEEP IN TOUCH!! RON

Alles Gute und viel Glück. Wir werden Dich vermissen. Stefan

Best of Luck always— —Sue "

I'm feeling a bit blue that you're leaving but wishing you well none the less. good luck! Mark

Good luck Adam. Tho

sorry to see you go adam... Robin

GOOD LUCK ADAM... SO SORRY TO SEE YOU GO!! STAY ON THE SUNNY SIDE OF THE STREET. Tricia

YOU'VE BEEN A "BRIGHT LIGHT" AT JSA. GREAT GRAPHICS, TEAM PLAYER AND JUST PLAIN FUN! YOU HAVE A GREAT FUTURE AHEAD. GOOD LUCK. Jim

SEE YA! RICK

HURRY BACK, North

ADAM, BLAH, BLAH, BLAH. JOE

ADAM 12 GOOD LUCK AND TELL MS. STONE I SAID HI STAY IN TOUCH. KRISTOPHER

Good luck in your new job. Claude.

Best of Luck! Jerry

SURF INTO A MOST REWARDING AND PLEASURABLE FUTURE. DRINK TEA & STAY IN TOUCH. MARKUS V. Z.

So get outta here already! TOM E.

ADAM, It was nice almost getting to know you. Buy you a beer sometime. Tom W.

ALL THE BEST! Good Luck JIE!

GOOD LUCK ADAM STAY IN TOUCH... WE'RE ONLY A HAPPY HOUR AWAY! —SANDRA ☺

GOOD LUCK & HAVE FUN! GARY

YOU'RE A GREAT KID, HAVE A GREAT SUMMER! ☺ EVEN THOUGH YOU SAT AT THE OTHER END OF THE LOFT, WE STILL ALL KNOW THAT: YOU DE MANN! —TRACY

BEST OF LUCK TO YOU. KEEP IN TOUCH Tom H.

Catch that wave! Eileen

Φ

Introduction

ARCHITECTURE TODAY is subjected to a continuous barrage of critical and theoretical analysis, often with a particular ideological or political subtext. In contrast, this book aims to address the complex variety of issues that underlie contemporary architecture in a single sweep, without an agenda, or an axe to grind. It introduces many new topics, such as ecological and populist architecture that are just beginning to emerge, and each of the chapters that follow provides a marker through the confusing labyrinth of current architectural activity. There have been other attempts to provide such a verbal map, but these have not been comprehensive, contemporary, or unbiased. There has also, hitherto, been a hesitancy to make the markers clear by either naming names and identifying recognizable movements, or by providing visible examples of them. Such identifications are admittedly risky, but the time has come to dispel confusion. The verbal map in this instance has been made as legible as possible, to be accessible to a wide range of interests without excluding or patronizing its readers.

Architects, and others interested in what they do, are visually oriented and the issues presented here are, therefore, put forward in tandem with images of the buildings involved. This juxtaposition of expressed intention and built reality allows the reader to judge the extent to which theory has been transferred into practice. The concern has been with what we, as those who experience architecture, see in the world and how architecture can shape our lives. We not only see the built environment in a phenomenological sense, we also experience it as an integral part of our daily routine. Because of this focus, reference to specific buildings plays an important role in the discussion of each issue that is undertaken here, whether stylistic, regional or global. These examples, built and unbuilt, are predominantly recent, but include the foremost buildings completed by each movement. The result is a concentration of much of the significant architecture of the last thirty years; however, this has been generated by the framework of the discussion of the issues involved, rather than the desire to create a compendium. The images of architecture, as an integral part of our lives and our collective cultures, are used to draw the reader into the debate; the single volume format, rather than a series, was selected to focus that debate and facilitate the cross references that weave through the chapters.

These chapters have been organized thematically expanding in refraction through the lens of Chapter One, 'The Modernist Legacy', which has to be the starting point of any analysis of the contemporary situation. The extent to which many of the strands of the Modern Movement have survived and thrived, and have also perfected their own distinct personalities and *raisons d'être*, has provided a framework that moves from the specific to the general. The chief proponents of each of the strands that immediately follow the modern legacy, whether high-tech, rationalist, classicist, vernacular, ecological, or new modern, for the most part adamantly deny that they advocate or practice a 'style'. Demetri Porphyrios' famous caveat that 'Classicism is not a Style' could just as easily be adopted by any of the other directions discussed here, and for similar reasons. The purpose of Porphyrios' disclaimer is to draw attention to the fact that 'style', thanks mostly to the post-modern practice of layering, now implies the superficial application of formal elements intended to evoke a certain historical period or to reinforce a polemical stance without being integral to deeper philosophical intentions and is, therefore, derogatory. Recent comparisons between certain kinds of architectural expression and corporate packaging substantiate and expand Porphyrios' point. The increasing commodification of architecture is keeping pace with that of other art forms, and many would argue that it is leading them in its adaptation to popular culture. The notion of style as the ordered application of a certain belief system, in a positive sense, has become as increasingly suspect as positivism itself. The physical evidence of such applications is indisputable, however, presenting the critic with the problem of how to refer to the belief systems behind them without being fooled by appearances.

After each of these 'styles' or movements, which are often arguably regional in the sense that they can be identified with a certain locale, the sequence of chapters progresses to two global and two *sui-generis* conditions. These are respectively megastructures and world cities, and Los Angeles and Japan, which are larger in scope and defy inclusion among the first refractive directions; the latter two because they are intentional manifestations of a national imperative. As with the earlier chapters, these also cover a wide time span out of necessity, since it is difficult to reach any conclusions without discussing historical background or taking a wider chronological sample. Los Angeles has generally been considered to be a bellwether for America and has fostered that identification through the appropriation of image-making itself. As the final frontier in a country obsessed with boundaries, LA makes much of freedom of expression, the most critical component of the American dream, which it valorizes.

Japan remains similarly singular. Like Los Angeles it has been given a chapter here because it is also an anomaly, a seemingly infinite source of architectural innovation. The reason behind this, and the meaning of the work itself, remains elusive, but is essentially the result of two forces: an unprecedented period of social isolation, during which highly individual cultural conventions were firmly established, and an equally unparalleled, forced introduction into a different value system imposed by the American occupation following the Second World War. This intrusion set the stage for the phenomenal transformations that have taken place in Japan since that time. Because of the extreme circumstances behind that change, Japan remains a unique case study of the effects of the clash between tradition and technology, a country that transcends the usual 'first' or 'third' world categories and by doing so provides a prescriptive model for all.

FRANK GEHRY,
Guggenheim
Museum, Bilbao,
1991-7

From what might be termed two national object lessons in the directions that architecture may take in the near future, based on the interconnected premise of testing new urban typologies in Los Angeles and reconciling entrenched traditions and environmental integration with rapid urbanization and technical change in Japan, the chapters on megastructures and world cities chart the dramatic expansion of our conventional frame of reference at different levels of familiarity. 'Megastructure' is not just another name for a skyscraper, but conveys the international position that a new breed of high-rise towers now occupy. Superseding the city-centred high-rises of the past which were a source of civic or national pride, megastructures are digital beacons with multi-national allegiances that disregard borders. Respect in this context is proportionally equated with size, and megastructures have become totemic symbols of an interconnected system of global finance.

'World Cities' are the urban equivalent of the international position these towers occupy. The same global

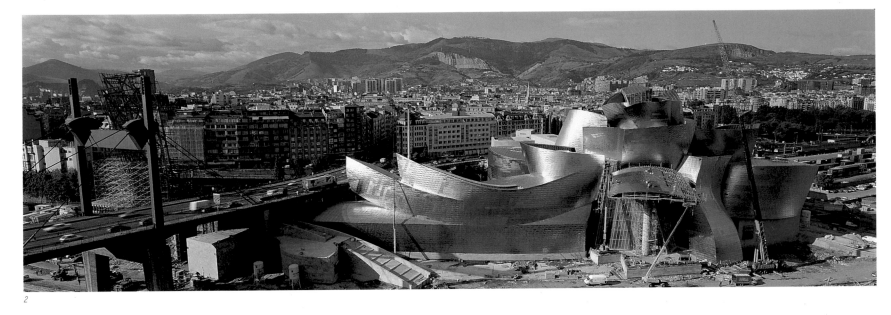

2

forces that have given megastructures wider status have also removed cities from their historical natural moorings. The transfer, in the last fifteen years, from an industrial to service economy in the developed nations and its corollary of industrialization in their developing counterparts has produced a second industrial revolution of greater magnitude than the first. The disparities of privilege and destitution which accompanied that upheaval are also present now; and the social and political factors that gave rise to the various initiatives leading to the formation of the Modern Movement in architecture are present again at a much greater magnitude. The final chapter brings this story, which is entering a new cycle, into focus.

The result of this cycle for architects, city planners and others involved or interested in the design professions, is an opportunity to learn from previous experience, to use history as a guide, to take direction from unprecedented past and present visionaries, and become involved in the numerous debates that are outlined here.

Attempting to interpret the beguiling array of colours that make up the spectrum of architecture today can be confusing, since the strands that connect the various movements, as well as the edges that separate them, are difficult to discern. The refracting prism that has created this spectrum is Modernism, however improbable that may seem.

Modernism, despite repeated declarations to the contrary, is far from dead; however, at the turn of the twentieth century, the very belief in progressivism, or the teleological notion that history moves inexorably forwards and upwards, that Modernism served to inculcate and sustain, has been called into question. Yet there is a growing realization that the modernist project is far from over and, indeed, may now be entering its culminating phase. That realization includes the caveats that

2

'functionalism' — as Modernism was characterized by its critics when they pulled out the long theoretical knives in an attempt to slay it in the early 1970s — is as inadequate a justification for design as the deliberate silencing of historical or cultural imperatives is as a method of levelling social differences. There is no doubt that an awareness of the irreparable damage caused by the culmination of rapid industrial growth in the West has, since the 1960s, made people question the goals of increasing technological change, and seek to broaden the definition of both technology and development to include concepts qualifying these terms, such as 'intermediate technology' and 'sustainable development'; and yet, Modernism — and the ideals that it symbolized — remains a powerful force, co-existing with and modifying further the refractions that it has created.

There is, of course, an explicit danger involved in attempting to identify distinct movements in contemporary architecture. Nominalism — or the urge to attach names to discernible trends or ideas — is increasingly generated from the rising influence of consumerism that now guides architects and critics as much as it does every other facet of contemporary life; and it is now rampant, making it difficult to separate fact from fantasy, or reality from the hype surrounding the latest commercial enterprise masquerading as theory. If this danger is viewed differently, however, and used to advantage, the task of differentiation becomes much easier. The intriguing feature of nominalism is that in our own increasingly image-conscious world, the act of giving something a title has the effect of making it real. In retrospect, this is not a new phenomenon; the term 'gothic', for example, was used by Renaissance artists and architects as a pejorative to define a competing theoretical construct which they wanted to characterize as barbarian: the destroyer of the classical tradition they were trying to revive. More pertinently, the Modern Movement — which is the starting point for each of the discernible initiatives discussed in this book which react to it in either a positive or negative way — was not itself legitimized until the publication of *The International Style*, written by the young Philip Johnson and his co-author Henry-Russell Hitchcock following the pioneering Modern Architecture: International Exhibition they curated at the Museum of Modern Art in New York in 1932. The basic dynamic evident in that act — of a name being allocated to a distinctly identifiable activity by discerning observers and that name, once recognized, causing consolidation and legitimacy as well as notoriety for those involved — established a pattern that has continued ever since.

The plethora of sub-styles and 'isms' that can be detected today can mostly be traced to the moment when the Modern Movement was conveniently declared deceased by critics in the mid-1960s; and each time a new movement is isolated and a name coined for it, the length of the cycle tends to accelerate, leading to a shorter and shorter 'half life' or fewer minutes of fame. This is due in part to the rapidly diminishing tolerance for stability in a world that has become accustomed to novelty and change, and the cycles of fashion and consumption have also begun to overlap, making parts of the spectrum even more difficult to discuss in isolation. The need for such a discussion, however, is long overdue. William Curtis, who has been one of the few historians to attempt a measured overview of the significant theoretical directions of twentieth-century architecture, sums up the issue best when he says: 'The historian who identifies with the interests of a single school or clique sacrifices the possibility of a balanced view ... Events, ideas, personalities blend into longer perspectives [and] movements once claiming complete opposition to one another are found to have shared some common ground ...' The problem with trying to formulate such a balanced view, however, is that the various 'schools' and their identifiable agendas tend to blend together, making comparative assessments difficult. Mindful of the sacrifice that Curtis identifies, this book is an attempt to make some sense of the myriad claims to truth being made by architects and critics today by first specifying what they are, and then examining their primary features, using key examples to illustrate their chief characteristics. The selection, divided into regional, stylistic and global influences, identifies a number of distinct areas, each of which represents an important contemporary issue. In doing so, it offers a survey of the disparate architectural activity of the last thirty years, but maintains, at the same time, a weather eye on the future.

Amid the scepticism that now surrounds the idea of progress, it is difficult to recall that there was a time, little over a century ago, when people believed that the future could be better than the present or the past. Modern architecture, which is now regarded as the singular tectonic manifestation of that belief, actually sprang from many apparently disparate sources over an extended period of time before being identified as an International Style as we have seen. The common theme that unifies these strands is the Industrial Revolution and the social changes that derived from it: factory production rather than domestic manufacture; the concentration of production and workers in cities, and the social upheaval that this caused. On another level, the new activities that industrialization fostered made it necessary to conceive new building types without historical precedents for architects to fall back on.

The history of modern architecture from the middle to the end of the nineteenth century is one of coming to terms with these two phenomena: radical social change and new building types executed in materials not previously available. The challenge to French neoclassical doctrine, as taught in the Ecole des Beaux-Arts, and presented by architects such as Henri Labrouste in his use of an iron structure inside a masonry shell in both the Bibliothèque Ste-Geneviève and the Bibliothèque Nationale in Paris of 1840 and 1868, respectively, comes to mind, as does the Auditorium Building in Chicago, 1889 by Adler and Sullivan, each of which exploited new technologies behind highly crafted external envelopes. Contrast these attempts to reconcile changing conditions with the impassioned lectures delivered by William Morris, the founding father of the English Arts and Crafts Movement, about the adverse effect of industrialization on the traditional art of architecture, which he characterized as: 'helpless and crippled amidst the sea of utilitarian brutality ... on the one hand it is cut off from the traditions of the past, on the other from the life of the present'.[2]

Some historians point to the demands of a far-flung Empire, as well as the profit to be made from developing it, as the reason why the ethic of production, or what has been called 'the élan of twentieth-century

1 (Previous page)
LE CORBUSIER,
Villa Savoye,
Poissy, 1928-31

2 HENRI LABROUSTE,
Bibliothèque
Nationale, Paris,
1868

3 LOUIS SULLIVAN
AND DANKMAR ADLER,
Auditorium
Building, Chicago
1889

3

4

5

industrialism' evolved in Germany and not Britain. Germany was so eager to compete for the markets that Britain had established that it: 'systematically studied the products of [its] competitor and by typological selection and redesign helped to forge the machine aesthetic of the twentieth century'.[3] In lieu of the colonial source of low-cost resources, and a similar market for its goods that Britain enjoyed, Germany focused on product differentiation through high quality. The Deutscher Werkbund, founded in 1907, was dominated by the personality of the architect Peter Behrens, who had by then also been appointed head designer for one of Germany's largest industries, the giant electrical concern AEG, in Berlin. The Werkbund was committed to the ideal of synthesizing industrial production and craft, and this ideal was further refined at the Deutscher Werkbund Exhibition in Cologne, 1914, which stressed mass-production, high standards and perfected 'types', in combination with individual creativity in order to increase the national share of global markets.

The success of this campaign is unfortunately most evident in the killing power of the armaments produced for the First World War, which followed shortly afterwards. Germany's defeat in that conflict, and the financially crippling effects of the Treaty of Versailles, led to its sudden economic collapse. Peter Behrens wrote in 1920 about food shortages, runaway inflation, the decline in public services and transport, and the public demoralization that resulted, calling for a 'transformation' that would lead to a 'passionate, moral renewal of puritanical severity' based on 'the imagination of the mind and the power of the idea'. It is crucial to an understanding of this formative stage of modern architecture to appreciate the missionary zeal with which this transformation was sought. Many of the leaders of the movement, such as Walter Gropius and Mies van der Rohe, had fought in the trenches and saw industrial production as the only salvation from the morass that Behrens described. The Werkbund Pavilion in Cologne, designed by Gropius and Adolf Meyer, illustrated the level of idealism accorded to production before the War, the close association between industry and cultural identity, and the essential relationship between this new means of expression and the academic tradition. Hermann Muthesius, who had praised the British Arts and Crafts tradition in *The English House*, published in 1904, proposed a craft-based curriculum in design education, integrated with industrial standardization as the most direct route to German technical superiority in the international marketplace.

The Bauhaus, founded after the War in 1919, marks the change in philosophical direction that the conflict caused. In its proclamation, Walter Gropius called for 'a new guild of craftsman, without the class distinctions which raise an arrogant barrier between craftsman and artist'. He envisioned the unity of art and architecture implied in the name of the school, based on the word

Bauhütte, or mason's lodge, reviving the gothic ideal that Morris promoted. It was no coincidence that Lyonel Feininger's woodcut for the cover of the Bauhaus proclamation was a stylized gothic cathedral: nascent Modernism in the German crucible of social crisis held on to its moral, aesthetic and religious Arts and Crafts origins which were pragmatically adapted to nationalistic purpose. Kenneth Frampton has shown how this was manifested in other contexts: Le Corbusier's 'Classical Mechanism', for example, was based on 'Greco-Gothic principles', and many German architects, such as Heinrich Tessenow, sought a 'will to form' based on 'a purified vision of the English Arts and Crafts movement'.[4]

Mention of Tessenow, who is known for his attempts to reinterpret a vernacular syntax in a normative manner, also raises the issue of traditional roots in

6

Modernism. These are manifested in such diverse forms as Charles Rennie Mackintosh's efforts to combine the Scottish vernacular with methods of industrial production at the Glasgow School of Art, 1897–1909; Mies van der Rohe's craft-based roots in Aachen, Germany; and Behrens' project to romanticize industry in his AEG Turbine Factory in Berlin, 1909, which carries with it formal echoes of traditional German barns, perhaps to make its newly urbanized rural workers feel more at home.

Whatever the extent of Western needs after the First World War, those in Russia were greater. Industrialization was underdeveloped and the housing crisis was severe. The common assumption that Le Corbusier with his Centrosoyus Building in Moscow, 1929, was delivering modernist wisdom from on high to a primitive Eastern outpost is superficial, however; Russia in the post-revolutionary period gave as much to the fledgling movement as it got. The Constructivists, who enjoyed a brief pre-eminence until Stalin frowned his disapproval, demonstrated the results of unrestricted experimentation as well as opportunities to realize significant projects, and Russia was an architectural testing ground of enormous and greatly underestimated importance. The creative crucible that Moscow represented at that time is recorded in projects such as Ivan Leonidov's proposal for the Lenin Institute of Librarianship, 1927, which offers a synthesis of form and function every bit as compelling and sophisticated as that of Le Corbusier and his contemporaries in the West.

Russia was also a magnet for Western architects, eager to observe such new developments at first hand,

Bauhaus, for example, both came to lead architecture schools in the United States — Mies at the Illinois Institute of Technology, and Gropius at Harvard — where each was to have a profound influence on an emerging generation of American architects.

For architects like Le Corbusier, who remained in Europe throughout the War, early post-War approximations of a utopian future such as his Unité d'habitation at Marseille, 1947–53 eventually gave way to a more humane alternative in the mid-1950s, prophesized by his chapel of Notre Dame du Haut at Ronchamp, 1950–4. By then, of course, the seed pod of Modernism had been successfully borne to the United States by German émigrés such as Gropius and Mies, but they, like Le Corbusier, spawned far less talented imitators who aped their style but did not share the ideological history of the movement. When the architect hero Howard Roark in Ayn Rand's novel

7   8

and to exhibit work of their own. Gropius, Mies van der Rohe and Erich Mendelsohn all held exhibitions in Moscow, arranged by the architect El Lissitzky who was one of the most important conduits between the USSR and Western Europe; he is generally credited with exposing Europe to Soviet art, a generator of the *Neue Sachlichkeit* — New Objectivity — in Germany in the mid 1920s, which was later proposed by Le Corbusier as a formal alternative to Expressionism and was ratified as doctrine by the Congrès Internationaux d'Architecture Moderne (CIAM) conference in 1933. Begun in 1928, CIAM was a formative device in the many housing programmes launched in Germany before the Second World War.

The War, of course, brought the first phase of the Modernist project in Europe to an abrupt close, and many of its greatest proponents fled from the tide of Nazism that flooded across the continent: the two former heads of the

The Fountainhead, published in 1943, refuses to design and later threatens to destroy a building that does not conform to his strict principles, readers are encouraged to equate modern architecture with purity of character; and it is clear that in the 1950s, Modernism in Europe and the United States was still synonymous with strong moral and social imperatives. However, the carefully woven and unselfrighteous monastic skein of the Modernists' garb, as well as the attempt to make Modernism the official architectural language of a socially responsible society, was ultimately lost in its commercialized translation from Europe into the United States mainstream.

All that remained of the modernist equation of unlimited possibilities and a better life through good design after its dislocation in the United States was an awareness of the product, not the process. However, the desire for a style of architecture that could accommodate a more leisurely way of life after the War was very real, and Modernism initially held out the promise that it could deliver it to an increasingly demanding consumer society. Initiatives such as the Case Study House programme in Los Angeles in the late 1940s and early 1950s showed the American public how modern architecture could be both homely and affordable, and its sponsoring publication, *Arts and Architecture* magazine, encouraged its readers to follow the example of pioneers such as Charles and Ray Eames – whose own house, Case Study House #8, 1945–9, is perhaps the most famous of the series – and to build in steel and glass, taking advantage of the benign local climate, and abandoning the tradition barriers between inside and outside in the process.

By the end of the 1960s, however, the architectural climate had changed. With the onset of the media age, lingering idealism, eroded by a decade of protest in Europe and the United States, was slowly converted to an obsession with image. Over the next three decades this became complete and public awareness of design, characterized by the Good Design movement of the early 1960s in Britain, focused on designers, name brands and product differentiation along with the increasing emphasis on advertising and consumerism that metastasized during the 1980s. Almost without knowing why, the public that had clamoured for ease of use and function after the War began to turn its attention to acquiring 'designer' goods, and fashionable social status increasingly became dependent on wearing or collecting the correct selection of designer labels. Furthermore, the increased leisure time that was expected to result from labour-saving devices, which started to become available on a mass scale in the 1950s, has remained a chimera. Paradoxically, technology has increased working hours as instantaneous electronic communication makes it easier to remain in touch with headquarters, while the home office remains elusively out of reach.

What has happened to Modernism – the only architectural movement ever to concern itself with the general public welfare – in the process? Public agencies and planning departments have largely usurped the architect's traditional role in the city; and paradoxically as urban populations continue to grow, and the housing crisis worsens, 'public housing' has become a pejorative term. It is no coincidence that it was the highly publicized razing of just such a public housing project in 1972 – Minoru Yamasaki's award-winning Pruitt Igoe development in St Louis, Missouri, 1950–4 – that was popularly seized upon by the critics as the final death knell of Modernism. The American architect Denise Scott Brown, has argued more insistently than many others, that a rising tide of elitism has been responsible for architects abandoning the modernist mandate to improve the lot of the masses. Unwilling to have their principles soiled in the marketplace, she maintains, they abdicated this responsibility at a critical time, during the rapid growth of suburbia in the late 1950s and early 1960s, leaving the field wide

9

10

open for developers. The New Urbanism that is emerging in America today may best be understood as an attempt to recapture that territory; the social responsibility that modern architecture ascribed to itself is best represented in this growing initiative; the first architectural movement to issue a charter and write a manifesto since the War.

The continuing crisis in public housing in the West, a silent but potentially devastating issue, is overshadowed, however, by the one billion people who lack shelter elsewhere in the world, raising the pertinent question of the global position of Modernism today. The transition in Western economies from a heavy industrial to a service or information base that began in the 1970s means that the industrial activity that caused all the furore in the first place is happening *again* and will continue, in successive stages, for some time to come.

11

This pattern of upheaval is matched in so-called Third World economies. The rise of a middle class in India at the end of the 1990s, based on the increased production of consumer goods, is one startling example of such change, and there are many others. In such instances all of the phenomena that accompanied the first Industrial Revolution — such as rural—urban migration, urban overcrowding, poverty, pollution, resource depletion and environmental degradation — are taking place again, on an even greater scale than before. Meanwhile, Modernism has suffered the indignity of becoming just another historical style, and as such is the architectural style of choice in many developing countries in the throes of this process. The reasons for this mostly revolve around image. Having taken second place in the race towards 'progress' over the last century and a half — or

even worse, having been exploited to make the race possible — these emerging nations, for example, Malaysia, now appropriate all the physical trappings of the West as they begin to achieve economic success, and modern architecture in cities such as Kuala Lumpur is the most symbolically potent commodity available.

The cycle of progress is faster this time around, however, as the social complications that are beginning to emerge in Japan indicate. The signs of anxiety and stress that are beginning to be evident in this model of post-war industrial development indicate how much the cycle from optimism to a sense of loss has accelerated in the last two decades. In many instances, other than in Japan, architects from the developed or post-industrial world are providing the majority of the modernist images and this time they seem determined to get it right. Wherever such renewed attempts occur, there is a sense of returning to an incomplete project hastily abandoned before its time. Claims of universality are tacitly understood no longer to be possible in an increasingly pluralistic age; nor is the expression of complete faith in progress, or in public institutions described through monumentality. What is still evident, however, is a reopening of the dialogue about the architect's role in the public realm, as a steward of natural resources and an unparalleled generalist, along with the secret wish to believe in the potential of technology and the power of the individual imagination.

Evolutionary psychologists have initiated a new field of scientific inquiry into what they propose is a mismatch between our genetic makeup and the dynamics of the modern world. In the course of studies on the human brain and the way it has changed as a result of natural selection they have put forward a 'mismatch theory' which connects higher levels of anxiety, depression, alienation, suicide and social violence to the advent of the industrial and post-industrial age. In America alone, they note, rates of clinical depression have been doubling every ten years and after automobile accidents and homicides, suicide is the third most common cause of death among young adults. Anxiety and social and environmental alienation can cause such unhappiness to develop into chronic, debilitating depression or what has been characterized as 'the disease of modernity'.[5]

This dislocation is the first clue to the difference between Modernism, as a historical period, and modernity as the contemporary condition. The threshold was crossed when optimism about the future changed to pessimism; Fredric Jameson has suggested that the assassination of President Kennedy in 1963 — possibly the first truly communal media event and the real beginning of the media age — is the psychological dividing line. As tempting as that theory is, the real issue is more complex, and a whole host of additional factors as epic as international financial disaster, the threat of nuclear destruction, and incurable viral plagues, have to be brought into the argument, along with many other possibilities.

It now takes a determined leap of faith to recall that the fruits of industrial production were once enthusiastically embraced as the means to unlimited possibility and that the complex group of forces now termed 'modern architecture' represented that belief, as well as the ideal that those advantages could be shared by everyone. The diversity of directions that will be described later indicate the extent of the attempts to rediscover this faith — or to propose viable contemporary alternatives — that can be found today.

The conventional view of recent history is that Modernism, seen as a unified architectural aesthetic, was supplanted by Post-Modernism in the mid-1960s. Modernism, however, was far from singular and continues to thrive in various manifestations, each of which has a distinct tradition of its own. Considered in the order in which they are discussed in this book, the review of significant contemporary influences begins with European Rationalism, which now has an especially devoted following in Germany, Luxembourg, Belgium, Northern Italy and the Ticino but is not exclusive to these areas. It is extrapolated from that part of the modernist aesthetic that promoted a Platonic ideal of universal beauty, continuing a tradition that extends from the architects of the French Enlightenment, through the Ecole des Beaux-Arts, to architects such as Giuseppe Terragni and Le Corbusier, whose work of the 1920s and 1930s perhaps represents the position best. Le Corbusier's concept of Purism, which draws on rationalist precedent, is clearly a rendition of the primacy of ideal form over the exigencies of function that was also to concern the rationalist Louis Kahn for much of his career. In such a view, the possibility of alternative forms for a given programme is impossible, since only one ideal solution to each specific problem exists.

After Kahn's death in 1974, the full responsibility for sustaining the search for pure platonic form fell upon the European Rationalists once again, led by architects such as Aldo Rossi, Mario Botta, Giorgio Grassi, Leon and Rob Krier, Oswald Mathias Ungers, and Josef Paul Kleihues, as well as the 'School of Madrid'. Each of these architects projected a particular layer of theory over that endeavour, ranging from Rossi's determination of types that have made up the formal structure of the city throughout history, to Vittorio Gregotti's premise about territory, expanded by Mario Botta into principles related to 'building the site', to Ungers' construction of 'cities in miniature' in a single building to offset atrophy in the urban environment. Europe generally has a better established civic tradition at higher densities than does North America, but expanding consumerism, so clearly explained by Fredric Jameson, has mechanistically begun to eradicate even this fundamental difference, pushing Rationalism into retreat on both sides of the Atlantic shortly after Kahn's departure from the scene. That situation has now changed, along with more realistic economic expectations and the rise of the political Right in Europe.

12

13

14 Jean Prouvé,
Maison du Peuple,
Paris, 1937-9

15 Ludwig Mies van
der Rohe, Crown
Hall, Illinois
Institute of
Technology,
Chicago, 1956

16 James Stirling,
History Faculty
Building,
Cambridge
University,
1964-6

17 Cedric Price,
Fun Palace, 1961

18 Team 4,
Reliance Controls
Building,
Swindon, 1966

14

15

16

Rationalism is finding a fresh voice and a newly enthusiastic following on the continent once again, irrespective of personal readings that individual practitioners layer over the hard-core principles of the movement.

Rationalism is relative and atectonic, in the sense that it is afunctional and unconcerned with details in the conventional modernist sense, focusing on typologies instead. This distinguishes it from the technological tradition, and the attempts of architects and engineers to come to terms with new building types, such as factories and railroad stations at the turn of the last century. The two traditions thus diverge at the point where pragmatic empiricism is required to solve unprecedented construction problems.

The willingness to embrace technology that characterized the architects of the Deutscher Werkbund and the early Modernists also underpins the contemporary High-tech movement which has emerged as a powerful direction in its own right. High-tech primarily focuses on fulfilling the socially ameliorating potential of technology that various branches of Modernism aspired to, but never achieved. Le Corbusier proclaimed in 1927 that architects should aim at fixing standards in order to address what he called 'the problem of perfection' and the adoption of new technical standards. He correctly identified a new spirit in architecture in which industry could provide new high-precision methods of construction, capable of revolutionizing the way architects build. His Cité de Refuge in Paris, 1929–33 was one of his most convincing attempts to carry that spirit into practice, and it initiated the idea of standardization that his contemporary, Jean Prouvé, was actually able to implement in projects such as his Maison du Peuple in Paris, 1937–9. This was also in part the inspiration behind James Stirling's attempts to substitute 'ready-mades' for prefabrication at the History Faculty Building in Cambridge of 1964–6 and the Leicester University Engineering Building, 1959–63, which are on the periphery rather than in the mainstream of the high-tech aesthetic. They were not as successful as Prouvé's adaptation of industrial systems, however, since Stirling's off-the-shelf parts eventually required custom fitting and led to serious problems of maintenance and poor functional performance.

Most easily recognizable in the highly visible and frequently publicized work of such proponents as Norman Foster, Richard Rogers and Nicholas Grimshaw, High-tech has evolved from the Miesian search for 'universal space' as exemplified in his Crown Hall, at the Illinois Institute of Technology in Chicago, 1956, along with an emphasis on the industrialization of building components as propounded by pioneers such as Prouvé. This synthesis is exemplified in the systematic expression of domestic functions achieved by Charles and Ray Eames in their house in Pacific Palisades, and the Fun Palace project by Cedric Price, 1961, among other precedents which have each compounded the ideal of an internal environment freed from the uncertainty that nature is prone to, and made perfect by technology. This technological utopianism is the primary identifying marker of the high-tech movement, whose participants adamantly refuse to be bracketed under the banner of a 'style'. In their celebrations of engineering excellence — which can be seen as the fulfilment of Mies van der Rohe's mandate to 'express the technology of the times' — high-tech architects have nonetheless created a recognizable idiom, based on the articulation and amplification of the means of production of each of the components and the systems that comprise a building. Other typical features of the genre include an undivided shed-like enclosure — as exemplified by Team 4's Reliance Controls building in Swindon, of 1966 — fed by either a serviced wrapper or clusters, housing mechanical, electrical, sanitary and transportation systems to provide optimum 'flexibility' of use and to make the internal environment as climatically independent from the outside and as free from mechanically sourced energy systems as possible. Perhaps the ultimate exemplar in this regard is the

17

18

Centre Pompidou, designed by Renzo Piano and Richard Rogers in 1971–8, which draws together all these threads, taking the Fun Palace as its point of departure and signalling a new way of approaching the viewing of both art and building in the city, and raising the notion of a mechanically serviced 'machine for culture' in the process. Along with European Rationalism and High-tech, Minimalism is the third most obvious regional manifestation of a distinct aspect of Modernism today. It represents an aesthetic and social reaction to contemporary consumerism, which in retrospect, can be traced to Mackintosh's remarkable efforts to eliminate the suffocating clutter of the Victorian parlour, following Morris' axiom of having 'nothing in your house which you do not feel to be beautiful or know to be useful' and the inspiration of spare Japanese interiors which were just beginning to be published in Europe and America towards the end of the nineteenth century. In the early twentieth century,

19 Luis Barragán,
Egerstrom
Residence and
Stables ('San
Cristobal'), Los
Clubes, Mexico
City, 1968

20 Ludwig Mies
van der Rohe,
Farnsworth House,
Plano, Illinois,
1945–51

21 Donald Judd,
Arena,
Installation
View, Marfa,
Texas, 1992

22 Demetri
Porphyrios,
Battery Park City
Pavilion, New
York, 1990

23 Adolf Loos,
Chicago Tribune
Tower Competition
Entry, 1922

19

20

21

Mies van der Rohe's edict that 'less is more' took the Arts and Crafts mission forwards into a belief system directly related to the free flow of space between inside and outside that Modernists such as Mies were trying to foster.

Contemporary Minimalism, however, goes far beyond such faith in reductivism, and has been fed by explorations in the fine arts and especially in sculptural installations by artists such as Donald Judd. Judd's crossover into architecture in the 1980s is a graphic indication of the close ties that have been established between the two disciplines in this area; ties which are frequently overlooked in discussion about repairing the schism that supposedly exists between art and architecture today. While it is seemingly antithetical to the high-tech celebration of production through a virtuoso display of materiality, structure and servicing hardware, Minimalism, especially as defined by architects such as Alvaro Siza, Tadao Ando and John Pawson, emanates from

22

the same space-positive tradition; reductivism in their hands accentuates planar geometry and inner volume. There is a similar root in the work of architects from earlier in the century such as Luis Barragán and Mies van der Rohe. Mies' attitude towards expressing technology further implies the engineering concept of design excellence, of reducing a component, volume or spatial system, to its essence. In buildings such as the Barcelona Pavilion, 1929, or the Farnsworth House, of twenty years later, which have become the iconic Miesian models of such minimalist reduction, this credo is evident at every level, from the way materials are joined, through space planning, to furniture design.

Minimalist art and architecture gained momentum in the late 1960s in opposition to the growing popularity of its Pop alter ego. Both movements, however, share a common search for essentials. In populist architecture, as in its Pop artistic equivalent, this has been related to discovering the conventions of representation in an attempt to uncover the way in which tectonic messages are sent and received. In minimalist architecture this exploration goes far beyond a reductivist aesthetic into the realm of renewed spatial exploration and subtle social protest.

In stark contrast to the minimalist position, the classical revival in architecture which offers pockets of entrenched anti-modernist resistance in Europe and the United States is viewed by its proponents as the continuation of a centuries-long tradition and part of an ongoing attempt to find renewed meaning in the classical language of Greece and Rome, which is considered by its proponents, such as Demetri Porphyrios, Jaquelin Robertson and Quinlan Terry, to have timeless significance and infinite possibilities for personal expression within established convention. Such a position, however, is peculiarly myopic, since Classicism represented a rich generic source during the formative period of modern architecture. Among the various streams of that source, it should be sufficient to mention the Beaux-Arts basis for Rationalism, as well as Henri Labrouste's structural explorations, which expanded rather than denied his classical training by drawing in Greek examples to be added to the Roman prototypes upon which the Academy restrictively insisted. As additional references, there is the enormous influence that Karl Friedrich Schinkel and especially his Altes Museum in Berlin, 1830, had on modern pioneers such as Mies, as well as the philosophical struggle that Adolf Loos flaunted in his conviction that Classicism represented the clearest example of a historical vernacular and that contemporary architects had to come to terms with its disjunction. His famous submission for the Chicago Tribune competition of 1922, in which he proposed a Doric column converted into a high-rise tower, was less tongue-in-cheek than is often assumed. He saw it as a clear symbol of the conflict between the most enduring historical vernacular system of all and the fragmentary nature of contemporary culture.

Classicism has also been the wellspring for Post-Modernism, which should not be surprising, since this movement is a commentary on, rather than a refutation of, the Modernism it is often erroneously characterized as replacing. Robert Venturi, who is usually given paternal responsibility for starting the commentary with his *Complexity and Contradiction in Architecture* published in 1966, came to the association through his intense analysis of Renaissance architecture, his winning the Rome Prize, and the patronage of Jean Labatat in Princeton. The house that Venturi designed for his mother, Vanna Venturi, in Philadelphia, of 1963, is generally accepted as one of the icons of nascent Post-Modernism. Venturi's friend, Vincent Scully, whose own brilliant study of the integral connection between Greek temples and prominent landscape features in *Earth, the Temple and the Gods: Greek Sacred Architecture*, which became required reading for

23

post-modernist converts in the late 1960s, has painstakingly described the depth of the classical connection in another Venturi project, the Delaware House, 1978, in which a loggia with flattened Doric columns is placed in front of the intentionally barn-like structure, meant to echo local rural vernacular buildings. The cartoon-like columns, according to Scully, are intended as a didactic reminder of the deciduous source of the classical orders, and the column as stylized tree, a connection that is prompted by the forest which forms a backdrop to the house.

Michael Graves, who along with Charles Moore, is the third most influential original protagonist of post-modern architecture, converted to Classicism as a resource because of the anthropomorphic rather than organic connections it has. His dramatic shift away from a strictly Corbusian language in the 1970s and 1980s, in projects such as the Plocek House, 1982, was prompted as much by a desire to establish a more overtly human link with his architecture as it was by his perception of the limits of the Corbusian Five Points.

The tendency towards didacticism, which Venturi shares with the late Louis Kahn, continues as a theme over

pure vision being mangled by less talented interpreters, was acerbically addressed by Venturi in his Walter Gropius lecture at Harvard University in 1982.[6] In it, he decried the rejection of Modernism as an ethos as well as a style by an army of theorists who jumped on the band wagon he had inadvertently helped to construct.

Rather than being *post facto*, as much of post-modern theory has tended to be, Deconstructivism seems to have been willed into existence, *a priori*. Post-Modernism evolved through its own pioneer phase, from a diverse first wave of interpreters including Venturi and Scott Brown, Moore and Graves, through a second that included but was not confined to Robert Stern, Paolo Portoghesi, James Stirling and Hans Hollein. Deconstructivism, on the other hand, has been more focused, with a much shorter period of development and list of perpetuating instigators that includes Peter Eisenman, Bernard Tschumi, Zaha Hadid and Coop Himmelblau. All these architects draw strength in one way or another from the theory of French deconstruction philosopher Jacques Derrida, with secondary layers of intention evident in some instances.

24

25

26

the three most influential decades of the firm. Through deliberate lack of seriousness, heightened superficiality and irony, rather than sheer historicism — which places it firmly in the post-modernist camp — Venturi and Scott Brown turned the Sainsbury Wing extension to the National Gallery in London, completed in 1991, into a post-modern polemic, showing that it is difficult but entirely possible to make distinctions between free-style Classicism and its more knowing stylistic cousin. Few movements have generated as sizable a theoretical apologia as Post-Modernism has, and with so little effect, and promoters of Post-Modernism are still trying to argue that it is a viable style. The original aspect of commentary engaged by Venturi and Scott Brown, Moore and Graves soon degenerated into a hermeneutic dialogue that was devoid of any intention of popular communication, of finding a historically and culturally meaningful semiotic system in architecture that could psychologically and emotionally engage the public in the same way that Classicism combined aesthetic pleasure with cultural mythology. The additional parallel with Modernism, of a

The brevity of the half-life of Deconstructivism, as well as the small number of its practitioners and the narrow source of their theoretical base, does not seem to have detracted from an equal capacity for confusion, a surprising dearth of explanation amidst an avalanche of supposition. Deconstructivism, based on a philosophical position related to the deconstruction of text, has ironically generated reams of it, as well as a great deal of paper architecture, the last gasp of architectural graphics before the computer revolution began in earnest. Tschumi and Hadid have both established a delineated corpus of work that has been equally as influential as its built equivalent; the formal over-statement of the game with its acute angles and intentionally distorted perspectives paradoxically the product of the media age. They have each evoked Constructivism and Suprematism respectively, layering these Russian variants over Derridean theory, and returning the argument to the egalitarian modernist experiment that they represent.

The connection that leading Deconstructivists have made to important sources of Modernism has been

27

28

overt, as a polemical move to reinitiate a debate that was abruptly repressed. The connection between modern vernacular architecture and such sources is less directly traceable, but equally important. Post-modernist diehards, who refuse to concede that the fifteen minutes of fame allotted to this movement is over, have attempted to characterize instances of contemporary vernacular expression as a continuation of Post-Modernism because of its historicist component.

That view, however, is as superficial as most Post-Modernist architecture. The more interesting and critical issue is the extent to which the proponents of a rediscovery of an appropriate vernacular language have been influenced by Modernism, whether they acknowledge it or not, and the implications of such influence on a reconciliation between the pervasive inroads of a new 'international style' and regional traditions. Seminal vernacularists, such as the Egyptian Hassan Fathy, have sought to exorcise their cultures from what they saw as a continuation of the colonial yoke, reconfigured in concrete, glass and steel, but could not finally free themselves from the subliminal intellectual constructs of that colonial past. This dilemma is crucial because it means that it is virtually impossible to recapture a pure tradition since all interpretation has now been compromised by external values. A second generation of architects, such as Balkrishna Doshi in India, have realized that this compromise exists and have been more realistic in attempting to formulate an appropriate tectonic language for their country. Doshi is in a particularly fortuitous position to attempt such a formulation, given his experience of working with both Le Corbusier and Kahn, and his broad knowledge of Indian architectural and cultural history. His deliberate attempt to perfect the modern project in India by bringing it into conformance with historical precedents and environmental imperatives indicates the potential of modern vernacular today. Other talented advocates of this position, such as Rasem Badran in Jordan, and Abdel Wahed El-Wakil in Saudi Arabia, have yet to reach this point of acceptance, but their work presents a similar synthesis nonetheless, focused towards the reaffirmation of cultural singularity in their particular situations.

The quest for individuality of a different sort is the main concern of an identifiable contingent of architects referred to here as the new expressionists, who are reinventing the rearguard action that slowed Le Corbusier's doctrinaire institutionalization of functionalism at the CIAM Conference in 1933. The founders of the expressionist movement, among them Erich Mendelsohn, Hans Scharoun, Bruno Taut, Hugo Häring, and Hans Poelzig, were of the belief that individual imagination is equally as valid as rational determinism as a means of fulfilling the modernist desire to blend craft and industrial production, to express the nature of materials, and the primacy of space through structure, circulation and light. This tendency has been framed differently in Europe and America with Frank Lloyd Wright forming the role model for the

latter. His followers, branching out from Bruce Goff, call their work 'organic' in direct reference to Wright's attempt to blend architecture and nature, and they defy theoretical analysis by claiming to disdain it. The contemporary European resurgence differs from its American counterpart in being more cerebral and more theoretically focused. The conditions that have forced a softening of the rationalist position have been seized as a sign of freedom by European expressionists. They have taken the opportunity to recover ground lost during the formative phase of Modernism, and finally fulfil the visionary methodology perfected by architects such as Taut and Hans Scharoun during their 'Glass Chain' Correspondence in the early 1920s. Contemporary architects, such as Günther Domenig and Zvi Hecker, among many others, have breathed new life into the expressionist movement. Hecker's Heinz-Galinski School, 1990, is an impressive indication that this approach, which was believed to have virtually died out in Berlin after Hans Scharoun's Philharmonie in the mid-1960s, is gaining new strength there, bringing the story around full circle at its point of origin.

The organic imperative is equally powerful in ecological architecture, but without the expressionists' insistence on individuality. Also called 'sustainable', or 'green', architecture, it has now generated a flurry of commentary. However, as much as people continue to talk about it, no one really seems to understand what it means. Of all the issues discussed here, sustainability is the only officially conceived, conference-driven movement, in the sense that it has been intentionally formulated through a series of United Nations sanctioned initiatives. The evolution of this movement can be seen as a reconciliation of the growth – or development orientated – and no-growth, environmentally protective factions that had fought to a draw by the end of the 1970s, with a view towards understanding what constitutes ecological or sustainable architecture now. Contrary to a popular perception, this is not a continuation of the energy-conscious, self-sufficiency drives that proliferated in the West after the oil shocks of the mid-1970s; nor is it a fringe or factionalized movement. Rather, an increasing awareness of the environment, and the importance to present and future generations of the conservation of basic natural resources, has developed among architects of every stylistic bent. Proponents such as Norman Foster and Future Systems, for example, in the international high-tech camp, are matched in their quest for a 'greener' architecture by contemporaries such as El-Wakil, or Ken Yeang, who bring particular regional considerations to bear on the problem. Rather than individual self-sufficiency the emphasis is now on global resource preservation and eco-system management which transcends conventional geopolitical boundaries. This requires architects not only to act locally, but think globally about all their design strategies and material choices, and to be aware of international politics, debt burdens related to the north–south imbalance in resource

29

30

31

32

use and environmental economics that price these scarce natural resources more realistically.

Increasing complexities, such as these, have also been factored into an international renewal of the modern aesthetic, a ground swell of commitment to explore the principles of the movement but without adopting its ideological agenda. The new moderns, as they are referred to here, share a respect for the explicitness of the modernist position without always being aware of, or agreeing with, the social premise that was originally behind it. This is partially due to the translation that took place when Modernism was formally introduced into the United States by Hitchcock and Johnson and later made viable as a vehicle for developers, as in the Lever House tower, of 1951, by Gordon Bunshaft of Skidmore Owings and Merrill. The 1932 MoMA exhibition focused on formal rather than theoretical issues; the forms, in turn, were copied, packaged and marketed without regard for what they symbolized; their shock value was seen more as an advantage in product differentiation than as the model of a new order. Paradoxically, current interpretations from a wide range of individuals of many different nationalities ranging from Richard Meier, Gwathmey Siegel or Steven Holl in America, Arata Isozaki in Japan, Henri Ciriani and Christian de Portzamparc in France and Jo Coenen in The Netherlands, represent a collective ennui with experimentation and offer persuasive evidence that a newly invigorated International Style is emerging. Unlike its predecessor, which was largely a forced attempt to find commonality among many diverse ideological strands, this confluence is actually being overlooked in the media and is more real. These widely diverse national attempts reveal a consensus of disillusionment with the idea of following trends and of architecture having become a prisoner of the consumer cycle of planned obsolescence and renewal. Modernism is regarded by these architects as the most stable antidote to that attitude. There is a palpable yearning for a cessation of the fashion spiral, of having to await the next 'ism' at the risk of being stuck in the last 'wasm', and a younger generation of architects are increasingly returning to Modernism in the process.

In the meantime, the populist resurgence that the Post-Modernists unsuccessfully sought to define has taken place of its own accord, fuelled by the expansion of an unfettered consumerism that began in the early 1980s. This has been primarily served by developers and entrepreneurs, rather than architects, as a phenomenon related in direct lineage to world expositions, amusement parks, and theme parks, such as Disneyland. The critical transformation that has taken place is that 'theming', as an intention, has expanded into the public sector, having been recognized as both a commercial opportunity and civic panacea, and the answer to a perceived social need. The Post-Modernists, especially the pioneers, correctly assessed popular discontent with restrictive architectural expression. However, they singularly failed to predict the

33

34

ability of non-architects to provide an alternative. Fed by rising urban and suburban paranoia, as levels of crime and communal dislocation rise, theming offers the psychological security of familiar historical images, and the real security of controlled, and patrolled, environments. The greatest significance of populist architecture and its escape from the confines of the theme park into the urban arena has been the pressure it has put upon architects to come to terms with both its public acceptance and its difference from conventional practice. In sponsoring famous architects such as Frank Gehry, Robert Stern, Michael Graves and Arata Isozaki, the Disney Corporation has created something of a crisis of conscience in the profession and the long financial tentacles of that global giant have also encouraged the transition of theming into the public commercial market place.

The globalization of finance that has fuelled theming has also augmented a transformation of the venerated profile of the skyscraper as a well-known commercial urban typology into the contemporary

35

'megastructure'. Paradoxically, in an age of heightened environmental sensibilities, high-rise towers are not only continuing to spring up in cities all over the world, but are getting taller and more assertive. Megastructures are important signposts of an international shift in economic status as well as the way in which capital is transferred; they are the new totems of corporate power as well as civic or national identity and while there is little news in that, there has been a distinct transfer of the location of that power as well as an amplification of the scale of the buildings used to express it. This phenomenon has been particularly evident in Asia, where the high-rise has been selectively appropriated as an iconic status symbol for reasons that go beyond spatial efficiency and high land values. Highly visible examples of this transformation, such as Cesar Pelli's contributions at Canary Wharf in London, 1986, and the Petronas Towers in Kuala Lumpur, 1992–7 or the proposed Millennium Tower in Tokyo by Norman Foster, among many others, indicate the extent to

which the skyscraper of the past has now become a totemic beacon of national economic success and corporate power. The megastructure today not only symbolizes participation in the high stakes game of global finance, but is also an indicator of the way in which that game is going.

The bi-polar capitals of the Pacific Rim, where most of that change has occurred, are Los Angeles and Tokyo; the state of flux that characterizes those cities has made both Los Angeles and Japanese architecture predictors of another sort. The avant-garde in each instance is producing work that is *sui generis*, self-referential, packed with contextual and historical meaning, inspirational, confusing, and endlessly original. The discussion of Los Angeles here extends the premise put forward in an earlier book, *Los Angeles Architecture: The Contemporary Condition*, which is that contrary to popular opinion, there are historical precedents in the city that outsiders always assume has no past, or at least admits to none. In the sense that the last second can constitute the past, the concept of history is relative, and even though Los Angeles has only existed for little more than a century, it is home to many of the first Modernist architectural experiments in the United States by architects such as Richard Neutra and Rudolf Schindler. These paradigms continue to inform the best contemporary work, surfacing in unexpected ways, even though these may not be immediately evident. As evidence of this connection, consider the Schnabel House as the final resolution of a long exploration of residential prototypes by Frank Gehry and its basis in the Barnsdall House by Frank Lloyd Wright, 1916–21, or the Mission Revival and Irving Gill quotes used by Koning Eizenberg in their 31st Street house. The use of urban typologies — such as the freeway and movie lot warehouse so peculiar to Los Angeles — by Eric Owen Moss in his Samitaur, and other Culver City prototypes, and the enduring power of the Case Study House programme and the architecture of pioneers such as Charles Eames and Pierre Koenig on the work of young architects such as Cigolle-Coleman, are further indications of an awareness of history in the city. Each of these enduring influences has been augmented by the immigration phenomenon that has overwhelmed Los Angeles, turning it into the late twentieth-century equivalent of Ellis Island in New York as *the* immigrant gateway into the United States. This has induced a collective paranoia in the city, and multiculturalism has displaced 'autoculture' as the first major screen that deflects critical recognition away from the genuine pattern of urban experimentation that exists in LA. Perhaps the most drastic change detectable is an increasing tendency towards introversion, a *volte face* away from one of the most benign natural environments imaginable.

Nature still remains a strong generating force in Japan, however, and architects uniformly respond to it in either a directed or a reflexive way, but never ignore it or take it for granted as Los Angelenos now seem to do. Nature and history coincide in Japan; the first buildings were carved out of the earth and then evolved in direct response to the environment entirely in natural materials. Increasing industrialization and American occupation after the Second World War altered material sensibilities but the attention to detail that such a hermetic relationship with the environment had encouraged has remained as a distinctive characteristic of contemporary Japanese architecture, combined with a desire continually to redefine the things that set this nation apart. A growing awareness that many traditions that inform this redefinition are being lost has contributed to a new sense of urgency as the older generation of architects who grew up in parallel with Japan's post-war industrial expansion, such as Kenzo Tange, consistently tried to accommodate Western conventions in the modern style. Tange's generation is followed by

36

37

38

architects such as Fumihiko Maki, Kisho Kurokawa and Arata Isozaki, each of whom have a long list of projects that illustrate a similar attempt at assimilation. The story of the dramatic changes that have taken place in the direction of the Maki, Kurokawa, Isozaki triumvirate, which has virtually dominated contemporary Japanese architecture after Kenzo Tange's influence began to wane, is an epic tale of three enormously powerful individuals who have each held sway in their profession during a formative period in Japan. That epic is beyond the scope of this book and still awaits its historian, but revolves around three distinctly different personalities who have each struggled with profound changes occurring in their country, trying to resolve them in architectural terms, as best they can. The function

39 RUDOLPH
SCHINDLER,
Schindler/Chase
House, Hollywood,
California,
1921-2

40 FRANK LLOYD
WRIGHT, Barnsdall
House, Los
Angeles,1916-21

41 KENZO TANGE,
Fuji Television
Building, Tokyo,
1995

39

40

played by tradition in this reconciliation has differed, but has been present in each case, making comparisons between the three an even more tantalizing task for a future analyst. There have, of course, been many more architects in their generation who have made important, sustained contributions that are acknowledged here, but these three leaders have come to represent the difficulties and possibilities inherent in attempting to reconcile two different cultures in a way that few others can even approximate, and this gives the efforts of each additional resonance. The generation they represent now begins to yield to a younger group that has quite a different perspective. The Japanese talent for assimilation without loss of cultural identity, so evident in their domination of electronic technology, has also been applied to architecture, and even the early translations of Western models still manage to convey a certain Japanese individuality. After Metabolism, which was a nationalistic attempt to submit Modernism to organic principles, to culturally personalize it, Japanese architecture has emerged as a continually renewing force in its own right. The key figures in what might loosely be thought of as the younger generation of Japanese architects, including Tadao Ando, Kasuhiro Ishii, Toyo Ito, Itsuko Hasegawa and Shin Takamatsu, have each displayed an intense concern for cultural expression of proud national independence in an era of diminished expectations. Not having the advantage of unquestioned, unlimited artistic expression granted to the generation before them, they have unexpectedly proven able to channel intense national pride into a different form of cultural expression without rejecting technology. Ando has achieved this through stunning simplicity, and an ability to penetrate to the essence of each different design problem, while Ishii, for example, has led the way in renewing explorations into tradition crafts, particularly in timber construction, which plays such an important role in Japanese architectural history.

Japanese singularity is only the most obvious and sustained attempt to retain cultural identity in the face of creeping homogeneity; the final chapter on 'World Cities' indicates the extent of global interconnectedness in the urban context. By the turn of the century a majority of the people in the world will be living in cities and the litany of problems usually associated with urban life, such as pollution, traffic congestion, overcrowding and poor to nonexistent services, will become everyone's problem, especially with regard to the environmental destruction that these primary factors cause. The global rate of urbanization is not uniform, however. North America, Latin America and Europe continue to lead the race; more than 75 per cent of the population of each continent is predicted to live in cities by the year 2000, followed by approximately 35 per cent in Africa and Asia, respectively; but Asia, and especially China, are gaining ground fast. Questions of style and 'schools' of design philosophy, or the influences of a particular avant-garde movement pale

41

42

43

alongside the prospect of the seeming inevitability of a global population doubling in the next half century and the potential lack of basic shelter, health and sanitation that will confront those yet to be born.

Quite unlike their counterparts at the beginning of this century, architects today contribute only a small proportion to the built environment, even though the media would like us to believe otherwise. If architects in the future want truly to have a significant impact on the way people live, the scope of their inquiry, interests and involvement must significantly change. A growing number of architects, architects in training, and others committed to the built environment who realize that such change is necessary, are also beginning to understand that we have been here before, albeit at a different scale and in other historical circumstances. The well-known warning about the dangers of repeating history if you fail to study it, has never been more timely. The lesson of the past century is that the problems the Modern Movement in architecture attempted to proscribe have now expanded to global proportions, but the basic nature of the problems remains the same. Social inequities — perpetuated by formal congruencies in what Michel Foucault has identified as an architecture of power — acute housing shortages; the dilemma of the destruction of craft by technology, and of individual expression by rationality; the role of history in providing precedent; the potential of architecture itself, as inspired construct of materials, structure and processional ritual, creating spaces to affect the human condition, are still the critical themes of architecture today.

Those who understand the helical character of history and the architectural significance of the re-emergence of these issues, recognize that the modern project has already laboriously ground the lens that can help to bring them into focus once again. The resilience of the essential philosophies of that project, regardless of certain formal considerations which have now become a historical style of their own, have impressed even Modernism's severest critics who have failed to put forward a workable alternative. This recognition has proved liberating, as more and more designers realize that they are operating within a premise of fulfilment rather than negation, and that the difficult ground work which has already been accomplished has provided a solid platform on which they can stand as individuals.

42 SHIN TAKAMATSU, The Ark, Kyoto, 1980-3

43 TADAO ANDO, Chikatsu-Asuka Historical Museum, Osaka, 1990-4

44 TSAO AND McKOWN, IMC Building, Kuala Lumpur, 1996

44

1 (Previous page)
ALDO ROSSI,
Bonnefanten
Museum,
Maastricht, 1994

2, 3 ROB KRIER,
White House,
Ritterstrasse,
Berlin, 1977-80

European Rationalism is founded upon an intellectual tradition which was born in classical philosophy, refined in the French Enlightenment, and survived intact until the Second World War, before it came to be severely threatened during the 1980s. In that consumer-oriented decade the rationalist, Cartesian defining statement 'Cogito Ergo Sum' — or 'I think, therefore, I am' — appeared finally to have been subsumed into situational ethics justified by 'if it feels (or looks) good, it can't be wrong'. Trust in reason rather than experience in the search for truth, so carefully channelled into architecture by the Abbé Laugier and JNL Durand during the Enlightenment and introduced into the Modern Movement through the Beaux-Arts system and modernist pioneers such as Le Corbusier, appeared to be too restrictive for post-war generations grown increasingly accustomed to hedonistic consumerism, instant gratification and visual and experiential sensationalism. Contemporary rationalists in the Benelux countries, Italy, Germany and northern Spain, where most of the movement's contemporary protagonists are concentrated, have begun to compromise to survive. The nature and extent of the compromise in each instance is a compelling theoretical micrometer, a way of measuring what these practitioners believe must remain immutable in the theory, and what is so significant in the winds of change that it must be adopted in order to perpetuate the basic philosophy.

The Luxembourg-born architect brothers Leon and Rob Krier, who are both high-profile leaders of the rationalist position and have done much to further its objectives, give a strong indication of what those immutable, bedrock principles are, particularly as related to the concept of typology and urban experience. In his book *Urban Space*, published in 1979, Rob Krier undertook the Herculean task of codifying all the perpetual urban conditions that he believes bear continuing, such as arcades, corners, courtyards, entrances and stairs; these he categorized, drawing all the common variations in the process. To understand the importance of such categorization to the Kriers and all other contemporary rationalists, it is necessary to recall that typology as a fundamental principle of Rationalism was established through a critical historical escalation of ideas. Abbé Laugier, in his *Essai sur l'architecture*, published in 1753, speculated on the essential elements needed in the 'primitive hut' — such as roof, column, door and window — which can be seen as the tectonic equivalents to Descartes' primary, rational thesis. These were extended by Durand into historical period, function, and most importantly, form. Such categorization, promoted through Durand's teaching at the Ecole Polytechnique in Paris, was aimed at solving the formal problems presented to architects by new building types, new materials, and changing social needs.

Relative to the urban explorations of the Kriers, the most important contribution to the theory of types was a definition of the nineteenth-century Beaux-Arts

architect Quatremère de Quincy, who clarified its difference from a model. For him, 'type' represented the idea of an element which served as a rule for the model, rather than an image of a thing to be copied. As he explained, 'Everything is precise and given in the model, everything is more or less vague in the type'.' Regarding precedent, Quatremère describes typical form as a result of operations carried out on prior forms, so that historical precedents become an inescapable factor in the generation of form from the rational standpoint. With regard to use, he suggests that some forms are more appropriate to certain kinds of functions than others.

A basic objection to typological theory is that, as a vestige of the pre-industrial age, it is a frozen mechanism that denies change and emphasizes automatic repetition. The Kriers note that this argument ignores the distinction between type and model that Quatremère highlights; a model is a final form, but a type is a guide that is liberating in that designers are not forced to repeat it exactly and many extraneous choices are eliminated by adopting predetermined precedents, allowing precious time that would otherwise be wasted to be invested in new kinds of exploration. Rob Krier's intellectual leadership in the context of the Internationale Bauausstellung (IBA) redevelopment of Berlin has meant that typological design standards, derived indirectly from Quatremère de Quincy, have been instituted, with individual designers appointed, as necessary or appropriate, to complete each allocated block.

The 'White House' project on Ritterstrasse in Berlin, of 1977–80, was intended by Rob Krier to be a prototype for the rebuilding of Kreuzberg, a historical part of the city which was almost completely destroyed in 1945, and which suffered the further humiliation of unplanned development from the 1950s to the 1970s. Indiscriminate, market-driven renewal resulted in banal isolated towers standing in a bleak urban wasteland, and Krier sought to re-establish the traditional urban framework of low-rise blocks that had characterized this district before the war. This housing unit, as part of what Krier calls his 'dream plan' for this section of south Friedrichstadt in the western part of the city, is bounded by Lindenstrasse to the west, Alte-Jacob-Strasse to the east, Oranienstrasse to the north, and Hollmannstrasse to the south. It is a typically rationalistic intervention because it straddles a road to set up the pattern of the blocks that will, or must, follow it, rather than being placed in an indeterminate location with less prescriptive power. Krier's dream plan, which followed the original publication of *Urban Space* in German — *Stadtraum*, published in 1975 — seems to be a testing ground for all of the typologies he identifies, especially for public spaces.

The window patterns of the H-shaped White House building vary from small punched-out squares in the central span, to larger squares in the wings; while the lack of trim or ornament is reminiscent of Aldo Rossi's Gallaratese Apartment Complex in Milan discussed later in this chapter. The window sizes reflect the kinds of units

2

3

4

behind them; there are twenty-three apartments, ranging from one to three bedrooms, and the larger units — which sometimes have two-storey-high living spaces — are concentrated in the wings, facing the common gardens. The larger openings below the parapet of the central span, in contrast to the smaller windows below, have been compared to the crenellations at the top of a medieval gate; this gate, however, is not so much a barrier to the pedestrian route through the middle of the block, as a filter that allows a view into the communal outdoor space, but discourages casual entry into it.

While Rob Krier has reinforced his theoretical stance by building on a broad scale, Leon Krier has largely confined himself to proselytizing through drawing. He has almost single-handedly attempted to reverse the destruction of the traditional fabric of the European city by means of widely publicized polemical articles, which are typically accompanied by visually engaging graphics — including bird's eye views of real and imaginary cities, restored to preindustrial integrity through the application of the principles he advances, which include a reliance on the typologies identified by his brother Rob. These principles have also been appropriated widely, not least by the New Urbanist cause in the United States. The efficacy of Krier's seductive, even romantic, hand-drawn graphics (also discussed in Chapter Five) raises the issue of the importance that representation has had in promoting rational ideals during a period when architects were given few opportunities to build in such a manner. Krier has created a considerable and compelling imaginary body of work of his own which has given him as much, or greater, authority than many architects with more built work to their credit. This underscores, once again, the power of perception in today's image-conscious electronically guided world and the potential that representation has to be accepted as reality.

The Italian architect Aldo Rossi — who like Krier is almost as famous for his graphics as his architecture — is perhaps the most powerful contemporary proponent of the tradition of rational analysis in Italian architecture that was crystallized in the work of Giuseppe Terragni in Como in the 1930s. In his book *Architettura della Città*, published in English as *The Architecture of the City* in 1982, Rossi categorizes the typologies found in the city, as either 'perpetuating' or 'pathological' permanencies. The 'perpetuating' variety, Rossi explains, are like the Basilica in Vicenza which last because they can adapt to change, or even inspire it. 'Pathological' varieties, which he does not specify, but which are exemplified in complexes like the Alhambra in Granada, and are consistently valorized by architects, are dead because they specifically represent social patterns that have now drastically changed; they have been unable to adapt to new conditions or uses and are moribund as typologies: therefore they cannot be relied upon as models.

From his argument, Rossi deduces that perpetuating typologies, such as the arcade, can safely be extracted

and abstracted as design elements because they have been historically successful, proving continuing social relevance. An important distinction, following Durand's classification of continuity of form, is that such abstraction can be implemented regardless of function, so that typologies in Rossi's hands are used as so many mimetic parts, assembled according to an afunctional, symbolic agenda. An early example of this in Rossi's work is the Gallaratese Apartment Complex in Milan, completed in collaboration with Carlo Aymonino in 1970. In the block that he designed, Rossi relies on the use of an arcade as a civilizing device in a long bar-like apartment building, recalling the streets of traditional Italian cities; the public space is the equivalent of the private accommodation above. The windows of the apartments are square in continuation of Rossi's, and most rationalists', preference for platonic geometries, such as circles, squares, and equilateral triangles, since these are most readily susceptible to mathematical proof. The windows, like everything else in the apartment block, are devoid of ornament,

5

which is deemed unnecessary. The Gallaratese project elevated Rossi from being a local, cult figure to one of international acclaim, but it was his San Cataldo Cemetery, Modena, designed in 1971–8, that solidified his reputation, as well as his commitment to a more complex psychological agenda.

In the Modena complex the Gallaratese arcade reappears, as do the severe square openings. Stacked and ranked cubicles are provided for inhumation or the interment of ashes; and the names of the deceased, together with their photographs, are attached to facilitate the local custom of celebrating significant days in the life of lost family members, such as birthdays, or anniversaries, with an extended visit to the cemetery. Rossi emphasizes the rather macabre purpose of the complex in his anthropomorphic arrangement of the central elements of the master plan, in which the projecting bars of the main building are set out in incrementally shorter lengths — forming a V-shape — becoming the ribs

4 ALDO ROSSI WITH CARLO AYMONINO, Gallaratese Apartment Complex, Milan, 1970

5 ALDO ROSSI, San Cataldo Cemetery, Modena, 1971-8

6, 7 Aldo Rossi,
San Cataldo
Cemetery, Modena,
1971-8

8 James Ingo
Freed, Pei Cobb
Freed and
Partners, United
States Holocaust
Memorial Museum,
Washington, DC,
1993

6

7

in this skeletal plan; a conical smoke stack, meant to symbolize the penis, rather macabrely marks the crematorium. In Rossi's perverse joke, the source of life, the phallus, becomes a device for the destruction of flesh and bones, and the 'ribs' of the scheme hold the bones that remain after exhumation. Rossi's macabre view is underscored by another, perhaps unintended, reference to Nazi concentration camps, in his use of wire railings, metal bridges, and malevolent towers, that were surely the prototype for the United States Holocaust Memorial Museum in Washington, DC, designed by James Ingo Freed of Pei Cobb Freed and Partners, and completed nearly twenty years after the inception of the Modena Cemetery in 1993.

The difference between Rossi's Modena Cemetery and Freed's Holocaust Museum, quite tellingly, is one of presentation of similar imagery, a relative trust in the ability of space to convey meaning to its audience. The Holocaust Museum contains many of the same metaphorical devices that Rossi uses, such as metal bridges wrapped in wire mesh fence, and materials are used in a severely plain way to convey a sinister impression. Freed, however, has assumed the responsibility of providing a public institution intended to receive millions of visitors each year. It is a national memorial to one of the most horrific events in world history, an attempt to present the indescribable. It should come as no surprise, therefore, that such an attempt sometimes falters, given the scale of the task. The Hall of Remembrance, with its single central flame, has a sacred quality that almost defies people to enter it, yet such sanctity is difficult to maintain throughout. Other, more literal configurations, such as an effort to convey what it felt like to be crowded into a cramped railway car on a final ride to a death camp, sadly degenerate into thematic kitsch.

Rossi's emphasis at Modena, however, is on the external conjunction of symbols as related to typological exploration, rather than a sequential progression through internal episodic spaces calculated to elicit certain emotions. As befits a dedicated rationalist, Rossi's architecture is more cerebral and subtle, concentrating less on the human capacity for inhumanity, as exemplified in a monstrous campaign of genocide in the past, than on the inhuman conditions of contemporary life that we continue to perpetuate, which he evokes by the image of the concentration camp.

Beyond these earlier studies of the arcade typology in the Gallaratese and at Modena, which conform to Durandian notions of form rather than function, Rossi has moved towards perfecting what has been termed 'a science of empty signs' that communicate with the collective cultural subconscious, in projects such as the Carlo Felice Opera House in Genoa, of 1982. The flytower technology of movable curtains and sets that exists today is as much an Italian invention as opera itself, and this theatre is based on that symbol, stripped down to its essence.

8

9 ALDO ROSSI,
Hotel Il Palazzo,
Fukuoka,1989

10 ALDO ROSSI,
IBA Social
Housing Block,
Berlin, 1989

11, 12
(Overleaf)
ALDO ROSSI,
Bonnefanten
Museum,
Maastricht, 1994

The marvel of Rossi's expansion from Italy into other countries in the late 1980s and early 1990s, as his international reputation increased, has been his ability to adapt his mimetic skill to diverse settings. The IBA Social Housing Block in Berlin of 1989, the Hotel Il Palazzo in Fukuoka, Japan of 1989, and Bonnefanten Museum in Maastricht, The Netherlands, of 1994, all perpetuate his commentary on the basic contemporary dichotomy between extraordinary advances in science and technology and the feeling of spiritual emptiness and loss that accompany it. It is this ability to create empty metaphorical landscapes that makes him the architectural equivalent of the painter Giorgio de Chirico, whose haunting, depopulated surrealist canvases convey the impression of cities full of people who are eventually all alone. Reversing the effect of Edvard Munch's painting

9

10

The Scream (1893), which invites empathy with a lone screaming figure, the heavily-shadowed, empty plazas in De Chirico's paintings seem to draw viewers into the composition, inviting them to join the search; perhaps for a past that cannot be recaptured, or answers to the abstraction of the present, which do not exist.

Rossi's work seems equally to present a puzzle. There are no windows on his Hotel Il Palazzo, its monumental facade is as much of a cipher in this regard as the conundrum that Rossi posits in all his work: how do we look for meaning when meaning is no longer to be found? The Bonnefanten Museum is one of the most deliberate attempts that Rossi has made to respond to physical context serrating the edge to let nature in and yet the metaphorical aspect of isolation still predominates.

11

For Rossi, memory has become the necessary layer that combines with typology to become the analytical moment of architecture, and this is identifiable in urban artifacts where memory and reason are most condensed. An insight into this approach is offered by Alan Colquhoun, who has argued that the whole notion of precedent is pointless in the current 'vacuum' that exists as compared to the past when there was a substantial 'body of traditional practice'; for Colquhoun, 'what appears on the surface as a hard, rational discipline of design turns out rather paradoxically to be a mystical belief in the intuitional process'.[2] In this view, rationalists, such as Rossi, are perpetuating typologies from institutions that no longer exist in contemporary society, or at least have lost their cultural mandate.

It is hard to reconcile Colquhoun's argument with the cold reason evident in the work of Rossi's fellow Italian Giorgio Grassi, who is one of the most extreme rationalists operating today, and who furthermore has a strong belief in the power of institutional typologies; for example, his student housing in Chieti, Italy, of 1976 makes even Rossi's 'empty signs' look verbose. His tall rectilinear porticos recall masters from earlier in the century such as Erik Gunnar Asplund, Giuseppe Terragni, Pietro Lingeri and Adalberto Libera, and evoke the height of rationalist influence just prior to the Second World War. And yet, Grassi, like Rossi, is also an urbanophile, who is concerned with the character of the city and the interchange of architectural forms that takes place there. He further admits to being 'concerned with the whole scale of choices contained in the forms in relationship to daily life in the city and the wealth of choices which are aesthetic choices, as well'. So, if the purest rationalist of them all can admit to the importance of aesthetic choice, Colquhoun's argument would appear to be correct, and the metaphorical and aesthetic values that are seen to overlay the typological readings by Rossi are present even in Grassi's severe dialect.

The Ticinese architect, Mario Botta, and the Ticino 'school' that he leads, is a graphic exemplar of such deliberate aesthetic choice, since he is so frequently identified with the quasi-functionalist, quasi-rationalist motives of the transitional Modernist Louis Kahn. Botta visited Kahn's office while the Congress Hall for the Venice Biennale was being designed between 1968 and 1974; that building, which typically began as a circle symbolic of assembly, but was converted to a linear wall that bisected the edges of the circle because of tight site constraints, had a profound influence on Botta, who developed his theory of 'territory' from the project (which translates from Italian more accurately as 'place', or 'context'). Briefly stated, this theory involves the idea that architecture must make a positive intervention into a pre-existing context, whatever character it has. It must be seen as an ordering device, an opportunity to guide future growth, rather than a singular contribution, and has ramifications

13

14

13 **Giorgio Grassi**, Student Housing, Chieti, 1976

14, 15 **Mario Botta**, Secondary School, Morbio Inferiore, Ticino, 1972-7

15

16 MARIO BOTTA,
House in Riva San
Vitale, Ticino,
1973

17, 18 MARIO
BOTTA, Casa
Rotonda, Stabio,
1982

16

far beyond the legally designated property lines shown on a site plan. While Kahn failed to capitalize on this potential aspect of the Congress Hall, Botta recognized it and began to use this technique soon afterwards. His Secondary School at Morbio Inferiore, designed in 1972–7, is just such an intervention: a linear phalanx of repetitive stacked classrooms separated by access stairs, that partitions a mountainside behind it from a rolling lawn in front, allowing only controlled access between the two. Botta's single-family house in Ligornetto, completed in 1976, is another example. This small residence visually separates the town from the countryside, providing a regional marker reminiscent of the triumphal arches used by the Romans to mark perceived points of demarcation between two distinct zones of influence.

Another equally small, but equally significant house in Riva San Vitale, completed in 1973, has an even smaller frame of tectonic reference, but Botta once again chose natural territory as the premise, shaping the house and site as a marker between the mountain and the lake at the bottom of the slope below. However, rather than seeming to be an isolated domestic outpost in the foothills of the Alps, the house actually conveys the authority it was intended to have, mostly because of a judicious use of massing, based on cubic Platonic solids. Botta places the entrance at the upper level of the house, at the end of a slender steel bridge from the garage, repeating a tactic used quite effectively by others, such as Frank Lloyd Wright at the Freeman House in Los Angeles of 1922, and Richard Meier at the Douglas House in Michigan of 1973. At Riva San Vitale, Botta could not afford the luxury of complete transparency, since this would have compromised his territorial agenda, detracting from the visual strength and solidity of his marker. The tower therefore opens up slowly on descent to reveal carefully controlled views across the lake, creating a balance of solid and void that skilfully maintains the fiction Botta is proposing — that architecture can mitigate between one territory and another, even if one zone in that territory is a vast expanse of Alpine lake and the other is a mountain rising out of it. Botta's Casa Rotonda of 1982, in Stabio, Switzerland, is an equally defiant commentary on a negative context. Having found nothing to delineate in the rather nondescript neighbourhood in which it is located, Botta chose to circle the wagons instead and turned the house inwards. Like a defensive medieval tower, the house holds its ground, but gives hints of a more humane world inside, as the Ligornetto house does, through a crystalline veil of windows suspended in recesses in the masonry wrapper.

Increasing international recognition in the decade following these modest residential projects has given Botta the opportunity to design larger commissions, such as the vast drum-like Cathedral in Evry, France, of 1995, and the Museum of Modern Art in San Francisco of 1994. While they are accomplished and decisive works, the

17

18

19 MARIO BOTTA,
Evry Cathedral,
1995

increased scale and a different context have made each of these important projects more abstract and less connected than Botta's earlier work, which is culturally and contextually specific. The Museum of Modern Art was, however, a difficult assignment and Botta has managed to gain a relatively high degree of control over a problematic, pre-existing jumble of facilities in Yerba Buena Gardens, which is effectively a cultural theme park run amok. Each prior contributor to the development has introspectively focused on the requirements of their own facility: Fumihiko Maki on the Center for the Arts Gallery and James Stewart Polshek on the Center for the Arts Theater, both with heroic but essentially token formal gestures to the setting, or lack of it. Given a mid-block site on the eastern side of Third Street, wedged between the Theatre and Maki's museum, Botta has used a stepped facade to create a powerful civic landmark when seen from a distant vantage point. This impression is reinforced by the truncated, striped stone cylinder that lights the central rotunda of the museum. This impression diminishes with proximity, however; it is precisely this monumental tactic which exacts the price of lack of continuity on the plaza itself. Botta's strategy is predictably formulative, given that he has opted for the grand gesture and he alone has attempted to use his contribution in the city as a unifying piece to solve a complex urban puzzle. This search for connectedness is, perhaps, most obvious in his submission for the Lido Film Theatre, of 1990, in which he found himself in competition with Aldo Rossi and Carlo Aymonino, who were also invited to participate. Botta's theatre, which relates to a popular pre-existing hall, brings the Kahnian influence, where Botta's notions of territoriality began, around full circle. Like Kahn's Biennale Congress Hall, this theatre is also used to form a wall; the only difference being a fanciful roof which makes a multiple reference to the sails of a *caravale*, or the hat of a reveller, which are a part of the ritualistically festive part of Venetian history.

Two other members of the 'Ticino School' that have been identified with Botta and who should be mentioned in regard to the rationalist notion of transforming the context are Aurelio Galfetti and Luigi Snozzi, although the 'school' is not restricted to them. The Bellinzona Public Swimming Pool and Tennis Club to which Galfetti has made incremental additions from 1967 to 1985 is a classic instance of using architecture as a framework for further growth. His initial move was to connect the town of Bellinzona via a pedestrian bridge to the Ticino River. This spine marches across the landscape like a Roman aqueduct, irrespective of topographical irregularities beneath it, and is used as a datum for the swimming pools and park land, which are connected to it by stairway below. The Roman metaphor is further reinforced by the tennis courts complex, which was completed in 1983. The eight courts are organized two to a quadrant, in a recreational version of a Roman camp plan; the *cardo maximus* is a grand allée

20

22, 23, 24
MARIO BOTTA,
Museum of
Modern Art,
San Francisco,
1994

22

23

24

25 AURELIO
GALFETTI,
Bellinzona Public
Swimming Pool
and Tennis Club,
Ticino, 1967-85

26 VITTORIO
GREGOTTI, ENEA
Research Centre,
Rome, 1985

25

of trees leading to and from the locker rooms, which act as a wall facing the parking lot. Like Botta, Galfetti makes a virtue of contingency; the entire complex, which is rendered in reinforced concrete, textured in various ways, achieves a great deal with as little material as possible.

The Bernasconi house by Luigi Snozzi of 1989, in Carona, Switzerland, is the Ticino version of Le Corbusier's Villa Savoye, but with some revealing differences. As with Botta's Riva San Vitale House, this residence is located on a steep slope, which is terraced in response to it, but in this instance it is placed parallel to the grade to act as a line of demarcation between the steeper part of the slope above it and a flatter part below. Like Le Corbusier's iconic translation of progression from nature into habitation, followed by a ritualistically reflexive turning back to consider the figurative distance that has been travelled — as if the house maps the entire progress that has been achieved by civilization in microcosm — this house also makes a statement about the difference between outside and inside. In truly pragmatic, almost brutal, rationalistic fashion, however, this statement is about controlling nature, rather than transcending it. The house is like a dam that metes out the precise amount of undulating lawn it will allow to flow past it into the valley below. A linear lap pool, stretching out as a perpendicular line from the living room, terminates in a pergola that frames the distant landscape. However, rather than allowing recollection of the path just taken — as the cut-out in the parapet of the Villa Savoye does — this frame seems to indicate territory still to be conquered.

The rationalist connection to Classicism, which was fostered by the French Ecole des Beaux-Arts, is less substantial in northern Europe than it is in Italy, where the cultural connections are more obvious. The Roman tradition, which is evident in Rossi's interpretation as related to the city, is also manifest in the urban focus evident in the magazine *Casabella* and clearly present in the work of its editor, Vittorio Gregotti. His ENEA Research Centre in Rome of 1985 is a clear example.

As a centre for testing the reliability of research related to information processing, these laboratories, designed for the National Board of Alternative Energy Sources, are located on an extensive site in the Casaccia industrial park near Rome; their purpose is to technically reproduce environmental conditions and events with computerized instrumental systems. The complex contains two large testing laboratories, with offices, smaller research facilities, meeting rooms, and other service spaces. Gregotti selected a standard planning module equating to the width of a standard door which is used in both plan and section. The circulation path through the project is straightforward. The two large testing laboratories are located at the centre of the plan with single laboratories around them. Each large laboratory is connected to workshops and services. Auxiliary spaces are lit from skylights and borrowed light. The structure is reinforced

26

concrete, with a curtain wall of prefabricated square panels, coloured iron grey, which are varied to deal with special conditions such as corners, parapets and a plinth base. Setting the windows flush with the interior wall surface seems like a simple decision, but the result is intentionally dramatic, as shadows on the elevation convey a sense of thickness, mass and depth, conveying a powerful classical simplicity that is a hallmark of rationalist architecture.

This enduring cultural empathy with the classical past which has been so carefully abstracted into a precisely ordered and hard-edged definitive intervention by Italian rationalist architects is, however, sublimated in the Mediterranean rationalist tradition. The divergent strains that surface in the work of Antonio Gaudí, for example, which include Catalonian mythology, gothic mysticism, Arab typologies and attitudes about non-representational ornamentation, are the most obvious clues to strong antithetical undercurrents, particularly in Spain.

Juan Navarro Baldeweg has reconfirmed the meaning of symbolism in architecture in this region in his Congress and Exhibition Hall in Salamanca, 1992, which is a clear example of the attachment to the land that is layered over the rationalist ethos there. Baldeweg used the site of this combination of open-air theatre, domed 1,200-seat auditorium and 400-seat concert hall, positioned along the old walls below the historic centre, to make the building a symbolic citadel or gateway into the city. It is a distilled explanation of the joining of an urban typology with topography: a synthesis of the natural and built environment. The *tour de force* of this fusion is the main auditorium ceiling, a stepped dome with a glazed central oculus that seems to float above the space since its pendentives have no visible connection to the corners of the room. There are numerous significant references here, both intentional and inferred: to the fundamental corbelled dome of the ancient Etruscans; to the Palazzo di Congressi in Rome by Adalberto Libera of 1937, where the lightness of the roof accentuates rather than negates its primary historical role as the parallel of the sheltering sky vault; and, finally, to an abstracted recollection of the dome of the cathedral in the city centre, which constantly appears in Baldeweg's sketches of the project.

This coincidence between past and present traditions is also clearly illustrated in the literal layering that Baldeweg's fellow countryman, Rafael Moneo, has accomplished in the design of his National Museum of Roman Art, in Merida, of 1980–6. Intended to interact with the archeological remains of part of the ancient Roman city that have been excavated on the site, the museum delicately straddles them as an organized framework of bridges that allow a clear view of the foundations and walls seen, as if in plan, not far below. The remarkable fact is that Moneo has been able to derive a module of regular bays that work with the old Roman plan without destroying any of the ancient fabric. By using thin, wide,

27, 28 JUAN NAVARRO BALDEWEG, Congress and Exhibition Hall, Salamanca, 1992

28

29

30

elongated bricks and arched bays, he has been able to evoke the feeling of what once existed there without literal reference to it, and has reconstructed mosaics of a quality only found elsewhere at the Bardo Museum in Tunis; these are judiciously placed on the walls to complete the message the architect wants to convey. Light, penetrating down through a glass monitor running along the entire roof ridge, washes the regular series of parallel bearing walls, casting ghostly shadows on the ruins that serve as a graphic reminder that, for the Romans, Rationalism was the equivalent of pragmatic empiricism. Their engineering skill improved through experience; and the typologies they developed, of triumphal arch, basilica, thermal temple and courtyard house came long after their initial appropriation of Greek, Hellenistic and Etruscan models during the early Republic, when growing imperial confidence and identity required that these be adapted and changed. The spatial awareness evident in Nero's Garden House (Domus Aurea) and Hadrian's Villa, for example, is substantial historical confirmation of the invention that is possible inside clear typological guidelines and Moneo's museum is enduring proof that he understands this lesson.

The northern European rationalist tradition may best be understood through the work of architects such as Oswald Mathias Ungers and Josef Paul Kleihues, who each have an extensive background in that aesthetic. Ungers' German Ambassador's Residence in Washington, DC, completed in 1995, has an austerity reminiscent of the work of Gunnar Asplund, but the strict formality of its monumental nine-bay facade inflects in response to internal function. Rather than approaching this design as a residence, Ungers saw the building as an architectural symbol of German culture, deserving 'a certain restraint, coolness and formality' which he felt was appropriate for an official government building. At 30,000 square feet, the structure is hardly domestic, however. Spaces for public functions, such as reception and dining rooms, occupy the ground floor with living, private dining, bedroom, bath and guest quarters on the first floor, above. The concrete frame is covered with Vermont limestone and the portico, overlooking the Potomac River, recalls a Greek Revival House that once stood on the same site; the theoretical crossovers are intriguing.

The typological component and Ungers' belief that 'the theme and content of architecture can only be architecture' is even clearer in his Architecture Museum in Frankfurt am Main, Germany, completed more than ten years before the Ambassador's residence in Washington, in 1983. Heinrich Klotz, the director of the museum during the design period, shared Ungers' philosophy of architecture in the city as a commentary on urban continuity. Ungers has wrapped a wall around a refurbished turn-of-the-century Italianate villa that provides, in sequence, skylit vestibule, circulation access and galleries, but the core is literally the central message,

31

an abstracted gabled house that metaphorically recalls Abbé Laugier's primitive hut.

Josef Paul Kleihues' Museum of Contemporary Art in Chicago, of 1996, similarly explores the purpose of symbolism and monumentality in architecture, the appropriateness of the public and private realm, and the link to previous references. Rather than following the contemporary trend of placing the main entrance at grade, to encourage public access and remove the mystique of the museum as a temple of art, Kleihues has placed his building on a 16-foot-high plinth base, clad in limestone to relate to the Watertower, an important Chicago landmark, nearby. A grand stair leads up to the main floor and ingenious planning keeps the galleries 'isolated with the art', at the perimeter of a grand four-

32

storey atrium. Kleihues' references in the building range from Otto Wagner's Post Office Savings Bank in Vienna of 1904–6 – obvious in the exposed bolts that attach the sandblasted cast-aluminum panels to the structural frame – to Karl Friedrich Schinkel's balance between transparency and containment in the Schauspielhaus of 1821, and Louis Sullivan's Carson Pirie Scott store in Chicago, of 1899–1904, in the careful arrangement of functions in a geometrical plan. Less obvious is the heritage of Mies van der Rohe in Chicago. Even though classically symmetrical, the museum extends the modern tradition in its rational clarity and returns to a belief in the uplifting role of culture as the highest and best achievement of society.

In addition to Ungers and Kleihues, Gottfried Böhm has provided ample evidence of an identifiable

33

34

Teutonic edge in the combined contemporary rationalist contribution, especially in terms of the importance of retaining a sense of dignity and monumentality in urban institutions. Many in the movement feel these must be protected against further erosion of the kind evident during the late 1980s and early 1990s, and Böhm's University Library in Mannheim, Germany, of 1988, represents the stabilization of two of the most important Western institutions into one. This library has been likened to a warehouse for books, but is more accurately a fortress and church combined in the tradition of Mackintosh's library in the Glasgow School of Art of 1908. Here, as there, the nave of this protective cathedral, where books are treated as sacred objects, is the reading room, or 'realm', as the architect refers to it. The impression of a fortress is reinforced by the massive solidity of the exterior walls, penetrated only by small portholes, with most natural light admitted through clerestories.

Böhm's aggressive stance at Mannheim, which may have seemed necessary during the time of social flux when it was built, seems extreme in retrospect. But the issue of how to maintain institutional continuity through architecture, brought to a head by such notable counter-insurgencies as James Stirling's Neue Staatsgalerie in Stuttgart of 1977–84 (see Chapter Six, pages 185–187), which questioned formality and monumentality, remains a critical concern among rationalists. With the substantial shift of awareness of the threat to individual cultural identities related to globalization that has taken place during the mid- to late 1990s, however, the pendulum has now swung back towards a general desire to preserve not just the built historical legacy of the past, but also the values that generated it.

Perversely, an impetus similar to that driving current interest in popular, or 'themed', architecture as described elsewhere here, is now also bolstering the rationalist's position. This derives from a wish to consolidate after the overheated experimentation of the 1980s, to rediscover social bearings through reference to familiar markers. This explains the unlikely, but evident, connection between Leon Krier's design for the new town of Poundbury, based on existing English village typologies of the past, and Disneyland, since both seek to offer reassurance as alternatives to a chaotic present and uncertain future. The future for the rationalists, however, judging from the mood of the faculty and students at Mario Botta's new school in Lugano, and the rising influence of this movement in the areas just described, is very bright, since the compromise of individual interpretation, layered over the bitter pill of reason, has finally made the rationalist ideology a desirable and readily administered palliative for social insecurity.

High-tech architecture, so-called, represents an earnest, perhaps even a passionate attempt to rekindle the technological spirit of early Modernism and, in particular, the ethos of pioneers such as Mies van der Rohe, who believed that modern architecture should express the technology of the times. After the Second World War mounting hostile criticism of modern architecture concentrated on its practical and systemic failures. International Style Modernists cared nothing, it seemed, about the effects of glare, overheating, draughts, leakage and functional issues in general: appearance and style was all. The high-tech initiative can be seen to be partially rooted in this popular perception of the Modern Movement's failure, but it is equally grounded on a firm conviction that the basic tenets of Modernism were right; they had merely become obscured in the hands of the less talented successors of the movement's pioneering visionaries.

High-tech is often regarded, with some justification, as a largely British phenomenon, continuing a proud tradition of adapting industrial mass production to the needs of the construction industry, an approach that can, indeed, be traced back to Isambard Kingdom Brunel's bridges and railway stations or Joseph Paxton's great Crystal Palace of the mid-nineteenth century. The Industrial Revolution was born in Britain and the new large-span building types that it generated in manufacturing centres such as London, Birmingham, Sheffield and Glasgow were designed by engineers rather than architects, who were generally content to provide ornamental, historicist claddings for the structures that resulted. The contribution of engineers has continued to shape the architecture of the twentieth century; the present-day successors of Owen Williams and Ove Arup continue to play an important role in the contemporary construction world, where the carefully crafted industrial shed has become a staple modern building type.

It has been argued by at least one historian that the British High-tech movement has it roots in London's architectural schools in the late 1950s, specifically the Regent Street Polytechnic and the Architectural Association, which generated respectively the magazines *Polygon* and *Archigram*.[1] The view that was propounded in those publications, that the emergent functionalist building types — the early train sheds and conservatories — were the 'real' architecture of the nineteenth century and the proper foundation for that of the twentieth, was promoted by influential teachers such as James Stirling and Peter Smithson, both of whom were enthusiasts for nineteenth-century engineering structures. They in turn inspired architects such as Richard Rogers and Norman Foster. But the impetus behind High-tech was, to an equal degree at the very least, transatlantic.

Rogers and Foster — who both, incidentally, reject being classified as 'High-tech' — are arguably the most famous proponents of the movement, and both are products of British architectural schools of that period —

Rogers of the Architectural Association and Foster of the more pragmatic Manchester school — and both subsequently studied together at Yale University in the USA. The Southern Californian Case Study House programme of the 1940s and 1950s, particularly the contributions of Charles Eames, Raphael Soriano, Craig Ellwood, and Pierre Koenig had a formative influence on both these architects. Koenig's Case Study House #22 became one of the most famous of the series, perhaps because of the magical, widely published photographs of it taken by Julius Shulman. Koenig has continued building into the 1990s: the Schwartz House in Pacific Palisades, Los Angeles, of 1993 is as matter-of-fact as any steel-framed house of the 1960s, though the highly expressive, even romantic, shifting structural frame can be seen as a response to more recent Californian architecture.

For all the lip service paid by the early Modernists to 'breaking the box' and encouraging the free flow of space between inside and outside, the classic glass curtain wall between columns still effectively kept nature at bay. The Case Study houses were an attempt to change that, in response to the post-War demand for a more casual, outdoor lifestyle and particularly to the benign climate and relaxed culture of southern California. These houses, and especially the residence — Case Study House #8 — that Charles and Ray Eames built for themselves in Pacific Palisades in 1949, held out the promise that Modernism could be humanized, that nature need not be excluded, and that architecture could relate to its surroundings sensitively without compromising its essential integrity.

Equally optimistic and inspirational — and a particular influence on Norman Foster — was the visionary work of the American pioneer of lightweight structures, Richard Buckminster Fuller who continued working, and inventing new structural systems, until his death at the age of eighty-eight in 1983. Foster once said of Fuller, 'the thing about Bucky is that he makes you believe anything is possible'. Though Fuller's grander visions — which included a glazed dome over the whole of Manhattan — remained unrealized, his Dymaxion House and Geodesic Dome projects expressed the potential of an anti-monumental architecture based on standardized parts and the frank expression of services. Fuller stumped architects by asking them: 'How much does your building weigh?' But Foster saw the rationale of the question. His response to the Fuller imperative (the two men collaborated on a number of projects between 1968 and 1983) was reflected in the temporary air structure for Computer Technology and the Fred Olsen Terminal at Millwall Dock, both dating from the earliest period of his independent practice. The quest for lightness was to be a constant high-tech preoccupation, while the idea of mass-producing buildings, like cars, underlay the preoccupation of high-tech architects with 'technology transfer', applying the technical advances made in the automobile and aeronautical industries to the cause of better building.

1 (Previous page)
RICHARD ROGERS,
Lloyd's Building,
London, 1978-86

2 PIERRE KOENIG,
Schwartz House,
Los Angeles,
1993

3 RICHARD ROGERS,
House in
Wimbledon,
London,
1968-9

4, 5 (Overleaf)
RENZO PIANO AND
RICHARD ROGERS,
Pompidou Centre,
Paris, 1971-7

3

Rogers and Foster, along with Wendy Foster and her sister Georgie Cheeseman (later Wolton), began their practice, Team 4, after their return from America in 1963. The Reliance Controls Factory in Swindon of 1966 — probably the best-known building that they produced together — relies heavily on Californian quotations, particularly ones from the work of Eames and Ellwood. However, these are edited into a tauter, more classical language, which speaks more authoritatively in isolation on its bleak industrial site. The highly crafted objectivity evident in this pristine, low-rise metal box remained a key theme for both Rogers and Foster after their split in 1967, albeit manifested in quite different ways.

After the dissolution of Team 4, Rogers designed a house for his parents in Wimbledon, south-west London, in 1968–9 that reflects his amplification of the Case Study House agenda. More daring was the Zip-up House project of 1968, which featured a 'zip-up' gasketed panel cladding system which was designed to facilitate rapid on-site construction and a high degree of user control. These principles were realized at a far larger scale in the Universal Oil Products Headquarters at the Tadworth Industrial Estate, using a mass-produced cladding system. International recognition came Rogers' way soon afterwards. The Pompidou Centre, Paris, designed in partnership with Renzo Piano in 1971 and finally completed in 1977, was a systematized ultimate realization of Cedric Price's 1961 Fun Palace project and of the visionary projects of Archigram. Its influence over the last thirty years has been considerable and remains strong even today.

The Pompidou Centre embodies a revolutionary concept that takes Rogers' earlier investigations into systems, prefabrication, and the articulation of structure, skin and services into a highly visible public forum. The Centre was a turning point in the development of the high-tech sensibility, the very embodiment of the building-as-machine ideal. The one-million-square-foot building, located in the Beaubourg quarter of Paris and facing a great piazza cut into the dense surrounding urban fabric, was intended as a cultural bazaar, a challenge to the idea of museum as monument. Renzo Piano recalls it as 'an act of loutish bravado', while Rogers sees the building as a vivid expression of the radical ideas of 1968, the year of student rebellion. Embracing concepts of flexibility and demountability, the architects wanted to create a people's palace, open to the life of the streets, not a place apart.

Quite apart from its social project, the building's structure represents a remarkable undertaking. Immense metal trusses, more than 15 feet deep and spanning more than 150 feet, were prefabricated off site and trucked through the streets of Paris before dawn to avoid traffic jams in the narrow streets of Beaubourg. They were then dropped on to a tubular column frame in the best Joseph Paxton/Crystal Palace instant-construction tradition. Huge cantilevering extension arms — named gerberettes after the engineer who devised them and supervised their

6

casting – were conceived in collaboration with the structural engineer in charge of the entire project, Peter Rice of Ove Arup & Partners. The gerberettes project out from the same tubular columns that hold the clear-span trusses and define an external service zone, which puts the innards of the buildings – which are more usually concealed in internal mechanical ducts – on public display as brightly colour-coded technological art.

The monumental, raw-boned pronouncement that the Pompidou Centre represents has frequently been criticized as being destructive of the intricate scale of one of the world's best-loved cities. Conversely, it is also billed as the most popular high-tech building ever built and the most visited Paris landmark. It has been defended by Piano as a logical extension of the gothic system of construction – which began in and around Paris in the late twelfth century – and the analogy seems apt. In the Pompidou, as in Notre Dame, engineers took the best materials available at the time and stretched them to their physical limits, exposing the structure outside a diaphanous glass skin to provide unfettered soaring spaces within. Both buildings now seem inseparable from the city and the Pompidou underwrites Rogers' contention that architecture can and must enliven the urban scene, serving the needs of the people who live and work in the city. In fact, the social message that the Pompidou carries is conceivably more important than its undoubted engineering achievements.

The new Lloyd's Building that the Richard Rogers Partnership designed and built between 1978–86 is an equally powerful statement about the nature of the city, though built for a great commercial institution rather than a public patron. Its structural and servicing strategy is similar to that of its Parisian predecessor – services and circulation are pulled to the perimeter, leaving clear floors inside – but it uses a concrete rather than a steel frame, and its floor-to-floor heights and vertical scale are significantly greater. Confined within a tight perimeter, delineated by the adjacent Leadenhall Market and the surrounding, basically medieval, street pattern, the Lloyd's Building plan became tighter than that of the Pompidou; as a result, dramatically vertical service towers, which are pushed to the corners of the site, replace the Pompidou's more relaxed linear service zone along the perimeter which take advantage of the streetscape. The towers, like the rest of the building, are clad in stainless steel, an entirely modern but highly prestigious and expensive material, the latter-day equivalent of stone or marble, appropriate to the City of London. Even more than the glass-walled Pompidou Centre, which has six evenly distributed floors, including a ground or plaza level, the Lloyd's Building amply demonstrates its lineal connections with Paxton's Crystal Palace; its soaring central atrium which rises the full height of the building above the market floor, terminates in a spectacular glass barrel vault which is strongly reminiscent of the

8 RICHARD ROGERS,
European Court of
Human Rights,
Strasbourg, 1995

9 RICHARD ROGERS,
Channel 4
Headquarters,
London, 1994

Crystal Palace's great nave. Given its sensitive location and the wave of architectural conservatism that began to crest at the time, as well as the the internal problems which began to affect Lloyd's even before the building was finished, it is remarkable that the Lloyd's Building was built at all. Rogers' Coin Street project of the same period, which translated the Lloyd's vocabulary to the South Bank of the Thames, forming a sweeping barrel-vaulted arc toward Blackfriar's Bridge, suffered a more predictable fate and foundered on the rocks of political and 'community' opposition. It remains an urban ideal still to be realized. In Coin Street, Rogers provided a vision of a new London where public as well as private interests might be served. His return to the South Bank and the remodelling of the arts complex there in the late 1990s may finally see that vision brought to reality.

The work of the Rogers office in second half of the 1990s reflects the changing sensibilities of the decade, not just in its greater environmental awareness, but also in its radical response to great institutions. As a continuation of the thought process followed by James Stirling in the Neue Staatsgalerie in Stuttgart in 1984, which resulted in a very different architectural expression, Rogers' European Court of Human Rights in Strasbourg, completed in 1995, extends the dialogue about the relative importance of monumentality at the century's end in a less historically referential and ironic manner. The vocabulary is still, in essence, that of High-tech and the building is anti-monumental — in the traditional sense — though it is clearly looking towards a new language of civic design for a democratic and participatory society.

The *parti* at Strasbourg is straightforward. The European Court and the Commission on Human Rights each occupy circular drums that rise out of a common public rotunda and each has a 'tail' containing judges' chambers, offices and administration, separated by a courtyard. The 'tails', which step down as they move away from the drums, curve to conform to a bend in the adjacent river, creating a nautical silhouette when seen from the water. This impression carries over into the interiors; the view up into the circular drum is reminiscent of the conning tower of some giant, futuristic submarine about to surface. Air conditioning is restricted to the large public zones; this is indicative of a growing trend among the leaders of the High-tech school to seek a balance between high technology and low energy, as part of a widening campaign for 'green' credentials. Concrete construction is used in this instance to provide thermal mass; and Venetian blinds — in combination with natural ventilation assisted by the breezy riverside location — keep the office interiors cool on even the hottest days. The question which cuts to the heart of the issues involved here, however, is whether this 'conflation of entomological, nautical and industrial imagery [has] the weight and resonance that we traditionally expect from monuments'.[2] Determining the appropriate style for a public institution

9

10, 11 NORMAN
FOSTER, Willis
Faber Dumas
Building,
Ipswich,
1975

12, 13 NORMAN
FOSTER, Sainsbury
Centre for the
Visual Arts,
University of
East Anglia,
Norwich,
1978

10

11

in a world that is sceptical of traditional notions of authority is not easy, but any such attempt must reflect the core values of society and its priorities, which are increasingly ecological. Rogers' Strasbourg Court is a court for the people, from whom it derives its authority, and while the imagery of the building may be mechanical, its inherent message is humane, even anti-authoritarian.

Carried over into the city, this humanist agenda is equally evident in Rogers' London headquarters building for the independent television company Channel 4, completed in 1994. Local planning restrictions required a mixed-use development, a prescription that was happily in tune with the architect's visionary view that the city should be a forum for all people. Unfortunately, the residential element of the scheme was subsequently handed over to other architects and designed in a pedestrian post-modernist manner. The core of the Rogers' project consists of administrative offices. There is just one broadcasting studio, which is small since the station does not actually produce its own programmes but commissions them from others. The Channel 4 building and the associated housing surround an open central quadrangle. In theory, social, commercial, civic and environmental needs are balanced, though the jarring juxtaposition of Rogers' building and the inferior housing upsets the equation. The headquarters building itself is organized in an L-shaped plan, forming two sides of the courtyard with the main entrance at the apex. Offices occupy the four floors and accommodate 700 staff. The 'gateway' entrance to the building is suitably civic, flanked by an antenna-like tower on one side — which contains transmitters — and a stack of what appear to be oversized television sets — actually conference rooms — on the other. It is one of the few obvious instances of humour that this architect, with his serious and much needed sense of mission to save London from mediocrity, has allowed himself.

Seen in retrospect the Willis Faber Dumas building of 1975 was the equivalent of the Pompidou Centre for Norman Foster, epitomizing his talent for making a virtue of adversity, and using the most sophisticated technology to do so. A corporate decision by the client to leave London, because of rising accommodation costs, and relocate to the unremarkable Suffolk town of Ipswich, was seen as a challenge by the architects. Willis Faber Dumas' staff members were used to the density and vitality of London, and they were expected to relocate to an overgrown country market town, with few recreational facilities. Foster's building sought to reassure them by providing a building that boasts its own swimming pool and expansive roof-top garden — amenities that were unheard of in office buildings at that time. Foster deflected the objections of local planners to the intrusion of a large corporate headquarters into the historic town centre by employing an architectural strategy focused on reflection and transparency. He created, in effect, one building by day and another by night. Instead of using a conventional plinth base, mullion glazed middle, and cornice top, the Willis Faber Dumas facade was conceived as a single undulating glass surface, with barely visible stainless-steel plates connecting the glazing, via glass fins, to the concrete floor slabs behind it. The result is that the building virtually disappears during the day, assuming the reflected image of the smaller scale buildings across the street. After sunset, however, the backlit glass curtain wall becomes transparent, and the concrete structure behind emerges with an identity of its own. This strategy was made more effective by building up to the very edge of the site, so that the structure abuts the pavement, in the manner of Ipswich's older buildings. The use of a deep plan, with vertical circulation zone at its centre, also serves an environmental purpose, offsetting the increased heat gain and loss from the all glass perimeter; the building's mass effectively becomes an insulating barrier. This, and much of Foster's subsequent work, once again illustrates the obsession with High-tech equals low energy. Modern architecture, Foster and others argue, cannot and should not seek dominance over nature, but rather find harmony with the environment and a natural way of life.

The close relationship with context that Foster utilized so skilfully in Ipswich was confirmed as a personal signature in the 1978 Sainsbury Centre for the Visual Arts at the University of East Anglia that followed soon afterwards. Ostensibly a sleek hangar-like shell, with all the spatial attributes that such a profile might suggest, the building has another layer of 'connectedness' and energy efficiency. The building's eleven-foot-deep perimeter structural zone provides the flexibility that is mandatory in the high-tech genre — which is usually gained by grouping services within the depth of the external envelope as they are here — and serves the same environmental purpose as the deep plan at Willis Faber Dumas; the cladding panels that wrap around the building are mounted directly on to the outer chord of the truss structure, and louvres are suspended from the inner chord forming an adjustable lining. The panels, which are either solid aluminium or glazed, can be easily removed and redistributed with a screwdriver; and simply by resetting a computer, the louvres can respond to new patterns of sunlight, deflecting solar gain. Through this strategy, as well as by sensitive orientation that takes advantage of the best views on the site with minimal heat gain or loss through the glazed hangar ends, the architect avoided heating and cooling the building in the conventional mechanical sense. The building's computer, reading the density of the clouds in the ever-changing East Anglian sky, drives the louvres all day long, and their muffled cranking offers an audible expression of the interaction of architecture, nature and technology.

This perimeter services arrangement, which allows open flexible space in the Sainsbury Gallery, becomes a 'saddlebags' system in Foster's Hongkong & Shanghai Bank, whose structure was inspired by suspension bridges like

12

13

San Francisco's Golden Gate. The building's services are concentrated in pods located outside the vertical structural piers, allowing a clear span inside, corresponding in this instance to the landing axis of the Kowloon Ferry and connecting to a public park behind the building. Structure is once again, in Foster's hands, put to the service of the high-tech ideal of universal space as well as contextuality. The suspended office floors allow the crowds leaving the ferry to walk under the tower directly to the park. Escalators whisk the bank customers among them up through air locks in a glass underbelly slung between the bridge piers, a clear protest against the legacy of Le Corbusier and against the all too familiar modernist landscape of sterile space that exists below buildings elevated on *pilotis*. Foster's sensitivity to terrain extended in this instance to consulting local

14

Feng Shui experts; geomancy is taken seriously in Asia, and especially in Hong Kong. They concurred with the alignment of the tower, acting as a gateway to the city from Kowloon, but advised that the triangular cable configuration, from which the progressively diminishing stacks of floors are suspended, be flipped so that the tip of each triangle points up, keeping energy and positive forces intact. The designs were suitably amended.

The Hongkong & Shanghai Bank, which was completed in 1985, set a standard of excellence for those who subsequently entered the phenomenal skyscraper sweepstake which overtook growing cities throughout the world, and Foster's proposed Millennium Tower, of 1997, designed for the heart of the City of London (see Chapter Thirteen, figure 26), may not yet be his final word on the

subject. A burgeoning corpus of other projects, including new and renovated museums – such as the Carré d'Art in Nimes, 1985–93, and the new galleries at the Royal Academy, London, completed in the same period – reflect an ever-growing concern with civic and urban values which form a continuing subtext in Foster's work. The Nimes project was a particular landmark in Foster's *œuvre*. The site, occupied by the fire-gutted remains of a nineteenth-century theatre, faces the third-century Maison Carrée, one of the best-preserved of all Roman temples, at the heart of the historic city. The brief was for an integrated arts centre – 'the Pompidou of the South' – although there was no attempt at achieving the flexibility that inspired Pompidou, and conventional gallery and library spaces were specified. Elevated on a 'podium', its deep canopy supported on slender steel columns, Foster's building evokes clear memories of the imposing classical frontage of the lost theatre. Timeless, yet entirely modern, and imbued with the sense of calm that Foster has increasingly sought in his architecture, the Carré d'Art demonstrates the ability of high-tech architects to work in tune with even a highly sensitive context.

The terminal building at Stansted, London's third airport, completed in 1991, is a development of Foster's earlier sublime sheds such as the Renault Distribution Centre in Swindon. Designed to sit effortlessly in the flat Essex landscape, Foster's minimalist, rational and highly transparent terminal building marks a conscious return to the straightforwardness of the pioneering airport buildings from the early part of this century. The passenger facilities are all located at entrance level and travellers have a clear route from the parking area or railway station through check-in and security to the train service that takes them to departure lounges and their aircraft. Few Foster buildings illustrate more strikingly the architect's complete mastery of space, services and natural lighting. The essence of Stansted lies, indeed, in its servicing strategy. By placing all the services in the undercroft, rather than in boxes at roof level, Foster was able to create a simple lightweight roof, punctuated by roof lights and supported on structural 'trees' through which lighting, ventilation and other services are distributed upwards. The contrast with more conventional terminals, in which services clutter the ceiling, could not be more striking. The tranquil but purposeful interior of Stansted is one notable example of the search for an appropriate image for the airport, which is as much an archetype of the twentieth century as was the railway station of the nineteenth. While Stansted is already recognizable as one of the enduring landmarks of post-war British architecture, Foster has continued to build on a vast scale internationally, gaining an enviable reputation for spatial mastery and technological excellence in the process.

The Reichstag project in Berlin began spectacularly with Christo's 'wrapping' of the historic parliament building, while Foster's remodelling has given the building a less

15

16

17

18

ephemeral quality of wonder. Following the historic decision in June 1990 to move the seat of the unified German
government from Bonn to Berlin, Foster's redesign of the
old Reichstag building to accommodate the new united
German Parliament has introduced an unexpected twist to
the original concept by opening up the original *piano
nobile* to members of parliament and general public alike.
This is a clear statement of acceptance of the social
changes that have taken place in Germany since the
Reichstag first opened in 1871. The architectural expression
of democratic restructuring continues in the assembly hall,
which is wrapped in glass to symbolize the accessibility of
the new parliament; this hall replaces a maze of rooms that
were inserted into the shell of the building, which was all
that remained of it following the Soviet bombardment of
Berlin in 1945. The dome, which was the enduring symbol of
the pre-war Reichstag, has not been renewed in replica,
but has been replaced with a new glass roof of an entirely

17 NORMAN FOSTER,
Stansted Airport,
Essex, 1991

18 NORMAN FOSTER,
Chek Lap Kok
Airport, Hong
Kong, 1997

19 NORMAN FOSTER,
Reichstag
Project, Berlin,
1997

20 (Overleaf)
MICHAEL HOPKINS,
Mound Stand,
Lord's Cricket
Ground, London,
1987

19

different profile, and the contiguous roof-top parterres
have been converted into public terraces, offering
panoramic views out over the city.

Foster's office in Hong Kong, which was established as a result of the Hongkong & Shanghai Bank tower,
has expanded the aesthetic of highly sophisticated technology in the new Hong Kong Airport at Chek Lap Kok. The
project required the creation of an artificial island large
enough to accommodate a terminal the size of London's
Heathrow and John F Kennedy in New York combined; it is
intended to handle thirty-seven million passengers a year
in phase one and eighty-seven million by 2040. One
consistent hallmark of the Foster approach has been the
use of structure to organize and rationalize complex
functional programmes. In this case, a wide-span truss
is set at rising elevations along a 107.25-foot square grid
to form elongated bow-shaped bays that stretch from
the land-based road system outward to a Y-shaped

30 Eva Jiricna,
Joseph Shop,
London,
1989

31, 32 Eva
Jiricna, Addition
to Ove Arup
House, London,
1991

31

32

33

34

affinity between the high-tech aesthetic and the classic High Modernism that the original house (designed in 1957 by the Rhodesian architect Erhard Lorenz in collaboration with Ove Arup) represents. Jiricna's commission involved restoring the integrity of the existing house, as well as accommodating additional facilities requested by the new owner, including a small gymnasium, sauna and outdoor lap pool. The sauna and gymnasium are housed in two stainless-steel and glass pavilions. A circulation spine links the existing house with the new pavilions and leads on to the pool, which forms a liquid line between the house and a vast expanse of lawn. Structurally interconnected, pin-jointed columns support the diaphragm roof of the pavilions, which have double-glazed, structural glass walls that allow unrestricted views over the lawn and Hampstead Heath beyond. A grey Spanish limestone floor provides continuity with the existing house. Jiricna is popularly identified with highly refined engineering details in stainless steel and glass, but this project also demonstrates her considerable spatial design skills; the functionalist, free flow of space seen in the original Arup house is well integrated into a new coherent whole. Precision detailing – such as the elegant translucent screens – of course plays a part in the project, lifting it into the high-tech realm, not least because of the obvious pride taken in making and presenting these elements and the delicate wedding of architectural and engineering considerations that the project represents.

Jan Kaplicky and Amanda Levete, of the London-based practice Future Systems, have reinforced the transparent and environmental subtext of High-tech in two notable projects which could not differ more in terms of their scale. The first, the Hauer-King House in London (1995), for a leading restaurateur and his wife, superficially resembles a giant steel and glass roll-top desk. Looking oddly at home in the context of Georgian and Victorian terraces, the house is contained within two parallel side walls of London stock brick. But these flanking walls do not have a structural role. Three *in-situ* concrete floors, which seem to float within a great internal space, are supported by an over-arching steel frame: the brick is merely cosmetic. The suspended floors – really a series of decks – provide a vertical space for living that is typical of London. But there is none of the sense of enclosure and solidity found in an eighteenth- or nineteenth-century London terrace. Instead, there are vertical views through the house and, to the garden side, views out through a tremendous, sloping wall of glass that forms one of the principal elevations. An elaborate battery of devices, including electrically operated blinds, is provided to address the problem of solar gain. To the street, the house is translucent, some privacy being provided by the use of a classic Modern Movement – and high-tech – material: glass brick. The Hauer-King House is quietly revolutionary. At home in its setting, it restates the case for the modern house with a quiet, but unswerving, passion and is an

39, 40 ODILE DECQ
AND BENOÎT
CORNETTE, Banque
Populaire de
l'Ouest, Rennes,
1990

41 (Overleaf)
RENZO PIANO,
Menil Collection
Gallery, Houston,
1981–6

spaces, continuing the precedent set at the Institut du Monde Arabe. The vault is lit internally at night, casting off a red glow like a living membrane and giving it the appearance of a large faceted jewel. This reclaimed space has been used for additional balconies and a ballet studio directly under the curve of the roof, the new profile recalling Palladio's Basilica at Vicenza, which Aldo Rossi, in *The Architecture of the City*, praised as one of the most memorable and durable of urban monuments. In Lyons, Nouvel has attempted to bring a venerable art form, and its equally venerated container, into the twenty-first century, with some success. The Opera House is one of the most prominent built schemes by an architect of visionary power; his sadly unbuilt *Tour sans Fin*, intended for the office city of La Défense, Paris, demonstrates his continuing preoccupation with illusion and artifice, the breaking down of the barriers between reality and illusion, and with the art of film in particular. The point where the semi-transparent tower ends and the sky begins is made deliberately ambiguous; an effect that is enhanced by the grey northern light which often clouds the French capital.

This search for lightness is an underlying theme of the Banque Populaire de l'Ouest in Rennes, France, of 1990, by Odile Decq and Benoît Cornette. It has a spectacular double-glazed, suspended all-glass facade supported by a metal structure located 6 feet in front of it. This innovative structural solution was engineered by Rice Francis Ritchie — proof, if needed, of its high-tech credentials — and carries the emphasis on glass found in the work of English architects such as Grimshaw and Jiricna. Decq and Cornette resist the high-tech label, preferring instead to characterize their work as 'soft technology'. The source is unmistakable, however, and by following the high-tech route the designers were able to achieve the degree of transparency and the progressive image that they wanted for the building.

The great engineers of the nineteenth century, with their visionary application of structure to the daunting challenges of new building types made possible by unfolding industrial development, would not be surprised by the current possibilities that such development now offers in the late twentieth century. The work of Renzo Piano, post-Pompidou, is interesting for its great diversity, its sophisticated urban response and its undogmatic handling of the established language of High-tech. Piano's gallery at Houston, Texas, built in 1981–6 to house the Menil Collection, has an ordinary enough setting in the suburbs of the Texan boom city. The revolutionary ideas behind the Pompidou Centre were not entirely laid aside in the programme for this relatively modest, yet unforgettable, art museum since the client wished to encourage research and show a varied collection in an unconventional and thought-provoking way. The interior is notable for its masterly use of daylight, filtered through a roof made up of 'leaves' of glass-reinforced concrete, and the exterior of the gallery is clad in timber boarding like that on nearby houses, further evidence of Piano's interest in context.

40

*42, 43, 44, 45
(Overleaf)*
RENZO PIANO,
Kansai
International
Airport, Osaka,
1988-94

The terminal building for Kansai International Airport in Osaka, Japan, which Piano completed in 1994, is typical in this regard, and is certainly his largest work to date. In fact it is one of the largest buildings of the twentieth century. With its graceful organic structure which relies on the repetition and gradual diminution of a dinosaur-like skeletal tensile beam assembly along the entire length of the terminal, Kansai reveals the constant line of argument in which the high-tech architects have been engaged, extending back to the mid-nineteenth-century. It is a building that invites superlatives: the world's longest building, built on the world's largest artificial island in Osaka Bay. Steel caissons were sunk to create the perimeter of the island and two nearby mountain tops were

42

levelled to provide infill after settlement exceeded the 36 feet originally predicted, leading to the cropping of a third mountain for additional ballast during construction. In addition to these formidable technical problems, the engineers had to protect the airport from possible earthquakes and typhoons. For Piano, for whom context is as important – if not more important – than it is for Norman Foster, the detachment of the island originally caused conceptual difficulties, but in time he, along with partner Noriaki Okabe, found ways to incorporate the waves and the sunlight on the water metaphorically into the design. Trees, planted heavily around the island edge, soften the impression of artificiality on the side behind the terminal and penetrate the interior wherever possible. The multi-level terminal building – in which domestic and international flights are dealt with on different floors and where planes dock along extended boarding wings – lent itself to a graceful, wing-shaped sectional curve in the central portion, which reverberates out into the extensions on either side. Transparency assists in orientation, and automated transport on the landside of each boarding wing links to international gates, diminishing the distances that passengers have to travel, and contributing to flexibility. The concentration of concessions on a separate level between the domestic and international floors contributes to this transparency by allowing clear views through the terminal at apron level, without the visual clutter that typically occurs in other airports. The well-established high-tech emphasis on service zoning contributing to flexibility is also evident here; there are strong parallels with Foster's Stansted Airport, notably the common emphasis on transparency and clarity. The key point of difference, however, is that while at Stansted the structure is neutral, almost determinedly non-directional and undramatic, at Kansai the avionic section of the building points the way to the planes.

Renzo Piano collaborated extensively with Ove Arup & Partners on the Kansai project, along with Nikken Sekkei, and the close co-operation between architects and engineers is most evident in the sophistication of the stainless-steel skin, the geometric discipline of the structure and its complex curved forms, and yet the evident standardization that they have been able to achieve. Conceptually, the roof was considered geometrically as portions of a cylinder of different radii; the boarding-wing roof, for example, is set out on a ten-mile radius inclined at 68 degrees, to form the horizontal. This is a 'soft' rather than a rigid geometry; Kansai embodies the pervasive late twentieth-century interest in expressive structure, achieved even at the expense of strict adherence to a functional programme, and Piano's terminal building expresses the language of flight as effectively as Eero Saarinen's TWA Terminal at JFK in New York did in the 1960s.

The wish to imbue such structures with a natural dynamic force is not new; such experiments can be traced to early attempts such as the Oxford Museum by Deane and Woodward of 1856, which was a Ruskinian riposte to the lack of natural reference in Paxton's Crystal Palace of five years earlier. High-tech architecture, its proponents would argue, is not style-bound, but rather offers a response to changing technology which needs to be harnessed and utilized in the service of society. At its best its mission literally to enlighten – to conserve resources by doing more with less – allows high-tech architects to achieve maximum results with minimum means – an imperative which matters more than ever in the ecology-conscious 1990s. As a movement it also points to the resilience of the modern tradition at the end of the century: more than a simply passing phase in the history of modern architecture, High-tech continues to enrich the mainstream of architectural invention.

43

44

Mies van der Rohe's famous dictum 'less is more' is for modernists a defining statement. For minimalists, however, it has become a kind of mantra to be repeated daily as they pursue their quest to strip away unwanted detail. For the true minimalist the object of all design is to define the true essence of any given piece, whether it be a piece of cutlery, a gallery space or a house in the landscape.

As a reinforcement of Modernism in architecture, as well as its manifestation in all of the arts, Minimalism may be traced back to the beginning of the Arts and Crafts Movement and the move away from Victorian clutter. It is rooted in the efforts toward simplicity made by William Morris, among others, who established the groundwork for the modernist principles of honesty of materials and structure, and the 'total work of art'. Minimalism, as evident today, most obviously stems from the philosophy and architecture of Mies van der Rohe and the reductivist tendency that finds its ultimate expression in his work. By taking this desire for simplicity to the extreme in buildings such as the Barcelona Pavilion, constructed 1928–9, and

2

the Farnsworth House, 1945–51, Mies intended to maximize the feeling of a free flow of space between zones in the interior, and between inside and out. Mies' reduction of details was not an end in itself, but the means of achieving a more general fusion between architecture and nature. Glass, however, arguably the most important material for the early Modernists, always intervenes between the two, keeping unpredictable, dangerous forces at bay. Glass provides a visual, but not actual, connection with the external world, abstracting it from experience and presenting it as a pattern on a transparent wall. Mies's development of this abstraction in the three decades that separate the Barcelona Pavilion and the Farnsworth House is obvious: the former has a direct relationship with the brick country villas that Mies had designed previously, with long tentacle walls extending out into the countryside, while the latter, in contrast, is completely detached from its site, a glass box riding high above the ground on steel columns. In his Glass House in New Canaan, Connecticut, 1949–50, Philip Johnson, Mies'

chief disciple, echoed this detachment. Johnson was able to make all the walls from glass, relying on the protection of his extensive wooded estate for privacy. Like the Farnsworth House, nature is treated as a remote backdrop, a changing panorama to be observed from an immutable, crystalline capsule.

The change that has recently taken place in this reductivist sensibility lies in the way it has been adapted by various architects throughout the world to answer to particularized agendas, and to develop a new awareness of a revised attitude to nature in general. Tadao Ando, Antoine Predock, John Pawson, Alberto Campo Baeza, Donald Judd and Ricardo Legorreta, who follows in the footsteps of the late Luis Barragán, are just a few of those now seeking to achieve a balance between architecture and nature through simplicity of form, surface and detail.

Chief amongst this group, Tadao Ando disproves the notion that architectural Minimalism is the built equivalent of artistic abstraction and the anti-representational reductivism that stemmed from it. Closer inspection also reveals that these architects, while superficially seeming to fall into the same category, must each be taken on their own terms. While Ando freely admits to an ongoing reverence for the work of Le Corbusier (the first books he bought in his remarkable struggle to teach himself architecture were Le Corbusier's Œuvre complète), he cannot be dismissed simply as an inspired disciple, taking the 'Five Points of a New Architecture' to their extreme. Instead, he has taken an entirely different direction specifically related to his own background. Consistent with the intention of Minimalism in art in its initial phase in the mid-1960s, Ando's aim has been to force a conflict between the person in a space and its surroundings. Whereas minimalist art can be seen as a reaction against commercial vulgarity, the commodification of culture and the overabundance of riches provided by industry, as well as testing the limits of non-representation, Ando's architecture presents a wider three-dimensional vision. Like minimalist artists, he seeks a reaction and sets up the spatial conditions to get it, but rather than calling the value of representation into question, he focuses on nature itself as the historical focus of Japanese architecture. The relationship with nature, Ando admits, 'is very troubled today', and he seeks to draw attention to the extent of this threat: 'by dynamically integrating the opposition between abstraction and representation. Abstraction is an aesthetic based on clarity of logic and transparency of concept, and representation is concerned with all historical, cultural, climatic, topographical, urban and living conditions. I want to integrate these two in a fundamental way. What appears on the surface may be geometrical abstraction. However, inside there must be much that is representational. Architecture exists in conflict between abstraction and representation. Into this relationship another element, nature, is introduced, which occupies a different plane.'[1]

3

1 (Previous page)
ALBERTO CAMPO
BAEZA, Casa Gaspar,
Cadiz, 1991

2, 3 TADAO ANDO,
Koshino House,
Tokyo, 1981

4, 5 TADAO ANDO,
Nakayama House,
Nara, 1985

This positive reversal in Ando's strategy is to use a refined version of the modernist language to combat its denial of context. The column, wall and window are taken as weapons against the homogeneity they once combined to create, and Ando manipulates them in covert ways to restate the case he feels has failed. One example is the Children's Museum in Himeji, 1987–9, which allows for an appreciation of the outside from the inside, in an attempt to change the meaning of nature through architecture. In this instance, Ando expands the attempts by minimalist artists to make viewers aware of the absurdity of the concept of museums in the first place, since the introduction of this genre during the Enlightenment was the beginning of the removal of art from its primary ritualistic function in the real world. Ando's equivalent to minimalist black canvases that force people to look elsewhere,

5

preferably at the space itself, are glass openings that prompt them to look at nature instead. The contemplation and comparison of difference, between inside and out, is most of his message.

Ando's Koshino House in Tokyo, 1981, is buried in a slope, with a curved wall defining a protected zone in which two separate rectilinear volumes are located, intended, according to Ando, to form a 'composition sprinkled with various scenic locations that describe the processes of the natural world and develop in complicated ways as the viewer moves through them.'

The Nakayama House of 1985, located in a new housing complex in the Nara Prefecture, is a two-storey rectangle divided longitudinally into an enclosed living area and an open court. By reducing the materials used to

6 TADAO ANDO,
Chikatsu-Asuka
Historical
Museum, Osaka
1990-4

7, 8 TADAO ANDO,
Water Temple,
Awaji Island,
1990

mainly concrete and glass, Ando has heightened the presence of light, shade and shadow, approximating what he describes as a sublime state.

The Kara-za Theatre of 1987, however, shows that this achievement is not limited to his use of concrete. The 600-seat structure, which the director requested be demountable, is based on the traditional timber Kanamaruza Theatre in Shikoku, but is executed in tubular metal scaffolding that is readily available world-wide. Ando's innovation here was to produce a set of drawings that can be faxed anywhere in the world where the troupe is booked, so that the theatre can be constructed locally, making this an architecture which is truly a product of the information age that Japan has done so much to make a reality.

The Chikatsu-Asuka Historical Museum in Minami-Kawachi near Osaka, 1990–4, underscores the architect's responsiveness to precedent, since this prefecture has over two hundred *tumuli*, including four Imperial tombs of great historical importance. Rather than just displaying archeological objects, Ando has taken the novel approach

7

of making the museum roof a stepped stadium from which visitors can view the *tumuli* across the lake. The site has been landscaped with blossoming plums and other deciduous trees that produce vivid foliage, providing a foil for the building in their midst.

The Water Temple of 1990, on Awaji Island, Hyogo Prefecture, is intended to completely alter preconceived notions of what a Buddhist temple should look like. This building is placed below an elliptical lotus pond, the flower symbolizing the state of enlightenment, instead of beginning with the axial alignment that is typically used. Entry is gained by a stairway which descends through the pond, giving the impression of sinking into it. Inside the circular temple, lattice screens, organized along a grid, divide the space into zones related to the divisions between transparent wisdom and phenomenal experience described in Tantric Buddhism. The entire hall, which is painted vermilion, is orientated to face the setting sun, and the walls glow fiery red at sunset.

The circle is used again in the Naoshima Contemporary Art Museum, finished in 1992, on Naoshima Island,

6

Kagawa Prefecture, in conjunction with a rectangular block attached to it at a diagonal. Serving as an open atrium reception space, the circle guides people to the galleries, guest rooms, cafe and restaurant, eventually ending the circulation sequence on a terrace overlooking the sea. This use of a time-honoured technique from Japanese landscape architecture called the 'borrowed view', which brings the natural environment into the exhibition experience, is typical of Ando's reliance on traditional Japanese themes where they are appropriate to his needs.

The Church of the Light, completed in 1989, is a paradigmatic example of Ando's special vision. It is located in a quiet residential neighbourhood in Ibaraki, Osaka Prefecture, and is perhaps the ultimate minimalist statement, a pure example of the combined power of space and light. Planned as an addition to an existing church and manse, the new building is positioned to complement the older structures as well as for solar orientation, which is particularly important to the design. A diagonal wall, lower than the ceiling height of the nave, intersects the plan to create a lobby. A high, narrow slot in this plane allows worshippers into the church and, after turning to move along this axis, they are presented with a cross cut into the concrete wall behind the altar, which allows sunlight to glow through its cruciform slots. Seats are made out of rough boards, partially for tactile reasons, partially to control cost. Ando explains the limited range of materials as a device to heighten the senses, since light becomes brilliant only against a very dark background: 'The only natural element here is sunlight. Nature has been rendered in extreme abstraction. The architecture, adapting to this light becomes purified. I am convinced that substances such as wood and concrete are invaluable materials since one becomes aware of the true quality of architecture, in those parts of the building that come into contact with the human hand or foot.'

This simple but spiritually powerful theme is restated in Ando's drum-like Meditation Space for Unesco in Paris, 1995. Built alongside the Unesco headquarters, in commemoration of the organization's fiftieth anniversary, the space is intended as a place of prayer for eternal global peace for all peoples of the world transcending their religious, ethnic and cultural differences and conflicts. It relies on a poetic reiteration of Le Corbusier's statement that 'Architecture is the magnificent and orderly play of solids brought together in light', providing a pure Platonic form whose interior is washed with daylight from above; it represents space in its essence and is both powerful and affecting.

If, as has been claimed, Minimalism has its real roots in the clash between American democratic ideals and their compromise in capitalism, the architects practising in the United States should provide an important clue to several critical attributes of the sensibility. Donald Judd is an especially important figure because he was both artist and architect, a transitional designer who

10

11

9, 10 TADAO ANDO, Church of the Light, Ibaraki, 1989

11, 12 (Overleaf) TADAO ANDO, Meditation Space for Unesco, Paris, 1995

bridged both disciplines in a way that has eluded others, such as Frank Gehry, who have tried to follow a similar path. Judd crossed this divide when he became frustrated with the inherent, two-dimensionality of painting and decided to make objects that enclosed space. Rejecting the idea of reductivism, he also attempted to avoid order and structure, declaring instead that he wanted to produce 'work that doesn't involve incredible assumptions about everything. I don't begin to think about the order of the universe or the nature of American society. I don't want to make a statement about what is universal, or claim too much.' Judd's work has slowly moved out of the confines of the museum. He has undertaken outdoor projects using metal, and in the 1980s in Marfa, Texas, he completed a series of concrete cubes that stretch for almost a kilometre. In each of the outdoor pieces, then and since, as the sculpture has also become habitable, an integral relationship with the land became a key ingredient in his work.

Ando's implicit conflict at the Children's Museum in Himeji indicates the extent to which his work differs from Judd's. They are most similar in instances when Ando has dramatically altered the topography. This may result from the feeling of openness in Texas — a state with endless horizons that represents a country that has institutionalized a frontier mentality even though it no longer has a frontier — in contrast to the density of Japan. The Block, in Marfa, Texas, completed in 1974, is one of Judd's largest structures, a sensitive conversion of two aircraft hangers and another existing two-storey, wooden-framed building. He surrounded all three with a high adobe wall to unify and screen them from the main interstate highway nearby. For all his denial of order, the Block is the essence of it, as the outer wall brings the chaotic grouping into focus like a walled Roman city. This could be due to the fact that, not surprisingly for an American, he prefers assertiveness to quaintness in his architecture: 'I don't understand buildings that are complicated, or produce a lot of commotion, which most of the buildings do now. Everything is every which way these days, why not have something that's easier to deal with'.

Judd's work at the Chinati Foundation, Marfa, Texas, is also a renovation, involving two existing artillery sheds in this instance. He gutted them, and replaced the doors with custom-designed windows, made openable to allow cross-ventilation. The Arena, which was the former gymnasium for the fort that the artillery sheds supplied, underwent a similar stripping-back, and is now used as a display space for Judd's art.

Antoine Predock, who also practises in the southwestern United States, has chosen a less polemical stance which primarily involves a pared-down historical commentary. Avoiding the subtlety of offsetting abstraction and representation, or making architecture as habitable, but not necessarily functional, sculpture, Predock has opted for barely indicative cultural references.

13

The crosscurrents that surface in discussions throughout this book arise again here: doesn't Predock's historicism place him in the contemporary vernacular, or even post-modern, camp? It can be argued, however, that his predominant tendency to abstract and clarify is the main issue in his work, which outweighs other strains that are arguably present. Rather than establishing a diametrical relationship between abstraction and representation as Ando does, or making such representation detailed, superficial or detached, and hence post-modern, Predock tries literally and figuratively to attach his work to each site. His Las Vegas Central Library and Children's Discovery Museum in Nevada, of 1986, in stark contrast to Ando's museum in Himeji, defines the plaything as a sanctuary in the desert. Nature is only admitted, as it often is in his buildings, as a planned, sequential, diurnal shifting of patterns on the walls. If he shares Ando's delight in setting up a progression of spatial surprises, they remain more introspective and controlled. Predock's sites are invariably severe landscapes, which may account for his building's internalization, and, typically, the past that he recalls focuses on societies with a strongly developed sense of privacy, whether Hispanic, Navaho or Sioux. He adopts the social divisions of the cultures that preceded the present inhabitants of the areas he works in, and, when none prevail, he focuses on a natural connection.

The Mandell Weiss Forum, completed in 1987, is something of an anomaly in Antoine Predock's *œuvre*. Built on the University of California's San Diego campus, this building is a fantasy related to the theatrical experience it provides: both a commentary on reality and its dramatic depiction, and the difference between fiction and fact. To do this, Predock uses the classic combination of point, line and plane, set against a processional sequence between the common point of arrival, the car park, and the final destination of the audience, the auditorium. The line and plane of the composition is a long, angled glass wall fixed to a dark background, creating a mirror that reflects the audience going into the theatre, as well as the natural environment. The point of entry is also the point of demarcation between the real world outside and the imaginary conception of it on stage. Through this twist, the audience itself is put on stage, made to regard itself and then finally to determine if reality isn't a fantasy and the play they are watching isn't more real than life itself. This also expands the minimalist dialogue about perception, the difference between inside and out, and establishing a connection between the two. The paradox that Predock creates upsets the usual rules, forcing a reconsideration of what these opposites really are.

The Nelson Fine Arts Center on the Arizona State University campus in Tempe, finished in 1989, is more familiar as an example of Predock's style, providing massive load-bearing walls against a hot, arid climate. Yet, in much the same way as the Mandell Weiss Forum, these walls are used not only as shelter, to mitigate heat and

13 DONALD JUDD, Concrete Pieces, installion view, Marfa, Texas, 1992

14, 15 ANTOINE PREDOCK, Mandell Weiss Forum, University of California, San Diego, 1987

14

15

16 **Antoine
Predock,** Nelson
Fine Arts Center,
Arizona State
University,
Tempe,
1989

17 **Antoine
Predock,** Venice
Beach House, Los
Angeles, 1989

16

glare, but are moderators of their physical surroundings, comprising a psychological measuring device. Predock uses a hierarchical system of penetration throughout, from arcades to perforated screens, to mask incremental penetration into the complex; the Arts Centre buildings are graded registers of accessibility, monitors of the climatic change they create, and massive sundials marking the passage of time. The architect's playfulness, in his abstraction of the Sphinx at the entrance to the complex, for example, remarking on the similarity between the climate in Tempe and Egypt, has been interpreted as an indication of post-modern, even thematic or popularist tendencies, but the complex's simplicity, almost to the point of severity, dominates. This, and the extent to which the architecture is used to explain environmental circumstance, places the centre firmly in the minimalist camp.

At a smaller scale, Predock's Venice Beach House, 1989, located on the misnamed Boardwalk in the seaside suburb of Los Angeles, is a notable exception among its more ostentatious neighbours along the beach. It is a refreshingly straightforward addition to a rank of detached houses that run the gamut from Bay Area-styled Arts and Crafts plagiarisms to Frank Gehry's Norton House, with its abstracted lifeguard stand, attached to satisfy the owner's nostalgia for his past. Predock, however, avoids fantasies of any kind, and in this design they are only present in the minds of passers-by, who envy such a pristine coastal retreat. This jealousy is not deliberately elicited, but is an almost inevitable consequence of the architect's attitude: an insistence on openness and unobstructed views that also provide clear sightlines into the house through large glass windows from the Boardwalk. The largest of these windows, flush with the *piano nobile* and raised on a plinth to separate the residents from the day-trippers ambling by in droves outside, has a large centralized hinge, allowing it to swivel to a horizontal position, removing all barriers to the ocean nearby. The plinth incorporates an ingenious fountain that runs along the entire facade, at eyelevel for the strollers outside and at floor level for those sitting inside. Pressure is precisely gauged to just cover the marble face of the fountain with a film of water which cascades into a shallow moat filled with long beach grass, running along the edge between the base of the fountain and the Boardwalk. Like the glass wall leading into the Mandell Weiss Forum, this fountain is very popular, and few people, especially children, can pass it without stopping to look or letting the water run over their hands.

It is tempting to categorize such devices as mere gimmicks, 'smoke and mirrors' that detract from serious consideration; yet, when positioned within the larger framework, Predock's architecture continues the minimalist dialogue between inside and outside, nature and the human construct. The pivoting window finally achieves the Miesian vision of a free flow of space between architecture and the environment, eliminating the crystalline hermetic

18 SHIRO KURAMATA, Issey Miyake Men, Seibu Store, Tokyo, 1988

19 SHIRO KURAMATA, Issey Miyake Boutique, Bergdorf Goodman Store, New York, 1984

20 (Overleaf) YOSHIO TANIGUCHI, Municipal Museum of Art, Toyota City, 1995

seal that has become a constant in the work of other new modern architects, such as Richard Meier, putting nature on display like a panoramic image on film or a butterfly under glass. The window allows interaction between people and enclosed and open space, and the fountain continues this relationship visually: a sliver of water, when seen from the house, that acts as a liquid foreground to the expansive marine horizon beyond.

Antoine Predock is not the only minimalist to resort to special effects. The Issey Miyake Boutique on Madison Avenue in New York, 1987–8 by the late Shiro Kuramata and Toshiko Mori, which has since been remodelled, continued the stylistic themes begun in the Miyake Boutique at Kuramata's Bergdorf Goodman Store of 1984. Kuramata and Mori's interior was like a fashion catwalk flooded with light, ready for the cameras and action. The illumination emerged eerily from below, producing an underwater aesthetic. A triangular slash in the terrazzo floor allowed light to penetrate into the shop via a radiating grid of beams, through which visitors had to negotiate their way on the steel treads of a narrow stair that seemed to pre-select the size and fitness of prospective customers. The metal stair and railing extended the original metaphor from oceans to ships, and a keel-like blade running down the middle of the ceiling reiterated the nautical imagery, making the customers unsure if they were in a boat or underneath one. The axial arrangement of the shop lent itself well to the logical display system, with hanging clothes to the right of the stair upon ascent, and folded clothes on shelves to the left. The outfits were hung on steel cables, acid-washed to match the corrugated aluminium used on screens in front of the sales counters, bar, bathroom and side walls. The cables ran the length of the shop, criss-crossing the room to emphasize the triangle of the stair, and were hung with nautical hardware. Only one sample of each outfit was displayed, with other sizes stored at the source of light in the basement – a key decision in this minimalist chess game that transformed a normal rectangular commercial space into an other-worldly environment. Similarly, in Kuramata's store Issey Miyake Men in Tokyo, completed in 1988, he explored the potential of steel mesh as a structural material that also defines space. This interior has also subsequently been remodelled, as is often the way in contemporary retailing.

Light, from a natural rather than an artificial source and on a much bigger scale, is also the generating concept behind the design of the Toyota Municipal Museum of Art in Toyota City, Aichi Prefecture, 1995, by Yoshio Taniguchi. Toyota City was originally known as Koromo before the motor corporation built its main factory there. The castle next to the museum site, built in 1787, was the focal point of the older city. In organizing the three basic components, a permanent, temporary and donor gallery, Taniguchi decided upon a Janus-like concept that looks to the castle as a symbol of the past and the new city to the west as the hope of the future, with light used to join the disparate parts. An elegant sheath of translucent curtain

19

21

wall creates an almost mystical ambience in the central permanent galleries, while light is introduced into the temporary exhibition space by skylight. Taniguchi has exploited the site's slope by placing the main entrance at the mid-level, across a constructed pond, and a garden with a visual connection to the castle at the highest level. Massive forms, such as a solid wall next to the main doorway and a flanking tower, bring the chiselled glass wrapper into even sharper relief: a skilful contrast of fragile and durable in judicious balance.

Once the basic components of functional relationships, topographical connections and restricted material palette were established, Taniguchi allowed the juxtaposition between elements to come into play. Such restraint is critical to the minimalist *modus operandi*, combined with a faith in, and understanding of, the power of the dynamics themselves to become the architecture.

Luis Barragán was one of the first architects in the Western hemisphere to fully appreciate the power of formal distillation, taking the Miesian dictum 'less is more' to its extreme using elements essential to his own culture. The monumental towers that he designed with Mathias Goeritz in 1957, for an area of expansion in Mexico City called Satellite City, demonstrate his refined eye and understanding of human perception. The main highway leading from the old city is on a relatively steep gradient, a fact critical to a full appreciation of the project as the architects have used solid concrete towers as a gateway into the city, sculpting the edges to conform to the changing perspectives of motorists as they climb the hill. The visual distortion is compounded by the deliberate elimination of any indications of scale, making the towers seem taller than they are, as well as the use of saturated colours from the hot end of the spectrum, which makes them seem to advance. These tricks are only revealed when the motorist is next to the 'towers', which are really not much higher than a three-storey building rather than the twenty-storey monoliths they appear from afar.

Antoine Predock, then, was not the first to use special effects, although applying the basic principles of visual perception and colour theory falls into a different, more natural category than hydraulic pumps, hinges and mirrored walls. Barragán's Plaza y Fuente del Bebedero, built between 1958 and 1961, in the Las Arboledas section of Mexico City, and his Egerstrom Residence and stables of 1968, located in Los Clubes, Mexico City, both extended his reliance on such principles.

Barragán had invented his own elemental architectonic idiom, related to essential cultural symbols, three decades before Predock began to search for his own. He was the minimal cultural expressionist *par excellence*, able to evoke a national spirit with walls, water and colour in ways that American minimalists can only envy: Judd increasingly introduced colour, yet showed less assurance when applying it than in crafting sculptural space, while Predock's colours are powerful, but are not studies to the

extent that his predecessor's are. Barragán had the rare ability to convert colour into a physical presence, to give it dimensionality, the third realm that Judd turned to architecture in order to experience. The El Pedregal landscape gardens, Mexico City, 1945–50, utilize colours that vibrate and show Barragán's intuitive understanding of colour theory; blue, at the cool end of the spectrum, emits less energy and seems to recede visually, while red, at the warm end, emits more energy and seems to advance. Barragán chose his palette very carefully according to these simple principles and combined them with other architectural elements to extraordinary effect: a single blue wall at the end of a long straight water trough seems to stretch the line of water to infinity with the combined image of linear acceleration and coolness, while red and ochre walls near the desert sand compress space and shimmer in the heat.

Ricardo Legorreta would not agree to being called a disciple of Barragán, but there can be no denying that he was profoundly affected by his ideas, especially his deft selection of the massive wall, vibrant colour and water as being essential to Mexican architectural character. Through his association with the Museum of Contemporary Art, Monterey, Legorreta was responsible for bringing Barragán to international attention by organizing an exhibition of his work there, and resolved to implement his ideas outside Mexico. Following on from an earlier design for the Camino Real chain in Mexico City, his Camino Real Hotel, Ixtapa, completed in 1981, is cut directly into its cliff-top site, giving all rooms an unobstructed view of the Pacific Ocean. The range of colours is relatively muted here, letting the walls that run parallel to the slope communicate most of the visual story, with water in an arc-like cove already present.

If the plane is a natural vista for Ando, a prison meant to become space for Judd, a sunlit interior for Predock, and a colour-saturated wall for Barragán, several British architects take yet another direction, dealing with a predominantly urban environment.

John Pawson, who emerged as a leading minimalist of international stature in the early 1990s, is frequently credited with establishing oases of calm in London, New York and wherever else he designs. The most important oasis of all, as far as he and his family are concerned, is their own home in Notting Hill, London, completed in 1995, which takes the self-denial of this aesthetic to new extremes. The building, a Victorian brick terrace house stripped to the bone, has been compared to a monk's cell as the interior contains only the bare necessities, which are each amplified by the choice of location and material: the floor is made from planks of Douglas fir, while the kitchen counter is a slab of Carrara marble. The only bathroom in the house has a tub carved from stone, that becomes a minimalist fountain as it overflows, the water being drained by hidden outlets in the tiled floor. The result of this self-discipline is a surprising sense of

23 JOHN PAWSON
AND CLAUDIO
SILVESTRIN,
Neuendorf House,
Majorca,
1989

24 JOHN PAWSON,
Pawson House,
London,
1995

25 JOHN PAWSON,
Calvin Klein
Store, New York,
1995

spaciousness not usually associated with terrace houses, but it comes at a high personal cost. The Shaker axiom of 'a place for everything and everything in its place' takes on added significance in this controlled interior environment where one item left askew can destroy the sense of order.

As Pawson's fame spread he began to attract high-profile clients, such as Calvin Klein who asked him to design his flagship store in New York in 1995. As is the case with many minimalist buildings, this one is also a renovation, but the word is mundane considering the results. Klein chose the building — the Guaranty Trust Company, dating from the 1920s, with a grand double-height banking hall — carefully, realizing that even talent has limits if the raw material is poor. Pawson began by putting single panes of glass between the facade's fluted limestone columns, creating large windows which provide an unobstructed view of the showroom beyond. The alterations inside are equally decisive: floor-to-ceiling doors with no lintels, no mouldings throughout, and screen-like walls that provide a sense of continual surprise, perhaps a legacy of Pawson's long visits to Japan in the 1970s as a student. The similarity of approach by architect and client, of using a limited palette of exceptional materials — sand coloured York paving stones in conjunction with ebony-stained walnut floors — may explain their compatibility, and this project has undoubtedly been very important for Pawson. The city is his turf, a context he understands well, and architecture, rather than nature, is the refuge he turns to, a solemn shelter against the chaos on the streets beyond the walls.

However, not all of Pawson's designs have urban settings. The Neuendorf House, completed in 1989 and designed with Claudio Silvestrin his former partner, is located in the hills of Majorca. The house is preceded by a long wall running perpendicular to the front entrance, a slot leading into a courtyard surrounded by high walls. The L-shaped plan wraps around the square court, and serves effectively as an outdoor living room in this sunny Mediterranean climate. The long wall leading up to the house, as well as the external walls, is concrete with a trowelled-on, pigmented stucco covering, derived from the high iron content of the local soil which makes it appear red. The ground floor of the house has a dining area, with a built-in stone table and a low stone wall separating it from the kitchen. Large square wooden doors that slide into the walls, can be completely opened to connect the dining room and the courtyard, creating one continuous space. A main internal stair, behind the kitchen, leads up to the first floor, where the master bedroom and bathroom are located. The other three bedrooms, and a smaller bathroom, are arranged along the hallway on the internal face of the courtyard, forming a separate wing.

In contrast to the wide openings facing the courtyard on the ground floor, the only fenestration on the first floor is orientated to the landscape surrounding

24

25

the house. Internally, the first floor presents a solid wall to the courtyard. In the master bedroom wing the windows, square punched openings in the thick concrete mass, are organized along the outer wall like a continuous dotted line. The windows in the other wing are more staccato and less frequent, grouped around the central axis of each room.

Locally quarried stone, which is similar to travertine and is used consistently in local vernacular houses, has been used on all floors. Strategically placed roof openings wash the walls and floors on the first floor with light, altering their colour throughout the day, just as the appearance of the external walls changes according to the intensity of the sun. The entire house is a receptacle for nature, plain surfaces providing canvases for

energetic than Pawson's massive wrappers. Flat formal surfaces at the front of the house give way to a terrace at the back, defined by a concrete portal, separating the house from the wood beyond. As a renovation and extension to an existing load-bearing brick house most of the new structure is also brick, so the change of texture and material on this portal is particularly significant. Similarly important is the way this frame combines with the large square, single-pane glass window and suspended skylight to create a dialogue between inside and outside. As a contemporary open-air conservatory, this terrace presents a welcome alternative to the vulgar, prefabricated stick-on models found in many middle-class suburbs, offering several unconventional spaces for outdoor habitation in a country with very uncertain weather.

Tony Fretton is a third contender for minimalist fame in Britain. The new wing for the Lisson Gallery, designed in 1986, is an extension to an eighteenth-century town house which provides much needed space to a respected institution, and is much more than a response to urban conditions around it. The purchase of a block on Bell Street around the corner, enabled a subsequent extension in 1992 to accommodate five floors, including a basement level, and two studio flats that house visiting artists. The three exhibition spaces are stacked one on top of the other from the basement, with the artist's lofts occupying the two upper storeys, with slight offsets signalling each floor in elevation. In addition to the offsets, Fretton has used various types of natural lighting to differentiate the exhibition spaces, and has dropped the main gallery just below ground level, separating it from the street with only a clear glass wall. The consequence of this disarmingly simple gesture is to add a new dimension to the inside/outside argument and the diversionary visual tactics of early minimalist artists. Rather than excluding the city Fretton puts it on view, making it the iconic equivalent of nature, while from the outside the art is decidedly commercialized, as if behind a shop window. Whereas early artists of the same sensibility sought to draw attention to the dilemma of commodification with blank canvases, or moving art from the wall to the floor, and finally out of the gallery completely, Fretton calls attention to this process by exaggerating it in an unmistakable way.

The influence of Le Corbusier has been shown to be pervasive among the new moderns who come to terms with it in either a positive or negative way, but rarely remain neutral. The Bibliothèque Nationale de France by the French architect Dominique Perrault is classified here as minimalist because of its simplicity of form, geometricity and strictly controlled palette of materials, but the eerie resemblance to the towers of Le Corbusier's Ville Voisin, designed for Paris in 1925, is a graphic reminder of the modernist roots of the reductivist sensibility and the fine line that separates the two. Following the *grands*

26

different patterns of light and shadow, which is quite unlike Pawson's urban retreats which are more introspective, protecting the individual against city noise and polluted air.

David Chipperfield, another British architect rapidly establishing a name as a minimalist, is not quite so austere in his civic, or even suburban, responses. The Knight House in Richmond, London, completed in 1989, caused great controversy when built and includes many deliberate gestures that frame nature in the style of Ando. These are part of an elevational puzzle of shifting, interlocking and layered planes that seem to open and close, depending on what they are facing, in a situational response to context that is less momentous and more

projets of François Mitterrand's first term — the Grande Arche at La Défense in 1984–9 and IM Pei's glass pyramid at the Louvre, 1983–7 — the competition for a national library, announced during the president's second period of office in 1989, was held in an atmosphere of heightened critical expectation. Located east of the Gare d'Austerlitz, along the Seine in the 13th *arrondissement*, the library was envisioned as the heart of a new city intended to grow around it. To this end, Perrault has used four L-shaped towers to bracket the corners of the site, forming and protecting a sunken garden inside. In spite of all of the vicissitudes that occurred in the evolution from competition winner to final building — the increase in the brief to twelve million books requiring half of the towers' volume for storage — Perrault's initial concept of readers sitting in a garden sheltered from the bustle of the city has been realized.

28, 29, 30
DOMINIQUE PERRAULT,
Bibliothèque Nationale de France, Paris, 1996

29

30

In spite of the obvious, and frequently voiced, criticism of the scheme — that half the windows are wasted, that books do not belong in glass towers where they may be damaged by solar gain, especially when the users are stuck underground — the amount of material required to be stored is phenomenal and the towers are arguably similar to vertical bookshelves, albeit much enlarged. Like the minarets added to the four corners of Hagia Sophia in Istanbul by the Turkish conquerors, the towers of the library define a rectangular space that is an effective barrier for the interior, a notional wall built in the mind. These invisible lines are the ultimate minimalist statement, creating mental architecture that needs no material at all. If the vertical city that is expected to surround the library materializes, the zone of learning that these lines protect will be very precious indeed.

The next minimalist stronghold also lies in Europe, in Spain and Portugal. Chief among the architects working there today is the Portuguese architect Alvaro Siza. His Centro Galego de Arte Contemporaneo in Santiago de Compostela, Spain, completed 1994, is a *tour de force* of spatial progression, movement and skilful control of light within a tightly controlled vocabulary. While a political agenda may be absent here, the context is a constant reminder of the monastic associations of Minimalism, since the town was an important medieval pilgrimage site and remains so today. The museum is near the seventeenth-century Santo Domingo de Bonaval, which Siza has also partially restored, and its baroque facade, which has a double entrance, was instrumental in his placement and treatment of the museum entry. The museum's external cladding of local granite and carefully placed wall openings constantly refers back to its historic neighbour. After entering the museum a large vestibule leads the visitor into a series of galleries joined by a skylit spine, running through the entire building from north to south. The museum has a large walled garden that once produced food for the monastery; Siza restored the garden and it now serves as a public park. As in the monastery, his intervention in this restoration has been controlled, noninvasive and is meant to appear undesigned.

The approach of the Spanish architect Alberto Campo Baeza is not as historically grounded as Siza's, but is more related to the ideal climate of the region, especially the clear blue sky. In the modestly scaled Casa Gaspar, Cadiz, constructed 1991, he has taken every opportunity to utilize the minimalist, plain white, local courtyard typology. In larger projects the strategy has been similar, a geometric puzzle of advancing and receding white planes, positioned to receive or reflect natural light.

The crossover into the art world that minimalist architects such as Tadao Ando, John Pawson and Tony Fretton have made, is echoed in the work of the Swiss duo Jacques Herzog and Pierre de Meuron. From their base in Basel they are rapidly establishing themselves as Europe's leading purveyors of minimalist architecture to the art community. Their Goetz Art Gallery in Munich, 1989–92, for a private art collector is a cool platonic box, the solid central section of which appears to float weightlessly between an obscured glass base and a balancing clerestory. It forms a perfectly neutral container, against which the art can be appreciated. Herzog and De Meuron consolidated their reputation in 1995 by winning the competition to convert the disused Bankside Power Station in London into a new contemporary art museum for the Tate Gallery. This recent combination of industrial architecture and the minimalist aesthetic can also be traced in their early work. The Signal Box in Basel (1992) is a six-storey concrete structure concealed behind a banded sheath of copper, which renders it as an abstract autonomous box in

31 ALVARO SIZA, Centro Galego de Arte Contemporaneo, Santiago de Compostela, 1994

32 Alberto Campo
Baeza, Casa
Gaspar, Cadiz,
1991

33 Jacques Herzog
and Pierre de
Meuron, Signal
Box, Basel, 1992

34 Jacques Herzog
and Pierre de
Meuron, Goetz Art
Gallery, Munich,
1989-92

32

33

its tough industrial setting. This mission to conceal, which one finds also in Pawson's architecture, is characteristic of Herzog and De Meuron, who have argued for an equivalence between the work of architecture and the work of art.

These examples, drawn from all over the world, provide an indication of the range of developments that have been possible within the framework of principles and underlying themes that constitute Minimalism. Once understood, these create the necessary matrix with which to negotiate a deceptively simple, but ethically complex landscape. If the American agenda in minimalist architecture revolves around the elemental schism between capitalism and democracy, it is interesting to speculate about the possibility of the political and spatial implications of this position in Britain, and even France, as this obsession with individuality and cultural singularity, made manifest in open space, is less evident in Europe. It is worth noting that minimalist art began in the decade when the worldwide concern for individual rights and social justice reached its zenith, and the boundaries between public and private, the permissible and the forbidden, art and non-art were becoming indistinct. Richard Wollheim, however, the philosopher who was one of the first to explore the theoretical underpinnings of Minimalism, explained it as reflection of the fact that the labour, or craft, involved in the production of art, is more important than the commodities produced by industry. The minimalist architect's emphasis on materiality, and how things are made, exemplifies this perspective, as does his insistence on eliminating unnecessary objects from interiors. The paradox, of course, is that achieving less often costs more, and minimalist architects frequently find themselves facing exactly the political dilemma that so troubled William Morris, whose workshops were kept employed providing furniture for the emergent industrial middle class, rather than for the working classes whose skills he so valued. It is also important to remember that Modernism, while it advocated a reductivist aesthetic, had a universalist mandate, rooted in a clearly defined social agenda. The minimalists, on the other hand, whose credo superficially echoes that of the early modernists, appear to have boxed themselves into an exclusive corner, however beautifully detailed and crafted it might be.

34

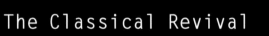

2

As a style, Classicism boasts connections to a tradition that goes back to ancient Greece and Rome via the Renaissance and several subsequent revivals. Contemporary proponents of Classicism interpret this diverse history in a variety of ways. The historian Michael Greenhalgh reminds us that: 'We must be careful to distinguish between Classicism simply as a style, which is of course open to anyone, and Classicism as part of a broader and hence more pervasive tradition, which arguably requires some range of common values as well'.[1] These common values have historically had social, artistic and political components, and architecturally are rooted in a series of rules, models and typologies which form the basis of the classical language and the classical tradition. It was these classical values that formed a common strand through architecture from antiquity right through to the mid-nineteenth century when industrialization and other social and architectural upheavals began to pull upon the thread.

This notion of a classical tradition has been explored thoroughly by the architect and theorist Demetri Porphyrios. He has consistently maintained that: 'Classicism is not a style: it transcends the vicissitudes of time and fashion as an enduring set of principles and in those things we call classical we recognize a kind of timeless present that is contemporaneous and at ease with every historical period'.[2] For Porphyrios, the emphasis is on fundamentals, the origins of architecture as shelter, in the mimetic sense of providing an image of what shelter should be, rather than the pragmatics of what it is. His buildings have spanned the gamut of function: from pavilions (which can be seen as follies intended to delight the senses, while at a more didactic level also explaining the origins of the column and classical orders), through to farms, museums, offices, private houses and recently the new town extension of Pitiousa on the Greek island of Spetses. An examination of Porphyrios' work is clearly a good place to start any investigation into the contemporary manifestations of Classicism, and the motivations of its exponents.

Porphyrios is perhaps the most cerebral of the classical revivalists, and certainly his buildings have a humanist foundation and contextual propriety about them. His New Longwall Quadrangle for Magdalen College, Oxford, 1991, for example, extends the open-courtyard vernacular of the college, placing student accommodation and a lecture theatre around three sides of a new quadrangle which opens up to the east, facing a deer park. Architecturally, the buildings continue the local idiom of Magdalen and other Oxford colleges. The buildings are constructed traditionally, with ashlar stone walls and, with the exception of the theatre which is roofed in copper, have stone slate roofs. Porphyrios set out to produce an extension to the College that would avoid the introverted mega-structural posturing of so much contemporary building in Oxford; instead he has provided a quadrangle where a number of buildings of varying

4 Demetri
Porphyrios,
Belvedere
Village, Ascot,
Berkshire, 1989

5 Demetri
Porphyrios,
Pitiousa Village,
Spetses, Greece,
1993-6

4

character, dimension and scale 'co-exist like members of a family; creating open spaces to be enjoyed by the College community and in harmony with the existing landscape'. The urban quality of the scheme is reinforced by the contrast between the classical theatre and the more vernacular style of the halls of residence, which heightens the dialogue between their respective public and private natures, and the relationship of the project as a whole with the town and college to which it connects.

Porphyrios' sophisticated fusion of the classical and the vernacular in Oxford is matched in his Belvedere Village, 1989, which is set in the Surrey landscape close to Ascot. The development provides stables, cottages, a barn and other ancillary farm buildings arranged to form an analogous village, planned around a sequence of open spaces forming farm, residential and stable courtyards respectively. The farm court performs in this context as the village green, or square. A dovecot tower performs the role of a belvedere in this ensemble, giving the village a formal focus and marking the stepping route from the farm court up to the stable court. Like the Magdalen buildings, those of the village are constructed in local vernacular materials — red and yellow brick, and red tiles and dark-stained timber — which gives the ensemble a contextual coherence, despite the deliberate variety of its individual buildings. These two projects, and others such as Pitiousa Village in Spetses, 1993–6, support Porphyrios' view that vernacular sources are critical. Like all his work, they are characterized by a sense of the appropriateness of materials, which are generally indigenous and natural, and rely on harmonious proportions and a contextual correctness as a subtext to the overall principles adhered to.

The Luxembourg-born architect Leon Krier, like Porphyrios, has been a passionate advocate of classical architecture, and is keenly aware of its polemical potential. He sees Classicism as not just an alternative to Modernism, but opposed to Modernism and the social consumerism that continues to support it. He also reinforces the connection between the classical and the vernacular, or the collective and the individual components that comprise the classically organized city, offering these up as a set of complementary pairs: the monument and the urban fabric; the palace and the house; the public and the domestic. Krier uses Classicism as an analogue for the typological order and building hierarchy that have been lost to the modernist paradigm, which, he argues, was intended to 'revolutionize, invalidate and replace all previous architectural traditions and knowledge'. He sees the procedures and materials that are the symbols of Modernism, such as standardization, prefabrication, steel, concrete and glass, as superficial symptoms of a pervasive dogma that still attempts to be exclusive, and notes that this is the reason why Classicism is frequently not considered for inclusion in the pluralistic revolt against Modernism. Krier has been most effective in formulating

5

a substantial theoretical argument to counter this impression, and the argument has been advanced in built form, as well as in text and drawings. His evocative contributions to the Seaside New Town in Florida, 1988, as well as to the master planning of Poundbury in Dorset, England, show his architectonic skill at doing so. His most memorable graphic effort has perhaps been his speculative reconstruction of Pliny's Villa Laurentium, 1982, which captures the fine balance between power and repose that exists in classical architecture.

Classical architecture, Krier argues, is timeless because it raises vernacular building to a higher cultural level, as an art. It is, he says, 'concerned with imitating nature in its principles of beauty by means of a limited number of symbols and analogies, and is a language of construction and tectonic logic'.[3] This imitative process has been extended to encompass medieval models in his plans for Poundbury in an attempt to provide controlled growth for the town of Dorchester, avoiding the suburban sprawl that threatens to engulf the rest of southern England in the projected rush to make up the painful shortage in housing stock that now exists there.

Dorchester was founded by the Romans; it grew to cover more than one hundred acres, and boasted four thousand inhabitants before migration to larger urban areas reduced its stature during the Industrial Revolution. More recently, it was affected by the dramatic civic transformations that took place in Britain in the 1960s, taking on a largely administrative and commercial role for the suburbs that began to grow around it. As in other towns throughout the country, this growth put tremendous pressure on the historic core, causing traffic congestion and destruction of the older fabric.

In 1988 Leon Krier was commissioned by the Duchy of Cornwall to consult with local authorities in finding a way to reverse this trend. Krier studied the patterns of traditional Dorset villages: their typical grouping around a 'common', the hierarchy of street sizes, the types of buildings, and the materials used. Using this as a model, he proposed integrating uses rather than dividing them — as has been typical of planning practice since the end of the Second World War — and organizing future growth around several new village-sized districts, each under one hundred acres.

In conjunction with the local authority plan to phase the expansion of Dorchester over the next decade, Krier's scheme is based on four communities of no more than eight hundred households each. The first quarter, Middle Farm, is complete, and focuses on a central square with a tower as a landmark. High streets radiate from it, reaching out to the existing Victoria Park suburb, as well as to an improved public park and the new Poundbury quarters, which occupy higher elevations around Poundbury Farm. This is characteristic of the plan, which is defined by the local topography and the existing suburbs around it. The Poundbury quarters consist

6

7

6 LEON KRIER,
Villa Laurentium
Project, 1982

7, 8 LEON KRIER,
Poundbury Master
Plan, Dorset,
1991

8

9

of three urban districts, with traffic channelled in boulevards between them. These wide tree-lined avenues are laid out to focus on important natural and historical features.

Leon Krier's brother, Rob Krier, has also been instrumental in an exhaustive examination of the components that once made the traditional European city livable and memorable, before it was destroyed by the twin juggernauts of war and Modernism. In doing so, he has made the critical distinction that 'every period in history forms a unit with its own internal logic, which cannot be fragmented and interchanged with elements of other periods at will'. It is interesting that in America, architects such as Andres Duany and Elizabeth Plater-Zyberk, master planners of Seaside in Florida, have reverted to ordinances

9 TONY ATKIN,
Beach Pavilion,
Seaside, Florida,
1987

10 ROB KRIER,
Tiergarten
Housing, Berlin,
1981-5

11 LEON KRIER,
Belvedere,
Seaside, Florida,
1988

10

11

to restore a humane dimension to the towns and cities of the nation, while for Rob Krier that initiative has taken the form of discovering the typological elements that repeatedly occur in the city over time. Revealing the strong connection that exists between Classicism and Rationalism, Rob Krier has been searching for a rational system that will allow him to both understand and reconstruct the most compelling aspects of the traditional city that have been destroyed. To do this, he has divided the urban area into public and private spheres, noting that the behavioural patterns, although formal and informal respectively, have been remarkably similar at the deeper level in both. His conclusion, after detailed historical study, is that the way that public space has been organized has, in all periods, exercised a powerful influence on the design of the private realm especially with regard to housing.

Appropriately, Rob Krier has devoted a considerable amount of energy to the design and construction of apartment buildings and housing blocks, most notably in Berlin, a city whose architectural traditions were all but eradicated in the Second World War. Krier's housing on the Tiergarten, in Rauchstrasse in Berlin, 1981–6, is exemplary in this regard. In the context of the Tiergarten suburb, Krier felt that an urban-scaled block would be inappropriate. He therefore took as a model the old classically organized villas of the neighbourhood, matching them in size and scale. The housing is arranged around a lush central 'green' closed off by a gateway from the busy thoroughfare of Stülerstrasse, and all the apartments relate to adjacent green spaces, whether public or private, reinforcing the notion of this new development as both a coherent entity at a local scale, and as an integral part of the city in its wider sense.

In Britain, Quinlan Terry, Robert Adam, John Simpson and Julian Bicknell have also played an important part in the resurgence of the architectural legacy of Inigo Jones and Christopher Wren. Quinlan Terry may be the

12

easiest person to start with in a discussion of this group. Terry, in a more visible way than any of the others, has managed to revive what might be thought of as a national tradition of appropriating Classicism for the purposes of commerce, since architects such as John Wood the elder and younger, and John Nash were notoriously commercially minded; Wood's Circus and Royal Crescent in Bath of the late eighteenth century and Nash's Regent Street in London of the early nineteenth century were not designed for altruistic reasons, to simply beautify their respective cities, but were property developments undertaken for profit. Much of Terry's work is in the same spirit of enterprise as these interventions, which are now held in the highest regard by architectural historians and city planners. Moreover, in the competitive economic climate of today, such commercialism is often necessary to ensure a project's success, and the longevity for which classicists yearn.

Quinlan Terry, like Demetri Porphyrios, understands that imitation has been a central feature of Western architecture for millennia, and for him that

imitation is more robustly Roman than delicate and neo-Georgian as it is in the work of the rest of the neo-Palladians with whom he is often grouped. This is particularly evident in the exultation in luxury and detail shown in his Ionic, Veneto and Gothick villas built to complement the Regency architecture of John Nash in Regent's Park, London, 1987–8.

In both his buildings and his writing, Terry has done much to address what he considers to be unjust criticisms of classical architecture. His Richmond Riverside Complex, for example, completed between 1985–7, which contains offices, shops and restaurants stretched out alongside a wide grass parterre facing the River Thames, is perhaps his best-known project in Britain and proves that Classicism is not only commercially viable, but can be popular as well. It is not just a luxury for a few wealthy clients, but highly competitive in the market place. Terry has been able to achieve this synthesis because of his realistic assessment of the strengths of the approach he is using; he has encapsulated the principles of this approach in an apologia entitled *Seven Misunderstandings about Classical Architecture.* Summarizing these, and his response to them will help to explain his conviction. Terry counters the first commonly heard criticism that classical revival architecture is merely a pastiche, by reminding critics that in Palladio's *Quattro Libri,* no guidance is given on size, scale, materials and construction, forcing the architect to draw on far more comprehensive reserves of knowledge, experience and resourcefulness than would otherwise be necessary. Secondly, regarding functionalism, he refers to the symbolic aspects of the classical system which makes its use easier and clearer than many modernist precedents. As to the third criticism, about adaptation to new types of use, he points to its versatility, saying: 'had Bramante not been able to juxtapose the circular pagan temple with the Christian Basilica, we would not have the Renaissance church typified by St Peter's'. Fourthly, regarding the use of modern materials, he points to the durability and lower maintenance costs of natural materials compared to their industrialized counterparts, and to the fact that: 'they give pleasure to the eye and make us feel good — simple pleasure in natural things'. Fifthly, considering cost, he gives examples from his own practice to show how classical buildings can be economical, and actually generate cost savings (these are due primarily to energy savings, gained by reducing the use of glass in elevations, and other passive methods). The issue of value for money leads to the sixth question about the availability and expense of crafts and trades today, to which he replies: 'The truth is, that whenever there is good work to be done, there are people available to do it'. Lastly, regarding the political implications of Classicism, he responds by saying that it has represented such a wide variety of political and religious systems throughout history that each of the 'spiritual, political, material and temporal influences are crystallized in classical forms, rendering the grammar neutral'.[4]

Terry's Howard Building, for Downing College, Cambridge, 1989, represents a significant return to Classicism by the Oxbridge axis. It has also been a particularly vulnerable target, drawing fire in the British architectural press as a polemical statement far exceeding its scale. It is, in fact, a modest detached rectangular building located near the part of the campus designed in the Greek Revival style by E M Barry in 1873, and encloses Kenny Court which was added earlier this century. Terry has taken great pains to differentiate the northern and southern long facades of the block. The north face is formal, using a higher plinth base than the other buildings on the quadrangle it faces; flat pilasters with Corinthian capitals, located at the corners of the building and between the windows, rise between plinth and cornice, but give way to engaged columns with composite capitals flanking the central door. The south elevation, by contrast, has the same plinth, pilaster and cornice combination wrapped around its corners, but after that it is essentially plain, except for a single-storey Doric portico which is eventually intended to be carried around the quadrangle on that side.

The critical war of words that followed the Howard Building's debut highlighted much of the latent animosity that exists towards Classicism in general in Britain, as well as many of the specific charges usually made against it. The arch traditionalist critic Gavin Stamp accused it not for being classical, but for being 'bad' Classicism, calling the north facade extravagant and lumpen, and certainly not the elegant Palladian composition in the manner of an English country house that Terry imagined. He argued that Terry's use of the orders was static and ornamental to the extent that details rather than architecture became the issue, saying: 'This concentration on detail rather than on overall composition may explain the characteristic deadness of Terry's Classicism.' Stamp's additional criticism of the inappropriateness of the building's formal front and casual back, a 'disappointing' interior, and the use of blind windows does not outweigh this primary charge against Terry of being unable to use classical elements in a convincing way. The result, for Stamp, is 'an awkward and amateurish essay in provincial English Baroque'. The late John Summerson, himself a respected historian and classical enthusiast, argued in response that such criticism reflects the difficulty that has always existed in determining what real Classicism should be, speculating that such vehemence against it may stem from the fear of 'a Neo-Renaissance revolution'. He admitted that he got a 'rare shock of pleasure' from the entrance facade, which had 'something new to say in a language that I happen to understand and love'.

This debate shows that convention has been blurred through historical reinterpretation and that beauty depends largely on the eye and receptivity of the beholder. Which brings us neatly to Julian Bicknell, who perhaps more than any of the other English classicists considered here has been criticized for allowing detail to

15 QUINLAN TERRY, Maitland Robinson Library, Downing College, Cambridge, 1992

16

17

triumph over composition. His work reads like a trawl through the catalogue of past classicists, from Palladio to Lutyens, running the gamut of styles from the copy-book Palladianism of his Henbury Rotunda, Cheshire, 1984, to the high English Baroque of his Upton Viva in Warwickshire, 1990. The latter is an extravagant pile in dressed and rustic stone, weighed down with over-scaled keystones and an awesome array of dormer windows. These are just two of the many large country houses that Bicknell has completed over the last decade, and his client list continues to grow. His work demonstrates, perhaps more effectively than Terry's, that contemporary Classicism has a strong commercial component; not only does it 'sell', hence its attractiveness to developers, but people also want to buy into it; this is particularly true of the newly moneyed classes who typically commission a classical country house to speed them in their quest for social respectability, or to help apply a thin veneer of 'old-money' over their new-found wealth. This is hardly new, however; it is a situation that Lutyens would have recognized and gleefully worked around, and doesn't necessarily diminish Classicism's continuing relevance in a wider context.

In a broader response to Terry's *Seven Misunderstandings*, classicists or their apologists such as Summerson generally argue for the style's continuing relevance based on an original connection to nature, an argument which extends to include its hierarchical framework of order. Having derived from a timber vernacular architecture, Classicism has retained detailed indications of its origins, in the details of its architraves, entablatures, dentils and guttae that offer durable representations of hand-crafted components. The trabeated or column-and-beam system on which classical architecture relies, unites architecture and nature, establishing a medium in which neither one dominates. Trabeation joins architecture to the landscape around and behind it: the Stoa of Attalus in Athens, for example, remains a paradigm of the ability of classical column-and-beam structures to link visually to their surroundings. Today, at a time when the human primal instinct to subdue nature seems to have entered its last act, an equally strong instinct for peace and harmony with nature has begun to emerge and gather strength. Classicism lays claim to this instinct, boasting a much longer and better established aesthetic pedigree than other newer, ecological alternatives. Furthermore, Classicism claims an anthropomorphic origin; the capital shaft and base of each of the orders are analogous to the human head, body and foot, and the proportions of classical construction are derived to emphasize this equation. The tripartite division, present in the column, logically extends at a larger scale to the entire structure, the pediment, column and stylobate relating to this same human connection.

Classicism is also put forward as an antidote to disorder. The basis of this proposition is the idea that

16 JULIAN
BICKNELL,
Upton Viva,
Warwickshire,
1990

17 JULIAN
BICKNELL,
Henbury Rotunda,
Cheshire, 1984

18 JOHN SIMPSON,
Paternoster
Square Master
Plan, London,
1989

order is the essence of the fine line between nature and architecture. This is explained by Demetri Porphyrios when he says: 'Classical order sets form over the necessities of shelter and tectonics over the contingencies of construction and shelter. Whereas the diversity of the contingent world is constantly on the verge of dissolution and the forms of the real world blossom and wilt, classical order makes us see the immutable laws of nature by means of tectonic fiction.'[5]

The intensity of the debate over the Howard Building may explain why the case for Classicism became a crusade in Britain in the mid-1980s. This was particularly obvious in the proposed redevelopment of Paternoster Square in the City of London, an area whose post-war rebuilding compromised the historic relationship between St Paul's Cathedral and its surroundings, leaving a legacy of slab block office buildings and windy pedestrian precincts in which all traces of the site's medieval past had been submerged.

The Paternoster Square development looked as if it would give the classicists their greatest ever opportunity to prove that Classicism still had a relevant part to play in the architecture of the information age. The scheme was an attempt to cut down the forest of office blocks planned by Sir William Holford in the 1950s and to restore the traditional urban grain and character of the area. As a direct result of the intervention of the Prince of Wales, the original master planner for the site, Arup Associates, was ousted in favour of the arch-classicist John Simpson. The Simpson scheme attempted a return to the street patterns that existed around St Paul's before they were flattened in the Blitz of 1940. Simpson's new streets ran into intimately scaled public squares lined by arcades which framed four- to six-storey buildings with commercial use at ground level and open plan offices above, all encased in mock eighteenth-century English classical wrappers. The plan included a quarter of a million square feet of commercial space, three quarters of a million square feet of offices, together with residential accommodation and a large hotel. Simpson answered charges of facadism by replying that: 'to accuse anyone building in a traditional classical style of merely trying to rebuild the past is to misunderstand the nature of tradition. No one would dispute that Christopher Wren's design for St Paul's was modern for its day. A classical architect today is drawing on a cultural inheritance thousands of years old. It is the Modern Movement which is in fact perpetrating redundant ideas from the late nineteenth and twentieth centuries. It is because I do not desire to reproduce the past that I design traditional buildings'.

When Simpson's scheme ran into commercial and planning difficulties, the developers hired the English post-modernist architect Terry Farrell and the Americans Hammond, Beeby and Babka to assist him; and Farrell effectively took over the role of master planner.

18

19

20

21

Farrell's plan was more commercially hard-nosed than Simpson's had been; it increased the amount of commercial office and retail space on the site, and created a huge lower-level shopping arcade accessed via a pavilion in the middle of the reinstated Paternoster Square. Like Simpson's scheme, it too ran into difficulties and any prospect of it being built finally collapsed along with the London property market in the early 1990s. Although ultimately it failed, the scheme was successful in many respects. It showed that Classicism could be harnessed to commerce to provide a contextually responsive architecture capable of gaining popular support, and it brought together what had hitherto been a disparate and sometimes antagonistic group of architects and united them under a single classicist flag. It proved that Classicism can offer a consensual approach to intervening in the city, providing a stark contrast to the deterministic and dogmatic modernist precinct that it was intended to replace. The architects collaborating in this exercise — Terry Farrell, Demetri Porphyrios, John Simpson, Sidell Gibson, Quinlan Terry and the appropriately named Robert Adam on the English side, with the Americans Allan Greenberg and Hammond, Beeby and Babka — coordinated their proposals, but aimed at a deliberate stylistic variety in the scale and detail of the buildings they proposed, intending to bring a traditional architectural richness back into this quarter of the City. Thus Terry Farrell was to be found designing in the gothic style, proposing a fan-vaulted pedestrian arcade that might have come straight from Batty Langley's treatise *Gothic Architecture Restored and Improved* of 1742; and Hammond, Beeby and Babka produced a monumental office block which gave more than a passing nod of recognition to the inflated imperial neo-Classicism of Lutyens' nearby Midland Bank building.

While the controversy over Paternoster Square was in full spate, Simpson was also involved in a one-and-a-quarter million square-foot project called London Bridge City, sited on the South Bank of the Thames between London and Tower bridges. His scheme, which recalled the Piazza San Marco in Venice in the massing of its forms and the arrangement of its open spaces facing the water, was put forward as a more viable alternative to a proposal by Philip Johnson and John Burgee which looked vaguely like Barry and Pugin's Houses of Parliament, but clad entirely in glass. In 1993, Simpson also contributed a design for a market building, one of two public buildings in the main square of Leon Krier's Poundbury development. In keeping with its traditional function, this new building houses a covered market at ground level, with a public hall above. Due to its civic importance, but relatively small scale, Simpson has done everything possible to make the building seem more assertive: large stone block quoins, a solid plinth, stone arches, window surrounds, sills, finials and columns all contribute to the required impression of solidity.

27, 28 ALLAN
GREENBERG, The
News Building,
Athens, Georgia,
1992

27

Virginia campus, or his Monticello plantation. There are also obvious Roman influences in Greenberg's repertoire, such as the Treaty Room columns, which are copied directly from the Pantheon, but the scale and delicacy of the egg and dart moulding, the dentils of the cornice, and the Corinthian columns are reminders of the strong part that the Greek Revival style had in the Federalist period in America. In the Department of State Greenberg works the Great Seal of the United States into the capitals as a clear reference to the close connection between Classicism and patriotism in America, and Greenberg has become successful by aligning himself in this way.

Greenberg's News Building, in Athens, Georgia, completed in 1992, adopts the Greek Revival style for which this city is renowned, offering in Greenberg's phrase, 'an appropriate paradigm for the development of downtown Athens'. The building houses the offices of two prominent newspapers, the *Athens Banner-Herald* and the *Athens Daily News*, and is thus important as a local public and political forum as well as an architectural landmark. The entrance facade is dominated by a two-storey stone Doric portico, the detailing of which seems exactly observed. Behind the portico is a plain wall of brick with stone trim and industrial-section window frames. The portico in this instance appropriately forms a kind of 'masthead' for the whole composition. Behind is a double-height central hall in which the Doric is supplanted by the Ionic at the upper level. The columns here have a polychromatic decorative scheme, intended to recall the temples of ancient Athens, of which Labrouste would no doubt have approved.

Hammond, Beeby and Babka have also established a strong reputation as classicists in the late 1990s, although they were more often identified with Post-Modernism in the previous decade, indicating the fine, sometimes indistinguishable line that exists between the two camps. Their Washington Library Center, in Chicago, is a ten-storey, three-quarters of a million square-foot library facility for the Chicago Public Library, America's largest circulating library at the time of its completion in 1991. The architects felt that Classicism was the only means by which they could establish the degree of grandeur a civic building of this scale required, but combined it with a steel and glass roof, and cast-stone and brick facade to express a level of technical skill characteristic of the Chicago building tradition. Sculptors rendered the exterior ornament. The library holds over two million circulating books and serves four hundred staff and two thousand patrons. It has a four-hundred-seat auditorium, audio-visual broadcast studio, computer and language centres, computerized directories and information retrieval, a public restaurant and a bookstore. While the perimeter is fixed, the core of the building is flexible; fixed service elements such as stairs, elevators and toilets are relegated to the outer zone. Conceptually, it is a high-tech box in a classical skin, designed to give the public the reassuringly familiar monumental face they expect.

29 HAMMOND, BEEBY AND BABKA, Washington Library Center, Chicago, 1991

permits and old photographs, revealed diverse roof lines and weak corners. Therefore, the design group collaborated to unify the cornice line and create strong 'book-ends' at the corners of the block to terminate the row of townhouses. The result is an integrated statement, in spite of the diverse personalities and nationalities involved. One of these book-ends, on Lot One at the corner of the Rue de Laeken and Rue du Pont Neuf, by Gabriele Tagliaventi and Associates, is a five-storey tower, a skilful conservation of a private house that sets the tone for the remainder of the units. It acts as a signal to people coming into the city, announcing the presence of the newly restored quarter, and telling them that this is an area symbolizing the city's history of destruction and renewal. Lot Two, by Atelier 55, Marc Heene and Michael Leloup Architects, also centred around the conservation of an existing house, and their original submission was reworked to achieve this; it now contains many references to the Art Nouveau period which gave Brussels some of its finest architecture. Lot Three, by Sylvie Assassin and Barthelemy Dumons Architects of Barcelona, is arranged axially to create a symmetrical plan, organized around a passageway leading into a central courtyard. The rigour of the building's internal composition reflects the slight monumentality of its facades, which, in the tradition of Adolf Loos, are intended to be 'silent', in contrast with the rich interior.

Lot Four, designed by Jean-Philippe Garric and Valérie Negre, has a deliberately massive appearance achieved with thick walls and a volumetric simplicity that belies the variety of apartments inside. The building, which mediates between the street and the garden, is based on two complementary principles: simple, rational organization contrasted with typological diversity. Lot Five, by Javier Cenicacelaya and Inigo Salona of Bilbao, is irregular in shape to accommodate a neighbouring house; this required a creative approach to circulation, which is placed along the oblique party wall. This results in various visual sequences which the architects have used to advantage, and the surprise of a single-storey house at the back of the unit, facing the garden. Lot Six, by Liam O'Connor and John Robins, is divided into two distinct projects, dominated by an impressive spiral stair running between three apartment floors; all the apartments are laid out around a square hall, typical of a nineteenth-century Brussels house. Lot Seven, the final opposing 'book-end' by Joseph Altuna and Marie-Laure Petit, completes this elegant ensemble, and provides another assured solution to the problem of turning the corner.

It is not too much of a jump from this approach to suggest that Classicism itself might be about to turn the corner. Many contemporary architects have come to value Classicism as an alternative to Modernism, largely due to the latter's failure to provide late twentieth-century society with viable built responses to its social, cultural and environmental needs. The American architect Robert A M Stern, who includes himself in this camp, is notable as much for what he says as what he does; an accomplished historian and commentator, he has made this classicist *cri de cœur*: 'Classicism presents the designer with a codified system of symphonic complexity for relating the smallest detail to the overall structure, for balancing geometry with human measure, and abstract shapes with literal depictions of nature or with verbal ideas. Its synthesis of rational composition, representational details and emphatic form challenges the intellect of the initiate and delights the senses of the layman as they pause for second and third moments to contemplate the play of light on carved surfaces, the meaning of acanthus leaves, wreathes and garlands, or the literary text of inscriptions. To talk of a forest of columns indeed to walk among one, is to experience nature in metaphor. The language of Classicism not only embraces such metaphors, it embodies them: it has them built in.'[7]

Stern's architecture has followed an erratic line from Post-Modernism to Classicism and back again, with several stops in between, which makes his inclusion in this chapter slightly problematic. He has, however, shown that he can work in a classical idiom with great conviction and panache, as demonstrated by his Observatory Hill Dining Hall for the University of Virginia, completed in 1984. Stern's porch-like additions to an existing 1970s facility are intended to give a sympathetic classical face to what had been an intrusive modernist intervention in Jefferson's campus. Just as Jaquelin Robertson and Allan Greenberg have drawn successfully on this tradition, Stern's building seems invigorated by its Virginian ancestry and the American classical canon. An increasing awareness of the range and relevance of this canon amongst American architects is matched also in a European context and Stern's vigorous invocation of Classicism and a traditional way of building strikes an increasingly popular chord. Returning to Demetri Porphyrios' assertion that 'Classicism is not a style', it is possible to detect in classically motivated projects such as Rue de Laeken in Brussels, or Seaside in Florida, a return to architecture that offers both contemporary relevance and historical continuity within the framework of a universal language which transcends the superficial concerns of style or image that characterizes the output of so many architects today.

32

31 ROBERT A M STERN, Observatory Hill Dining Hall, University of Virginia, 1984

32 SYLVIE ASSASSIN AND BARTHELEMY DUMONS ARCHITECTS, Building on Rue de Laeken, Brussels, 1992

At some point in the mid-1960s, modern architecture reached a crossroads. The principles of Modernism, as articulated by CIAM (Congrès Internationaux d'Architecture Moderne), its official organ, had come seriously under review as planners and architects around the world began to challenge the modernist hegemony, and the failings of what it had actually achieved, in both social and structural terms. A common shock tactic amongst antagonists at the time was to proclaim that Modernism was either dying or dead.

However, a change in direction was more quietly heralded by the American architect Robert Venturi who, in his landmark book *Complexity and Contradiction in Architecture*, published in 1966, called for the development of 'an architecture that promotes richness and ambiguity over unity and clarity, contradiction and redundancy over harmony and simplicity'.¹ In example after example fired rapidly like a machine gun at the modernist edifice, he described delightful historical alternatives to the famous dictum of Mies van der Rohe, 'less is more', polemically proclaiming that, 'less is a bore'. His descriptions were accompanied by postage-stamp-sized black and white illustrations, organized in the format of a slide lecture which allowed it to be subliminally accepted as authoritative by academics. In fact, the book was a compilation of lectures given by Venturi at the University of Pennsylvania. According to Tom Wolfe, author of *From Bauhaus to Our House* (a satirical account of Modernism and its aftermath in America) Venturi's arguments indeed had far more impact because they came from within the academic 'compound'.

Venturi's book laid firm foundations for the growth of a distinctive 'Post-Modern' movement originating in the United States. This is not to say that Venturi's vision of a new direction for architecture was entirely novel or original. Several of the characteristics that were to become identified with Post-Modernism, largely as a result of *Complexity and Contradiction*, were already being explored by architects who did not necessarily subscribe wholeheartedly to the Modern Movement. Perhaps the most notable amongst these was Louis Kahn, who was Professor of Architecture at the University of Pennsylvania from 1957 to 1974, and with whom Venturi obviously, therefore, had close connections. In contrast to the mechanistic approach conventionally endorsed by Modernism, Kahn believed in the need for architecture to be in tune with the rules of nature, and explored the possibility of an architecture imbued with animistic force, in which different elements might in some way express qualities such as 'hope' or 'inspiration'. Kahn's was the architectural equivalent of method acting, in which he projected his own aspirations into the most vital parts of an inanimate system. It was closely connected to an idea of habitable structure, in which the building and the people who use it become indistinguishable.

Kahn is well known for his essays into historical allusion, in projects such as the Richards Medical Research Building at the University of Pennsylvania, 1957–64, and

Bryn Mawr College dormitories, 1960–4 (modelled on the Italian hilltown of San Gimignano and a Scottish castle respectively). This reliance on historical allusion is usually regarded as being Kahn's primary contribution to the popular move away from modernist abstraction; it also became a design technique central to the vocabulary of Post-Modernism. Kahn's idea of the habitable structure may also have had a bearing on Venturi's seminal notion of the 'decorated shed' in which an appropriately characterful facade could be imposed on a bare functionalist box, thereby creating an architecture to suit any situation. A further device developed by Kahn, which was also to become a key motif in Post-Modernism, was the idea of 'wrapping' space, as in his scheme for the Mikvah Israel Synagogue in Philadelphia, 1961–72. While never realized, this design is based on the idea of cylindrical towers that surround the worshippers like circular sentinels shining with refracted light and resonating with the sound of music. These towers were for Kahn the direct interpretation of the column filled with 'inspiration'; here, the 'column' has become large enough to contain a room at its centre.

As Kahn's reputation increased, international commissions followed and the column filled with inspiration gave way in tropical climates to the need to shield windows from the sun and prevent glare. In his project for the US Consulate in Luanda, Angola, 1959–61, Kahn realized that the construction of a second skin wrapping around the building, set at a certain distance from the primary fenestrated wall, would protect the interior of the building from the sun's glare and heat. However, in what is arguably his best-known building, the National Assembly Building in Dacca, 1962–74, a similar outer layer, or second skin, is randomly cut with playful geometric openings to underline the fact that it has no functional or structural purpose, environmental or otherwise. This represented a significant formal challenge to the modernist precept that the enclosing skin of a building must express its internal organization and function. Interestingly enough, Venturi had completed a headquarters building for the North Pennsylvania Visiting Nurses Association, in Ambler, Pennsylvania, a year after the design of Kahn's Luanda Consulate and two years before the Dacca building, in which he had similarly implemented the concept of layering at a purely symbolic, rather than functional or environmental, level. An arch built in inexpensive plywood, diagonally braced to the sidewalls, is used in combination with superfluous decorative mouldings around the ground-floor windows facing the street to create a sign or symbol of entrance as a separate layer in front of the wall holding the actual entrance door. This is perhaps the first modern instance of layering used for semiotic effect. However, the building which was to be widely hailed as the first built manifestation of the ideas explored in *Complexity and Contradiction* was Robert Venturi's Vanna Venturi House in Chestnut Hill, Philadelphia, 1963.

The Vanna Venturi House, a three-dimensional 'child's drawing of a house' is now regarded as an icon of Post-Modernism, and sets out its primary characteristics. Form is used as a symbolic rather than functional expression of elemental 'shelter', while historical reference to the shingle-style profile of early-twentieth-century McKim Mead and White buildings, regarded as indigenously American, are boldly mixed with Greek and Roman temple fronts. Layering, intentional disjuncture, and deliberate ambiguity in plan, elevation and scale generate a level of playfulness and humour in the project which was to become part of Venturi's signature in his later buildings. The formal street facade looks much larger than it actually is through the controlled balance of scaleless elements, giving a 'fun house' aspect that was anathema to ultra-serious modernists. In contrast to the purism and proselytizing zeal of Modernism, Venturi argued that architecture should reflect and express the whole range of emotions found in real life.

Venturi's Franklin Court Complex, completed in time for the Philadelphia American Bicentennial celebrations in 1976, is an excellent example of his incisive wit. Venturi was originally commissioned by the National Park Service to restore the private home of Benjamin Franklin, which was located in a walled enclosure behind the first American Post Office which he founded. However, Venturi responded by arguing that there was insufficient evidence of the building on which to base a competent restoration. He developed a proposal, therefore, in which steel frames approximate the outline of the house and its appendages as an alternative to conventional restoration. Venturi's scheme was based on extensive correspondence between Franklin, who was in Paris as Ambassador to France during the time the house was built, and his wife, who actually oversaw its construction. He also proposed a garden, reproduced according to Franklin's written description. The plan of the house was inlayed in white marble on the red brick pavement along with quotations from Franklin's correspondence. Visitors could view the foundations which survived the fire that destroyed the house, and explore an underground museum accessible via a ramp or stair inside an arcade along the garden wall. The proposal combines integrity, in refusing to attempt a restoration that would inevitably be flawed by incomplete information, and pragmatism in reproducing the parts of the original house that are known, with a wry take on the main character involved. The subterranean museum amplifies this inspired concept, describing a complex person. Franklin had many interests; he was the true product of the scientific curiosity that characterized the Enlightenment, a fascinating combination of nascent European Rationalism and Yankee ingenuity and thrift. The resulting mixture of pieces brings Franklin's personality alive, and evokes the circumstances of his life at the time the house was built, in a way that historic preservation could never hope to do. The ensemble sensitively rides the borderline

2

3

4

of decorum, eventually evoking a profound response in the viewer following an initial reaction of surprise and delight at what seems to be an outrageous solution.

Venturi's residential projects completed at this time, such as the Brant House in Bermuda, 1977, continue the application of intentional complexity found in the Vanna Venturi House, with an even more overt historicism. Bermuda has strict building codes, primarily due to water shortages, and Venturi had to find a way of getting his complex message across within this strict framework. The result is an amalgam of local vernacular and Southwestern American references, the connection between Bermuda and the Alamo never really being explained. An ocean-facing portico, also adapted from the Southwest, makes a more logical connection. Harsh glare is a factor in both contexts and the covered arcade is an effective answer to it. The three volumes in the plan of formal reception room/library, central residence, and guest wing collide in a deliberately awkward tripartite plan that is the antithesis of the modern 'suppression of conflict' in organization that Venturi deplores.

In 1983 Venturi completed Gordon Wu Hall, a new building for Butler College at Princeton University. In the red brick of its walls and limestone window surrounds, its large bay windows at both ends, and grand stair which doubles as an informal gathering place and indoor amphitheatre, it deliberately refers to the older neo-gothic buildings of the university. The entrance facade, however, clearly relates to the devices used both at the Vanna Venturi House and Franklin Court, where architectural form is delineated in a two-dimensional format. Over the entrance itself, and overshadowing it completely, the brick facade is interrupted by a panel of white marble patterned with simple geometric shapes executed in a contrasting grey. The effect is childlike, an irreverent gesture in an otherwise buttoned-up building.

It was Venturi's fellow American, Charles Moore, however, who really shocked the architectural establishment with his forays into humorous and ironic historical commentary, in projects such as the Piazza d'Italia in New Orleans, designed in conjunction with the Urban Innovations Group, 1975, or the Beverly Hills Civic Center, 1985. The Piazza d'Italia was a ludicrous send-up of the Italian hill-town model to which Louis Kahn had paid his sincere respects. Ironically perhaps, Moore was also part of Kahn's orbit; he recalls driving up to Yale University in New Haven with his students to hear Kahn lecture in the early 1950s. However, his interest in breaking with the canons of Modernism was based primarily in populist concern rather than on formal issues. The *Yale University Journal*, in which excerpts of *Complexity and Contradiction* first appeared, also published an article by Moore on the social role of the architect, entitled 'You Have to Pay for Public Life', in which he warned of the dangers of modernist reductivism and identified the irrepressible character of popular taste. In contrast to

6 CHARLES MOORE,
St Matthew's
Episcopal Church,
Pacific Palisades,
Los Angeles
1980

7 CHARLES MOORE,
Faculty Club,
University of
California, Santa
Barbara, 1968

Venturi's encyclopedic methodology, Moore relied on regional examples from his more localized experiences in California, where he did much of his early work, to make his point that architecture had to address an irrevocable change in the nature of the public realm brought about by the fact that: 'as the population grows phenomenally, the people who comprise it come from all sorts of places and owe no allegiance to any establishment'.[2]

It was this concern about the apparent vacuum of interest in the public realm, based on a utopian notion of culture, that led Moore towards his forays into Post-Modernism. He always denied any intention of pioneering Post-Modernism in architecture. Rather, he preferred to regard himself as part of the regional San Francisco Bay tradition along with architects such as Julia Morgan, Bernard Maybeck and William Wurster. His Faculty Club at the University of California in Santa Barbara, 1968, recalls Maybeck's Faculty Club at the University of California in Berkeley in its studied compartmentalization of surfaces used to create different internal and external impressions, but also expands the theme of layering found in the work of Kahn and Venturi at that time. Moore's all-out assault on the modernist tenet of the integrity of the external wrapper, and the implicit division between nature and technology which that signifies, escalated significantly in 1973 when he designed Kresge College at the University of California in Santa Cruz around an internal pedestrian street entirely faced with such layered walls. By cleverly locating the essential functions at the end points and junction of this L-shaped street, Moore ensured a captive audience for the musical scores duplicated in the structure of the walls, positioned like stage sets in front of the forest beyond.

Moore liked to poke fun at ceremony, perhaps as a way of criticizing cultural forms imposed from above. Saint Matthew's Episcopal Church, in Pacific Palisades, 1980, shows the sophisticated extent of his skill in this regard. While usually described as a community effort, since it was partly the product of the atelier that Moore liked to coordinate, the final design is a kaleidoscope of colour, light and surface that could have only one source. It is a forced marriage of a traditional, linear basilica plan with a more centralized proto-Justinian model, as seen in San Vitale in Ravenna, or the Hagia Eirene and Hagia Sophia in Istanbul. By choosing such opposing prototypes Moore not only recalls the essence of the liturgical controversy surrounding their use, but also guarantees a crystalline space which certainly meets Venturi's criterion of complexity.

Moore was fond of telling the story about a lecture he once gave at a major university in Brazil, in which he criticized Post-Modernism for having become superficial and banal. He was interrupted by one of the organizers of the lecture, taken backstage and told how disturbed the students and staff were to hear this, since he had been invited specifically because of his reputation as one of the founders of the movement. They had all hoped he would

7

encourage those in the school who were being deterred from using the style. The story is less trivial than it seems, on two levels. First, it shows that Moore did not intentionally set out to start a new style. He was curious about the world, had a playful, vibrant intellect and wanted to include many ideas in his architecture, rather than being restricted to only one, yet he was critical of the lack of awareness of historical connection or context in the most publicized examples of post-modern architecture. The stylistic label he now carries was given to him by others. Second, the story indicates that the threat to 'progress' that Post-Modernism posed has been perceived as very real, especially in academia.

Alongside Moore and Venturi, Michael Graves is generally considered to be the third most critical protagonist in the initial phase of American post-modern

8

architecture. Unlike Venturi, however, Graves has had no particular connection with the University of Pennsylvania (he has taught at the University of Princeton since 1962), or with Kahn. He underwent a high-profile conversion from idealistic modernist to committed populist as a result of dissatisfaction with the Corbusian paradigm. In the Hanselmann House, 1967, Graves ostensibly follows Le Corbusier's five-point canon of column grid, free plan, free elevation, strip window and roof garden as a way of breaking with traditional, load-bearing wall construction. The approach to the entrance is dramatically delineated by a bridge, underlining the modernist principle of progression, or 'procession'; but at the same time, the insertion of a solid wall – cut to resemble a staircase – into a glass curtain wall makes the point that this is only a quasi-serious homage to the master.

Graves' homage was considered serious enough to merit inclusion in an effective and extremely influential media exercise, a publication entitled *Five Architects*, which appeared in 1972; it presented the work of five like-minded neo-Corbusians — the remaining four were Richard Meier, Charles Gwathmey, John Hejduk and Peter Eisenman (see also Chapter Eleven) — and was suitably restricted to a black and white format. It included copious bird's eye axonometric black line drawings of each project and was intended to demonstrate the possibility of individual creative expression under the umbrella of Corbusian theory, thus obviating the need to break away from it. Ultimately all five architects were to develop in very different directions, but Graves was the first to break ranks. The Snyderman House, 1972, marked the end of his attempts to work within the framework of the five points. The grid seems not so much a generator as a cage, unsuccessfully attempting to contain a pulsating creative force inside it, and the elevation is not only free, but aggressively searching for escape. Graves also uses colour here in a definitive way for the first time, his artistic training evident in the way it balances form. Brown calms down curved surfaces and literally brings them down to the earth it signifies, while blue is reserved for flat planes, to render them less oppressive and connect them to the sky.

Graves' Plocek House, 1982, comes as no surprise in the context of this evolution, but nevertheless its appearance was accompanied by a media fanfare. At this point Graves felt he had exhausted all options in the Corbusian pedagogy and wanted to move on to more fertile ground. At the time the Plocek residence was being designed he wrote: 'While any architectural language, to be built, will always exist within the technical realms, it is important to keep the technical expression parallel to an equal and complementary expression of ritual and symbol. It could be argued that the Modern Movement did this; that as well as its internal language, it expressed the symbol of the machine and therefore practised cultural symbolism. But in this case the machine is retroactive, for the machine itself is a utility. A significant architecture must incorporate both internal and external expressions. The external language, which engages inventions of culture at large, is rooted in a figurative and anthropomorphic attitude.'[3]

Looking for something more enduring than Le Corbusier's *Towards A New Architecture*, that would allow him more room for invention, Graves rediscovered Classicism and its human connection, the column as a tripartite tectonic replication of foot, body and head, and the temple division into stylobate, column and pediment, as a larger expression of the same division. While Graves' Plocek House doesn't actually look classical, it is based on the same tripartite division, using the same colour code which Graves had experimented with in the Snyderman House, to anchor the base to the ground and lift the middle and top towards the sky. Once he had undergone his

9

11 MICHAEL
GRAVES, Humana
Building,
Louisville,
Kentucky, 1983-6

conversion to the classical, Graves never looked back and an impressively large body of work completed since the Plocek House demonstrates the remarkable consistency of his subsequent approach.

The Portland Building in Portland, Oregon, completed in 1983, was Graves' first dramatic announcement of this conversion in the public realm, and it caused a public uproar. The architectural profession saw it as proof that Post-Modernism had ceased to be an elitist game within the architectural academy, and had been sanctioned by the establishment. Based on the same tripartite division and colour coding logic as the Plocek House, and decked out in a variety of decorative 'add-ons', as Venturi has coined them, the Portland Building was quickly followed by the Humana Corporation Medical Headquarters in Louisville, Kentucky, begun in the same year and completed in 1986. This Post-Modern skyscraper instantly became an important urban landmark and a source of civic pride. By the late 1980s and early 1990s, Michael Graves was riding the crest of a commercial wave, with close to seventy projects in design, including museums, office towers and hotels. One of the largest of this latter category is the Dolphin and Swan Hotel complex for the Disney Corporation in Lake Buena Vista, Florida, completed in 1990. By the time he completed these buildings, however, Graves had fallen into the trap of formalism, the 'figurative language' he had been searching for in the 1970s had become a set speech, with few remaining surprises. Only the over-scaled swan and shell finials on these hotel buildings relieve the predictability of an established formal pattern.

Venturi, Moore and Graves can arguably be described as the founders of the Post-Modern Movement in America, responsible for the majority of the most visible post-modern architecture, and for a paradigm shift which took place in American architectural culture. Although there had always been alternatives to Modernism (most notably, of course, Frank Lloyd Wright always remained outside it, carving his way in a distinctively 'American' idiom, as opposed to the International Style) the architectural establishment had remained very much in its thrall since the arrival of the Bauhaus founders. Post-Modernism seemed to open the way for an exploration of an architecture more rooted in, and expressive of, American culture than Modernism could ever offer. A notable indication of the shift in attitude which occurred at that time was the apparent apostasy of Philip Johnson.

In 1932 Johnson had organized, with Henry Russell Hitchcock, an exhibition on what they termed the 'International Style' at the Museum of Modern Art in New York. Johnson's subsequent design of a Miesian replica in his own Glass House in New Canaan, Connecticut, 1949, and his partnership with the German master in the realization of the iconic Seagram Building on Park Avenue in New York in 1958, firmly established his ideological credentials — or seemed to, until the design of the Pennzoil Place towers in

11

Houston nearly twenty years later. These buildings, which mutated the Seagram Building's Platonic rectangular form into a series of parallelograms, heralded a significant change in Johnson's style. This was given its final flourish three years later when, in 1979, he designed his own post-modern corporate sensation, *à la Graves*, in the shape of the American Telephone and Telegraph Corporate Headquarters (AT&T) Building in Manhattan. In a city where corporate towers had sported regulation flat-tops since the 1950s, Johnson dared to let his hair down, giving the building a profile as distinctive as those of its Art Deco predecessors. Its flat central shaft and pedimented roofline led to its popular characterization as a 'Chippendale tall-boy'; and its stone cladding, altogether more sleek than that of Graves' Portland Building, gave it a more sophisticated suit in which to go to the big city, thus making the American post-modern corporate sensation bicoastal.

Johnson's flirtation with historicism was soon consummated with the completion of the Republic Bank Center in Houston, 1981, and the Pittsburgh Plate Glass Tower, 1981, the formal costume of which was inspired by the stepped gables of Amsterdam canal houses and a gothic cathedral respectively. Together they provided irrefutable evidence of his final break with the modernist legacy —this by an architect who had perhaps done more than any other to make Modernism welcome in the United States.

The fact is that Post-Modernism struck a chord with the commercial, entrepreneurial spirit which arguably built American society. Big, bold and brash, the new post-modernist buildings shouted 'look at me', in dramatic contrast to the essentially European understatement and reserve of the International Style. Fredric Jameson, in his book *Post-Modernism: The Cultural Logic of Late Capitalism*, offers a cogent analysis of Post-Modernism as a commodification of culture in an era of post-industrial capitalism. He argues that, whereas Modernism was based on the understanding that materialism should be the subject of critique, culture in the post-modern period has been 'dilated' into the 'sphere of commodities' alone, so that it has itself become a product. Jameson identifies this repackaging of society's notions of culture as the birth of a 'media society', driven by electronic representation rather than production on the assembly line model, which allows it multinational scope. The defining moment of its inception, marking the break between modern and post-modern sensibilities, was, he argues, the Kennedy assassination, because it was the first entirely national event, in which collective consciousness was caught up in the controlled electronic representation of reality, and modern ideals were crushed in such a graphic way, endlessly replayed in slow motion, frame by frame. Jameson further argues that 'aesthetic populism' has transformed the economic basis of capitalism, as defined by Marxism, so that: 'aesthetic production today has become integrated into commodity production generally: the frantic economic urgency of producing fresh waves of ever more novel-

seeming goods (from clothing to airplanes), at ever greater rates of turnover, now assigns an increasingly essential structural function and position to aesthetic innovation and experimentation.'[4]

Jameson's theory effectively describes the post-modernist phenomenon, but it is most directly related to the experience of Post-Modernism in America. In Europe, the story of Post-Modernism has been rather more ambiguous, and owes much, on the one hand, to the influence of architect—theorists such as Aldo Rossi or Rob and Leon Krier, and their investigations into the morpho-typology and reconstruction of the European city; and, on the other, to the work of French philosophers such as Jean-François Lyotard in the field of language and semiotics. In Lyotard's hypothesis, the world of post-modern knowledge can be represented as a game of language. He argues that the status of knowledge is altered as societies enter the post-industrial age; for Lyotard, Post-Modernism represents 'a period of slackening' of the teleological experimentation that characterizes the modern ethos. Eclecticism, fed by diverse cultural influences from around the world, now takes precedence over the unified vision of Modernism. Whereas Modernism advocated abstraction, on the basis that the sublime or 'unpresentable' could never be represented, Post-Modernism is based on the belief that reality is representable, and so discards abstraction in order to be more in tune with real rules. Monet, for example, did not really believe that he could reproduce the complex beauty of the lily pond at Giverny in pigment on canvas; the 'sublime' aspect of the scene he paints, which he concedes can never be captured in the medium he is using, is 'the unpresentable' that Lyotard describes. Photography upsets this tacit assumption, being a medium which can come closer to capturing the sublime or unpresentable, and for this reason it was described by David Hockney as the precipitator of a 'crisis of representation'. Hockney's photographic collages are a commentary on what he regards as the hubris of the earlier assumption, which he uses to define the crisis and make it comprehensible. Rather than recognizing the limitations of the unpresentable or nostalgia for the maintainable, as Modernism does, Post-Modernism, according to Lyotard, is based on the belief that if such forms are discarded the approach to the unpresentable becomes clearer. The paradox he proposes is crucial: the post-modern artist or architect discards abstraction in order to be more in tune with real rules, since reality is considered to be representable. Lyotard's statement that these rules are 'what the work of art itself is looking for',[5] sounds remarkably like Kahn's assertion that design consists of discovering what a building, or material for that matter, 'wants to be'. The post-modern artist/architect, according to Lyotard's paradox, 'is working without rules in order to formulate the rules of what will have been done.'

Jameson's exegesis of an elusive cultural upheaval inflected by this trend supports Lyotard's

conclusion. To emphasize his point about the appropriation of traditional representation by the photographic image, he compares Van Gogh and Warhol through the former's painting of work boots, and the latter's silk screen of a photograph of women's shoes. The limitations of depicting reality, which are evidently assumed in Van Gogh's painting, contrast with the ephemeral representation in an infinitely reproducible image, implying multiple sales, in the Warhol silk screen, which saw the 'end of style' at work. The transfer that this example depicts has been given various names, from simulacrum to derealization, by different philosophers, and marks a capitulation to the impossibility of representing reality, as well as a devaluing process in which essence is reduced to an outline to be framed as a poster on a million walls for profit.

Perhaps as a result of the rather different cultural climate, the American post-modern architects, notably Venturi, Moore and Graves, have hardly been made welcome in Europe, with the possible exception of Venturi at the National Gallery in London. When he and Denise Scott Brown won the competition to design the Sainsbury extension to the gallery in 1986 there was public outcry, as much because the scheme was perceived as poking fun at the European architectural tradition as because of the circumstances of the contest. Indeed, the scheme itself seems to occupy a somewhat uncertain position *vis-à-vis* Post-Modernism, perhaps due to the European context of its making. The skin of the building is animated by a series of classical pilasters, in various orders, moving across the limestone surface like so many superimposed, moving neon images on a billboard in Times Square. The columns eventually crowd together and appear to slide behind, or crash into, each other at the main entrance, a modernist nod to an emphasis on the location of the front door. From the entrance, a monumental main stair clearly indicates a line of progression into the building, where a curtain wall reminiscent of the early heroic phase of Modernism removes all doubt about the architect's intention to say that this is a modern building, in spite of its columnar mask.

A key moment for Post-Modernism in Europe was the Venice Architecture Biennale of 1980, organized by the Italian architect, Paolo Portoghesi, one of the most vocal proponents of the movement. Entitled 'The Presence of the Past', its contents were subsequently published by Portoghesi in his book *Postmodern*. He explained: 'The return of architecture to the womb of history and its recycling in new syntactic contexts of traditional forms is one of the symptoms that has produced a profound "difference" in a series of works and projects in the past few years understood by some critics in the ambiguous but efficacious category of post-modern.'[6] The exhibition contained a special 'tribute' to Philip Johnson, alongside the Italian architects Ignazio Gardella and Mario Ridolfi, and a selection of international architects which included Graves, Venturi, Moore and various other, mainly Pennsylvania-based, Americans, alongside a collection of

influential or emerging European architects such as Leon Krier, Oswald Mathias Ungers, Josef Paul Kleihues, Hans Hollein, Christian de Portzamparc, Rem Koolhaas, Ricardo Bofill, Maurice Culot, Jeremy Dixon and Edward Jones, Terry Farrell, Aldo Rossi, Franco Purini and Massimo Scolari — all of whom were to play their part in shaping architectural Post-Modernism in Europe.

One notable absence was that of the British architect James Stirling, who was subsequently to become one of the most notable converts to the movement. In 1984 he completed his ground-breaking Neue Staatsgalerie in Stuttgart, a building which could not have offered a greater contrast to his earlier work, such as the Leicester University Engineering building (Stirling and Gowan), 1959–63, or the Cambridge History Faculty building completed in 1967. While in these buildings Stirling seemed, as Kenneth Frampton has noted, to have 'absorbed the fundamental contradictions of the initial Brutalist position by recombining the canonical forms of the modern movement with elements drawn from the industrial and commercial vernacular of [his] native Liverpool', the first real move away from a modernist position may be traced to his plan for Derby Civic Centre, 1970, and the U-shaped, unrealized omnistructure that he used here to reconcile the difficult considerations posed by an existing twisted warren of medieval streets. At the time, Leon Krier was working in Stirling's office and it has been suggested that his traditionalist civic concerns influenced the scheme. The move towards a more contextual, self-effacing approach was consolidated in Stirling's entry in the competition for the Museum for Nordrhein-Westphalia in Düsseldorf in the mid-1970s and many of the ideas explored there were to reappear in the Stuttgart scheme several years later.

The Staatsgalerie repeats the scale, materials and formal configuration of its eighteenth-century predecessor, while achieving through its veneered sandstone and travertine walls and natural stone paving a 'casual monumental effect'. Stirling wanted to make a statement about the dichotomy between the formality of museums in the past and the more populist, informal approach promulgated today. It was hailed as a great success and, as a result, James Stirling Michael Wilford and Associates were appointed to prepare a town-planning study two years later that included adding a Music School and Theatre Academy to the new museum complex, which were completed in 1995. The additions frame a new plaza on the north and east sides, which becomes the nodal point for a whole series of new pedestrian and vehicular routes around the site. The new buildings are treated externally in a similar way to the Staatsgalerie, with a grid of stone pilasters used to establish a visual order on walls where the random positioning of windows relates to the varied size of rooms. As at the Staatsgalerie, vines will cover the walls giving the building the romantic aspect of a discovered ruin. The dining room is intended to be a meeting place for students and to contribute to the liveliness of the community, so that, both

13 JAMES STIRLING AND MICHAEL WILFORD, Music School and Theatre Academy, Stuttgart, 1995

14 ROBERT VENTURI AND DENISE SCOTT BROWN, Sainsbury Wing, National Gallery, London, 1986–91

14

15 JAMES STIRLING
AND MICHAEL
WILFORD, Neue
Staatsgalerie,
Stuttgart, 1984

16 (Overleaf)
JAMES STIRLING
AND MICHAEL
WILFORD, Cornell
University
Performing Arts
Center, Ithaca,
New York, 1983-8

17 JAMES STIRLING AND
MICHAEL WILFORD,
Clore Gallery
extension to Tate
Gallery, London,
1985

18 TERRY FARRELL,
Charing Cross
Station Development,
London, 1987-90

formally and programmatically, the new complex rein-forces the urban fabric of the city. The whole development represents a major civic investment for Stuttgart.

The contextualism and historical metaphor employed in the Stuttgart scheme were continued by Stirling and Wilford in their design for the Cornell University Performing Arts Center, 1983–8. The new build-ing, a teaching faculty and performance centre, serves as a gateway to the campus and stands as a transitional element between the town and the university, to be used by both. It is organized along a spine terminated by a tower, which evokes at an abstract level the metaphor of an Italian hilltown, a notion that is reinforced by an internal plaza, campanile and 'church' – the theatre itself. The plaza contains a pergola and seats and provides a place for students to meet, while the entry to the building from the plaza is via a loggia framing views across the gorge towards the campus and views towards the lake beyond. Once again, as at Stuttgart, the building is clad in stone, but the detailing is such that it is less monumental in feel than a traditional educational or civic institution.

However, Stirling's most blatant foray into Post-Modernism was the Clore Gallery extension to the Tate Gallery in London, 1985, which generated a frenzy of media comment, and underlined the ambiguity of atti-tudes towards Post-Modernism in Britain. Amongst the critics of the building, there was a fundamental sense that it lacked both gravitas and integrity. There was also a strong tendency to link Post-Modernism with commercial-ism, specifically American capitalism. According to the English architect Terry Farrell, much of the dislike of Post-Modernism was fuelled by an element of anti-Americanism in the British cultural establishment.

Terry Farrell has played a more prominent role than any other architect in Britain in introducing Post-Modernism into the architectural vocabulary. Farrell pursued part of his architectural education in Philadelphia with people such as Kahn and Venturi, although he always maintains that his work has never been close to American Post-Modernism, but rather to that of European so-called post-modernist architects such as Stirling, Hans Hollein or Aldo Rossi. Farrell has achieved considerable success in London, producing post-modern buildings such as the headquarters for the breakfast television station TV AM, 1981–2, and the Charing Cross station redevelopment, 1987–90. Most of his work was designed for commercial clients; his status as purveyor of large corporate buildings developed to such a degree that a building he had designed speculatively in 1988 for a site on the Thames at Vauxhall was leased by the British Government to house its intelligence services, MI6. The exaggerated classical vocabulary which he uses in pop art caricature on the TV AM facade and logo and in its internal central court, and as a monumental civic syntax at Charing Cross, typifies the confluence between Post-Modernism and commercial development that took place in London and elsewhere in

17

18

19

20

the financially overheated 1980s. At some point, architects like Farrell, business leaders and bank managers simultaneously reached the same conclusion: that the consumption of easily digested historical images was equated in the public consciousness with what has been termed by Magali Sarfatti Larson in *Behind the Postmodern Facade*, 'the constitutive dimension of post-industrial economic activity', in which it became more important for the facade of a building to convey an idea of an organization's status, than to express the functions it served. Classicism provided the most easily recognizable building wrapper, and thus became 'the lifeblood of late capitalist commerce'.[7] Perhaps the most outrageous appropriation of Classicism for this purpose occurred on the other side of the English Channel in the Palais d'Abraxas designed by Ricardo Bofill at Marne-la-Vallée, one of the new towns outside Paris. Built episodically between 1978 and 1983, the quasi-classical elements of the building are obviously overscaled, inaccurate and superficial. Coloured precast-concrete panels are used in a clumsy attempt to glorify what are essentially conventional housing blocks, in order to boost status and prices. The fact that Bofill has been largely unable to continue working in this way in the 1990s is indicative of the style's purely economic motivation, which died along with the inflated construction boom of the previous decade.

By contrast, the British architect John Outram has engaged with Post-Modernism at a much more intellectual level, fuelled by his interest in Vedic imagery. He has executed a small number of significant buildings in Britain and America, in which he has explored the possibility of reinstating architecture as a system of signs that can be easily read by the general public, in much the same way that imagery was used in the architecture of past societies. The Cambridge Management Centre, completed in 1995, is a flamboyant, multicoloured essay on this theme which belies the building's more sober programme. The earlier Storm Water Pumping Station, 1985–8, on the River Thames in London, which pumps overflow surface water and sewage from the Isle of Dogs, recalls the solidly constructed, serviceable public works of the Victorian period, in which historical reference served an allusionary purpose. The allusion here is to a 'temple of storms'. The building is faced with Staffordshire blue engineering bricks with bands of red and yellow stock bricks, and the column capitals are formed from highly coloured precast concrete ribbed casings which, along with interlocking glazed green clay tiles on the roof, are intentionally evocative of the organic origins of the classical language, as suggested by the nineteenth-century French architect Henri Labrouste. In his controversial search for the essence of the classical canon during his visit to Paestum, which shook up the established understanding of the orders at the Ecole des Beaux-Arts in Paris, Labrouste came to the conclusion that it was by means of decoration superimposed on an underlying structural order that the Greeks conferred specific meaning on their buildings.

Like Michael Graves' exaggerated use of elements, such as a sculptural stair, an extracted or displaced column, or a protruding wall in the final trio of neo-Corbusian houses that preceded the shockingly different experiment with the Plocek House, Outram's Pumping Station uses the syntax of column and roof in a deliberately semiotic way, exploring the connections that Post-Modernism suggested between linguistics and architecture. However, there is also a strong mythical–mystical content to Outram's work which might be seen as part of a specifically English tradition going back to the writings of the nineteenth-century architect and theorist WR Lethaby. Such interests are also to be found in the work of the Austrian architect Hans Hollein, who was a friend of Stirling's and is generally regarded as having the same importance as a transitional marker of the change of sensibilities that began to reach epidemic proportions after their respective well-publicized heresies. Hollein declared in a lecture in 1962: 'Architecture has no purpose.

19 TERRY FARRELL,
TV AM, London,
1981-2

20 TERRY FARRELL,
Vauxhall Cross,
London, 1988

21 RICARDO BOFILL,
Palais d'Abraxas,
Marne-la-Vallée,
France, 1978-83

22 JOHN OUTRAM,
Storm Water
Pumping Station,
Isle of Dogs,
London, 1985-8

21

22

Speaking in terms of a pre-calculated material utilization, it is purposeless ... The origin of architecture is sacred. The human need to build manifested itself at first in the erection of structures with a sacred purpose, with a magical significance, of a sacred sexual nature.' Fundamental to Hollein's concept of architecture was the idea that it had to be conceived as a communication medium, 'as a sign — a ritual and semiotic architecture'. His first clear built foray into these ideas was an interior for the Austrian Travel Bureau in Vienna of 1976–8, which includes myriad references to the exotic destinations that lie at the far end of an airline ticket purchased inside the vaulted space — which is itself a clear homage to the Post Office Savings Bank in Vienna, of 1904–6, by Otto Wagner. However, the first building by Hollein on a civic scale in this mode was the Städtisches Museum at Abteiberg, Mönchengladbach, realized between 1972 and 1982. This *tour de force* parallels the site-specific contextualism of Stirling's Staatsgalerie, and marks the start of Hollein's increasing tendency to dig his buildings into the earth in some way. At Mönchengladbach he turns the museum into a series of subterranean caverns inside an artificial mountain, with floors eroded in certain places to form terraced gardens, resulting in a kind of sacred repository of culture. This organicism provides a sharp contrast with the more normal, rational solution to the perpetual circulation quandary that the museum building type typically presents: how to provide a relatively flexible and clear path of movement through collections that must also remain secure. Unlike Stirling at Stuttgart, or Venturi and Scott Brown at the National Gallery Sainsbury Wing, which both stick to the usual enfilade of rooms implying the modernist shibboleth of a logically mapped out 'procession', Hollein uses a uniform field of square exhibition spaces, thus achieving a higher degree of

23

freedom and clarity which is more in tune with the post-modern emphasis on multiple possibilities and directions.

Hollein's Museum of Modern Art in Frankfurt, realized between 1982 and 1991, turns the traditional relationship between urban space and the architectural object inside out. An internal plaza is used as an antidote to the noisy traffic surrounding it outside, while the galleries are stacked around it, thus rejecting the city beyond. In the Haas House in Cathedral Square in Vienna, 1987–90, the debate about urban space is continued. In contrast to the concept of civic space encoded in the 1748 Nolli map of Rome, and analysed by the urbanist Camillo Sitte in the nineteenth century, where the buildings of a city become secondary to the spaces around them, or negative in relation to positive space, the Haas House embodies an artificial, hermetic world inside itself that is at the same time less lyrical and more commercial than the idea of the city contained within the Museum of Modern Art. This is the most overtly post-modern of the three civic projects, in its blatantly attention-grabbing reflective glass wrapper, recalling Fredric Jameson's criticism of the amorphous space around and inside the Bonaventure Hotel by John Portman in Los Angeles as a reversal of the symbolically significant utopian spaces of Modernism.[8]

The literal erosion and deliberate contradiction of the modernist premise is also evident in the German architect Gustav Peichl's Bundeskunsthalle, or Federal Art Gallery, in Bonn, 1986–92. It is a 30-foot-high, square fortress with three pointed skylights, which resemble rocket nose-cones, on the roof. The building has to be read in conjunction with the similarly proportioned Kunst Museum by Axel Schultes next to it, the two separated by a rectangular plaza. The complex is pervaded by the spirit of Le Corbusier, which may be read as both a recognition of his dominant position in the history of architecture and a commentary on the changes that have taken place since his death. Le Corbusier had designed an unrealized museum based on the idea of a square perimeter and a right-angled path moving in a constantly decreasing route towards the middle: a rational labyrinth. Peichl's scheme is a cliff-like edifice in which crevices open up to a wavy glass wall forming the main entrance, and a stair leading to a sculpture garden on the roof, so that the primary curvilinear abstraction of nature is once again balanced by a linear axial recollection of the notion of 'procession'. Schultes challenges the concept of the single-minded sequence by employing the Hollein tactic of a field of rooms, deliberately broken on the plaza facade facing the Bundeskunsthalle to ensure that the iconoclastic anti-Corbusian symbolism is clear. Peichl has chosen a revisionist roof garden as his contribution to this game of 'guess the modernist source of the reference'. All roads in this building lead to the axial stair that leads to the roof. Instead of the utopian city in the sun, complete with running track and cafe for residents that Le Corbusier provided on the roof of the Unité d'Habitation in Marseille, however, Peichl has created a surreal roofscape closer to Gaudí in spirit, if not detail. The rooflight cones are the mountains in this artificial landscape, populated by the Nana statues of sculptor Niki de Saint Phalle amidst patches of grass and trees which allow an unrestricted view out on to the real countryside in the distance. The relationship to nature expressed here suggests a parallel with its exaggerated depiction in David Lynch's film *Blue Velvet*, now regarded as a post-modern classic because of its incongruities and the sharp juxtaposition of good and evil — a contemporary morality play in which the meaning of morality itself is questioned. In one key scene, the young male protagonist finds a severed ear in the grass that leads him on a search for its owner. Grass and trees are hand-tinted almost as picture postcard images of reality. The shock of finding a grisly, mutilated body part in

24

25

an otherwise idyllic natural context is heightened by this technique and, while Peichl's juxtapositions are hardly as macabre, there is a similar kind of contrast at work.

A similar but far less subtle tactic has been used to throw nature and architecture into sharp, almost artificial contrast, by the Miami partnership Arquitectonica. One might suggest that Arquitectonica's work tempers American Post-Modernism with a specifically Latin element of surrealism, making it quite distinct from either the work spawned by Venturi, Moore and Graves, or, indeed, the European angle on Post-Modernism informed by urban typology and linguistic analysis. The team, comprising Laurinda Spear, Bernardo Fort-Brescia and Hervin Romney, first made international headlines in the early 1980s with their Atlantis and Babylon apartment complexes in Miami. The Atlantis, completed in 1982, is a traffic stopper on Brickell Avenue. The reflective glass wrapper is pierced with a huge square opening that frames the usually azure Florida sky. The south side of the long narrow building is adorned with a large blue stucco grid laid over the legible grey floor slabs and balcony railings, and a yellow cube of the same dimension as the punched-out opening, housing an exercise room and squash courts, reads as the fallen solid piece of the 'sky court' above. This childlike play with building blocks continues with a series of bold red forms on the roof, which is itself expressed as a simple triangular cutout reminiscent of Robert Venturi's Vanna Venturi House, 1963. It is hard to imagine the Atlantis located anywhere else. Despite its Hollywood aura it could not easily be transplanted to Los Angeles. It is contextually specific through imagery, as well as siting, its simplified shapes and brash primary colours making it a 'billboard for Miami' in the most elemental Venturian sense.

Arquitectonica's ability to capture the essence of the image of a place in a non-literal way is also evident in the Lima headquarters of the Banco de Credito, 1988, a commission won in competition during a more expansive financial climate in Peru. To remind the bank of the country it is serving and the original source of its wealth, Spear and Fort-Brescia, with landscape architect Mercedes Beale de Porcari, successfully argued against levelling an existing rock formation on the 8-acre hillside site, enclosing it instead within the square perimeter of the building as a microcosm of the natural topography around Lima. The decision was fortuitous, since Inca ruins were uncovered during construction, transforming the atrium into an archaeological zone. Beale de Porcari convinced owners of some of the best private conservatories and gardens in this arid region to part with prized specimens for the atrium and, along with waterfalls fed by three elaborate pumping systems, they give the inner court the aspect of an overgrown lost kingdom. This lush interior is a shock after the five-storey cliff-like external wall, clad in black marble tile and relieved only slightly by thin blue glass bands. The possible oppressiveness of a forbidding external perimeter has been alleviated by

26 GUSTAV PEICHL, Federal Art Gallery, Bonn, 1986-92

27 ARQUITECTONICA,
The Atlantis,
Miami, 1982

28 ARQUITECTONICA,
Banco de Credito,
Lima, 1988

28

29

raising everything except an auditorium and branch bank office up on *pilotis*. This also increased security by allowing entry to be restricted to an immense glass block drum, which contains escalators and stairs that lead to a single first floor check point. This sheer glass cylinder is pierced by a black marble balcony which continues the inside—outside formal play seen in the Atlantis project.

The best of the post-modern architecture produced in the three decades since the publication of Venturi's *Complexity and Contradiction in Architecture* has achieved much by exploring a commentary on the relationship between nature and architecture or history and architecture, both of which are fundamental to the existence of architecture itself. At the same time, however, Post-Modernism offered a style that was easily imitated and exceptionally vulnerable to commercial debasement, and as a result it spawned a flood of poorly designed speculative buildings throughout America and Europe that effectively eroded serious intellectual respect for the movement. Indeed, Venturi himself, in an annual Walter Gropius Lecture at Harvard University, delivered in 1982, nearly twenty years after the publication of his book, and later published as an article in the journal *Architectural Record*,[9] charged Post-Modernism with superficiality, and with having lost the force of its original pluralistic vision – although he himself continued to work within the style. Shortly after the National Gallery Sainsbury Wing was opened, he completed work on the Seattle Art Museum, 1991, which was criticized by some as a rather weak reworking of typical Venturiesque gestures: two grand staircases, one internal and one external, a striated side elevation giving an exaggerated sense of perspective, and the adornment of the facade with red, yellow and white terracotta panels, with the words 'Seattle Art Museum' cut into the limestone above in huge letters.

Worst of all, Post-Modernism had, just like Modernism before it, reverted to being an exclusive language designed by and for architects, neglecting the people it was intended to serve. Image-generated 'hyper-space' had replaced humanistic functionalism, cynical commodification had displaced zealous altruistic social improvement, and episodic spontaneity had superseded teleological, diachronic planning. At one extreme, Post-Modernism's intentional expression of a level of social fragmentation might be regarded as having resulted in the shattering of nation states. Ironically, all of these accusations amount to the inescapable conclusion that Post-Modernism has ultimately emerged as a cynical byproduct of the modernist agenda rather than, as was always intended, its absolute antithesis.

As Post-Modernism became increasingly commercial-ized and appropriated by developers in the overheated construction market in Europe and America in the early 1980s, a new architectural avant-garde became increasingly restless, and the public began to expect something new. Post-Modernism fell victim to the con-sumer mentality it celebrated, only able to manage a lifecycle half as long as that of the modern canon it originally sought to displace. It was displaced by Deconstructivism, in which the pattern that Post-Modernism had established of using a polemic to explain and promote both built and unbuilt work was repeated with a subtle twist.

2

In 1988, a seminal exhibition, Deconstructivist Architecture, curated by Mark Wigley and Philip Johnson — who effected his shift of loyalty from Post-Modernism as easily as he had formerly abandoned Modernism — was held at the Museum of Modern Art in New York. In the cat-alogue, Wigley defined the new movement as one which marked 'a different sensibility, one in which the dream of pure form has been disturbed. Form has become contami-nated'. Wigley and Johnson traced the roots of the move-ment to Russian Constructivism in the early twentieth century, which 'posed a threat to tradition by breaking the classical rules of composition, in which the balanced, hierarchical relationship between forms creates a unified whole. Pure forms were ... used to produce "impure", skewed, geometric compositions ... placed in conflict to produce an unstable, restless geometry'. Similarly, Deconstructivism sought to challenge the values of 'harmony, unity, and stability', and proposed the view that 'the flaws are intrinsic to the structure'.[1]

The exhibition included projects by seven architects, of whom three were based in the United States, and four were European. Amongst them was the American Peter Eisenman, who, despite Wigley's claims that the projects 'did not ... derive from the mode of contemporary philosophy known as "deconstruction"', was particularly influenced by the theoretical manifesto then being developed by the French philosopher Jacques Derrida, who explained that his philosophy of deconstruction: 'starts with the deconstruction of logocentrism [through] parasitology or virology ... the virus is in part a parasite that destroys, that introduces disorder into communication. From the biological standpoint a virus is a mechanism that derails communication, the body's ability to code and decode'.[2] Derrida's philosophy had the added appeal of a tectonic promise: the potential of 'the interplay between architecture and the home in which philosophy, aesthetics and discourse are located'. By focusing on the destruction of logocentrism, the primacy of language and text, Derrida is obviously at odds with the entire semiotic structure of Post-Modernism. Even though it has been argued that deconstruction is an extension of the post-modern project in that it is critical of positivism, this difference of opinion over language is the crucial distinction.

Peter Eisenman was the first to attempt to transform this idea of an ever-changing text into architecture, by emphasising the 'de-centering' of the human subject. Reacting to what Marshall Berman has described as the 'maelstrom of perpetual disintegration and renewal',[3] Eisenman began to search for an aesthetic that was not just a reflexive response to the consumer society. His Wexner Center for the Visual Arts at Ohio State University, 1989, represented the ideal opportunity to explore these issues because of its position between two existing buildings, and the memory of a pre-existing armory which might also be partially reconstructed as an additional source of commentary on the theme of disintegration and renewal. The scheme developed out of the idea of an excavation between the two buildings, resulting in a site which essentially represents other sites through a superimposition of grids: the grid of Ohio, the grid of Columbus, and the grid of the University campus. Historically, the university campus had maintained a distance from the city, but Eisenman extends the city street grid into the campus as a new pedestrian route forming a ramped east–west axis. A north–south passageway, half enclosed in glass, the other half in open scaffolding, undermining the traditional architectural symbolism of permanence and shelter, runs perpendicular to the east–west axis. The crossing of the two forms a literal 'centre' for the visual arts.

Eisenman employed the same theme in the Aronoff Center for Design and Art at the University of Cincinnati, Ohio, 1986, which is also wedged between two buildings. Like the Wexner Center, its form derives from this pre-existing context, but the central internal street is more decisive and legible and progressively etches into the ground plane, eventually becoming a ramped, sunken cavern illuminated by slivers of natural light sliding down the walls. The complex layered visual planes of the Wexner Center are accentuated even more in the Aronoff Center, completely fulfilling the condition of 'betweenness' that Eisenman believes to be one of four key elements necessary to 'displace' the traditional way that architecture has been conceptualized. These included a seeking out of the 'uncanny', or a sense of unease and disquiet, through an anti-intuitive design process; the representation of 'absence' of previously existing traces in what he calls 'two-ness'; and a pursuit of 'interiority' as delineating the 'unseen or hollowed out'. In addition to these elements, 'betweenness' avoids dominant meaning in favour of: 'something which is almost this, or almost that, but not quite either. The displacing experience is the uncertainty of a partial knowing ... Again, this between is not a between dialectically, but a between within'.[4] Given Eisenman's expressed intention to displace conventional representation using these four devices, the Wexner and Aronoff Centres become more understandable as deliberate manifestations of them.

Eisenman's project for the Gardiola Weekend House in Santa Maria del Mar, near Cadiz in Spain, 1988, is the most graphic example of his alignment with the Derridian notion of the demolition of shelter. Derrida questioned the hypothesis of the influential German philosopher Martin Heidegger, who drew an analogy between language and the house, as establishing a 'general opposition between an inner world of presence and an outer world of representation'.[5] Derrida rejected the idea that philosophical thought should be based on logically constructed architectonic models or solid sheltering dwellings. The Gardiola House was intended as an investigation of the changing meaning understood in the idea of place, which challenges received ideas of order. Such challenges, Eisenman claims, 'have been repressed by traditional reason, but ... can no longer be repressed'. The creation of place has traditionally embodied a proud announcement of the destruction, or conquest, of nature; the key point in architecture is whether this is still necessary or important, since, as Eisenman believes, nature is in any case on the verge of complete collapse. He also believes that, as a result of technology and the questioning of the framework of logical reasoning, our traditional understanding of what place is has broken down, and that the old topos/atopos (place/non-place) dichotomy embodies an inherent contradiction.

As an alternative Eisenman offers the idea of a receptacle, in the Platonic sense of a recording of

3

5, 6 Peter
Eisenman, Columbus
Convention
Center, Ohio,
1992

movement, something between container and contained.
The Gardiola House is his attempt at such a record,
representing the antithesis of a static position. It is best
described by him as 'figure and frame simultaneously
[with] tangential L-shapes [that] penetrate three planes,
always interweaving'. He avoids the traditional lines
of demarcation between inside and outside, trying to
convey a notion of constant change, impermanence and
'controlled accident'. As part of a relentless effort to break
down the conventional language of architecture begun in
a series of houses, numbered House I through to House X,
of which Houses I and II were described in the publication
Five Architects, 1975, the Gardiola House is intended by
Eisenman to be difficult to discuss on a purely functional
level, with pragmatic fixtures such as bathtubs and sinks
almost seeming to be unwelcome intrusions into what is
essentially a sculptural experiment.

     The Columbus Convention Center, Ohio, complet-
ed in 1992, was taken as a larger scale, more public
opportunity to continue the discussion about place and
what Eisenman perceives to be the changing nature of

5

urban life, related to the information revolution behind the
phenomenon of globalization. 'What is called for now,' he
believes, 'is a new monumentality, a civic architecture of
the between, which celebrates the many small transactions
necessary to the dynamics of a vital city'. Rather than the
literal expression made possible by pre-existing conditions
at the Wexner Center, Eisenman concentrated on the
broader transitional quality of this open site and the
particularity of a residential district along one edge of it.
This texture, along with railroad tracks to the east, and the
wish to convey his preoccupation with the information age,
led to the building's division into curved, bar-like strands
that are meant to recall train sheds and fibre-optic cables.
These end in 'plugs' articulated in brick and glass to
conform to the more defined texture along the main street
front. The plan of the Center, despite its metaphor-laden
envelope, could not be simpler, and Eisenman's functional
goal of redefining what is typically a scaleless, amorphous
building type into a more human-scaled, legible 'gathering
place' is generally considered to be more successful than
the costly contortion of the perimeter. In contrast to the

French counterpart André Le Nôtre represents the less organic and more formal tradition of purposefully demonstrating that nature should be kept in check. The abstract basis for the Parc, divided into a series of points, lines and planes, reveals the mechanical approach that Tschumi has taken, pushing the French tradition to the extreme. The 'points' are 'folies', continuing the idea of deliberately constructed 'ruins' used as distant focal points in large landscaped English gardens. Tschumi's 'folies', however, illustrate a complete rejection of their romantic precedent, since they are machines. The machine in the garden, which was a favourite modernist theme perfected in Le Corbusier's Villa Savoye, changes here to the machine *is* the garden; the 'folies' also become the trees. Greenery is replaced by concrete, asphalt and steel, which Tschumi believes make the park more appropriate to the twentieth and twenty-first centuries.

The constructivist connection, partially incorporated into Tschumi's language, is perhaps more obvious in the work of the London-based Iraqi architect Zaha Hadid, who was also included in the MoMA show. Her architecture refers specifically to the suprematist variant of

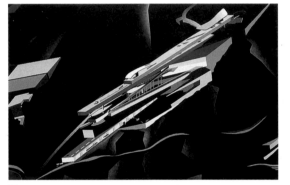

12

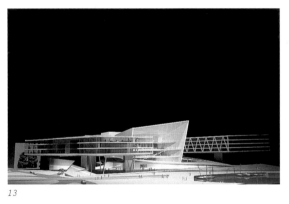

13

Constructivism first proposed by Kazimir Malevich at the school of Vitebsk in 1919, where Lissitzky and the painter Marc Chagall were also teaching. Malevich believed that artistic style was a cultural system that could only be implemented incrementally by individual interpretations. Rather than reacting to purely formal issues, as Constructivism did, Suprematism made direct analogies between certain colours and social conditions. In a pamphlet on Suprematism produced at Vitebsk in 1920, the artist explained his idea of the canvas as 'a window through which we discover life', and said that: 'Suprematism is divided into three stages according to the number of black, red and white squares … their constructions are based upon the chief economic principle of conveying the power of statics or apparent dynamics and rest upon the planar surface alone'.

Hadid stresses the anti-gravitational component of Suprematism rather than strictly adhering to the spectral analogies that Malevich proposed. While confining herself to a similar palette, she implements it in an aesthetic rather than systematic way. On her large canvases, colour is used as a psychological signal, with the energy

level of each choice carefully calculated to open or close the visual and psychological distance between a particular area of the composition and the eye of the viewer. By also frequently selecting a point of perspective that seems to levitate her buildings, and which would be very difficult to achieve in reality, she deliberately tries to give them dominance. Her paintings appear to defy gravity — the most ancient enemy of the architect — and she is able to detach her work from the rigorous restrictions that mass has always imposed, allowing other possibilities to emerge before immutable, physical laws are factored back into the final design equation. Having first come to international attention with her winning design entry for the Peak Competition in Hong Kong in 1982, which was never realized, Hadid has consistently adhered to the patterns of design exploration through painting which she displayed in that submission.

In her winning competition project for the Cardiff Opera House, 1994, which is one of her largest projects to date, and has also not been realized, a similar aesthetic is evident. This competition, to design a new home for the Welsh National Opera, was taken as an opportunity to address what Hadid has identified as the 'mutually exclusive paradigms of urban design, by attempting to be both a monument and a space'. To achieve this, she created a continuous linear form that acts as a foil to the oval harbour nearby, and breaks down the orthogonal arrangement of traditional theatres. The building takes the form of a 'necklace' with the concert hall as the pendant and its subsidiary appendages as the jewels on the strand.

The Opera House was envisaged as a strong figural landmark near the waterfront, with the main opening in the deformed perimeter carefully calculated to encourage public access, as well as providing an arena for outdoor performances, and to enhance views of the Inner Harbour and Cardiff Bay. The perimeter block defines the secluded internal space within a 'single continuum', and the plaza is extended, in a continuous warped plane, into the central courtyard over the entrance.

Despite the fragmented appearance of the design, the plan is in fact highly resolved and hierarchical, with theatrical functions arranged around the central court, and office and support functions located around the perimeter. There are also direct, functional relationships between the seemingly spontaneous form and the operation of the backstage area, and the theatre's acoustic performance and structural design.

Had it been realized, the Cardiff Opera House would have represented Hadid's most successful and sophisticated marriage of function and image to date, and a step forward from her last completed building, a fire station for the furniture manufacturer Vitra, in Weil-am-Rhein, Germany, 1990–3. As several commentators have observed, the Fire Station is a problematic building on two levels. Functionally flawed — it served only briefly the purpose for which it was designed — it

highlighted the difficulty that Hadid, and those like her, face in translating such highly developed visionary designs into buildings. One commentator was prompted to question: 'whether the design in its artistic representation as an image, is not more exciting than the building in reality [and] whether the desire for immortality is not more compelling and visionary than the earthly realization which can only appear banal by its side.'[6]

This is a dilemma faced by many deconstructivists, not least the Polish-born architect Daniel Libeskind, who trained at Cooper Union in New York under John Hejduk. Libeskind, despite his inclusion in the MoMA exhibition, claims no allegiance to any existing manifestos, and in his early work, art became an expanded cursive technique of inquiry with which to communicate his impressions of the physical world. As with several contemporary artists who have been fascinated by the graphic power of writing, Libeskind used it not only to accompany his art and architecture as an explanatory text, but also as an integral part of each, confusing its intelligibility through sheer repetition and volume and turning it into mere pattern in the process. While his earlier architectural collages were used as an instrument of liberation from functional requirements as well as from the subliminal expectation of traditional means of representation, his art is free of all such responsibility, and has a frenetic, calligraphic energy that seems, in its weightlessness, to reflect his restless and seemingly boundless intellect more accurately. In voluntary, self-imposed polygraphics, colour plays a supportive, rather than a descriptive, role, almost seeming to be a pale subcutaneous fluid released by a pin moving erratically across the canvas. Because of the additional inquisitive potential that it offers, Libeskind uses art and the new language that he invents within it to test the physical and dimensional boundaries of reality.

The text of Libeskind's 1985 Theatrum Mundi series called *Confessio Fraternitatis* is less Joyce-like than most of his writing, in that his intention is to combine certain words for resonance rather than meaning. This same intention is obvious in his proposal for a memorial to Ludwig Mies van der Rohe in Berlin, and his Jewish Museum extension to the Berlin Museum which was won in competition in 1989 and is approaching completion at the time of writing. It is a veritable lightning-bolt of a building clad almost entirely in zinc that displays the sharp points and edges that have become a signature of the deconstructivist style, through the legacy of Constructivism, along with the Derridian disregard for space and the people that might inhabit it.

Either time or more pragmatic commercial concerns have softened the edges of Libeskind's later work, most notably his 1996 competition-winning project for the Boilerhouse extension at the Victoria and Albert Museum in London. Housing a multi-media gallery and additional space for temporary exhibits, the extension will have

15 DANIEL LIBESKIND, Jewish Museum Extension to the Berlin Museum, Berlin, 1989-97

16 DANIEL LIBESKIND, Boilerhouse Extension to the Victoria and Albert Museum, London, 1996-

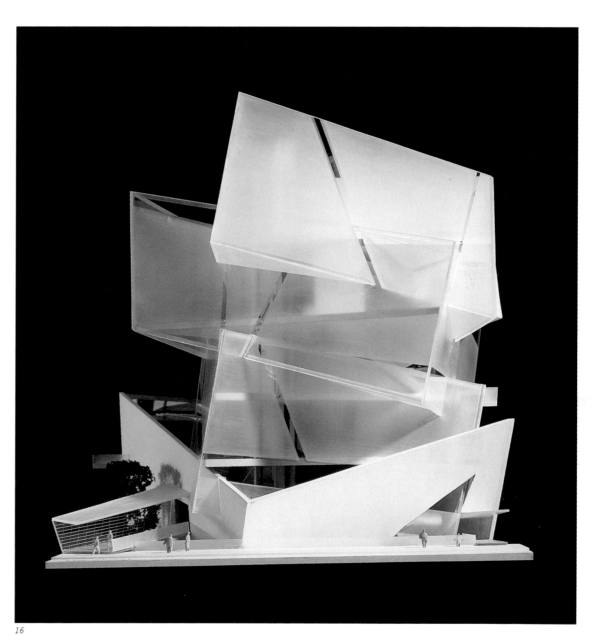

16

17 Coop
Himmelblau, Attic
Remodelling for
Falkestrasse 6,
Vienna, 1983-8

18 Coop
Himmelblau, Funder
Factory Works 3,
Vienna, 1989

computers that allow visitors to log on and be guided through the exhibits available in this and other museums. By the time the extension opens in 2001, most museums will store their exhibits electronically, allowing international connections to be formed in cyberspace. Libeskind was chosen as the architect specifically in order to demonstrate a rupture from the past and a more forward-looking approach to museum design. Described by him as 'an Arachne's thread leading into the main building' – which was itself controversial when it was built in 1899 – the seven-storey extension has the appearance of an interlocking stack of tumbling triangular boxes, faced with the same tiles used by NASA on space shuttles to absorb heat on re-entry orbit. Once inside, visitors can enter an express lift that will take them up to a perilously tilting glass observatory at the top of the stack from which they can look down into the Pirelli Garden in the museum's main courtyard. Like Hadid's Cardiff Opera House, Libeskind's 'Spiral' is remarkably conventional in its space-planning, once you get beyond the external wrapper. The impact of that initial shock, however, is deep, generating a debate in which the question of context seems to be all-important.

The Vienna-based practice Coop Himmelblau, which was also represented at MoMA, has generated an equivalent amount of shock in and around Vienna with its rendition of Deconstructivism aimed at revising preconceived notions of civic propriety. Its two founders – the Austrian Wolf Prix and his Polish partner Helmut Swiczinsky – have formed what they refer to as a 'Blue Sky Cooperative' which has adopted a more aggressive strategy than any of the other principal figures engaged in this dialogue, if that is possible. They are determined to follow the advice of their fellow Viennese, Sigmund Freud, by diverting the energy expended in suppression into their projects, to upset what they consider to be 'the safe and sound world of architecture'. The roof conversion for Falkestrasse 6 in Vienna and the design of the Funder Factory Works 3 on the outskirts of the city, completed in the late-1980s, established the ground rules, or rather the lack of them, and Coop Himmelblau has been consistently breaking them ever since. The Groningen Museum in The Netherlands (designed and built between 1990 and 1994 by Coop Himmelblau, Alessandro Mendini, Philippe Starck and others) is the largest example of their iconoclastic approach, which Prix has gleefully described as having been initiated through freehand sketches, completed with eyes closed, and then scanned into the computer: this is quite literally a stream-of-consciousness methodology that yields predictably chaotic results. Their largest building in Austria, following the Funder Factory and Vienna attic conversion, is the Seibersdorf Office and Research Centre, 1996. Rather than mere displacement, they advocate architecture that is 'smooth, hard, angular, brutal' as well as 'colourful, obscene, voluptuous, dreamy and alluring'. This translates at Seibersdorf into a 120-foot-long

18

double-height steel truss on splayed concrete *pilotis* grafted onto an existing laboratory to create an 'interstitial space'. The two-storey office wing also acts as a gateway to the complex. Following the emphasis on language, the logocentric focus of Derrida, the cursive sketches of the Constructivists, the palimpsests of Eisenman, Tschumi's events and fragments, Hadid's artistic explorations, and Daniel Libeskind's verbal transformations, these seismic simulations continue the discourse on graphology that is evident as a consistent thread in Deconstructivism, presenting a more specific example of casual relationship between lines and form without premeditated rational intention.

In the frenzied rush to satisfy the public hunger for new theories and a fresh style, there was a perilous attempt on the part of the international architectural media and certain academics at naming and categorizing, in the course of which several members of the so-called Los Angeles School, such as Frank Gehry and Eric Owen Moss, were included in the deconstructive camp as it was first defined. Indeed, Gehry was included in the MoMA exhibition. Several carefully constructed apologias appeared to substantiate this claim but none of these originated from the architects in question, who steadfastly maintain that they have not deliberately set out to interpret a specific theory or historical aesthetic. Gavin Macrae-Gibson, for example, in *The Secret Life of Buildings: An American Mythology for Modern Architecture* makes a compelling argument for a link between Gehry's perspective distortions and the mystical parallelograms of the Russian constructivist painter Malevich. Fredric Jameson just as forcefully denies it, and others try to make a case for Deconstructivism being just another manifestation of Post-Modernism. Gehry makes no secret of his admiration for Constructivism, but his lack of deliberation, in comparison to that of the architects discussed previously, seems to eliminate him decisively from this category, and Eric Owen Moss as well, for similar reasons.

With Moss, however, the issue is somewhat confused by his constant references to chaos theory, which, alongside Derridian philosophy and constructivist aesthetics, is often considered a third theme running through deconstructive rhetoric. Chaos theory, however, has been largely appropriated by deconstructivist theory, rather than generating it, since it was developed in the physical sciences at the same time that Deconstructivism began to emerge. Rather than feeding the style, as Derrida's post-structuralism or the historical propositions leading to Suprematism have separately but jointly served to do, chaos theory has been used to validate it. Resulting from irreconcilable divergences that have consistently occurred in the results of experiments conducted using the conventional scientific method, chaos theory has resulted from a closer study of the way hypotheses are formulated and measurement errors are accounted for. These studies have shown that experimental results are not only

19 COOP HIMMELBLAU, Groninger Museum, The Netherlands, 1990-4

20

contingent on the way that a research problem is framed, but also on the external variations that may affect it; a sensitive dependence on initial conditions can, therefore, lead to a wide variation in the final results. Beginning in meteorology and computer predictions of weather patterns, which were shown to vary according to the parameters used, chaos theory was used as a basis for observation of seemingly random events which have been found to have a hidden order after all.

As previously mentioned, Gehry and Moss cannot be consistently aligned with deconstructivist intentions, but they may be interpreted as filters for an eccentric urban sensibility (as described in Chapter Fourteen on the Los Angeles avant-garde). The American firm of Scogin, Elam and Bray, however, is more definite about its intentions and presents no difficulty in classification. The Chmar House in Atlanta, Georgia, 1989, is convincing as a demonstration of their alignment, literally replacing a large tree that had fallen on the heavily wooded two-and-a-half-acre site. *Pilotis* isolate the house from its natural setting, raising it above the ground so that it appears like a large mechanical heron picking its way across the forest landscape. The interior of the residence is intended to conform to the 'multiplicities and dualities' of the owners; space for intro-spection is set in conflicting juxtaposition with more social, public zones in the longest wing of the L-shaped plan, with a more conventional organization of bedrooms and a bath in the shorter leg, which also supports a long stair down to the forest floor.

In their extension to the Arizona State University College of Law, Tucson, 1993, Scogin, Elam and Bray have adopted an even more discursive, collage-like approach intended as a foil to the formal symmetry of the existing college building. As in the Chmar House, the concept was derived from the idea of countering the landscape, in this instance related to the 'mis-readings' that they saw in the nearby desert where 'plants look like animals, animals look like rocks, rocks look like animals, plants look like rocks, animals look like plants'. This is nature distorted rather than disregarded or superseded, adding to the extensive and unexpected litany of such commentary in the deconstructivist *œuvre*.

The negative commentary on nature is evident in name only in the Karbouw (Dutch for buffalo) Office and Workshop in Amersfoort completed by the young Dutch architect Ben van Berkel in 1992. It is an inward-looking office structure in an industrial park. Based on the idea of circulatory crossing points, the steel-wrapped prow-shaped structure has an upper floor that seems to swivel on a concrete and tile-faced base. The position of the director's office, facing the main road, was the reason behind this alignment, as well as the long strip of inward-leaning green glass that relieves the solidity of the facade. A second decision, to interconnect all administrative offices, led to a complex, curving roof structure, which is hardly legible from the outside, except in the arcing curve near the entrance.

20 SCOGIN, ELAM
AND BRAY, Chmar
House, Atlanta,
Georgia, 1989

21 SCOGIN, ELAM
AND BRAY, Arizona
State College of
Law, Tucson, 1993

21

Van Berkel's Erasmus Bridge, 1990–6, a connection between the northern and southern sections of The Netherlands before reaching Rotterdam and the North Sea, is far less detached from its physical surroundings, and less evident as a consistently deconstructivist statement about what the architect sees as his role of 'rediscovery' in a 'multiplicitous, incoherent and non-directional practice'. The bridge depends on the water to explain its structural concept fully, since it is only in reflection that its bow-like configuration becomes clear. Its soaring blue steel pylon, intended as a prominent landmark, is meant to combine architectural, structural and urban metaphors in one expressive, sculptural form, which is especially dramatic after sunset. When reflection is no longer possible, special lighting creates a silhouette, dematerializing the daytime image. The notion of dematerialization which has obvious resonance with the central proposal of Deconstructivism, is important to Van Berkel, who fears that whenever a vision is appropriated by architecture, it is denied the opportunity of becoming what it might have been.

This belief, of architecture as a potential destroyer of the diversity of life, is shared by the German architect Günter Behnisch, who feels it must not be 'closed off' too soon, but must 'be kept living throughout the entire production process: open, adaptable, flexible so that many different influences can be taken into account'. Behnisch is not commonly regarded as belonging to the deconstructivist camp, because his architecture is so firmly rooted in the tradition of organicism developed through the work of nineteenth- and twentieth-century German architects such as Gottfried Böhm, Hans Scharoun and others. Nevertheless, his work has unmistakable formal parallels with that of the key deconstructivist architects, and the validity of such a connection has been considerably strengthened by the identification of chaos theory as a fundamental basis for the development of natural processes and forms. The result of Behnisch's commitment to an architecture capable of nurturing the diversity of life, the visible manifestation of which may appear chaotic, is evident in his German Post Office Museum in Frankfurt, 1990, in which a sweeping arc of glass floods the core of the building with natural light, and in the Solar Research Institute Building at the University of Stuttgart, 1987. The Solar Research Building was an attempt to balance equal programmatic priorities in 'free equilibrium' as an experiment in avoiding formal compromise. This attitude, along with a strict, short construction schedule, has resulted in a light, cursive character in the architecture. By contrast, because of scale and its public function, the German Parliament Building in Bonn, completed by Behnisch in 1992, is less spontaneous, and this project, more than the others, reveals Behnisch's conviction that Deconstructivism synthesizes rather than repudiates the principles of Modernism. This synthesis emerges in the Bonn Parliament in volumetric balance and Miesian restraint, mixed with uninhibited, almost fractured spatial treatment, which has been described as 'diachronic', meant

to dispel any impression of ideology, rhetoric or solemnity. Like the Postal Museum, the Bonn Parliament is inextricably connected to its natural context, the bank of the Rhine and the restored buildings nearby having been sensitively considered in the design. This contextualism, combined with his views on the possibility of a completion of Modernism, or at least its adaptation to suit more complex times, reveals Behnisch's detachment from pure deconstructivist dogma, a theoretically driven position which, in its strictest translation, rejects nature and humanity alike.

While the coining of the deconstructivist label proved useful in broadly describing the work of a relatively limited number of architects interested in challenging the apparent certainties of Post-Modernism, Deconstructivism never really achieved the status of a movement beyond the narrow academic sphere that Post-Modernism did. Nor would it be true to say that most architects embraced the full theoretical lineage of Deconstructivism — even though that is apparently much clearer than many of the diverse

23

24

strands that are manifest in the recent history of architecture, primarily because of the association with the deconstruction philosophy of Derrida and others: a philosophical hypothesis with an especially nihilistic basis. Additional strands borrowed from Constructivism and chaos theory have not proved to be sufficiently humanistic to leaven the mixture, and the notion of Deconstructivism as an extension of Modernism, introduced by the work of Behnisch and others, has yet to be sufficiently developed in enough detail to offset concerns that the movement, like a celibate utopian community, is based on the very premise that must eventually destroy it. With the advent of globalization and the necessity of cultural intercommunication which that entails, philosophers such as Jürgen Habermas are now seen as holding out more hope for the future, admitting that language is imperfect but it is, finally, the best device we have, and therefore it is not in the interests of humanity to take it apart as deconstruction philosophy has tried to do.

22 Ben van Berkel, Erasmus Bridge, Rotterdam, 1990-6

23 Günter Behnisch, German Post Office Museum, Frankfurt, 1990

24 Günter Behnisch, German Parliament Building, Bonn, 1992

2

3

There has long been a trend in many developing countries, fuelled by architects concerned about their national cultural identity, to find a more authentic regional voice for their architecture. This is a phenomenon that grew largely, although not exclusively, as the national independence movements of these countries gained momentum, with former colonies beginning to establish their own political and cultural roots following the end of the Second World War. Long-standing colonial structures in many developing countries had been completely shattered during the War, or seriously compromised by it, deeply undermining a system that had depended upon the myth of invincibility for its effectiveness. The pattern of emerging nation-states that spread across the globe in the 1940s and 1950s is testimony to this groundswell. Developing countries which were central to the conflict, such as Egypt and Jordan, offer perhaps the clearest examples of this resurgence, but others that were less strategically important, such as India and Mexico, are also relevant because of the pressure for independence, or consolidation after unification, which characterized their post-war development.

In many developing countries, however, the model of progress provided by the industrialized nations continued to be seductive, and the political and psychological patterns of pre-war colonial government remained largely intact, even after independence had been won. It was also common for architects who tried to recover some semblance of cultural identity in these circumstances, by attempting to return to vernacular expression, to be generally rejected in their own countries, finding only a small core of followers who appreciated the deeper significance of their efforts. Now, nearly fifty years later — with environmental conditions worsening, and concern about the loss of regional identity and heritage in the face of a mounting trend towards cultural globalization — there is a growing appreciation of the work of these pioneers, who are now regarded as visionary.

The Egyptian architect Hassan Fathy was one of the first to recognize, and speak out against, what he considered to be the aesthetic anonymity of International Style Modernism, and he began to investigate the possibility of a traditional national style. Egypt had suffered a particularly unhappy history of foreign occupation and colonial exploitation, and the inversion of power and values involved in such a negative relationship made Egypt the ideal testing ground for Fathy's investigations. The main thrust of Fathy's work was to reverse the progressive pattern of destruction of Arab architecture and decorative arts in Egypt that had resulted from successive colonial influences, first Ottoman and then French and British.

In 1938 Fathy organized an exhibition in a suburb of Cairo called Mansouria that has now been absorbed into the urban sprawl. The watercolours and gouaches that he produced for the show were quite unlike anything being considered in Egypt at the time, combining

elements that he determined had been typical in traditional Egyptian architecture prior to the Industrial
Revolution and the country's occupation by colonial
forces. These elements, or spatial typologies, discovered
in the dozen or so merchants' residences left in the
medieval portion of the city that remained from this early
period, were adapted by Fathy into formal compositions
meant to convey the essence of a national heritage.
Fathy's choice of Pharaonic conventions to illustrate these
ideas, including the flattening of picture planes to show
plan and elevation at the same time, indicated his awareness of assimilation, appropriation and continuity from
each of the great historical epochs in Egyptian history.

The traditional self-build construction techniques Fathy advocated to realize this new architecture
had the advantage of being less expensive than using
imported concrete or steel under the supervision of a
general building contractor. Fathy's first opportunity to
demonstrate how this system might work in practice
came when the Department of Antiquities called for an
inexpensive solution to the problem of relocating an
entire community of grave-robbers from Gourna, near
Luxor in the Nile Valley. Fathy's system, with its mud-brick
walls, simple vaults and domes, offered an ideal solution:
it was cheap, required few building skills, and relied on
locally abundant materials; but self-build requires motivation, and a willingness to move was certainly not high
among the Gourna community. Despite Fathy's energetic
commitment to reinforcing family and tribal connections
that would inform the design, and exhaustive surveys to
discover individual requirements within the traditional
village framework that he was attempting to provide, the
Gournii repeatedly sabotaged the project during the off
season when it was too hot to continue construction.
However, nearly one quarter of the scheme was constructed by 1945, which is remarkable considering that it was built
for such a reluctant population during the Second World
War while the Battle for North Africa was raging.

New Gourna remains Fathy's most important
project, and offers a succinct statement of his architectural philosophy. This philosophy has informed a
younger generation of architects in Egypt, among whom is
Abdel Wahed El-Wakil. He has achieved a high profile in
both the Middle East and Europe, due to an early association with Fathy and his highly publicized commissions in
the Gulf. He has also been helped in this regard by the
patronage of the Prince of Wales, and is now possibly the
best-known architect pursuing a traditional direction in
both those arenas. Born and educated in Egypt, he left in
the early 1970s to seek commissions from wealthy patrons
in Saudi Arabia, believing that the message his mentor
Fathy had tried to propagate had not spread because his
clients had not been influential enough. Before leaving
Egypt, however, he completed several important residential projects, and while his Halawa House in Agany, 1975,
which first brought him international attention, is more

1 (Previous page)
GLENN MURCUTT, The
Ball-Eastaway
House, Glenorie,
New South Wales,
1980-3

2 HASSAN FATHY,
Mosque, New
Gourna, near
Luxor, Egypt,
1946-53

3 ABDEL WAHED
EL-WAKIL, Halawa
House, Agany,
Egypt, 1975

4 HASSAN FATHY,
Hamed Said House,
Marg Plain, near
Cairo, 1942-5

4

familiar than his Hamdy House in Cairo, 1978, the latter is equally instructive of his attitudes towards residential design at a comprehensive scale.

In the Hamdy House, El-Wakil employed a proportional system based on the golden mean to help him achieve the most efficient plan within a small site and to give the house a sense of spaciousness and order. This resulted in a plan that is roughly one-third open and two-thirds closed. By using a continuously doubling spiral that is generated from the centre of the fountain in the open courtyard, and creating increasingly larger squares in the process, El-Wakil achieved a logical progression of spaces that evolved from the source of water, which symbolizes the beginning of all life. The interior of the house on the ground floor is a lesson in economical planning. The living room, or *qa'a*, as well as the dining room and kitchen are organized in a way that allows them to function as a single entity with maximum efficiency, and yet each space has an identity of its own. The *qa'a*, with its flanking loggias, or

5

iwans, is a surprise because of its grandeur and has a spacious feeling that is quite unexpected in such a diminutive envelope. As in Fathy's Hamed Said House at Marg Plain, 1942–5, or his own house at Sidi Krier, 1971, this *qa'a* takes on added importance because of the limited size of the project, combining a variety of functions in one, all-encompassing realm.

The Al Sulaiman Palace and Mosque, 1979, which was El-Wakil's first commission in Saudi Arabia, is of a much larger scale than the Hamdy House. Nevertheless, it continues the approach of his earlier work in Egypt, as well as attempting to translate it to the singular condition of Jeddah, which was a walled city until the early 1940s. El-Wakil has described his concept for this residence by saying: 'I wished to make explicit a philosophy of design of the traditional Arab house. Any architecture that serves society is dynamic and prone to change. The challenge is to maintain continuity within change by referring to constants and reinterpreting them in a new context.'

The palace is located in new Jeddah, to the north of the old city, and occupies a long plot alongside a wide avenue. Its plan extends on a horizontal axis; it has long elevations to the north and south which are used to take maximum advantage of natural light and the view towards the Red Sea. The sequence of spaces along this axis begins with a small courtyard which acts as an indirect entry into the palace. A large reception hall, or *majli*, located on one side of this court has continuous banquettes facing the exterior along three walls, typical of a traditional male reception room in this region. This adjoins a towering *qa'a* which is the highest volume in the long elevation. After the *qa'a*, there is a subtle shift in zoning towards an inner sanctum reserved for close friends, marked by a change in level and scale. This change of level is repeated in an even more exaggerated way between the next semi-private zone and the private area for the family at the end of the linear sequence, resulting in a tripartite division of public, semi-public, and private compartments. In this way, the architect has reinterpreted the divisions of the traditional Jeddah house, where these functions are stacked vertically, organizing them in horizontal sequence instead.

Following this project, El-Wakil attracted the attention of the Mayor of Jeddah, Said Al-Farsi, who has a keen interest in architecture. In the early 1980s he commissioned El-Wakil to build a series of mosques along the Jeddah Corniche. The third and largest of this trio, built as a part of Mayor Al-Farsi's beautification plan for the city, is the Al-Ruwais Mosque, 1987–90. It occupies a high knoll that allows the building to command attention when approached from the city centre. When seen from the opposite direction, the mosque still forms a dominant landmark despite its small scale because it is seen against the impressive backdrop of the Jeddah waterfront, as well as the city's growing commercial centre.

In all three of El-Wakil's Corniche mosques, he had to address natural ventilation techniques in order to receive approval for their construction from the municipality. As a consequence of this approach, the Al-Ruwais Mosque reaches its most eloquent formal expression in a rhythmical double series of catenary vaults that are stacked to draw in the maximum amount of sea breeze coming in their direction. Behind these vaults, the main dome above the *mihrab* (a niche indicating the direction of prayer) has been incorporated with two domes on each side to create an extremely effective system of air circulation, as well as a simple, but memorable, massing of forms. The gradual transition achieved in this banked composition of vaults and domes is extended further by the addition of two shallow domes, one above the other, of the symmetrical entrances to the prayer hall.

The system of catenary vaults employed by El-Wakil was made possible by a specially designed thin clay-tile brick that allowed compressive forces to be transferred and yet maintained the elegant curved profile

6

7

8, 9 RASEM
BADRAN, Sana'a
project, Yemen,
1987

10 ABDEL WAHED
EL-WAKIL,
Al-Miqat Mosque,
Jeddah, 1991

8

9

that the architect wanted. To accentuate the linearity of these vaults, which also intentionally echo the waves of the Red Sea nearby, buttresses were used to frame the front elevation; and the minaret, rather than being expressly vertical, is intentionally subdued in order to make the rhythmical sequence established by the tiers of vaults and domes read more forcefully in vertical harmony. To assist in the establishing of an unhindered flow of natural ventilation from the sea, while providing a measure of privacy from the road, from which good visibility was also required, this small mosque was placed on a fairly high base and was provided with open screens made of brick that fill the spans of three of its five main arches on the front elevation.

The Al-Miqat Mosque, 1991, is one of El-Wakil's most recent projects, intended as the gateway to Medina. The most basic of the compositional concepts employed by El-Wakil, and the one of principal importance in the design of the Al-Miqat Mosque, is that of the central courtyard used in conjunction with surrounding hypostyle galleries. This concept dates back to the beginning of Islam, when the first mosque, which evolved as an extension of the House of the Prophet, was organized inside a protective wall. As El-Wakil explains: 'This variation typifies the early mosques in Islam and is conceived by defining a plot of land through the erection of an outside wall and establishing a shaded area along the *qibla* wall facing the direction of Mecca. This gesture of defining space and consecrating it to the name of God and to his worship is the basis upon which space is converted from the profane to the sacred.'

The second important concept evident here, which results from the transformation of an original prototype and its commemoration at a smaller scale through a series of rotating squares, is the revitalization of the sacred geometries used in the past. As a plan form, the square is non-directional, with four sides that represent the cardinal points of the compass. When repeatedly rotated one inside another in a series of closed and open spaces, as they are at Al-Miqat, the sequentially diminishing squares strongly imply infinity. The Al-Miqat's minaret, which forms a vertical punctuation mark to reinforce this intention, is an appropriately soaring geometrical *tour-de-force*.

Viewed in chronological order, the Hamdy House, the Al Sulaiman Palace, the Al-Ruwais and Al-Miqat Mosques are representative of El-Wakil's approach to both secular residential and sacred architecture in form and detail; this approach could be considered intentionally derivative, elaborating on the formal mud-brick language evolved by his mentor Fathy. El-Wakil, however, has translated it to the traditional clay brick which is a more durable and publicly acceptable material. Indeed, the scale of El-Wakil's construction activity in Saudi Arabia can be measured by the fact that, at one point, a clay brick factory produced units almost exclusively for use in his buildings. Less of a purist in this regard than

Fathy, El-Wakil seems more cognisant of pragmatic issues, including the use of the computer as a design tool; and since his approach in uncovering past techniques involves a thorough knowledge of geometry, access to the computer has helped him considerably. He characterizes his role as that of a transmitter, or one who is rediscovering the way in which craftsmanship was implemented in the past and is re-implementing it again through building. This, he claims, is the positive function of derivation. While El-Wakil has frequently been criticized as 'acontextual' and 'anti-urban', it should be noted that the examples typically cited in support of this charge are the Jeddah mosques along the Corniche which were always intended to be read at an abstract level as 'functional sculpture'. Furthermore, in defence of these charges, there are many equally compelling instances of El-Wakil's ability to blend into a pre-existing architectural field, and his design ability, regardless of sources, remains unquestioned.

The outbreak of the Gulf War in 1991 brought El-Wakil's commissions in the Middle East to an abrupt halt, and he has since settled in the United States. His following in the region has consequently diminished and attention has shifted to the Jordanian architect Rasem Badran, who represents a completely different approach to the reinterpretation of a traditional language that El-Wakil has propagated. Unlike El-Wakil, Badran has used many of the major Islamic cities as his field of study, and has developed what might be thought of as a rational approach to investigating the lessons of the past. He has specifically studied the environmental and social differences in these cities and the way in which these variations are expressed in formal arrangements. He has described his approach by saying: 'The solutions for any architectural problem are bound to a set of interconnected factors related to socio-cultural, environmental, morphological, and technological issues. As for my role as an architect in activating these factors, I see it as giving value to human needs through emphasizing the character of place, its architectural and morphological patterns and giving meaning to the built environment [in order] to truly relate it to its inhabitants.'

Badran has consciously tried to avoid overt historicism or literal copying from past models. He has aimed instead to produce buildings that meet contemporary standards of utility and comfort, and exploit modern technology where appropriate, while developing the notion of a regionally-based or nationally-rooted architecture. Two of Badran's most recent projects for Sana'a, in Yemen, and Riyadh, in Saudi Arabia, reveal these more general concerns. In Sana'a, a project won in competition in 1987, he undertook an analytical study that began with a comparison between the characteristics of the urban architectural texture of the Yemeni city and those of other Arab cities, such as Cairo and Baghdad, to show the points of similarity and divergence between them.

10

11

12

The urban and particularly the residential formation of Sana'a was found to be quite different from other Arab models. Here residences are grouped vertically around gardens, which form the public spaces in the neighbourhoods, providing places where people can interact. In the other Arab cities he studied, the residential neighbourhoods typically spread horizontally around the internal courtyards, which provided the private spaces for each house. In Sana'a, Badran found that the vertical arrangement of these units resulted from the needs of a nomadic agrarian society and the special topography of Yemen, where agricultural land is very scarce. The houses have evolved in relationship to light and ventilation, with openings of various sizes cleverly placed to cut glare; yet they allow diffused light into the interior, as well as encouraging natural air movement. Badran also noted that, despite the social differentiation among the peoples of any given neighbourhood, the ornamental quality of the openings of the Yemeni house acted as a social leveller. More specifically, his typological studies, carried out mainly by personal survey with sketch book and pen, show a distinct methodology in the ornamental and architectural elements of the openings.

Badran has categorized urban typologies and their morphological patterns, studying the agricultural allotment, the mosque, the *suq* (or shopping area), the specialized commercial centre, and the well, in addition to gates, walls, streets, alleys and intersections. From this he determined the distinctive planning principles operating in Sana'a. Badran then applied these to an actual site similar in size to a traditional neighbourhood in the historic city, his aim was to create what he calls an 'integrated environment' which achieves a harmonious relationship between its physical, spiritual and rational activities. Amenities such as shops, offices, hotels and cinemas are located close to the public street, while the residential complex with its high towers is organized around a garden at the rear of the site.

The Riyadh project, for the construction of the Qasr Al Hokm Justice Palace and Al Jame Mosque, completed in 1992, is Badran's largest to date. By its very nature, the new complex has an important relationship to the old city of Riyadh, and occupies a strategic position in its urban fabric. In dealing with the design and planning of the project, Badran took several complex issues into consideration. The first of these was his desire to re-establish the cultural and urban centre of the city through studies of the inter-related elements traditionally found there and the use of these elements as an incentive to create new cities in the Islamic world. In the Justice Palace these strategies were specifically formulated to encourage its integration in the urban fabric. By replicating the morphology of the old city of Riyadh and some the elements of its traditional architectural vocabulary, such as walls, gates and towers, Badran has produced a complex that strongly relates to the scale and character of its locale.

11, 12 RASEM BADRAN, Al Jame Mosque, Riyadh, 1992

13 RASEM BADRAN, Qasr Al Hokm Justice Palace, Riyadh, 1992

13

Following historical precedent the mosque, an equally important component of the project, has been joined to the scheme's other functions rather than being isolated, as is generally the case today in many cities throughout the Middle East. To establish further the notion of continuity with the past, Badran has adopted a traditional system of construction and ornament, developing it to serve contemporary needs; the mosque's hypostyle columns, for example, resemble the tall palms that were formerly used as supports in the House of the Prophet.

As the range of issues presented in Badran's projects in Yemen and Saudi Arabia indicates, his concerns are far wider than those highlighted in El-Wakil's work. Badran's method of inquiry is heuristic, rather than derivative, generated through direct observation and sketching numerous examples, and focuses on typologies and slight variations within them due to different contextual conditions. This overview allows him to formulate progressions of those examples, based on the generic similarities that he has been able to define. While he is concerned with craftsmanship and detail, it is not his primary focus. He seeks to perpetuate types rather than techniques and forms. If the forms that result are similar to those used in the past, the synthesis is coincidental rather than intentional, based on local evolution of a certain type. This process tends to give his work an aspect of authenticity lacking elsewhere, and it continues to elicit a positive reaction from those familiar with it.

Because Badran searches for constants rather than superficial detail, he has consistently uncovered what the Italian architect Aldo Rossi has categorized as 'persistences' in the evolution of historical types and models, and he distinguishes carefully between the permanent and the transitory. In his exploration of a religious and cultural tradition that is recognized as having both great unity and great diversity, Badran has concentrated on finding the common denominator beneath these differences rather than perpetuating the historical symbols of one particular country. Through extensive graphic analysis, he has shown that these variations usually exist because of environmental and economic rather than philosophical differences. In spite of his rationalistic approach, however, Badran's architecture relies on a perceptive, rather than rigidly objective, study of the world he is examining. As a result, he has made many others aware of the seemingly infinite possibilities for creative expression that can exist within the framework of tradition.

Badran's allegiance to the principles that Fathy helped to lay down is mirrored worldwide in the work of other architects most of whom are from countries which have faced a perceived or real threat of foreign domination. Among the most influential are pioneers such as Dimitris Pikionis in Greece, Sedad Hakki Eldem in Turkey, and Luis Barragán in Mexico, and a present generation of well-established designers including Geoffrey Bawa in

Barragán's predilection for surface, volume, and colour, as well as water, has carried over into Legorreta's architecture. Legorreta's redevelopment of Pershing Square in downtown Los Angeles, completed in 1994, offers a translation of his Mexican architectural vocabulary into a sympathetic Californian context. At the turn of the century, the square was a lush, verdant oasis of elongated queen palms, intersected by paths that crossed it from corner to corner. Fifty years later, the palms had been removed and the 'park' was simply a cover for the garage beneath it, cut off from the city by access ramps to the parking level below. Promenading families had been replaced by drug pushers and prostitutes, and there were frequent confrontations between the police and the homeless who erected cardboard shelters there.

Legorreta was commissioned to re-examine the area in 1985 and, together with the associated landscape architects, he began to identify elements basic to the success of any urban park regardless of location; these included people, vegetation and water. The importance of people, as the first of these, is also the most elusive, since it is the most difficult to predict, especially in a city that is not known for public spaces. As refinements to the strategy of opening the perimeter to people rather than cars, Legorreta activated each corner of the rectangular site and identified a natural line of demarcation, or movement, across its centre which was used to divide the square into segments in order to reduce its scale. A slope from one end of the square to the other indicated the possibility of upper and lower elements, with the space between providing access to the underground parking. Legorreta's love of colour emerges here in a landmark purple tower holding a bright yellow sphere, and lower walls that are much reduced in scope from the initial concept. Part of his intention in this design was to highlight the existence of the growing Hispanic community in Los Angeles, something reinforced by the close proximity of a traditional Hispanic market, and to provide a place where different ethnic groups can meet and interact. Legoretta's characteristic use of colour, water and vegetation have helped to bring the square alive once more.

By opening up the corners of the rectangle, which is made possible by a stricter configuration of the ramps leading down to the underground parking garage, Pershing Square has been reconnected to the city. Raised *allées* of trees, with integral seating running their entire length, are intended to invite people to spend time here, and the transit station nearby will also make people more aware of the park. The queen palms that had been on the site and were later removed to Griffith Park have now been returned as a potent symbol that Pershing Square has been returned to the people.

Legoretta's Renault Factory in Gómez Palacio, Durango, Mexico, completed in 1985, offers further evidence of his commitment to a regional way of building, and his continuing exploration of the architectural power of the wall. The factory is located in a wide-open desert site and the building lies long and low behind flowing sand dunes. Legoretta's reaction to the site is revealing: 'The desert is magic, it is not possible to describe it, it only absorbs you. I found myself with desert and walls, walls that never end. I did not want to soften this emotion, so instead of landscaping the open areas, we covered the site with cobblestone, instead of a sweet colour, we used red. Instead of fighting the desert, we complemented it.'

The wall in this context becomes multivalent, and is integral to understanding and experiencing the building: when it thickens it provides security and thermal mass; when stretched or extruded it provides shelter from the sun; when punched through with openings it provides a sense of light and visual connection; when covered in vibrant colours it radiates warmth. These themes reemerge constantly in Legoretta's architecture,

17 RICARDO LEGORRETA, Pershing Square, Los Angeles, 1994

18 RICARDO LEGORRETA, Renault Factory, Gómez Palacio, Durango, Mexico, 1985

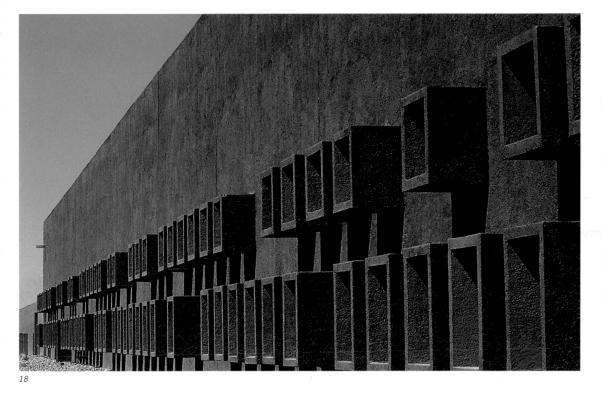

18

sometimes overlaid or complemented by others. His Metropolitan Cathedral in Managua, Nicaragua, 1993, is a powerful concrete monolith which replaces an earlier building damaged beyond repair in an earthquake. Here the wall is symbolic of strength; massive and sturdy enough to resist future tremors, its roughly cast surface has been chiselled by hand to represent the heroic strength of the Nicaraguan people.

Legoretta's fellow Mexican, Teodoro González de León, has adopted and developed another vernacular theme, that of the patio, and translated it in personal and contemporary terms. He has used patios of varying shapes and scales, sometimes open, other times partially covered or enclosed, but always invigorated with a traditional sense of space and population; usually given a central position in the plan, they become places of interaction

20 TEODORO
GONZALEZ DE LEON,
Supreme Court,
Mexico City,
1987-92

21 RICARDO
LEGORRETA,
Metropolitan
Cathedral,
Managua,
1993

which at the same time organize the circulation pattern of the building. In the design of the Supreme Court in Mexico City, 1987–92, González de León expanded the patio to become a broad internal street covered by a massive concrete pergola which continues the building's framed structure. The concrete here is monolithic and rough, bush-hammered to reveal a multi-coloured aggregate of local stone, reflecting the fact that human hands have been at work on it. For González de León, concrete is both a poetic and a pragmatic material; capable of being built at low cost, using unskilled labour, it also resists the passage of time, living up to Le Corbusier's definition of it as 'the stone of the twentieth century'.

The North American architect Antoine Predock (whose reductive work is also discussed in Chapter Four), has often been compared to the South Americans

20

Barragán and Legorreta, but the similarities mainly relate to a common historical heritage in the southwestern United States, through Mexico to Spain. Predock's Zuber House in Paradise Valley Arizona, 1989, was built for a couple after their two sons had grown up and left home, to confound the 'empty nest' syndrome. Characteristically, Predock chose to respond to the climate, vegetation and geology of the Sonoran desert, designing a protective enclosure that almost completely surrounds a square courtyard. The living, dining and kitchen spaces are organized along a more public edge, overlooking Phoenix in the distance to the south, while the master bedroom is perpendicular to this, located in a private zone that projects out past the central courtyard towards the south. Water has been introduced from the courtyard into the

house at ground floor level below the master bedroom wing, setting up an indoor–outdoor commentary around a metaphorical oasis. The house's prow-shaped forms recall Frank Lloyd Wright's Taliesin West in nearby Scottsdale, a building that is also based on a reverential synthesis with the desert landscape.

The architectural distillation of cultural essentials that characterizes the work of practitioners like González de León and Predock is not limited to Mexico or the American Southwest. The Australian architect Glenn Murcutt has been able to synthesize the spirit of Australian outback architecture, combining the pragmatic, durable and inexpensive corrugated metal siding found on farm buildings and sheep stations, with the more elegant materials associated with Modernism. In his distillations, which are comparable to the skilful selection of elements made by architects such as Barragán in their determination to capture a national spirit, Murcutt has interestingly chosen a singularly colonial model — the bungalow — since the notion of a pre-colonial prototype is unsustainable in an Australian context. His crisp renditions maximize exposure to nature when it is appropriate to do so, reflecting the popular Australian regard for the great outdoors, and their generally easy-going lifestyle. Murcutt's Ball-Eastaway House in Glenorie, New South Wales, 1980–3, exemplifies the poetic power of his distillation of an essentially Australian way of building. The house with its long thin plan, and vaulted corrugated metal roof, is inserted into its woodland setting in a sensitive, but nonetheless pragmatic way. Talking about his approach, Murcutt has said: 'I find myself strongly directed by climate when designing, allowing the penetration of the winter sunlight and excluding the sun in summer, thus modifying and affecting the micro-environment of my buildings. The use of gardens, pergolas and simple sunlight and wind filters establishes a temperature gradient between the interior of my buildings and the surrounding environment ... I am particularly interested in the language of a site, the question of appropriateness of building to landform, whether one designs merely a house on a farm or a farmhouse.'

The Hungarian architect Imre Makovecz is another singular example of an inspired translator of vernacular tradition whose work has acquired an almost spiritual dimension. Hungary, which experienced the same post-war love affair with technological growth and progress as Egypt and Mexico, did so within a completely different ideological framework, dominated as it was by a Communist regime that tended to punish non-conformity. As a non-member of the Communist party, Makovecz was an outsider, without access to the scarce supply of industrial materials that other architects and contractors within the party could claim. As a result, he was forced to turn to the vernacular, and has revived the Transylvanian tradition of carpentry as much out of political expediency as

21

from pride in his national heritage; or, more pointedly, as a personal, thinly veiled revolt against the ideological 'occupation' of his country. (His work, because of its strong expressive content, is discussed in greater detail in Chapter Nine of this book.)

While the characters in this international play may change, the elementary scenario remains the same; for many of the best translators, the re-invention of an indigenous architectural language is the first step towards an expression of cultural autonomy and pride, and tectonics become a semiotically loaded weapon against perceived or real cultural suppression. In India, this architectural language began as a respectful continuation of a dialogue rather than a diatribe. Le Corbusier's ambitious scheme for Chandigarh, which was implemented throughout the 1950s and early 1960s, had an enormous impact on an entire generation of Indian architects, most notably Balkrishna Doshi and Charles Correa, both of whom began their careers in the modernist mainstream, but have incrementally moved away from the Corbusian syntax to formulate bolder representations of their rich national history.

Doshi began his working life in the atelier of Le Corbusier in Paris, where he was closely involved in the design of Chandigarh. His personal move away from this influence can be measured by the intellectual distance travelled between the design of the Doshi Studio at Sangath, Ahmedabad, built in 1979–81, and the gallery he built in 1993 to house the art of M F Hussain near the school of architecture in the same city. The difference between them is enormous and represents a general trend in India towards self-realization in architecture. Sangath comprises a series of simple barrel vaults at various heights with the studio cut into the earth to mitigate against the heat. The Hussain-Doshi Gufa Gallery does the same, but its circular plan forms and sectional profile are a far cry from the environmentally adapted International Modernism evident at Sangath. The difference is reinforced in the references that the architect uses to describe the building, comparing it to a large black cobra 'turning and twisting as it does in the legends of Lord Vishnu and Sheshnag'. Made of wire mesh and ferro cement, the structure was built 'as in ancient times, by hundreds of men and women who compressed the mortar over the wire mesh with their skilful hands as if they were making flat bread'. Doshi acknowledges the gradual change that has taken place in his work, identifying it as part of a constant search for a more appropriate and relevant architectural future while holding on to elements of tradition: 'The dilemma that I face is having to look back at tradition, almost hypnotized by the past and without any clear view of the present and even a hint of the future. Perhaps we are too preoccupied with the past because we need a 'hook' to hold on to. It is also comfortable to be with yesterday which is known and predictable. To accept the present, that is today as it is, one needs to answer

22

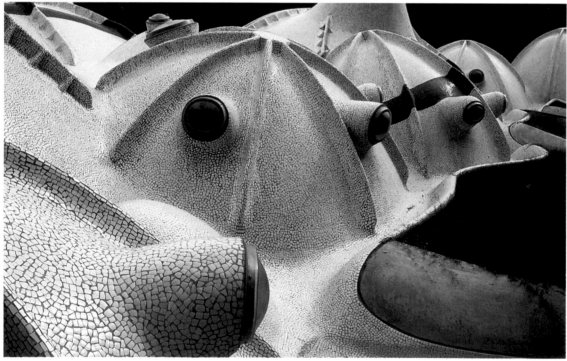

23

questions. What is today? What does it offer to us? And what are the attributes of today which we can use to grow and nourish? Apart from today, we have a greater problem of not knowing the morrow because it is too risky to dream, to speculate or predict. For that, we must understand today. This being the case, my architecture is constantly evolving and perhaps some day one of the buildings that I will design may answer the question of which is true, the dream or the reality, and find the link between the roots and the blossom.'

Doshi's contemporary Charles Correa shares these concerns and has undergone a similar process of questioning and revising his architectural stance. He is known for his culturally expressive and environmentally sensitive buildings which, while revealing his modernist background, seem perfectly rooted in his native India.

22 BALKRISHNA DOSHI, Studio at Sangath, Ahmedabad, 1979-81

23 BALKRISHNA DOSHI, Hussain-Doshi Gufa Gallery, Ahmedabad, 1993

24 CHARLES CORREA, Inter-University Centre for Astronomy and Astrophysics, Pune, 1992

24

His recurrent use of bright colour also hints at the 'blossom' to which Doshi refers. Correa's library and head-quarters for the British Council in New Delhi, 1992, is a characteristically cubic structure, clad in warm red sandstone, and planned on a linear axis that is cut by a series of punctured vertical planes; the axial route through the building is intended to represent the historic relationship between British and Indian cultures. The vista that unfolds as one travels this route moves through open to closed to open spaces, finally settling on a statue of the god Shiva rising above a pool of water which is drained via a spiral channel sunk into the ground. A mural by the English artist Howard Hodgkin, which offers an abstract representation of a banyan tree, is carried across the receding planes within the building's open entrance court, bringing a sense of unity to the composition.

25 CHARLES CORREA,
British Council,
New Delhi, 1992

26 RAJ REWAL,
Asian Games
Village, New
Delhi, 1982

The Inter-University Centre for Astronomy and Astrophysics that Correa built in Pune, in 1992, seems equally grounded in its place and culture. Here Correa sought to express architectural order as a cosmic phenomenon, and the plan is drawn from a Vedic mandala which is symbolic of the universe. The centre is organized around a *kund*, or stepped courtyard, and houses research, office and residential facilities. Formally it plays flat-planed elements against others that are deliberately dynamic, as exemplified by the entrance pavilion with its star-studded domed ceiling and its geometrically patterned floor. Correa is immersed in the architectural environment of the developing world, and has identified four 'issues of decisive importance' to architects attempting to build there. The first is concerned with living patterns in a warm climate; the second with the importance of energy conservation; the third with the tendency towards urbanization; and the fourth with the nature of change, as traditional cultures risk being swamped by globalizing influences. These concerns underpin his own architecture, but also provide an intellectual template against which others can measure their activities.

Like Correa and Doshi, the Indian architect Raj Rewal has sought to find an appropriate cultural expression in his work, but has remained more faithful to Corbusian or Kahnian models. His Asian Games Village in New Delhi, 1982, is a convincing effort to avoid the monocentric, architecturally anonymous statement that frequently characterizes such developments. What Rewal has provided instead is a contemporary version of a traditional Indian village, which briefly accommodated athletes but was converted to low-rent housing soon afterwards. There are three different types of units, organized in clusters along a strictly controlled central pedestrian spine, based on the village *gali*, a space where people can meet and spontaneous events, like street markets, can take place. The complex has a well-defined hierarchical order that easily lent itself to prefabrication, but still manages to avoid regimentation.

Rewal's National Institute of Immunology complex, also in New Delhi, which was built over the course of almost a decade, and completed in 1990, has a similarly modularized basis but is more campus-like in conception. Rewal sees this cluster of buildings — academic, laboratory and research facilities, with five clusters of professors' and student housing — as being analogous to an urban settlement. Located on a hilly site inside the Jawarhalal Nehru University precinct, the complex follows the traditional courtyard typology of the region, the courtyard being the plan generator for the individual building layouts and the site as a whole. The courts and blocks are linked by gateways and shaded pathways designed to give protection from the heat. The scheme follows a careful path between tradition and modernity; the concrete-frame structure is clad in

26

27 RAJ REWAL,
National
Institute of
Immunology, New
Delhi,
1984-90

28, 29
(Overleaf) RAM
KARMI AND ADA
KARMI MELAMEDE,
Supreme Court,
Jerusalem,
1987-93

concrete panels with a local stone aggregate, articulated by bands of red or buff sandstone which have resonances with other local monuments such as the historic Qutb Minar which is visible from the site.

This search for an indigenous architectural consciousness within the framework of a contemporary language has been an occasional modernist subtext, especially in nations where climate and landscape are dominant influences. In Israel, where International Style Modernism has a long and glorious history, the emergence of a contemporary voice for the vernacular tradition is a relatively recent phenomenon. A leading protagonist in this movement is Ram Karmi, a British-trained Israeli. Like others of his generation including Doshi and Rewal, Karmi began his career safe within the modernist fold, working

situation. Like Rewal's Institute of Immunology, Karmi's Supreme Court adopts an urban metaphor appropriate to the ancient city in which it stands; the plan is a collage of elements — open courtyards, enclosed public rooms and ceremonial routes which form analogues for squares, streets and civic rooms. It also explores the materiality of Jerusalem, the city of stone, and its walls, arches and pavements seem appropriately massive, establishing a sympathetic dialogue with the surrounding city.

This notion of a dialogue, whether at a regional or national level, becomes evermore compelling as the end of the twentieth century approaches. The age of mass communication, and the concept of a global village first predicted by Marshall McLuhan more than thirty years ago has finally become a reality. Accelerating developments in aeronautical and electronic engineering have changed the realities of space and time that have separated countries and cultures in the past, bringing modern technology to the most remote yurt in Tibet, for example, or thousands of tourists to the Galapagos Islands. In addition to breaking down physical barriers, this changing reality has also shattered many of the social and cultural distinctions that physical distance had once managed to protect, causing widespread changes. The media, or more specifically the medium of television, has not only brought a specific set of materialistic Western values into every corner of the world, but has also been responsible for the 'And now this' syndrome, in which tragedies such as war and mass murder are routinely and incongruously juxtaposed with advertising sales pitches. The final result of this confusion has been the destruction of traditional societies from Rwanda to Chiapas by the seemingly inexorable homogeneity of globalization.

Many see this process as a regrettable concomitant of modernity and go on to bemoan the demographic effects that have resulted; as we have seen, however, architects working in a contemporary vernacular idiom have refused to accept the inevitability of this situation. While seeming to repudiate all contemporary, consumer-orientated logic, they are merely recognizing a social phenomenon that others, in their search for individuality, have overlooked. They believe that people need a sense of identity with family, religion, friends, village, town and country, as well as a connection with their past in order for any of the technological gains that have been made to have any meaning for them in the future. While the anthropological evidence of this need, as well as the ranks of the culturally dispossessed continues to grow, those who are trying to address this problem through their architecture continue to be labelled by cynics as hopeless romantics; but for many, their message is valuable.

27

in the atelier of his father, Dov Karmi, one of Israel's pioneering Modern Movement architects. It was not until the 1980s and 1990s, in what might be thought of as his mature work, that Karmi began to seek a more profound sense of place and regional identity, developing a more responsive and eclectic compositional approach and confronting problems of symbolic expression and contextual resonance. The Supreme Court Building in Jerusalem, 1987–93, designed with partner Ada Karmi Melamede, gave Karmi the opportunity to address all these issues in a single

1 (Previous page)
ERICK VAN EGERAAT,
Nationale
Nederlanden and
ING Bank,
Budapest, 1994

2 HANS SCHAROUN,
Philarmonie
Concert Hall,
Berlin, 1963

The recent trend towards expression in architecture is really a resurgence of a clearly established historical position, which began in the early part of this century with the impulse to stress the spiritual rather than the rational and purely functional aspects of building. The source of this position is critical to an understanding of any new activity because the basic issues remain the same. To begin to trace the roots of Expressionism one must look to the genesis and foundation of the Deutscher Werkbund in 1907. Under the guidance of its founder, Hermann Muthesius, the Werkbund existed to foster closer links between German artists and industry, with the aim of improving the quality of German design and manufacture. The Werkbund's mandate also had a moral and nationalistic dimension, the belief of its founders being that the modernity and progressiveness of the German nation should find appropriate expression in the output of its artists and craftsmen. Muthesius, who was heavily influenced by the English Arts and Crafts Movement, advocated that similar methods of craft and economy of means should be followed in a German context and that a unified language of German design would naturally follow. However, the inevitable tension that resulted from Muthesius' alliance of industry and art led to a polarizing debate in which the mass-production ethos of industry, which demanded standard types, was contrasted with the formal freedom demanded by the artist. This split between *norm* and *form*, between normative typology and formal expression, is characterized broadly as one between *Typisierung* and *Kunstwollen,* or literally, 'will to form'.

By the time of the landmark Werkbund Exhibition in Cologne in 1914, Germany was preoccupied with focusing its industrial might on wartime production. Germany's subsequent humiliating defeat brought much soul searching among architects eager to use their professional skills to help the country they had fought for recover its pride and economic stability. Some took refuge in teutonic mysticism, and *Kunstwollen*, especially as embodied in the historical gothic model, took on a deeper patriotic significance; it was no coincidence that the name Bauhaus implies the *Bauhütte* or gothic mason's secret lodge. The principles of that famous school had first been put forward a year earlier by Bruno Taut, who argued that a new society could only be achieved through a revived architecture or 'art of building' which offered a cultural synthesis of each discipline involved. Taut's vision of the reunification of art and architecture was embodied in a group called the Arbeitsrat für Kunst (or Soviet for Art). The ideas of this group were developed in a series of letters between its members called *Die Gläserne Kette*, or the 'glass chain'; these correspondents included Bruno Taut, Walter Gropius and Hans Scharoun. Other architects, such as Hans Poelzig in his Grosse Schauspielhaus in Berlin, 1919, and Erich Mendelsohn in the Einstein Tower in Potsdam, 1917–21, and Petersdorff Store, Breslau, 1927, definitively put these ideas into practice. While it seemed

that this integral sensibility might prevail in the Modern Movement, it was effectively challenged at the first meeting of CIAM (Congrès Internationaux d'Architecture Moderne) held at La Sarraz in Switzerland in 1928. Hugo Häring was the main proponent of 'organic' expressionism at that conference, but Le Corbusier succeeded in having a functionalistic model adopted as a normative proposal, in such an effective way that it prevailed.[1] Hans Scharoun alone managed to carry the spirit of *Kunstwollen* forward in Germany into the period following the Second World War period, culminating his career with the design of the Berlin Philharmonie, 1963, but by then the normative mind-set had been so well established as the only possible modernist construct that he was marginalized and the concert hall was generally dismissed as idiosyncratic and excessive. Scharoun was not alone, however, in keeping the expressionist flame burning, and it still has many adherents worldwide.

Given its contentious background in Germany, it should perhaps come as no surprise that expressive, or 'organic', architecture has thrived more successfully in America in the last three decades of the twentieth century than it has in Europe. As the nation that has idealized the notion of the individual more emphatically than any other, the United States also has an exceptional paragon of freedom of expression in Frank Lloyd Wright, who extracted his entire philosophy from the theme of art and craft versus the machine. Wright is the architectural equivalent of the American transcendentalists Ralph Waldo Emerson, Henry David Thoreau and Walt Whitman, who advocated discovering personal identity in sympathetic competition with the vastness of the American frontier. Wright also nationalized English Arts and Crafts propositions, converting them to suit an American context. While identifying with his Welsh family ancestry, he was unmistakably attempting to find a distinctive American profile, and his Prairie-style houses are as singular as the Conestoga Wagons that settlers lived in while travelling across the central grasslands from east to west. Wright's Chicago period, however, and especially its early phase before 1905, still described Arts and Crafts affinities that began to be replaced by bolder personal expression as time went on; this 'organic' evolution was responded to by followers of Wright, such as Bruce Goff. Like Wright, Goff also had Midwestern roots, and was also mostly self-educated in architecture, learning through apprenticeship rather than formal academic training. As chairman of the University of Oklahoma School of Architecture from 1947 until 1955, he influenced several generations of students in the pursuit of a radically different direction from the modern doctrine sweeping the country after the Second World War, and it was heavily influenced by Wright's architecture. Goff never worked with Wright, which may explain his willingness and ability to interpret him so freely, rather than being constrained by the code of respectfulness to the Master that seems to have been adopted by Wright's apprentices. Goff adapted Wright's later formal language, visible in such examples as Taliesin West, 1938, the Marin County Civic Center, 1957–66, and the Beth Sholom Synagogue in Elkins Park, 1959, extrapolating geometries which he then used to generate surprisingly original design statements of his own. Goff's Bavinger House, 1950–5, in Norman, Oklahoma, is one of his best-known efforts; a shell of rock that spirals like a chambered nautilus around a mast, wrapping an interior collage of *ad hoc* materials including flocked carpeting on floors and walls, aeroplane parts, and pieces bought from a department store. The overall effect is something like Frank Lloyd Wright meets 1950s angular pragmatism, the characteristic popular style of a decade that endorsed new materials such as nylon and plastic which were made possible by the same scientific curiosity that produced the atomic bomb.

A professorial chair at Oklahoma, established in Goff's name, has included many of the most recognizable advocates of his architectural position, such as Gunnar Birkerts and Bart Prince, and the school's quarterly journal regularly features others including Fay Jones, John Lautner, Imre Makovecz and William Bruder. As a graduate of the Technische Hochschule in Stuttgart, Gunnar Birkerts is very aware of the Bauhaus attempt to integrate craft and industry, and the split that later invalidated the Gropius ideal, as the functionalist aspects of Modernism came to predominate. His Latvian ancestry has also made him especially sympathetic to the work of Finnish architects such as Alvar Aalto and Eero Saarinen whose terminal building for TWA at Kennedy Airport, New York, completed in 1962, remains one of the landmarks of expressionist architecture in the United States. Birkerts apprenticed in Saarinen's Bloomfield Hills, Michigan office from 1949 to 1954, opening his own firm in Birmingham, Michigan, five years later. The natural surroundings of Birkerts' adopted Michigan remind him of his native Latvia, and have been a constant inspiration for his own organic expression: 'I like to call my design process organic synthesis', he says, 'The process creates expressive architecture that brings into play the relationship between a structure's interior and exterior. The geometry I am attracted to is polygonal. The folded planes and bent lines respond precisely to programmatic needs'. While he admits to having been influenced by the rationality of Mies van der Rohe and other Modernists, he claims that his admiration stopped at the persistent dogma they presented. 'I believe in discipline in architecture', he says, 'but not in dogma. And I can honestly say that I have not benefited from anyone else's theory in my life ... whatever I have developed has come through the empirical method ... by testing things out'.[2]

Birkerts' visceral approach is a measured rebellion against the orthogonal restrictions of the rational mentality that prevailed in the Modern Movement; it also identifies his allegiance to what he prefers to call the 'expressive' branch of Modernism. He is able to identify an

2

3 Bart Prince,
Shinenkan
Pavilion, Los
Angeles County
Museum of Art,
1988

alternative position within its general parameters rather than being boxed into a total rejection of them. This is evident in his incremental additions to the University of Michigan Library, 1986, which he has placed almost entirely underground as a respectful gesture to the existing campus fabric. The angular skylights that bring light deep into the interior of Birkerts' new building send sharp crystalline forms slicing up through the earth; as the difference between these forms and the ground around them clearly demonstrates, Birkerts intentionally avoids emulating nature. Rather, he considers his method to be organic, analogous to crystalline growth. His plan for the Latvian National Library in Riga, begun in 1989, provides an appropriately peaked 'crystal mountain' beside the Daugava river. The profile is intended to evoke the mythic shining prow that it was believed would one day rise out of the water, although the library is the only evidence of a mountain rising near the river so far. The angles also recall ancient fortresses, vernacular barns and historic houses in Riga.

The University of Michigan project led to a similar commission at Ohio State University College of Law in Columbus, in 1993; this is an equally strategic campus planning addition, but without the contextual restrictions Birkerts faced in Michigan. Located in its own quadrangle, Birkerts' Y-shaped addition, with its stem pointing to the centre of the university, clamps on to an existing renovated facility that is completely engulfed in its outer limestone skin. Light also plays an important role here in defining the public face of the building, but because of its increased exposure, the fenestration is mostly recessed behind an arcade that announces points of entry. Birkerts' particular skill at adapting to existing conditions goes underground again in San Diego, in the Central Library expansion at the University of California, completed in 1992. The original library, designed in the late 1960s, is best described as an upside down ziggurat supported by a branching concrete frame. Reacting to the client's suggestion that the existing building should remain virtually untouched, Birkerts has once again resorted to a subterranean solution; this is mostly single storey below grade, with an earth covered second level that ties into the main floor of the existing library. The new addition wraps around the central core, and 'canyons', like those used in Michigan, light the interior.

Birkerts represents a direct, if transplanted, continuation of the European origins of Expressionism, while Bart Prince, as the second occupant of Goff's University of Oklahoma professorial chair, represents the home-grown version, which has an obvious affinity with Goff's idiosyncratic approach. Prince worked in Goff's office in the early 1970s and continued a collaboration with him after he had set up his own office. On Goff's death in 1982, Prince was asked by Goff's client Joseph Price to complete the pavilion at the Los Angeles County Museum of Art which Goff had designed to house Price's extensive collection of Japanese art. The Shinenkan Pavilion, which was completed in 1988, establishes the direct link between these two architects. Price himself, incidentally, can trace his links with organic architecture back a generation further; it was his father who, in the 1950s, commissioned Frank Lloyd Wright to design the Price Tower, in Bartlesville, Oklahoma. Price junior was responsible for supervising the project and thus worked closely with Wright. Almost hidden as it is behind the main entrance to the museum, the Shinenkan Pavilion is clearly in the tradition of Wrightian organicism; this stemmed from Wright's appreciation of Japanese architecture and its integral response to nature which was reinterpreted here first by Goff and latterly by Prince. Much more monumental and hermetic than any tea pavilion, the Prince design is one of the largest organic or expressionist examples from the Goff camp, its enormous stone cones and stylized functionless horns announcing its genealogy.

Prince's addition to the Spence House in Pasadena, 1986, extends a Mission-style structure, and establishes a further, smaller foothold for the expressionists in the Los Angeles metropolitan area. With this house, Prince has attempted to achieve a more comfortable relationship with the original building while showing an equal respect for nature and the existing trees on the site. He clearly defines inner and outer worlds, the building's sinuous walls hug the site contours, defining an inside 'garden'. The repercussions of the Shinenkan Pavilion, and its connection with the Japanese homage to nature appropriated by Wright, also extends to Prince's house for his patrons Joseph and Etsuko Price in Corona Del Mar, California, completed in 1989. The plan is organized to meet two quite different conditions: a band of rooms at the back of the site forms a protective zone alongside the adjoining properties while at the front it explodes outwards to take full advantage of the views of the Pacific Ocean. At the heart of the plan are three overlapping pod-like spaces, each one supported on a sinuous trunk of laminated fir and steel plate, which branches out at the top to frame the ceiling and walls. The internal gardens attempted for the Spence House in Pasadena become in this instance sculpted laminated wood trees in a wavy shingled wrapper; in Prince's hands the San Francisco Bay Area tradition introduced to Southern California by Julia Morgan and others is given a sinuous twist. Another house, for Henry Whiting, built in Sun Valley, Idaho, at the same time, has a less exuberant shingle wrapper, and no crafted enchanted forest interior, seeming more restrained than earlier work and perfectly suited to its expansive, grassy site at the base of a range of hills. The use of a banded, hull-like tube casing is a technique extended from Prince's own house in Albuquerque, New Mexico, completed in 1984, which is an extended wooden cylinder, wrapped into an oblong 'doughnut', and supported on four large tile covered *pilotis*, on an equally wide-open site.

5

6 BART PRINCE,
Price House,
Corona Del Mar,
California,
1989

The settings of the Price and Prince houses, like the wild flavour of Wright's Taliesin West in the Arizona desert, raise another issue that may be identified with the Wright–Goff variant of the American contribution to the New Expressionism: the implicit connection between an organic style and the freedom that the West subconsciously represents in a nation where individuality is plainly under threat. If the Arts and Crafts Movement really did attempt to recapture the rural English ideal, the Wright–Goff strain of Expressionism recalls cowboys and teepees and strong silent types who can live off the land and commune with nature. The frontier is the most enduring and powerful remaining American myth and the freedom implicit in American Expressionism consciously or subconsciously connects with it. Architect and client alike have a self-image of rugged individualism, seeing themselves as the contemporary version of the plains people who won the West. Silent types rarely theorize, however, and the need to justify or substantiate is seen as a sign of weakness; the work is intended to be self-explanatory, material emotion being the only reaction necessary.

Bart Prince hasn't been the only active expressionist in Los Angeles. The late John Lautner, who apprenticed with Frank Lloyd Wright at both Taliesin East, in Wisconsin, and Taliesin West, between 1933 and 1939, began his own practice in Los Angeles in 1940. In his fifty-year career, he stressed the machine aesthetic rather than the handcrafting of natural materials, and his Chemosphere House of 1960, which looks like an alien spaceship perched on a single concrete column, defined his approach. Silvertop, a house overlooking Silver Lake, which followed three years later, continued the theme of the cantilevered shell, and technological adaptation to the special difficulties involved in building on steep, geologically unstable hillside sites in a city where houses frequently slide away. Yet, in spite of Lautner's more industrial tactics, he too believed in the self-explanatory, non-theoretical approach that recurs like an anthem among expressionists. He wrote that: 'architecture, in its truest sense, may not be academically defined, it is a continuous search for basic human needs that include emotional and psychological requirements'. The Sheats/Goldstein Residence, one of the last houses Lautner worked on before his death in 1996, shows the remarkable consistency of his attitude. The house was originally built by Lautner in 1963 and was almost continuously remodelled by him from 1989 when it was bought by its present owner, Jim Goldstein. It occupies a mountainside site overlooking Beverly Hills, opening up to panoramic views of the city and the ocean beyond. From the street, the house is entered via a hall and dining area which has a low wood-panelled ceiling; this leads to a cavernous living space which has a vaulted concrete roof with hundreds of small glass lenses let into it; each acts as a tiny skylight, in Lautner's words, 'simulating the light in a primeval forest'. Lautner came to Los Angeles to superintend the

7 JOHN LAUTNER,
Sheats/Goldstein
Residence, Los
Angeles, 1989-96

8 FAY JONES,
Thorn Crown
Chapel, Eureka
Springs,
Arkansas, 1980

7

construction of Wright's Sturges House, and the spirit of the frontiersman that Wright encouraged in his apprentices supported him in this 'ugly' city as he struggled to establish his own independent direction. It also sustained him as he went on to produce a body of work that is completely at odds with the cool detachment of the other, more celebrated and effete currents of Modernism that thrived briefly in Los Angeles after the Second World War. It is perhaps fruitless to try to place Lautner in any particular stylistic camp. He saw himself in a school of one, preferring a comparison with engineers such as Pier Luigi Nervi or Felix Candela, rather than other architects, but his work seems nonetheless to represent the zenith of the Wright—Goff strain of American Expressionism and its 'will to form'.

Lautner is joined in this lofty eminence by other great names of American architecture, including Hendrick Bangs Kellogg who is a distant relative of the famous American landscape architect Frederick Law Olmstead, and James T Hubbell, who apprenticed with Kellogg. Chief, however, amongst Lautner's fellow devotees of Frank Lloyd Wright is Fay Jones. Jones first met Wright while he was teaching at the University of Oklahoma, while Bruce Goff headed the school, and subsequently spent time with him at Taliesin in the late 1950s. Jones has eloquently conveyed this Wrightian bond, as well as the reverence for nature that it represents, in the diaphanous Thorn Crown Chapel, 1980, which is now an accepted classic of the genre. The chapel occupies a wooded site in the Ozark Mountains near Eureka Springs in Arkansas; it has a simple rectangular plan and a soaring section that culminates in a high sky-lit roof. The interior of the building resonates with the forest that surrounds it; its grove of columns and the complex, canopy-like arrangement of the braced roof trusses, with light shining down through them, suggest a geometrically ordered glade, imbued with a sense of spatial drama that seems gothic in its origins. Jones admits to being 'nourished' by Wright, and has demonstrated an innate understanding of Wright's brand of organicism in a series of chapels, most of them, like the Thorn Crown Chapel, on wooded sites. A rare exception in this regard is the Marty V Leonard Community Chapel that Jones completed in Fort Worth, Texas, in 1991. Its broad shingled roof and 'forest' interior continue familiar themes, but its soaring form dominates its open setting, an effect that is heightened by placing the building on a wide brick podium that levels out its falling site. Its isolation may be uncharacteristic, but it helps to make the point that Jones' organicism is not simply another regional style — it has been christened the 'Ozark' style because so much of Jones' work is in the Ozark Mountains — rather it relies on well-founded principles which can be applied in any situation. Jones sets out three 'tenets' of organic architecture: a deep understanding of the site, what it is and how to enhance it; a sense of detail and how the smallest part of a building relates to the whole; and an honest approach

to the nature of materials. He sums all this up by echoing Wright's question: 'what is the nature of this thing?'

9 WILL BRUDER,
Phoenix Central
Library, Arizona,
1988-95

This question has been picked up, and reinvestigated by a younger generation of American architects. Prominent among this group is Will Bruder who remains something of a curiosity in contemporary architecture; like his architectural forebears Wright and Lautner, he didn't attend architecture school and indeed has had little formal training. Instead, he became an architect in the traditional perhaps 'organic' way, apprenticing himself to a succession of architects and forming associations with numerous others, including masters such as John Lautner and Bruce Goff, and rebels such as Paolo Soleri, with whom he completed a summer workshop in 1967 at Arcosanti. Perhaps because he is self-taught, Bruder is ready to admit to more recent influences, including the work of the Italian architect Carlo Scarpa, which he discovered during a stay at the American Academy in Rome in 1987, and the architecture of his fellow American, Antoine Predock (discussed in Chapters Four and Eight).

The complex range of influences that these architects have brought to bear on Bruder's work is evident in buildings such as the Theuer Residence, in Phoenix, Arizona, completed in 1992. It seems to take its cue from Lautner as exemplified by the Sheats/Goldstein Residence, juxtaposing precise machine-made elements with natural materials, and combining a Wrightian sense of spatial drama — the house opens up slowly to reveal a spectacular view of the gardens and the mountains beyond — with an attitude to shelter and site that seems to follow the pattern of traditional Southwestern houses, which have evolved complex passive systems for protecting their interiors from the harsh desert sun.

These themes are explored at a far larger scale in Bruder's Phoenix Central Library of 1988–95, which although it is located on the edge of an expanding town centre, seems to take its formal inspiration from the shear-sided table-like mesas of Monument Valley. This is a metaphorical connection that Bruder encourages and takes further, characterizing the library's five-storey high central roof-lit atrium as a 'crystal canyon'. These metaphorical notions are given appropriate physical expression; the slab-like longitudinal walls are sheathed in earth-coloured copper panels whose horizontal ribs suggest geological strata; and they are cut through on either side by a wide band of polished steel panels which are angled to reflect the sky and thus suggest that the copper cliffs have been rent apart by some giant natural force. These steel bands also mark the entrances to the building and suggest another kind of connection to the 'crystal canyon' beyond.

In his advocacy of liberation from 'justification, reason or theory', and his warnings against becoming 'a slave to a philosophy' the English architect Will Alsop, along with his German partner Jan Störmer, occupies an equivalent position to Bruder, Lautner and the

10

11

anti-theorists of the American expressionist school. It is not the intention of this book to try to wedge architects and their buildings into convenient pigeon-holes, and this is a good point at which to admit that any art-historical method has its limits. Alsop, like Lautner, seems to defy easy classification, yet he seems to be an inheritor of the 'will to form' that characterizes the work of architects such as Hans Scharoun and Bruce Goff; indeed, Alsop has challenged the old Modernist law 'form follows function', by asking 'why shouldn't function follow form?'

This challenge seems incidental to many of Alsop's buildings, such as his Hamburg Ferry Terminal, 1988–91, which appears formally restrained, even carrying echoes of the Deutscher Werkbund in its functionalist good manners, but Alsop's question hangs meaningfully in the air in his Hôtel du Département, Marseilles, won in competition in 1990 and completed in 1994. Its immense blue forms — the baguette-shaped *délibératif* and extruded box-like administrative floors — sit suspended in mid-air above a palette-shaped deck, spiked on an aggressive array of tilted cruciform *pilotis*. 'Le Grand Bleu', as it is popularly known, has a sculptural quality that has little to do with function. In this respect Alsop's architecture is reminiscent of Frank Gehry's (whose work is discussed at length in Chapter Fourteen). Gehry's architecture springs from his fascination with the model and the changing formal games — adding and subtracting, teasing and testing — that can be played as its scale increases; he prefers to work three-dimensionally from the beginning of a project, freezing it orthographically only once the formal and spatial issues have been resolved. Alsop also designs three dimensionally but, for him, the act of painting is analogous to Gehry's modelling process. Like Gehry, he follows an intuitive path; painting allows him to imagine solutions without thinking too closely about the programme or a particular problem; it is a way of opening up a dialogue, of creating a conversation between form and function which can be developed, rather than mapping out the specifics of a building early on.

Other architects, notably the Italian Massimiliano Fuksas, work in similar ways. Fuksas conceives his buildings either through painting or modelling using strips of paper and other bits and pieces that come to hand. He argues that one of the most welcome recent trends in contemporary architecture is that it has become possible to make connections between sculpture and building. Fuksas' architecture typically has a sculptural quality, whether it is the figurative strain of his entrance pavilion to the Niaux caves in France, 1988–93, executed in rusting corten steel, or in the minimalist tradition of his Michel de Montaigne University Art School in Bordeaux, 1993–4, clad in green patinated copper. Fuksas counts the Italian painter Lucio Fontana among the formative influences on his work. Just as Fontana crossed spatial boundaries in his paintings — slashing or piercing the canvas — Fuksas seems to be able to make the leap between art and architecture, providing habitable sculptures which can be enjoyed both abstractly and programmatically.

The free-style *ad-hoc* collages and assemblages of Alsop's fellow countrymen Piers Gough and Nigel Coates also seem to result from largely unpremeditated reactions to a particular place or condition. Piers Gough of Campbell, Zogolovitch, Wilkinson, Gough (CZWG) has been characterized as the court jester of English architecture, but as usual with such characterizations there is more to Gough than meets the eye. While certainly playful, his architecture results from a metaphoric reading of place and a manipulation of programme that is every bit as convincing as the work of his near namesake Bruce Goff. Much of Gough's and CZWG's architecture from the 1980s resulted from a development boom in London's Docklands area which was quickly established as a resi-

10 WILL ALSOP, Hôtel du Département, Marseilles, 1994

11 WILL ALSOP, Hamburg Ferry Terminal, 1988-91

12 MASSIMILIANO FUKSAS, Entrance Pavilion, Niaux Caves, France, 1988-93

13 MASSIMILIANO FUKSAS, Michel de Montaigne Art School, Bordeaux, 1993-4

12

13

dential district following the commercial demise of the docks. Gough's China Wharf, 1982–8, located near Tower Bridge on the River Thames, has three distinctive facades, each of which expresses an approach to building in this Victorian warehouse context. The river facade, for example, attempts to recreate the juxtaposition of warehouse and ship. It comprises a central solid plate, painted bright red, with flanged curves that suggest naval architecture; these flanges are pulled outwards on their horizontal edges to provide balconies with nautical railings. Just in case the point is missed, a small rowing boat, which forms the balcony for the lowest apartment, has been embedded in the facade at the high water mark. As Gough says of the building: 'Part boat, part pagoda and very red, it is definitely waving not drowning'. China Wharf's near contemporary Cascades, 1986–8, is another

14 CZWG,
Cascades, London,
1986-8

15 CZWG,
China Wharf,
London, 1982-8

16 CZWG,
The Circle,
London, 1989

14

15

residential development, this time on the Isle of Dogs and on a far more ambitious scale. Built in anticipation of the high-rise blocks of Canary Wharf which now tower above it, Cascades rises shear on three sides to twenty storeys, but 'cascades' towards the water on its fourth, where glass-covered escape stairs and balconies are arranged to suggest an immense geometric waterfall. Architecturally its sources are a rich blend of warehouse and nautical imagery; its brick facades are pierced with portholes and festooned with pirate-ship balconies. This theme, of warehouse brick and 'Treasure Island' detailing is picked up again in CZWG's The Circle, completed in 1989. Built behind one of Docklands' few surviving Victorian 'brick canyon' streets, it expresses this heritage in a direct way; its walls echo robustly the form and proportion of the neighbouring warehouses, but there is a surprise in wait. At the centre of the scheme, seemingly scooped out of the apartment blocks, is an immense drum-like space; its walls covered in glazed blue tiles, it forms a vast vat of colour. For Gough, this space stirs memories of the abandoned Victorian dyeworks that once operated nearby, where each floor was imbued with its own rich hue. It is offered as a gesture on a grand scale, expressing with a flourish the heroic urban quality the area once had.

Nigel Coates, who expanded into architecture via interior design, shares Gough's eclecticism and his fascination with technological flotsam, from aircraft parts to bits of ships and other heavy metal. Coates first came to critical attention when he set up NATO — Narrative Architecture Today — at the Architectural Association in London in 1983, proposing an architecture of fluid and unfixed forms that would express and interact with what he called the broader social matrix of the city. The city that has given him the greatest opportunity to experiment with form is Tokyo. Coates' Tokyo buildings rely on a playful synthesis of elements and influences from East and West. The Bohemia Jazz Club and Caffè Bongo, for example, both completed in 1986, each result from his aircraft fetish. The latter has a giant aircraft wing, complete with engines, embedded in its fragmented classical facade; it is a reminder simultaneously of Japan's fateful love affair with technology and the destructive influence it can bring to bear. The Nishi Azubu Wall commercial building completed in Tokyo in 1990 is far more earthbound but makes a similar commentary between the antique and the modern, appearing as an ancient palazzo that has suffered the indignity of conversion.

The Frenchman Philippe Starck, who like Coates is known as much for his furniture and product design as he is for architecture, has also made his mark in Tokyo, a city that seems to welcome and thrive on experimentation. This is best summed up by two projects which Starck completed at the very end of the 1980s: Unhex Nani Nani, an office building in downtown Tokyo, and the Asahi Beer Azumabashi Hall located next to the Sumida River close to the Asakusa Temple in the historical part of the city.

17 PHILIPPE
STARCK, Asahi Beer
Azumabashi Hall,
Tokyo, 1989

18 PHILIPPE
STARCK, Nani Nani,
Tokyo, 1989

19 NIGEL COATES
Caffè Bongo,
Tokyo, 1986

20 (Overleaf)
USHIDA FINDLAY,
Truss Wall House,
Tokyo, 1993

Nani Nani is an extraordinary piece, a headquarters building for a construction company that seems to delight in subverting the requirements of its conventional programme beneath an undulating green patinated copper roof, which looms above the rooftops in this low-rise district like the rising form of an aquatic monster emerging from the deep. In this building, Starck has taken the biomorphism of his furniture design to its surreal limits; indeed the building's adopted name results from the client's startled question when he was first presented with the drawings: 'What is it? What is it?', or in Japanese 'Nani? Nani?'

The Asahi Beer Hall starts from a more conventional standpoint but ends on an equally dramatic note. Like Nani Nani, the building has a nautilus-like plan form, organized within a rectangular site boundary. Approaching the Beer Hall by night from across the Azumabashi Bridge, one sees only the glistening black profile of its granite-clad structure, which forms an urn-like base for a gilded 'flame' that hovers on the rooftop and seems to flicker in the wind, beckoning people from across the city. Inside the building is a decorative programme that would challenge even Bruce Goff's ingenuity: velvet-covered walls, lead floors, frosted glass balustrades and twisted columns are intended to generate an illusionistic or even surreal sense of space. Here Starck poses a question of his own: 'Why shouldn't architectural design be free?'

Coates and Starck are not the only eccentric expressionists to be found working in Tokyo; Eisaku Ushida and Kathryn Findlay have produced a more futuristic example of the genre in their Soft and Hairy House, 1993, in nearby Tsukuba, Ibaraki Prefecture. The clients, who are art lovers, are particularly fond of the work of Salvador Dalí and took the name of the house from his writing. Located on a corner site in a neighbourhood of single family houses, this small residence takes the form of an extruded cylinder looped around the perimeter of the property line, forming a central courtyard. An egg-shaped bathroom projects into the courtyard as a curvilinear exception to an otherwise straightforward *parti*. The roof of the house is planted with a mixture of species from a local nursery – local grasses and wild flowers as well as herbs and vegetables – to transform the hairy image into a pragmatically edible urban garden. This house offers one of the most literal fusions of nature and architecture in a movement that is preoccupied with the link between the two. The Truss Wall House by Ushida Findlay, built in Tokyo at the same time, is more introverted because it is located alongside a main highway. The name of the house once again reveals the main design idea; the house is characterized by its walls. Ushida Findlay has devised a system of wall construction in which vertical trusses support a skin of wire mesh which can be formed to any shape and then sprayed with concrete. This allows the possibility of *poché*, whereby the walls and roof can vary in thickness,

18   *19*

21 RALPH ERSKINE,
The Ark, London,
1991

22 USHIDA FINDLAY,
Soft and Hairy
House, Tsukuba,
Ibaraki
Prefecture,
1993

23 JØRN UTZON,
Sydney Opera
House, 1957–73

creating spaces on the inside that relate only approximately to the forms apparent on the outside. At a practical level, the building's double-skin construction insulates it from extreme temperatures, and protects the occupants from the noise of passing traffic. The house becomes a kind of 'spatial vessel', an idea that is reinforced stylistically by the building's strategically placed portholes and an exterior that seems to result from a confabulation between an expressionist villa and a bloated pleasure boat.

Whether intentionally or not, the leading British expressionist, Ralph Erskine, has also appropriated the ship metaphor in his Ark, at Hammersmith, London, 1991. Visually dominant because of its prominence at the edge of the major western traffic gateway into London, and shaped in plan to adjust to the highways around it, the Ark is one of the most significant symbols of Expressionism in Britain, built by an architect who represents the continuance of the Aalto tradition. Born in England, Erskine moved to Sweden in 1939, just before the start of the Second World War. After the War, he studied at the Swedish Royal Academy of Art, and opened his own office near Stockholm, soon afterwards. His housing block at Byker, in Newcastle upon Tyne in the north of England, which began in 1969 and continued until 1981, helped establish his international reputation, and underscores the unfinished social programme of the Modern Movement which was partially realized here in co-operation with the residents. The fragmented, eccentric appearance of 'the wall', as it is called, put many purists off, but it has provided a viable alternative to the anonymous blocks of public housing that blot the skyline in major cities and towns throughout the United Kingdom, and offers a specific case study for comparison with the reductivist modern aesthetic. If Erskine's work is most characteristic of the British tendency towards Expressionism, albeit heavily weighted by his Swedish connections and the Aalto tradition, his position exhibits none of the technological phobias of the American Goffists, and can be seen, uniquely, to promote common, rather than individual aims.

In Scandinavia, Jørn Utzon also continues Aalto's manifest identification with natural abundance in a Danish rather than Finnish context. Outside that framework he is best known, perhaps infamous, for the Sydney Opera House, 1957–73. Cost over-runs, due to its complicated structure, severely damaged the architect's reputation, however, and perhaps led to the relative conservatism of his National Assembly Complex in Kuwait, 1972, in which the flourish is restricted to a tent-like porte-cochere rendered in concrete to signify the code of Bedouin hospitality. Administrative offices are flanked behind this grand, but structurally controlled, gesture in a pragmatic, legible grid, the uniformly flat roof over the offices that support the ceremonial government functions symbolized by the tent also announcing Utzon's intention to be pragmatic.

22

23

24

The Bagsvaerd Church in Copenhagen completed three years after the Sydney Opera House in 1976 also strikes a moderate, if more expressive chord than the Parliament Building, which is less accessible to the general public. Travel restrictions in Kuwait, compounded by severe damage during the Gulf War, have meant that the Parliament Building has remained a cypher, largely unknown to Utzon fans eager to see the work of an architect whose output has not equalled his talent. The Bagsvaerd Church, however, shows him at his best. It is a tightly controlled, virtuoso performance in local materials with many legible national references that avoid the metaphorical misunderstandings that have occurred in Sydney. Perhaps this sure-footedness comes from cultural familiarity as much as a desire to prove the efficacy of moderation.

In a European context, equal cultural assurance is evident in the Hungarian architect Imre Makovecz's renditions of Transylvanian skill in carpentry. While his agenda has been identified elsewhere in this book as related closely to the contemporary vernacular, there can also be no argument that his approach is also expressionistic. Makovecz's work, such as his Roman Catholic Church in Paks, Hungary, 1989, whose black shingled roof suggests the quivering haunches of some giant animal, was for many years known only to a relatively small cult following; but he has since gained wider international recognition largely due to his being selected to design the Hungarian Pavilion at the Seville Exposition in 1992.

Makovecz openly refers to his direction as 'living' and 'organic' and is extremely knowledgeable about the contributions of Frank Lloyd Wright and Rudolf Steiner to the tradition that he continues. His variation upon this expressionist theme is to expand the role of folk tradition within it, particularly its response to perpetual patterns of life, offering a humane view of coexisting with nature. The human being, in his view, is a curious combination of visionary dreamer and frail mortal vessel with evolutionary roots that are indisputably simian. Makovecz uses a compelling mixture of metaphysical symbols and pragmatic craft. These include a funeral chapel that looks like the inner rib cage of an ancient leviathan transformed into wood; a cultural centre steeped in ninth-century symbols when the Altaic people who settled in Hungary arrived from Asia; a Community Hall in Zalaszentlászló, 1983, that suggests a forest enclosed by an enormous roof; and an ongoing complex of buildings in Visegrád that responds to the medieval pattern of the town with a quasi-gothic language. As all of these examples show, Makovecz is interested in tracing origins, especially those of his people and the land that nurtured them. He is not content to express trees symbolically, but must show the roots as well, the hidden but equally important parts of the tree that form the conduits of life.

This notion was given literal expression in Makovecz's Hungarian Pavilion, at Seville, which contained an uprooted 'tree of life' at its centre. Perhaps because of its transplantation from its native country, the Pavilion seemed to overlay several powerful themes, not altogether successfully. Seven church-like spires punctured the upturned slate-covered hull of an enormous ark suggesting a contradictory reading of these two metaphors for salvation.

While its architect is Dutch, the Nationale Nederlanden and ING Bank, in Budapest, completed in 1994, represents the urban manifestation of Hungary's expressionist present. Erick van Egeraat, whose project this is, was a founder partner of the architectural practice Mecanoo along with Henk Döll, Chris de Weijer, Roelf Steenhuis and Francine Houben. They established a high-profile position in European architecture based predominantly on an output of houses and housing, or small-scale buildings such as the Boompjes Pavilion, completed in 1990, which overlooks Rotterdam Harbour close to the Erasmus Bridge. Van Egeraat left Mecanoo in 1995, taking many of the staff with him, and his departure signalled a new direction in his work, away from the New Modern style for which Mecanoo is noted, towards what he calls the 'modern Baroque'.

The ING Bank project is a renovation of a neoclassical nineteenth-century building situated on Andrassy ùt, Budapest's main ceremonial thoroughfare. Van Egeraat added two floors to the building, creating a great biomorphic structure which he calls 'the whale'. The whale's back rises above the roofline of the old building, while its belly hangs above a newly created atrium, made by roofing over an existing courtyard. The whale's 'bones' are laminated timber frames which are suspended from the steel structure that also supports the two new concrete floors. Its skin is part opaque and part transparent, alternating between zinc and curved glass panes; the whole thing floats in a sea of clear glass that lights the new roofspaces below. From both inside and outside, the whale is a dominating presence, adding an intriguing element to the Budapest skyline.

Like Van Egeraat's, the work of the Zurich-based Spanish architect—engineer Santiago Calatrava also has a strong biomorphic basis. And like Makovecz he made a powerful contribution to the Seville Exposition, where he designed the Kuwaiti Pavilion and the Alamillo Bridge. Calatrava is influenced by natural forms such as birds' wings and animal skeletons, which are abstracted and stylized in his structures. His educational background offers a clue to the synthetic nature of his work: after studying art and architecture in his native Valencia he entered the ETH in Zurich where he gained a doctorate in technical science, and his buildings seem to fuse art, architecture and engineering in a startlingly original way. Calatrava's Lyon—Satolas TGV Station in France, 1988—94, is a characteristic piece. Located at Lyon—Satolas Airport, the structure of the station hall roof appropriately echoes the extended wings of a flying bird, and its steel 'bone' structure is detailed to achieve a singular lightness of effect.

Managing nature, a concept that is central to the sustainable ideology, perhaps paradoxically reaches its extreme in another high-tech enterprise by Nicholas Grimshaw called the Eden Project, currently underway in Cornwall, UK, which attempts to replicate natural cycles. In this sense it follows the precedent of projects like Biosphere II in Arizona, constructed in 1991 (named after Biosphere I, the earth). The main difference between the two projects is that Biosphere II – sponsored by a billionaire interested in finding a fall-back position in case the current environmental crisis reaches the point of no return – was intended to be entirely self-sufficient, while Eden attempts merely to reproduce each of the earth's ecosystems in miniature, recreating hydrological cycles and using hydroponics for growing food. Unfortunately Biosphere II failed because of severe temperature swings which reduced anticipated levels of food production. It also aggravated the inevitable claustrophobia of the enclosure and resulted in bitter conflicts between the participants.

5

The Eden project is the brainchild of Tim Schmidt, who also created the Lost Garden in the same region of Cornwall. It will be constructed in an abandoned clay pit and will allow the study of plants at an unprecedented scale. When it is complete, the centre will be open to the general public, although it is intended to be heavily involved in scientific research which should be of immense ecological value. The architects have approached this living collection as the means by which different cultures of plants and people can interact, while the profits will be used to fund the type of programmes proposed by Agenda 21 – The United Nations Programme of Action, which resulted from the proceedings of the Rio Conference.

Botanists around the world have been consulted on which potentially valuable crop plants should be included, and the initial exhibition house will be the first enclosure large enough to accommodate a rainforest canopy. The design consists of a series of linked, climate-controlled transparent capsules referred to as bionomes.

7 MICHAEL
HOPKINS, Inland
Revenue Building,
Nottingham, UK,
1992-4

8 MICHAEL HOPKINS,
New Parliamentary
Building, London,
1989-

7

Ancillary greenhouses containing staff accommodation and visitor services, such as restaurants and an information centre, are arranged to allow maximum flexibility. The intention is that more bionomes will be added in the future. The bionomes have been designed as a microcosm of four key climatological regions — wet tropics or rainforest, dry tropics or semi-desert subtropics and Mediterranean — and priority has been given to threatened species. The obvious lineage of the scheme is the British tradition of horticultural glasshouses and the collection of exotic plant species from all over the world, epitomized by the Victorian Palm House at Kew by Decimus Burton. When complete, the Eden Project will be the world's largest greenhouse, stretching nearly one kilometre from end to end, and its tensioned trusses will span more than 100 metres at its widest point.

The project's enclosing skin is formed from a double-bowstring structure used in conjunction with a triple-layered pneumatic pillow, inflated by small electric fans, which forms an external transparent envelope around the plants. The fans are controlled by climatic sensors powered by photovoltaic cells in an attempt to reproduce the organic process of photosynthesis using technology. Despite the centre's dedication to biological research, the theme park aspect of the project, as well as its energy intensive and high maintenance requirements, raise serious ecological questions. There is no doubt, however, that it is a bold attempt to use technology to control the environment.

A further extremely convincing example of the appropriation of technology to the cause of sustainability is The Inland Revenue Centre, Nottingham, 1992—4, designed by Michael Hopkins and Partners, another practice previously associated with the high-tech movement. The sustainable strategy for the building begins with the organization of the offices into six separate clusters connected via internal circulation, intended to break down what might otherwise have been a massive depersonalized block into more human-scaled and environmentally manageable units. This division also provided the management staff with the flexibility necessitated by the organization, enabling them to close down individual units without affecting the operation of the others. Secondly, the practice researched the possibility of using local materials to reduce the energy costs involved in transporting the typical palette of components for an office complex of this kind. Traditionally, the clay pits in Nottingham had produced a distinctive red brick during the Victorian age, but unfortunately supplies had been exhausted and so a similar clay was located in Cumbria which enabled the building to respond sympathetically to its context. The choice of brick, however, was far more than a response to purely aesthetic criteria; for instance, as the construction is loadbearing, standard proprietary bricks would have been unable to meet the high-tolerances and crushing strength required, which

ruled out the opportunity to utilize local resources. Interestingly, despite the fact that loadbearing structures are normally built on site, a rather time-consuming and labour-intensive process, these bricks were preassembled into piers under factory conditions and then delivered by lorry to the site. This speeded up the construction process and dramatically increased accuracy and quality control.

Brick is an excellent material in sustainable terms as it requires relatively little energy to produce — compared to aluminium, concrete, steel or glass — and has an excellent thermal mass, preventing heat or cold from penetrating the material too quickly. By using this inherent quality to mitigate environmental extremes, the architects reduced the need for mechanical heating systems. This second strategy was augmented with a third decision to use natural ventilation wherever possible, despite the heavy occupation levels and number of computers. To facilitate this, the glazed stair towers are thermal chimneys which are used to heat the air contained inside. As it warms up the air rises, escaping through dampers at roof level, which creates a negative pressure, due to buoyancy or 'stack' effect, that draws fresh air through the facade and across the floor void of the offices, where it is cooled by the concrete floor slab. This system is also used to heat the building during the winter. This is achieved by sealing the stair towers so that the warm air is unable to escape and the thermal gain is transferred into the offices instead, augmenting the heat generated by the occupants and electrical hardware. A fourth strategy is the use of openable triple-glazed windows to provide thermal and acoustic insulation, and cross-ventilation when necessary. Solar shading is provided by 'light shelves' which help to minimize thermal gain in the offices and reduce the need for cooling; they also reflect sunlight into the offices to increase natural lighting deep within the building. General illumination levels are monitored and controlled by computers, while task-specific lighting can be controlled by individuals.

The New Parliamentary Building in London, currently under construction, is also based on reduced energy demands and the use of renewable resources. The project embodies three key generating concepts that could also be applied to the ecological mind-set in general. The first of these is that while a design may comply with the typical conservation profile of the late 1960s and early 1970s, it may still not be truly sustainable because the energy required to produce the materials and construct the building may exceed the energy saved during its lifetime. The second is that even though a scheme may have a conservationist design, it may not have a sustainable relationship with its infrastructure, making excessive demands on transport, communications, sanitation, maintenance and other services. The third is that quality of life is an implicit element of the ecological equation and extreme conservation measures, which treat the environment as an enemy to be conquered, often ignore the fact that light and air are important.

8

9

To answer these broader concerns the New Parliamentary Building was treated as an integrated unit, more like a mini ecosystem than a combined kit of parts, creating a compact, environmentally responsive building. However, like the majority of projects undertaken by the practice, the design has evolved out of the complexities of the brief and as a response to its site rather than fulfilling a preordained agenda; for instance, due to the heavily polluted nature of the site, fresh air is drawn in at roof level rather than through the facades as it is at Nottingham. Similarly, rather than articulating individual building elements into mono-functional components – such as a steel frame for structure, with separate glazing for the enclosure and bolt-on air-conditioning systems for environmental control – all of the elements in this building have been designed to be multi-functional. For example, the precast concrete floors are not only used as a thermal store, absorbing heat during the day and releasing it at night, but are also used to reflect light, both natural and artificial, on to the working surface below. Like the Inland Revenue Centre, sunlight, which is relatively rare during the winter in Britain, is reflected into the interior by light shelves. However, the ventilation strategy for the New Parliamentary Building is more elaborate. As previously mentioned, fresh air is brought in at roof level through the clearly articulated thermal chimneys to avoid pollution, and is then circulated by low energy fans through ducts expressed on the facade. Return air is assisted by the natural buoyancy created by heat gains absorbed within the glazing and blinds, thereby dissipating temperature increases and driving the exhaust air process, reducing the fan requirements. The air is eventually expelled through the rooftop chimneys, and to further minimize energy expenditure can be used to heat up incoming air via a high-level 'thermal wheel' or heat exchanger. The fourteen chimneys are critical to this design as they contain both air intakes and exhausts, as well as the necessary thermal wheels and low-energy fans. During the summer months, when the temperature of incoming fresh air may exceed internal comfort levels, it is cooled by ground water extracted from an artesian well below the building.

The technological component of these buildings relates to Hopkins' use of prefabricated components, allowing for a greater degree of quality control and much less time spent in on-site fabrication which reduces costs significantly; he has also relied on the use of computational fluid dynamics and new research and techniques. While not as visibly engineered as the high-tech examples by Grimshaw discussed earlier, Hopkins' environmental strategy indicates an extremely promising use of technology to achieve sustainability within sensitive contexts.

Future Systems is another practice that has been adapting its technological approach to environmental issues, albeit in a more experimental fashion. For the last two years the firm, in conjunction with the Martin Centre in Cambridge, has been concerned with the Zero Emission Development Research Programme funded by the European Commission. Together they have developed a number of solutions to a brief which proposes that buildings should produce more energy than they consume. Three separate European cities – Berlin, London and Toulouse – were identified as suitable locations, intended to provoke a variety of climatic responses. The proposals are certainly visually very different and dynamic, but as the co-founder of the practice, Jan Kaplicky, has pointed out, the real beauty of these projects is their 'attempt to marry the organicism of nature with modern technology' rather than superficial aesthetic modelling.

The plan for the 100-metre-high tower for London's Tottenham Court Road, a mixed-use office and residential development, validates this statement. Despite its science fiction aesthetic, its design is a calculated response to necessary environmental concerns; the streamlined hollow core being essential as it houses two wind-powered generators. Additional energy requirements are provided for by photovoltaic cells located on the solar-shading devices. The Berlin scheme, based on a similar brief, was dramatically different, however, mainly due to climatic differences between the two cities. Here large temperature variations led the practice to develop a linear earth-sheltered design. The large earth berms perform numerous environmental functions, from providing thermal insulation to the supply of grey water, while energy requirements are again produced by photovoltaics. Similar climatic variations resulted in the adoption of another sustainable approach in Toulouse, where, due to the availability of sunlight throughout the year, the design focuses on solar collection, heat dispersion and natural ventilation. The variety of these architectural responses, despite Future Systems' belief in the applicability of technology to the question of sustainability, illustrates that there are numerous approaches to ecological architecture. Yet, as Jan Kaplicky states, sustainable architecture: 'is at the beginning, it's the Wild West at the moment and so it would be foolish to claim that there is one way of doing it, but one thing is certain, that new forms will be created.'

The reliance on scientific methodology adopted by these architects highlights the fact that its application to solve problems related to environmental degradation is central to certain ecological advocates. However, many sustainable architects argue that technology, especially in an industrial context, is the primary cause of the destruction of nature, and that expecting it to provide a solution for environmental ills is like using the cause of the disease to cure it. Proponents of this approach argue that high-tech architecture is no more than a victory of marketing over ideology, and that the large amounts of embodied energy required to produce the industrial materials on which the aesthetic depends is sufficient justification not to follow it. The extent of the controversy surrounding the use of such techniques to produce an ecological architecture is highlighted by contrasting the preceding examples with a selection that searches for sustainable solutions in other areas, particularly through contextual or cultural fit, using technology only where appropriate.

The J M Tjibaou Cultural Centre by the Renzo Piano Building Workshop, to be completed in 1997, clearly demonstrates the possibilities of such an approach, and provides welcome affirmation that ecological architecture need not be ugly to be effective. The centre is located on the promontory that separates the Bay of Magenta from the small lagoon behind it, at the eastern edge of Nouméa, the capital of the Pacific island of New Caledonia. Currently under construction, it is organized in three clusters arranged along a wooden promenade facing the bay. Each group is made up of varying numbers of wooden, semicircular enclosures that Piano refers to as 'cases', perhaps because of their shell-like shape, while numerous others have compared them to villages. This is actually unsurprising as, in form and scale, they are modelled on the indigenous conical reed huts; although they have been bisected and positioned to face the bay in order to catch the prevailing sea breeze in their curves. In fact, the cases — made of laminated wood supported by steel cables — appear less like villages when they are lined up along one side of the promenade, but this arrangement maximizes natural ventilation. Wind tunnel tests prompted the extension of the cases to enclose three-quarters of the circular footprint, and enabled the architects to locate the necessary openings to allow the construction to adapt to various directions and speeds of wind, from a light breeze to a cyclone. As a result, these penetrations are located at the head, base and entrances of the enclosures. The sloping roofs tucked inside the laminated shells constitute the building envelope.

The complex is approached by a path, winding through the dense vegetation, which finally leads up a broad set of stairs providing access to the entrance court of the three cases and a four-hundred-seat auditorium. This first village is dedicated to exhibitions about the indigenous Kanak culture, local environment and natural history, while the second has administrative offices for the various disciplines required to research, plan and mount exhibitions. The third and final village contains dance, music and graphics studios, with a somewhat isolated position at the end of the sequence.

What identifies this complex as sustainable is the practice's attitude towards the indigenous culture, which is visible through its utilization of pre-existing typologies and local materials, as well as its attempts to achieve economies of scale through the clustering of activities, and its reliance on natural ventilation. This signifies a recognition of the primitive techniques that native inhabitants have developed to deal with this specific environment, as well as the efficacy of employing appropriate technology to improve on these tried and tested models.

10

11, 12 SHORT,
FORD AND
ASSOCIATES,
Queen's Building,
De Montfort
University,
Leicester, 1993

11

Short, Ford and Associates' Queen's Building, for the new School of Engineering and Manufacture at De Montfort University, Leicester, 1993, is another obvious case study when considering this inclusive approach to ecological architecture. The spotlight placed on Leicester in 1992, when it was designated the United Kingdom's 'environment city', prompted the university, in conjunction with the local council, to proceed with the construction of this building, the design of which had been commissioned four years earlier. Like the Inland Revenue Centre, this scheme also exploits the insulative quality of brick and natural ventilation, but amplifies the possibilities inherent in each to their maximum potential without relying on prefabrication. Rather than deep plans organized in clusters, the architects have utilized a thinner, linear profile with a north–south orientation to take advantage of prevailing winds for cross-ventilation. Each subsequent design decision was based on this initial premise. A central internal pedestrian street allows air to escape from the classrooms and laboratories which are arranged to either side; stale air is expelled through chimneys located on the roof above. The requirement for two centrally located auditoria presented the most difficult challenge, since environmental expectations for such spaces are high; as a result the size and location of additional ventilation stacks in these rooms had to be precisely calculated. These problems were solved by positioning ventilation grills under the stacked rows of seating, and heating the fresh air with finned hot water pipes as required; automated dampers in the chimneys are used to prevent draughts.

The Queen's Building was the largest naturally ventilated building in Europe when it was completed, and used the least mechanical equipment to assist it towards this goal. A similar determination to use as little energy as possible is evident in a much smaller, but no less significant, project by Abdel Wahed El-Wakil (who has been discussed at length in Chapter Eight). El-Wakil has primarily looked to traditional societies for inspiration, and his preference for what are now termed 'sustainable strategies' is generated through this connection. As a result, all his work displays a significant commitment to the ecological ethos, in particular his Al-Ruwais Mosque in Jeddah, Saudi Arabia, 1987, is most clearly sustainable. His patron, Mayor Said Al-Farsi, wanted to locate several small mosques along the Corniche, to symbolize his commitment to Islamic principles and the ideal of appropriating architecture as a creative, legitimizing force. His budget, however, was paltry, and El-Wakil had no recourse to water or electricity, forcing him to emphasize the sculptural character of the programme. Undaunted, he decided to expand on an earlier design he had worked on in Hassan Fathy's office in the late 1970s for a new community in the middle of the desert at the Kharga Oasis in Egypt. Due to a similar lack of infrastructure there, Fathy and El-Wakil had developed a ventilation system based on the Venturi principle of incrementally decreasing openings to

accelerate airflow, converting even the gentlest breeze into a rushing vortex. The dramatic result of this design feature was that perishable goods — the agricultural produce that was the financial backbone of the community — were able to be stored in naturally cooled rooms while waiting to be shipped to Cairo without reliance on refrigeration. El-Wakil utilized this same principle in the Al-Ruwais Mosque so successfully that he was able to convince local officials, who normally would not allow a mosque to be built without air conditioning, to approve his scheme, which, now that it is complete, is just as comfortable in the hot, humid climate as its mechanically cooled counterparts.

Another example of extreme contextual specificity is the fusion of architecture and landscape by the architect James Wines and his practice SITE, who quite literally attempt a reunion with nature: a philosophical and aesthetic, as well as physical synthesis with the environment. Since the late 1960s, SITE has used both sculpture and architecture, filtered through various social frames of reference, to promote a greater public understanding of ecological principles. More specifically, however, SITE's more recent work is intended as a departure from the conventional concept of architecture, as a spatial construct reliant on built form, towards an emphasis on architecture's narrative and environmental associations. This is a serious game which absorbs the mind as well as the body, and is intended to set up a dialogue that will tactically and psychologically educate the public in the principles of sustainability. Taking a cue from the media in its attempts to send this message, SITE realized that the aesthetics of the television set are not as important to viewers as the programmes they want to watch, and concluded that the container is not as important as the message it sends. SITE also believed that just as no contemporary industrialized society has a collectively shared cosmology or religious association with nature, so a new iconography had to be determined. It has labelled its attempt at such a framework as a theory of 'passages', a process it has described as involving, 'change and discovery ... a cartographical route through new and sometimes conflicting territory'. This map charts a theoretical approach, which like Hopkins' New Parliamentary Building, is a reconfiguration of conventional rules, but more closely tied to nature.

All of these concerns are combined in SITE's proposals for Trawsfynydd, North Wales, which were developed speculatively in 1994, inspired by the news that the local nuclear power station, despite being constructed a mere twenty five years earlier, was to be decommissioned. A BBC producer invited four international architectural practices — SITE, Ushida Findlay, Arup Associates and Alsop & Störmer — to develop an architectural strategy for the existing structures and surrounding area, with the intention of highlighting in a television documentary the environmental problems caused by the

16

17

basically flat, but has two shallow streams running through it that flood during autumn, the annual rainy season, while a mountain range that runs the entire length of the island protects the site from the prevailing winds, which can be cold in winter.

The Rogers plan addresses the problems of the area on a triage basis, tackling the most urgent first. Firstly, they proposed a cistern system to store storm water drawn from the surrounding area during the rainy season, which would otherwise run into the sea causing extensive erosion; this would be used to provide site irrigation and drinking water during the hot dry summers. The tanks are fed by an arrangement of weirs and lakes, and irrigation water is supplied by gravity, eliminating the need for pumps. Secondly, the architects have designed a series of agricultural terraces, which act like raised beds allowing the steep slopes to be farmed. The new land made available by the terraces and irrigation will make it possible to introduce new crops and dramatically increase the productivity of the existing range. Successful experiments in the burning of quick growing and easily renewable crops, such as sorghum and willow, have shown that they can provide a cheap fuel source.

The architectural components of the plan have been designed to complement the scheme's agricultural, hydrological and fuel strategies, and address the final issue of social mix. Taking a cue from traditional solutions they saw in Palma and throughout the island, the designers used the gently sloping site to locate compact neighbourhoods grouped around narrow streets that discourage vehicular use, keep the houses in shade, and decrease distances between locations, making it possible to walk or cycle between destinations. In contrast to Rogers' signature high-tech buildings such as the Pompidou Centre, 1971–7, or the Lloyd's Building, 1978–86, the Majorca master plan is mainly non-architectural, consisting of underground buildings tucked beneath agricultural terraces that gradually emerge as they approach the town centre, keeping the same low profile language. It is the planning process and the use of technology to ameliorate the environment that is most important here, not the architecture.

Even though it may suit critics to pigeon-hole architectural practices into distinct camps such as 'ecological' or 'technological', in reality things are rarely that simple. It is certainly true that some architects prefer technological to contextual solutions to contemporary ecological imperatives, while many believe the converse, yet within any system of classification there are those individuals who manage to fuse such contrary ideas. The Malaysian architect Ken Yeang is such an example; he has adopted an approach that has embraced both these concerns. Throughout his career, Yeang has attempted to reconcile his commitment to ecology with his desire to produce buildings that articulate the ambitions of the emerging Malaysian nation and the contemporary architectural typologies and technologies it demands. This is a

particularly difficult task given that, as with the majority of the Pacific Rim, Malaysia is undergoing a massive period of urban growth that is unfortunately motivated by monetary rather than environmental gain; and due to the sheer scale of the enterprise, this expansion threatens to eclipse Malaysia's fragile indigenous culture. Yeang is aware that this economic development is essential to the future financial security of the country, but realizes that unless the innate problems of this type of rapacious commercial development are addressed, it will irrevocably damage his country's environment.

Yet despite these immense pressures Yeang, in conjunction with his practice T R Hamzah & Yeang, has developed an approach that addresses environmental concerns whilst remaining financially viable in a market-driven economy (see also Chapter Thirteen). Yeang has managed to balance such diverse criteria without compromising his principles. This is illustrated by the fact that, rather than focusing on smaller projects, the practice has responded to the needs of the community and concentrated on producing environmentally friendly tropical high-rise buildings, which Yeang has characterized as 'bioclimatic' skyscrapers. The design of these structures is defined by their location and climate.

Although this approach produces very site-specific solutions, there are certain characteristics that are found throughout Yeang's work, which can be broken down into two specific agendas: whether they respond to wind direction or solar orientation. The former are typically referred to as the 'wind rose' projects, and tend to be used for either high-rise offices or clustered linear apartment blocks, while the latter are known as 'sun path' projects and are normally used for high-rise office buildings. The plans of wind rose projects are on the whole fragmented, opening to facilitate egress for natural ventilation throughout. To allow this process to function efficiently, the plan is arranged in relation to the prevailing winds, and other innovative features – such as wind walls, roof-level aerofoils and 'skycourts' that draw air into the internal spaces – are brought into play.

The MBF Tower, Penang, constructed between 1990 and 1993, is a multi-storey block split between office space and luxury apartments, which faces the north shore of Penang. It offers an excellent example of Yeang's wind rose typology. The project consists of large two-storey skycourts or terraces which are utilized to provide natural ventilation for the apartments and deck space for planting and recreation. The separation of the individual elements has enabled even the centralized lift lobbies to be naturally ventilated; open-air bridged walkways lead from these lobbies to the apartment units. Stepped planter-boxes located on the main facade of the building emphasize Yeang's attempts to integrate the natural environment completely with his designs.

Similarly, all Yeang's sun path buildings can be identified by a number of common characteristics. Like

1 (Previous page)
RICHARD MEIER,
Getty Center,
Los Angeles,
1984-97

2 RICHARD MEIER,
Museum für
Kunsthandwerk,
Frankfurt, 1984

3 RICHARD MEIER,
Smith House,
Connecticut,
1967

2

In the early 1970s the critics lined up confidently to predict the imminent demise of Modernism, united under the banner 'Modern Architecture is Dead' or 'MAID'. News of its death proved to be premature, however, and there remains today a growing band of architects whose stylistic and formal loyalties link them with the modernist mainstream of the early century.

The undoubted leader of this group is Richard Meier, whose characteristic all-white architecture suggests his position as the 'pope' in the New Moderns' broad church. Meier first emerged on the international scene with the publication in 1966 of the book *Five Architects*,' which presented the work of five New York architects: Richard Meier, John Hejduk, Charles Gwathmey, Peter Eisenman and Michael Graves. Although hardly a 'group' as such, they were distinguished by their loyalty to the 'white' architecture of Le Corbusier and their adherence to the compositional 'five points' that he identified. They were also united in their recognition that effective media exposure is very helpful on the treacherous road to fame. Le Corbusier's five points, of a grid, a free plan, a free facade, strip windows, and roof garden, can be regarded almost as a short-hand notation for Modernism, a check list of the professed advantages provided by using post rather than pre-industrial materials.

Richard Meier, who has, perhaps, applied the five points more effectively than any of the other advocates in *Five Architects*, began his independent career with the Smith House, 1967, in Connecticut. In his hands, the structural grid creates a complex spatial weave, the free plan explodes, the strip window is exaggerated to form all-glass facades, and the roof garden becomes the true 'fifth elevation' of the building.

Meier's first large-scale international commission was the Museum für Kunsthandwerk in Frankfurt, 1984, won in competition against Robert Venturi and Denise Scott Brown amongst others. Of all the entrants, Venturi, Scott Brown and Meier presented the most diametrically opposed recommendations for the museum, congruent with their ideological differences over the role that history should play in creating new architecture. The Venturi, Scott Brown scheme was strongly historicist, taking its architectural clues from the existing Villa Metzler which dominated the site. Meier's scheme was altogether more abstract, but managed nonetheless to integrate the villa within a coherent new master plan. The plan proportions of the villa formed the basis of a larger square framework, in which the villa's cubic mass, placed in the lower left hand corner of the frame, was repeated in the three remaining corners. Meier was careful to make the frame large enough to allow an open space in the middle of the four cubes to fulfil a competition requirement that there be unhindered pedestrian passage through the museum from front to back, in this instance from the Schaumainkai district to that of the Sachsenhausen beyond. Venturi and Scott Brown disregarded it at their peril, perhaps feeling that the strength of

4

their connecting tactics and the stark contrast between their building's formal front and more casual sunken back would win over the jury. They were thus disqualified on a technicality. Meier's beautifully fluid movement diagrams were conclusive and he won the competition.

The Museum für Kunsthandwerk was a breakthrough for both Meier and the style he has so effectively championed. In this building, an introspective quality prevails in contrast with the outward-looking Smith House where distant nature is dematerialized behind hermetic glass walls. Within the museum, fractured and abstracted elevations appear and disappear as the visitor moves up or down the central ramp. This is a device reverentially appropriated by Meier from Le Corbusier's work as an elegant way of visually unravelling space; a magic carpet that allows participants to gaze up as they move through the building, rather than casting their eyes down as they watch their footsteps on the stairs. Meier frequently uses

5

6

ramps to unite the succession of spaces in his buildings. They are not just functional elements, but also serve as didactic devices, showing the visitor how the various spatial elements of the building fit together. Meier's High Museum of Art in Atlanta, 1980—3, is especially instructive in this regard because it is intended as a functional, if not spatial, improvement on Frank Lloyd Wright's New York Guggenheim Museum, 1943—56, which is entirely predicated on using the ramp as a viewing space. In Frankfurt, Meier's building is as much a part of the exhibition as the crafts on display and the ramp makes this central theme coherent. The Museum für Kunsthandwerk is an archetype in Meier's increasingly large-scale and high-profile body of work. It set the scene for his Barcelona Art Museum, 1996, for example, and has had a profound influence on other architects, as well. It would be difficult to imagine concepts like Diener and Diener's Gmurzynska Gallery in Cologne, 1990, for example, being realized without it.

High Museum of Art

8

Meier has remained remarkably consistent in his commitment to the Corbusian version of Modernism. His Getty Center in Los Angeles, 1984–97, which many see as the apotheosis of his career, marks three decades of using the same approach, albeit somewhat deflected in Los Angeles by the impact of scale. Visualized as an acropolis of culture in a city bereft of such institutions, the Getty Center occupies an entire mountain top at the intersection of Sunset Boulevard and the 405 freeway. It is appropriately located at the nexus of the city grid and the Pacific Ocean, giving it an indisputable position of power. As at Mont St Michel, which was totally reconstructed to sustain the cathedral and monastery at its summit, the Getty Center is supported by a massive infrastructure at its base. The mountain has been removed and rebuilt to incorporate public parking, mechanical and electrical plant, storage facilities and a monorail that whisks visitors to the mountaintop. While it is completely pragmatic, the monorail is a clue to a prevailing attitude towards nature and culture that can be identified in all of Meier's work, which by extension, may be argued to be part of the modern condition. Both have been objectified and detached from life. This allows nature and culture to be treated as commodities, ultimately leading to the theming syndrome (discussed in Chapter Twelve). The monorail is also particularly familiar to Angelenos, whether it is used to view the increasingly bizarre rides at Disneyland, or to elevate them towards the cultural acropolis of the Getty.

While Meier's work may itself seem to be 'on rails' stylistically, Charles Gwathmey, the second of the New York Five, has found a varying tactical use for the Corbusian five-point checklist. In his hands it is related to questions of materiality and craft. A series of early houses for wealthy clients on Long Island, based on the free plan, were clad in an outer wrapping of weathered timber, which was cut away at strategic points to form abstract openings. The timber gives the houses a 'solidity' which Meier's transparent white cubes lack, but like Meier's buildings, they are exquisitely detailed.

As the frame and scope of Gwathmey's projects has grown, his commitment, with his partner Robert Siegel, to high-quality craftsmanship has not diminished. Gwathmey Siegel's restrained addition to Wright's Guggenheim Museum, 1992, proves this point. Wright was even more prone to shoddy detailing in his later work than were most Modernists. The number of leaky roofs and skylights that he designed is legendary. The prospect of adding to an iconic Wright building was daunting, but the museum desperately needed more space and the meticulously crafted tower block that Gwathmey and Siegel have provided is an elegantly pragmatic answer to this problem.

While John Hejduk, the third member of the Five, has chosen to restrict his polemics to the academic arena and to overlay the rational agenda of Modernism with a poetic counterpoint, Peter Eisenman has set about turning polemics into an art form, moving from Corbusian

Modernism through Deconstructivism to folding theory in the twenty years since *Five Architects* was first published. In a series of houses deliberately numbered one through to ten to isolate them from the identities of their owners, Eisenman pursued the idea of deep, or less overt, structure, expressing Le Corbusier's grid through its 'absence' as well as its presence in the horizontal and vertical dimensions. Recalling the intellectual background against which *Five Architects* was conceived, Eisenman has said that: 'it was a time when it was very difficult to talk about architecture, it was a wild time politically and socially. People were thinking of Vietnam, of black voter registration drives. Nobody wanted to talk about form, which is what we thought architecture should be about'.[2] Casting himself as a public intellectual, rather than following the almost monastic pose of John Hejduk, Eisenman went on to assist in founding the influential architectural publication *Oppositions*. It was his penchant for popularizing

9

10

theory that eventually drew him to the ideas of French philosopher Jacques Derrida and the heresy of deconstruction (discussed in Chapter Seven).

The architectural evolution of Michael Graves, the last member of the Five, has been even more startling than Eisenman's. He has moved, almost without pausing, from a modernist to a post-modernist language, or what has been intriguingly described as a 'cross between classicism and cubism'.[3] This change is illustrated in a series of early houses, or rather one playroom addition and two large houses, in the modern idiom. They were all completed just before *Five Architects* was published and two are prominently featured in it.

From the Benacerraf House addition, 1969, through to the Hanselmann and Snyderman houses of the same period, there is the sense of a frenetic search for meaning. Rather than being a celebratory proclamation of what was to become a life-long commitment to the formal

11

12

13

*11, 12, 13, 14
(Overleaf)*
JAMES STIRLING AND
MICHAEL WILFORD
WITH WALTER
NAEGELI, *Braun
Factory Complex,
Melsungen, 1992*

language of Le Corbusier, as the Smith House was for Richard Meier, this trio reveals Graves' growing restlessness and constriction. The clues of this discontent are evident at first in the Benacerraf addition in his playful syntactical conversion of the five points. Graves turns one column so that it becomes a horizontal handrail, displaces another so that it is shifted off the structural grid, and uses a detached stair as a sculptural sign for ascendancy, rather than as a functional necessity in what is essentially a single-storey extension. The stair symbol also proliferates in the Hanselmann House, which can be seen as a passably convincing Corbusian clone until the play of stairs is factored in. A monumental tribute to the *piano nobile* of Le Corbusier's Villa Stein at Garches, the first, actual stair, is recalled in a simplified virtual triangle flattened against the facade; the abstraction and displacement take time to register, appearing as a mocking rather than respectful gesture. In the Snyderman House, 1972, the last of the series, the grid becomes a cage, and the walls which move inside and around it are coloured for the first time. Rather than using colour to accentuate visual sensations of distance or perceptions of temperature, Graves uses it here as both a formal leveller and wider contextual reference. Light brown makes the curved surfaces seem more sombre and all of these eventually touch the earth. The use of light blue, on the other hand, tends to dematerialize the flat surfaces, and lift them towards the sky.

Graves' next major building, the Plocek House, 1982, unveiled the change of direction that his work has followed ever since. Graves was not alone in his disaffection with Modernism and the transition to Post-Modernism that one finds in his architecture can equally be traced in the transformation of other high-profile Modernists such as Philip Johnson, whose *œuvre* spans from his Glass House of 1949, to the 'Chippendale tallboy' tower he completed for AT&T in 1979. Others, including James Stirling and Arata Isozaki, have also followed this path. The trail is not always easy to follow, however, as two respective works by Stirling and Isozaki demonstrate.

The Braun Factory Complex in Melsungen, Germany, was James Stirling's last completed project before his tragic death in 1992. Ironically, resulting from the accolade he had received from Stuttgart, the Braun commission gave him the opportunity to reaffirm his modernist roots. The project has a monumental quality which Frank Gehry identified as being 'very Roman' the first time he saw it. The massive tapered piers with which Stirling supports the curved administration building make the Corbusian connection clear, and the laboratory block that is connected to it by a spine-like bridge is used as an opportunity to tell a metaphorical story about the beginnings of Modernism. It recalls the AEG Factory by Peter Behrens, representing a recognizable point at which historical representation was abandoned in favour of abstract signification. Behren's AEG Factory is literally a temple to industry, the stylobate made a structural plinth,

the columns becoming square piers, the pediment segmented to remind a once rural workforce of the barns they had left behind. The next iteration of Modernism, promulgated by Behrens' pupils, such as Mies van der Rohe and Walter Gropius, and subsequently Le Corbusier, took this abstraction for granted and moved beyond it, taking it to a second and third remove in which representation was obliterated altogether. This is the philosophical distance which Stirling spans so eloquently in his Braun Complex. It is a compound of modernist references and self-references, an abstract masterpiece by an architect whose work is ultimately untramelled by mere style.[4]

After Graves and Stirling, Arata Isozaki has been one of the most high-profile architects to question the modernist ethic. However, Isozaki's Museum, 1993–5, in La Coruña, Spain, can be seen as his equivalent to Stirling's Braun Factory, marking a return to a dialectic with Modernism, after a long flirtation with Post-Modern Classicism. It is a remarkable project, demonstrating Isozaki's consistent ability to probe the depths of a specific context; to elicit the essence of it. Once an island in the Bay of Biscay, La Coruña is now a peninsula and the site of the world's oldest continuously operating lighthouse: the 'Hercules Tower' built in the second century AD. The museum is located at the top of a rocky cliff nearby. On his many visits to the site, Isozaki was struck by its ruggedness and the ever-present northwest wind. He began to visualize a single smooth wall, like a mask, rising at the top of the cliff and receiving the full brunt of the wind, and another wall, like a folding screen on the bedrock, transferring the force of the wind longitudinally and providing support. The museum has two levels, related to the top of the cliff and a ledge further down its slope. The entry is at the top level, with exhibition rooms and a multi-purpose hall. A restaurant, recreational area, museum work and storage area, and loading deck are on the lower level, and there is a bridge that connects the building with the old lighthouse, on axis with it to the north. Little has been done to alter the rock face; the middle ledge has been used as a terrace in the recreational area. A large staircase which provides access from the coastal road moves up underneath *pilotis* which support the curved wall of the multi-purpose hall. Originally, the curved wall was to be faced with metallic grey ceramic tiles, to match the colour of the sea, but grey-green slate was substituted. The folding screen is made of thick granite blocks; Isozaki wants this museum to last at least as long as the nearby Hercules Tower.

The implications of the choice of the metaphor of a mask and a folding screen are important, a visual language that Isozaki has intentionally chosen 'as a deviation from the orthodoxy of modern architecture'. The point is that, in choosing a metaphor meant to convey understandable meaning or effect communication with the observer, the architect has returned to a dialogue with the abstract compositional concepts found in Modernism.

Rather than rejecting that dialogue entirely as he did in such projects as the Tsukuba Civic Center, 1978–83, his forms function on two intellectual levels at once. While making abstract associations of strength, permanence and equilibrium he also invokes temporal connections with the land, the lighthouse, and the historical links between Spain and Japan. There is also another more elusive parallel to the idea of the mask put forward by Adolf Loos, which was a generating force in the formulation of the blank, unornamented facade adopted by Le Corbusier, later parodied as the 'decorated shed' by Venturi, Scott Brown.[5] Although Isozaki utterly rejects that this project marks a return to 'neo-Modernism', he is attempting to strike a middle ground in an 'architecture of allusion and metaphor' that imbues abstract representation with more complexity and power, offering a readjustment to contemporary perceptual demands.

While Graves, Stirling and Isozaki have chosen to chart a risky course, several others have never altered. Arch-modernist I M Pei, for example, has consistently advanced a refined, geometrically based architecture. Following on from the coolly logical approach of his addition to the National Gallery in Washington, 1968–78, which is based on an isosceles planning grid that can be read from the largest central foyer to the smallest bathroom, and his remodelling of the Louvre in Paris, 1983–93, where pyramidal skylights pierce the Cour d'Honneur, Pei has carried through his geometrical approach in his new building for the Rock and Roll Hall of Fame in Cleveland, Ohio, 1993–5.

The design of the Rock and Roll Hall of Fame was begun during the construction of the Louvre pyramid, and the huge triangular glass wall that Pei has included in it, to make the building evoke the 'explosive energy' of the music it memorializes, is a continuation of the geometry and the transparency he has worked through in both the National Gallery and Louvre extensions. Pei explains: 'I wanted the building to express the music. But what is this music? It has a sense of rebellion, of breaking away from tradition. It has a dimension of energy. The generation that made rock music was much more transparent about its ideas than my generation. Everything is up front, whether you like it or not.'[6] It is difficult to imagine another architect in this situation producing anything quite as cerebral or controlled as this pristine monument to popular culture.

Romaldo Giurgola, who is another unwavering champion of Modernism, has been as much of a prophet without honour in his adopted home town of Philadelphia as was his theoretical mentor Louis Kahn. It has taken a major commission for the Parliament building in Canberra, Australia, 1988, to raise local consciousness of Giurgola's importance. But despite his prolific output, he is still not as well known in Philadelphia, or in the United States in general, as other architects of his stature. Giurgola's Canberra scheme is everything that Meier's

15 I M Pei, National Gallery addition, Washington,DC, 1968–78

16 I M Pei, Louvre Pyramid, Paris, 1983–93

16

Getty Center is not: dug into the hill it occupies, not perched on it, axial and integral rather than loosely assembled, with an imprecise distinction between the public and private realm. Giurgola took his cue from a 1912 plan by Walter Burley Griffin for what was then an uncharted colonial wilderness. Griffin's reaction to this setting is reminiscent of the ancient Roman attempt to fix infinite open space with a three-dimensional, cosmological axis and rectilinear grid that located it within their world. Axial, grid-iron plans were also favoured in establishing new cities in America for the same reason, providing a sense of order in what was considered to be natural chaos.

As an American Prairie School follower of Frank Lloyd Wright, Griffin had none of the imperial memory that

17 I M PEI,
Rock and Roll
Hall of Fame,
Cleveland, Ohio,
1993-95

18 ROMALDO
GIURGOLA,
Parliament House,
Canberra, 1988

18

otherwise might have inflected such a plan. His Camp Hill scheme was resuscitated by Giurgola who has used two granite-faced parabolic walls to frame the north–south axis, on which a formal sequence of spaces is situated.

An elliptical forecourt takes the visitor up to the great verandah of light red sandstone which recalls Ayers Rock and Australia's Aboriginal past and leads into the central ceremonial spine where all public spaces are located. The Senate and House of Representatives are located on the opposite, east–west axis just on the other downhill side of these gently arcing walls, with their related offices strung out like wings on either side of them.

While the Canberra Parliament project has had a critically mixed press, it stands as an admirable example

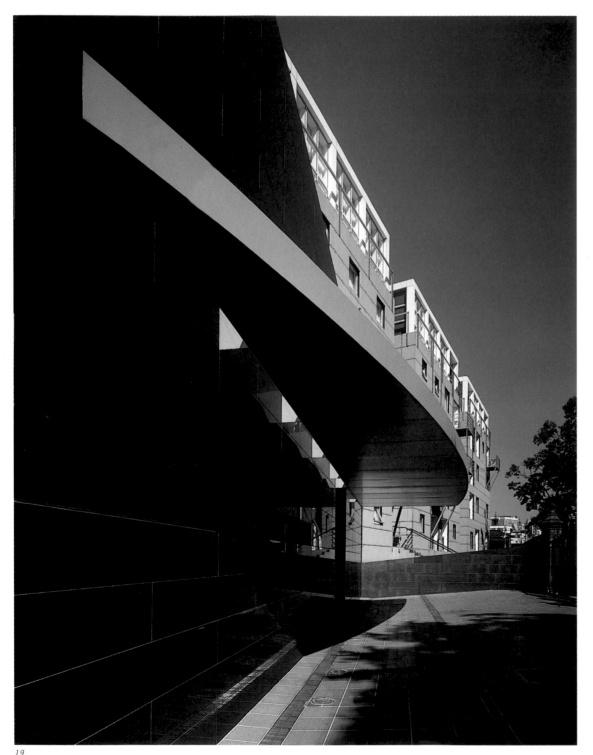

19

in the modernist idiom of how to integrate a building naturally with its site. It also marks the middle of an upward cycle of Australian architecture in general, of a wave now reaching full crest. Denton Corker Marshall is important contributor to that rise. It has made an even more elemental statement of the traditional Aussie love of the land in the Cowes house, 1994, dug into a hillside on Philip Island on the southeastern coast of the country. In reality a simple long thin rectangle, the house occupies one side of a square courtyard, on the edge facing the sea. In a description that reminds us of the soul of the Australian lifestyle, the punctured long wall has been characterized by Barrie Marshall as creating 'pictures of the ocean' from inside, so that every difference between outside and inside is eliminated. You live inside an outside environment and the views through the openings become the very essence of the building.[7] Taking the notion of abstraction to the limit, the architects have provided only the essentials needed for shelter, a Villa Malaparte buried underground, so that when approached from the landside the house is virtually invisible. Light enters from the courtyard through narrow slit windows, making the contrast with the picture wall, opposite, that much more intense.

These sensibilities, when transplanted in another country and extruded upwards to fit a more official, public programme, are less secure, if equally searching. Denton Corker Marshall's Australian Embassy in Tokyo, 1991, only 3 kilometres south of the Imperial Palace, plays a much more complex and self-conscious game of interacting with nature through inside—outside separation. Here the axial organizational device used by Giurgola at Canberra is used to connect open spaces. The formal arrival court from Mita Avenue is linked to a square central garden surrounded by chancery offices on the ground floor which leads finally to a 'moon viewing hill' in an informal garden beyond. This last is the beneficial residual of a southward slope which the architects have allowed to penetrate into the interstices of their E-shaped plan, in which the chancery block is the middle bar. The sinuous lines of the viewing hill, and the rectilinear organization of the embassy, is a reminder of the Katsura Palace, which is predicated on the best positions for viewing the moon, and which had a quite profound effect on such early modernists as Walter Gropius and Bruno Taut.

A common ancestry with these pioneers links surviving modernists worldwide. As two life-long adherents to the cause, Henri Ciriani and Colin St John Wilson must be highlighted in any discussion of modern principles, not because of any similarity in their work, but certainly due to their perseverance. Ciriani's Historial de la Grande Guerre, Peronne, France, 1987—92, and Museum of Archaeology in Arles, France, 1984—92, demonstrate the seemingly infinite variety he finds within the same Corbusian vocabulary used by Meier, but in a far less

19 DENTON CORKER
MARSHALL,
Australian
Embassy, Tokyo,
1991

20 HENRI CIRIANI,
Historial de la
Grande Guerre,
Peronne, 1987-92

21, 22
(Overleaf) HENRI
CIRIANI, Museum of
Archaeology,
Arles, 1984-92

formulaic way. At Peronne on the bank of the Somme, near the scene of the battle that took place from July until November 1916, Ciriani tapped into the two potent symbols available to him: the river and the ruins of a thirteenth-century castle, much reinforced with brick during the late sixteenth and early seventeenth centuries. Ciriani explains that everything began with the site and that: 'by emphasizing the horizontality of the main facade in relation to the expanse of the water, the new building enhances the site instead of weighing it down ... we wanted to develop the contact between the castle and our new building by allowing the two architectures to coexist ... playing on the notion of transition from one to the other'.[8]

The anomaly that Ciriani poses, of a contextually related translation of a topographically neutral Corbusian model, is reiterated in his Arles Museum, which has a far less emotionally charged, if equally important, cultural content. But at Peronne, Ciriani tries also to mitigate the unfathomable horror of a senseless battle that claimed the lives of 620,000 Allied and 450,000 German soldiers for a total territorial gain of 10 kilometres — a battle which has come to symbolize the futility of war itself — with calm lyricism and the inference in the foundation that war is a timeless curse. The less poignant, and more geometric museum in Arles responds to a different set of nationalized impulses: the Imperial Roman presence, perceived in the city's omnipresent archeological ruins, is as monumental, mathematically precise and boldly engineered as anywhere in the Empire, and more intact. In addition to forms, and graphic methods of conception, Ciriani also shares a love of colour with Le Corbusier — who considered himself an artist as well as an architect — and this takes on added resonance in Arles, because the Romans, like their Greek mentors, also loved to use primary colours on their architecture. Intensely saturated reds and greens, and a particular facade of Saint Gobain blue glass, vibrate in the bright sunlight that is as typical in the Midi as it is in Rome. Pieces of the building puncture the perimeter wall in places, reading like individual sculptures against it, but the real story occurs on the roof plane which is carefully modulated, in combination with interior spaces, to correct, modify or filter the strong sunlight. Clerestories guide light on to long solid walls; sawtooth monitors feed the temporary exposition hall; flat skylights convert ceilings into luminous overhead horizontal surfaces. Le Corbusier's much-loved ship metaphor, so obvious in the liner-like Villa Savoye, is alive here also. The plan triangle points to the end of a peninsula projecting out into the Rhone, and the long sleek silhouette of the building, with its pointed prow and mast-like central stair, conveys an equal impression of a vessel at full steam, holding a precious cargo of culture.

The New British Library at St Pancras, London, 1963–97, by Colin St John Wilson is an exhaustive cultural saga of more extensive proportions. Holding over twelve million volumes and serving close to 350,000 users every

20

21

23 COLIN ST JOHN
WILSON, New
British Library,
London, 1963-97

24 ELDRED EVANS
AND DAVID SHALEV,
Tate Gallery,
St Ives,
Cornwall, 1993

23

year, the new library has replaced a much loved neo-classical domed rotunda that many were sorry to see made redundant. Modernism has quite literally replaced tradition in this instance, and the high degree of public loyalty and affection claimed by the older structure has not made the transition easy.

Unlike the strictly classical symmetry of its predecessor, the new library is less formally axial, conforming to the incongruous trajectories of the Euston and Midland roads on the south and east, and Ossulston Street on the west. A 'plaza' at the southwestern corner of the site acts as an organizational device after entering from Euston Road. It acts as an open elbow that connects a linear building containing an auditorium and general science reading rooms on Midland Road, with another to the west, which also contains reading rooms, rare books, music and manuscripts. It could be argued that Wilson, in being as site-specific as Ciriani in a much more demanding urban context, has been equally thoughtful about the issue of responsiveness that runs as a leitmotif throughout the new modern sensibility. The new library has been criticized for its mute and ponderous shell, but the design intentions, best revealed in the interior, show a concern for place-making that goes a long way towards redressing its external inarticulateness.

Several practitioners operating in the new modern canon, such as Eldred Evans and David Shalev, and the Spanish architect Enric Miralles, have taken this issue of place-making to another level entirely, searching for more effective ties to site and local culture without compromising canonical principles of spatial purity, and formal and structural expression. Evans and Shalev's Tate Gallery in St Ives, 1993, for example, blends into its hillside site and the scale and texture of the local village without missing a beat, disproving the point made by James Stirling at Stuttgart that Post-Modernism is the proper approach to tricky urban texture. The Tate Gallery differs from the Staatsgalerie mainly in its specific refusal of literal historical reference and its mock-monumentality, use of colour and tricks of scale. The St Ives museum is tied directly to a local painting tradition, which the building has been custom-designed to accommodate, on an almost residential scale. However, despite their obviously divergent natures, the two museums do reveal some intriguing similarities. Both buildings use exhibition spaces in enfilade : the Tate has these in chronological order of the St Ives School painters that it celebrates; both have a grand circular public space as an organizing device: in Stuttgart it is open and planted to recall a ruin, in reference to the supposed emptiness of contemporary cities, while at St Ives the rotunda is a pure volume covered in glass. The same processional optimism shown by these two buildings is evident in countless modern predecessors from Wright's Guggenheim to Meier's High Museum, which in St Ives is recalled in equally hopeful and inspiring miniature.

25 ENRIC MIRALLES,
Igualada Cemetery,
Barcelona, 1986-90

26, 27 JO COENEN,
Netherlands
Architecture
Institute,
Rotterdam, 1988-93

In a piece entitled 'A Sense of Place' Eldred Evans and David Shalev have defined their general intention as: 'trying to create an entity which is both part of a larger one and a grouping of smaller ones ... we look at the place as it is and the place as it wants to be ... we are in search of an idea ... to us the elements of space are walls and light. Our buildings want to be white because of the light we want'. This ascription of human desire to inanimate space and 'the place as it wants to be' comes directly from Louis Kahn and his mystical personification of structure and material. As the key transitional figure between Modernism and Post-Modernism – 'John the Baptist', as it were – preparing the way for the revolutionary propositions put forward soon afterwards by Robert Venturi, Kahn is paradoxically also the prototypical new modernist. He presents an ideal model because of his basic humanity and realization of the imperative of continuity which only a sense of history can provide. Kahn sought a 'timeless' architecture that tapped into primal dissatisfaction with abstract detachment. Light, for Kahn, was more of a sacred than merely physical substance, connecting back to the early strain of Modernism, represented by Paul Scheerbart and Bruno Taut, in which light, as a natural life-giving medium, was sanctified.

Evans and Shalev's work runs closely with this Kahnian ideal; following it in their evocation of the essential character of a place through their architecture; their formal clarity and selective introduction of light to explain those forms, retreating only in materiality due to more restricted budgets than Kahn ever faced. Theirs, like Kahn's, is an architecture devoid of obvious reference to a particular movement or stylistic nuance. The dichotomy which Kahn represented and which Evans and Shalev perpetuate, includes the fact that high-period Modernism is now itself an historical style, since it can be quite clearly bracketed within a particular time-frame. To refer to Modernism from the standpoint of the late twentieth century is, therefore, to make an historical reference; and the canon of forms that are associated with Modernism are therefore symbolically loaded in just the same way as the Classical Orders.

In deviating from the modernist 'canon of forms' to connect to a more essential, rather than recreated past, Kahn created a viable alternative to the dogmatic reductivist tendency of Modernism. The poetry that Kahn used to convey his ideas was a welcome relief to an entire generation who felt deprived by Modernism's sterile dialectic. The importance of that poetic component in the making of places has been realized by several new modernists who have succeeded in taking it as their own.

Enric Miralles' Igualada Cemetery in Barcelona, 1986–90, is a sculpturally articulate example of this position. He has laid out the cemetery in a free-form complex that is as much land art as it is architecture. Kahn frequently spoke about seeking out beginnings, and Miralles' Z-shaped gashes, literally cut into the earth along the site

26

27

28 REM KOOLHAAS,
Kunsthal,
Rotterdam, 1987-92

29, 30 REM
KOOLHAAS,
Netherlands Dance
Theatre, The Hague,
1984-7

28

29

contours, come close to that intention, subconsciously recalling some forgotten prehistoric ritual. The banks of concrete tombs also serve as retaining walls, the sunken passages between them creating processional avenues that are as far removed from the rationalist streets in the sky that Aldo Rossi has created in his Modena Cemetery as it is possible to imagine.

Miralles' approach to the Igualada Cemetery, and the ritual scraping away of the earth, is recalled in a comment by the Dutch architect Rem Koolhaas about the new strain of Modernism that can be detected today. He believes that: 'the same process now leads everywhere to different results, to new specificities, new uniqueness. Even if you scrape the earth, the slate will not be absolutely clean, because there is previous history; the people who lived there once, who will live there in the future and the new communities that will bring specificities. The irony is that the obsession with history and specificity has become an obstacle in the recognition of these new realities'.[9]

Koolhaas first came to popular attention with the publication of his book *Delirious New York* in 1978 which took an off-beat but well-expressed and incisive look at the pattern of urban growth. He is the most visible, and certainly the most audible, representative of a growing number of talented architects in The Netherlands, which now has its strongest international voice and influence since the De Stijl movement of the early century. The Netherlands Architecture Institute, with a building by Jo Coenen dating from 1988–93, has been an important locus of this resurgence. Unlike many of his peers, however, Koolhaas thrives on confrontation and re-invention, he conserves his strength to make the boldest stroke, and his work has seemed to consistently increase in scale over the years. In his latest book *S, M, L, XL* (Small, Medium, Large, Extra Large) he praises 'bigness' as 'the ultimate architecture'. Koolhaas has usually achieved such bigness by grafting: the scale of his Netherlands Dance Theatre in the Hague, 1984–7, was amplified by joining it to an existing concert hall. The wild range of materials that he used, together with a cacophony of volumes, further asserted scale. In contrast, the interior of the 1,000-seat hall is plain and black, the action here restricted to a deep thrust stage. The audience in this theatre becomes as much a part of the drama as the actors on stage; transparency is used judiciously to add to the 'smoke and mirrors' approach of the architecture which has been described as relying: 'on whimsical shapes, colours and textures ... to create momentarily arresting but inescapably flimsy incidents in an underwhelming spatial envelope'.[10]

Koolhaas' Kunsthal, an exhibition space in Rotterdam, 1987–92, represents the next step in scale above the Dance Theatre, but it is still not yet 'big'. It is a more complex exercise in juxtaposition, the building perhaps forcibly generated from a large square site, traversed by the north–south axis of the nearby Museum

31 REM KOOLHAAS,
Grand Palais,
Lille, 1990-4

Park, and hemmed in by an east–west running highway parallel to Maas Boulevard on which it is located. The self-imposed challenge in this project became how to join these four segments of the site with a circulation sequence that made sense, while maintaining the strict functional requirements demanded by an exhibition space of this size. Unlike a museum, an art hall is a public institution with no permanent collection and so strives to be more egalitarian. Using the concept of a continuous circuit, which follows the site cross axis, and continues along a series of ramps that end in the Corbusian device of a roof garden, stepped in this instance to record the circulatory generation of form, Koolhaas leads the visitor through the building, while making formal play with the skewed grids created by the conflict between the circuit ramp and the horizontal, normative datum of the roof. The mullions of the window wall, being perpendicular to the ramp, do not align with the true verticals of the walls of the hall, showing two systems in dynamic competition, deliberately avoiding resolution to set up visual conflict. This tension also mirrors the confusion being orchestrated by the architecture; the building contains three major exhibition halls capable of being used for separate exhibitions at different times, or as one large exhibition space, in addition to an auditorium which can accommodate lectures, concerts or films, alongside a restaurant and a popular bookstore. The building has been mistakenly characterized as 'deconstructivist' by those who mistake its post-earthquake appearance for chaotic disorder instead of recognizing how it pushes the idea of the free elevation to the limit, while the columnar grid remains intact.

Only with Le Grand Palais in Llille, 1990–4, does Koolhaas finally reach 'bigness'. He has provided an all-purpose, hard-edged urban shed for the twenty-first century that is a single-handed attempt to revitalize the image of railway stations, generally considered to be a romantic relic of the Industrial Revolution. Located alongside an intermediate station on the Channel Tunnel railway line between London and Paris, and wedged, or more fittingly 'nested', on a triangular site at the intersection of the railroad tracks leading to the Lille train station and the motorway that crosses them going north, the Palais had to be assertive to survive and in this respect it surpasses all Koolhaas' earlier efforts.

Following his success in Europe, Koolhaas has begun to seek a greater involvement in Asia. In Fukuoka, Japan, his contribution to the Nexus World Complex, 1990, generally conceived by Arata Isozaki, is an attempt to reinvent the common perception of housing in the city. The site is located in an area that is as much an urban wasteland as anything Koolhaas has attacked in Europe. The project, reminiscent of the Weissenhofsiedlung — an exhibition organized in Stuttgart in the 1920s by Mies van der Rohe as a showcase for International Style public housing — is a similar pioneer for the New Moderns of the 1990s. Koolhaas' housing is a low-scale arrangement of

two blocks in linear ranks intended as an antidote to the prevailing tower typology he so dislikes. The blocks flank the formal entry road into an L-shaped agglomeration, located next to a more conventional scheme at the corner by the American architect Mark Mack.

Each of the different housing solutions at Fukuoka addresses the issue of privacy at either an overt or subliminal level, as well as cultural differences in the perception and use of public space and the difficulties involved when Western architects attempt to design in a Japanese context. The Mack project raises this issue most clearly. Mack has provided a 'piazza' at the intersection of the two blocks, but there is relatively little precedent for public space of this kind in Japanese history, let alone any model providing direct exposure to traffic in the Italian tradition on which this space is predicated. Isozaki's courageous comment about Japanese tradition being as mysterious to, and distant from, his own generation as it is for any foreign architect working in his country, is a graphic reminder of the price that nation has paid for its ability to assimilate and filter many external ideas, values and technologies. Conformity to Japanese tradition may no longer be relevant for foreign architects, since those values have themselves been extensively compromised. This view will undoubtedly upset many purists who view Japan's position in Asia as being the repository of a refined, individual culture; in the same way that France sees itself as unique in Europe.

Of all of the contributions at Fukuoka, that of Steven Holl is the most sensitive attempt at an explanatory interpretation of this process of cultural transformation. He has deliberately integrated Le Corbusier's idea of a proportional module with the Japanese concept of the *ken*; the regulating system embodied in the tatami mat that generates the sizes of the floor areas it covers, and which entranced early modernists such as Walter Gropius and Bruno Taut when they visited the Katsura Palace. This focus on determining an ordering system has been a favourite device for Holl, one that he also employed effectively in the Stretto House in Dallas, in 1992. The house, named after the overlapping stretto in music, is sited next to a sequence of spring-fed ponds formed by concrete dams. The house literally reflects these pools, which for Holl were suggestive of Bartok's *Music for Strings, Percussion and Celeste*, in which the stretto technique forms a central role; the piece having four movements, alternating between heavy percussion sections and light string passages. Holl has translated the differences in the sound of percussion and string instruments into light and space, dividing the house into four sections; heavy masonry cores as Kahnian servant spaces containing pragmatic elements such as the kitchen, bathrooms and stairways alternating with more open areas of living, dining and study, covered with petal-like roofs.

Holl has chosen to break through the perceived inflexibility and insularity of Modernism with an appeal to

32

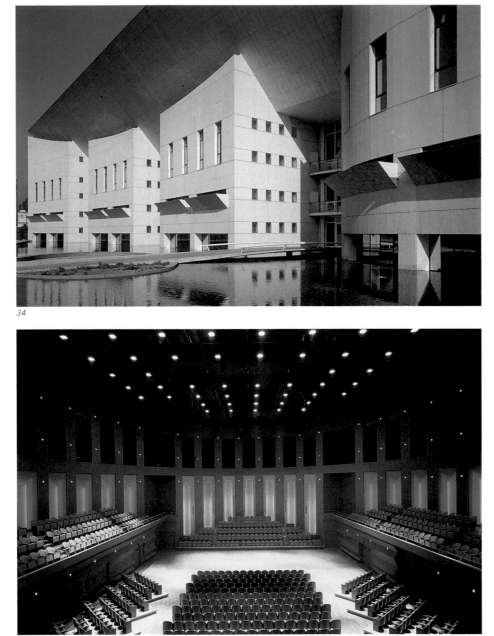

34

35

a heightened sense of spatial awareness, intensifying the contemplative, monastic aspect that has always been a central part of its philosophical underpinning. Holl, like Kahn before him, has gained a wide student following by tapping into the idealistic yearnings of a younger generation of architects. He has done this by moving beyond pure theory, which many began to find as sterile as the mute historicism of Modernism that it replaced. He stresses the fact that of all the arts, only architecture appeals to all the senses; light, colour, texture and tactile sensations, smell, sound, and spatial awareness all contributing to a total experience that 'holds the power to inspire and transform our day-to-day existence'. In this belief, he perpetuates the most basic modernist credo: that buildings have the ability to ameliorate social problems and change our lives. Holl's popularity indicates that young people ascribe to this credo once again.

Christian de Portzamparc, who has made a surprisingly post-modern contribution to the distinguished assemblage at Fukuoka, seems to personify Holl's plea for the recognition of sensual totality in architecture. Echoing Holl's analogy at a much larger scale, two of Portzamparc's largest projects at Nanterre and in Paris are both close approximations of the modernist characterization of architecture as 'frozen music'. His Paris Opera Dance School in Nanterre, 1983–7, is characteristically joined to its urban surroundings, in this case by an enormous transparent hall that allows clear sight lines through the school to a large park in the distance. This hall, which is also the terminus of the main entrance road, is the plan 'generator' in the Corbusian sense. A long, sinuous extension spins out from it towards the south, and the residential wing is curved to allow various vistas towards the park. This rather simple *parti*, of a large central block divided into dance studios organized around a circular central stair, and a flame-like tail of accommodation connected to it, prefigures the clean approach to form-making that Portzamparc has taken at the Cité de la Musique in Paris.

Conceived as a gateway to the newly-created Parc de la Villette, the Cité de la Musique, 1985–95, is also a small city in its own right, complete with all the typologies of streets, public structures, institutions, restaurants, shops and houses that this implies. The west wing was the first part of the Cité to be completed in 1989–90. It is a teaching facility for the National Conservatory of Music, organized in four solid bands with linear open spaces between them in a north–south axis perpendicular to the main entry road. The west wing is relatively orderly. Its strict plan organization allows an extensive grouping of educational spaces of various sizes, including practice rooms, group rehearsal spaces, a concert hall and offices, to be combined without confusion, in ways that retain acoustic isolation when necessary and allow for controlled public participation and attendance wherever possible.

The east wing, in contrast, completed in 1995, oscillates energetically within an elongated triangular enclosure. A formal, elliptical concert hall, which seats up to 1,200 people, is the core of this dynamic composition. It echoes the shape of the rehearsal hall in the conservatory, but is far grander in scale and finish, and substitutes the overtly Corbusian conical roof of the earlier space with a beret-like dome, jauntily tilted above the datum of the residentially scaled spaces wrapped around it. Like a nautilus shell, the ancillary spaces typically associated with a world-class concert hall protectively surround the ovoid chamber, separated from it only by what the architect has referred to as a 'musical street'. From a wide, funnel-like entrance, this street spirals past administrative offices, an information centre and café into the inner sanctum around the hall, where a museum is located. The museum, as well as student residential units, is the primary device that Portzamparc has used to break down the scale of what might otherwise be an overwhelming complex; both the exterior facades, as well as those facing into the 'street', have been treated as abstractions of residential elevations, painted or tiled in different colours in contrast to the white stone shell of the concert hall itself.

While Portzamparc's use of a hierarchy of powerful formal geometries and abstraction make his position in the debate about metaphorical representation clear, if one places him among the other New Moderns who share this approach, his concern for urbanity would appear to make him unique.

Rather than being content with singular formal statements, Portzamparc positions his architecture to establish complex connections both within the building and with the external realm. Of all the New Moderns he alone is responsible for attempting to recover the urbanistic mandate appropriated by the early leaders of the Modern Movement who took their cue from such diverse inspirations as *La Città Nuova* by Antonio Sant' Elia, the utopian visions of the Futurists and the startling civic proposals of Constructivists. Further comparisons with the early work of Le Corbusier can also be made. Portzamparc's volumes in the cone over the rehearsal hall of the west wing, and the tilted dome of the Cité, combined with a giant truss that slices past the concert hall, is a reminder of the persistent formal heritage that Le Corbusier has left us, and specifically of his unrealized Palace of the Soviets project, which was in turn inspired by the Constructivists and others. The aesthetic tenor of each epoch can be regarded as the culmination of all of the strongest creative forces that have preceded it: Le Corbusier's Palais represented such a synthesis in the 1920s and Portzamparc's tribute is testimony to the durability of memory today.

At the end of this epoch, the most viable contender for the role of the new modernist icon is perhaps the Tokyo International Forum, by Rafael Viñoly,

1990–6. This vast project combines many of the elements expressed individually elsewhere at an unprecedented scale and level of technical execution. It occupies a highly defined site wedged between the tracks of the Tokyo station on the east and 'Metropolitan Road AO2' on the west and is even more tightly circumscribed by the subway lines that hem it in below ground level. Viñoly has accepted the challenge presented by a difficult site and has countered urban adversity with a monumental scale and an assertive *parti*. He has solved the daunting task of placing four theatres inside this transportation framework by building a wall along the most extensive western edge, against the Metropolitan Road and Yokosuka subway line and then backing the four theatres of increasing size against it. To complete the concept of a walled courtyard, he has added an open, tapering 'glass hall' that conforms to the curve of the eastern site line.

The finely crafted appearance of the Tokyo Forum, and particularly its glass hall, so reminiscent of the Crystal Palace by Joseph Paxton in scale if not in form, would initially seem to classify this as a high-tech project. However, Viñoly's Forum goes far beyond the mere celebration of technological skill which such a classification might suggest, and sets out to define a more complex agenda, making it the ideal synthesis of the new modern aesthetic.

Viñoly has described the design of the Forum as 'a mission', both to resuscitate the tarnished image of Modernism in regard to technical expertise and to provide Tokyo with public fora at a scale commensurate with the city's leading role at the beginning of what many predict will be the Asian century. The Tokyo Forum is also an exemplary manifestation of Rem Koolhaas' mission of 'bigness' and mirrors his attempt at Euralille to come to grips with uncontrolled urban expansion as a phenomenon of the end of the twentieth century. It is also a reminder of Koolhaas' insight in *Delirious New York* that Modernist visions, proclaimed in numerous manifestos in the 1920s and 1930s, are now being realized, and that 'in many ways we are now living the actual implementation of all those ambitions that were inaccessible myths for the pioneers of Modernism: the speed of production, of volume, and engineering'. Viñoly refuses to accept Koolhaas' contention, however, that: 'while we weren't looking, architects seem to have lost almost all control over the potential of Modernism, lost any ability to find a connection with it once again'. Koolhaas has discovered a complete personal style in his belief that it is time to surrender such control. Viñoly, on the other hand, has constructed his project around the opposite conviction that such potential still exists and has more promise than ever because of new and unprecedented technological advances. The Tokyo Forum is testimony to the strength of his modernist convictions and now inspires all of those capable of sharing them.

37, 38 Rafael Viñoly, Tokyo International Forum, 1990-6

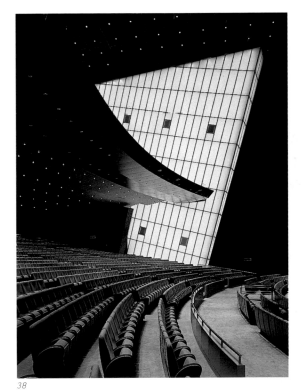

38

Often characterized by friends, family and associates as a child at heart, and with a lifelong fascination for an ever-expanding collection of toys, Moore was especially receptive to the message sent by Disney and the techniques used to realize it. As early as 1965, Moore made clear his admiration for Disney's understanding of people's deep-felt need for make-believe, to see and be seen, and for what had been achieved at Disneyland. He also identified the essence of the continuity between Disneyland and the world expositions and fairs of the previous century and their common separation from the real world.

Other serious students of Disneyland have identified the archetypal American image of Main Street, transported at seven-eighths of its full size from Walt Disney's hometown of Marceline, Missouri, as the most basic of the subconscious symbols first used there. The use of miniaturization and distorted perspective is also a staple of the cinema and scenography. The miniaturization of Main Street makes adults feel like children again and they become the central participants in their own, long-since forgotten fairy tale. Aside from artful reduction, the other important difference between the real Main Street and its simulacrum is the increase in commercialism that the latter heralds. The authentic Main Street was not as completely geared towards financial gain as its smaller cousin in California. This process of transformation reflects the impact of the communications revolution, in which the media as the prime source of information and entertainment is also paid for by commercials. This has made products and product differentiation more important than they ever were when the real Main Street thrived. Advertising aesthetics has been accurately described as 'an extension of the sphere of mass media';[4] and advertising has become the real contemporary art, as Andy Warhol most effectively illustrated. The mass media, especially television, now plays a crucial role in governing how people measure their place in society, define their values, structure their language, and construct an identity inextricably tied to particular products in a pattern called 'automatic adhesion reflex', which begins to give popular products — such as Coca Cola, for example — sociological anonymity. But, as Marcel Duchamp demonstrated, once this adhesion is broken and the functional purpose of the product is either amplified or destroyed — as by putting nails in the flat surface of an iron — its artistic value can be appreciated.

The Venturi, Scott Brown contribution to the formulation of a theoretical basis for populist aesthetics was to apply this concept to architecture. *Learning from Las Vegas* examined the unmasked commercial strip, the Main Street as reformulated by Disney. Venturi and Scott Brown exposed the Las Vegas Strip as a landscape of symbol in space rather than form in space; or to put it another way, as the antithesis of modernist values: with an ironic inflection towards their earlier statement that 'Main Street is almost all right', they declared provocatively that 'Billboards are almost all right', and staked a claim to the

6 JON JERDE,
MCA City Walk,
Universal
Studios, Los
Angeles,
1994

7 JON JERDE,
Fremont Street
Experience, Las
Vegas, 1995

6

present urban problems – and his achievement has been to transport the hyper-world of the theme park into the real-world civic realm. One of Jerde's first attempts in this regard was Horton Plaza, a 1.5 million-square-foot mixed-use redevelopment of a six-block historic district in downtown San Diego. Completed in 1985, it includes the usual components of such projects: 165 speciality shops and restaurants, four department stores, cinemas and extensive office space. These elements are united by arcades detailed to relate to a perceived indigenous architectural language suggesting the vitality of 'Latin' American streetlife. Jerde responded to a commercial consistency that he identified in this area of the city, despite its state of deterioration. He has accentuated the new development's connections to the existing city by cutting a diagonal pedestrian street through it, which picks up a route from the centre of downtown to the Pacific waterfront. This gesture, Jerde feels, 'captures the essence of what San Diego is, its Hispanic origins, subtropical climate, pastel colours, and deep shadows'. He composed many of the new buildings out of existing, or suggested, fragments of the old, such as the arcades of the Santa Fe Railroad station, also using the idea of towers to recall a perceived code of visible landmarks in the existing city fabric. All of the techniques now familiar from Post-Modernism are recognizable here – collaging fragments of history and layering – but Jerde has taken them a stage further, offering a heightened hyper-commodification of culture, and the sanitizing of history for commercial gain, at a much larger scale and in a more uniform presentation related to a central, if not necessarily indigenous idea.

Jerde's City Walk at Universal Studios, located alongside the Hollywood Freeway in Los Angeles, and completed in 1994, is a much larger, more obvious example of this ersatz approach. Designed in conjunction with the MCA Development Company, Universal City Walk institutionalizes a growing desire to create pedestrianized havens in Los Angeles, as exemplified in the 'real' world by the Third Street Promenade in Santa Monica, and Broadway, which is an attempt to restore the attractions of that street's theatres, displacing in the process a vital Hispanic commercial strip in favour of a more culturally homogeneous *cordon sanitaire* which is intended to rival its namesake in New York. Each of these artificial streets is home to a predictably ubiquitous collection of franchises: the same shops, restaurants and general commercial mélange are deemed necessary by overly conservative leasing agents in order to ensure financial success. Their implacable economic logic arranges the mix and position of these facilities according to perceived market forces. The resulting homogeneity is not only confined to pedestrianized, sanitized streets, or themed environments; the concomitant proliferation of retail and restaurant franchises has meant that city and town centres throughout the world now look disarmingly, predictably, and sadly, the same. Even the franchises themselves are being

'themed': witness the advent of 'Nike Town' stores in New York and other cities, which integrate architecture into an all-encompassing brand-reinforcing experience. Across the Atlantic, a city by city inspection of Britain illustrates the point. Every high street in every major urban area has outlets for the same conglomerates, from Body Shop and Next to Monsoon and McDonald's. The vista along these streets is depressingly similar; what they lack is precisely the variety and texture of the market squares of the past that the sanitizers claim to be recreating. Individual shopkeepers cannot compete with the marketing and advertising might, or the sales and distribution capability, that the conglomerates can muster, and so are inexorably being driven out of business. The cruel market mechanism involved ensures that the scenographic imitation of historical texture destroys the paradigm that it superficially seeks to replicate.

At Universal City Walk the plasticity of the sanitized street has now quite literally risen to new dimensions. The Universal Studios complex that exists on the 430-acre site contains the massive physical plant necessary for making movies and television 'soaps', as well as the headquarters buildings that house the executive and administrative offices. The backlot was once a maze of false-fronted sets, organized thematically into the streets of smalltown America – against which were shot such classics as *Leave it to Beaver*, about the daily dramas of an average suburban family – or faux frontier staging posts used for wild west movies such as *High Noon*; but they have long since outlived their usefulness, and the backlot has been converted into a highly profitable 'ride', setting the scene for Jerde's newly conceived street. In the Universal City Walk design, Jerde claims to 'speak to a collection of special interest groups: the family, the tourist, the non-specific citizen'. He searches for the essence of Los Angeles, which is like no other city in the world: a vast metropolis with no perceptible edges. City Walk is a commercial container intended to combat placelessness, and to provide a focused space which people can identify with closely and return to regularly. Huge parking structures form the periphery of the roughly linear pedestrian thoroughfare, which angles at the circular plazas that form elbows in its cash-producing arms. Jerde's architectural references range from 'Googy' recall – the angular, car-orientated, multi-coloured architecture that characterized Los Angeles in the 1950s – to the quasi-Mayan style introduced to Los Angeles by Frank Lloyd Wright's Hollyhock House in the 1920s, and continued by Donald Stacy Judd in the eclectic Melrose Avenue. The scale of the buildings increases towards the centre of the development, following the inverted, bowl-like contours of the site.

The irony of fabricating an artificial and completely commercial pedestrian 'street' far from any of LA's six emerging urban centres, and accessible only by freeway and feeder parking garages seems, however, to have escaped all those concerned. City Walk is really only

a new-improved backlot of artificial building fronts with batallions of cash registers ringing behind them. This phenomenon has become an underlying feature of these themed worlds, as the developers rush to cash in on the growing public paranoia over rising real-world crime and the perceived need for security, as well as the instinctive human desire for sociability.

Jerde's redevelopment of the Fremont Street Experience in Las Vegas is a far more straightforward proposition than City Walk; as the press announced when this four block-long attempt to rejuvenate Vegas' original 'glitter gulch' section of the city was completed in 1995, it is all 'lights, action, and excess', and it has no pretensions to civic respectability. The 'experience' is a street-level mall, 1,400 feet long, covered by a huge barrel-vaulted, steel-framed canopy held 90 feet above the ground by sixteen tree-like steel columns. This 'celestial vault' comprises an astonishing 2.1 million lights spread in an even pattern of pixellated clusters and a 540,000-watt sound system that combine to produce a spectacular multimedia show on the hour, every hour of the day. Economic competition between Fremont Street, whose casinos and fading neon charms were losing out to the burgeoning Strip to the south, was the driving force behind this development. The covered lobby that Jerde and Jeremy Railton & Associates have created connects the 'historic' casinos that line the street; and the 'experience' has had the desired effect, drawing thousands of sightseers and punters into the downtown. This has led to a commercial revival in that part of the city and a new 84,000-seat stadium and a performing arts centre, along with increased private investment, have followed in its wake.

The Fremont Street Experience is symptomatic of the mushrooming growth of what must be the most artificial city in the world; Las Vegas is predicated on the paradigm of theming and fuelled by the need for constant popular diversion and change. To quote one popular sports commentator: 'This is the nineties — it's gotta be entertaining!' The glitz and commercialism that held Venturi and Scott Brown in thrall in their study of Las Vegas casinos like the Excalibur and Caesars Palace in the 1970s has since been spectacularly exceeded in newly developed hotel and casino complexes such as New York, New York, which is designed to look like a congregation of the best-known Big Apple skyscrapers and landmarks. Designed by architects Gaskin and Bezanski with Yates and Silverman, and completed in 1997, this resort at the corner of Las Vegas Boulevard and Tropicana Avenue offers the Vegas punters a condensed caricature of New York spread over 20 acres at a cost of 400 million dollars. A replica of the Statue of Liberty at the corner of the intersection announces the complex, which features a tugboat in a miniature New York 'harbour', together with a 529-foot-high copy of the Empire State Building and a 500-foot Chrysler Building, both of which contain stacks of hotel rooms. The parodied replication continues in a 'Greenwich Village' — complete with

faux Brownstones and permanent fall foliage — a Motown Cafe, and Hamilton's Cigar Shop, as well as Times Square, Little Italy, a roller coaster called the Manhattan Express — recalling the elevated trains on Manhattan's east side — a stock exchange, City Hall, graffiti, crumbling concrete, and manhole covers that periodically shoot up steam. The New York, New York skyline is designed to appear as nine individual landmarks, but a quick investigation reveals that it is actually a megastructure housing 84,000 square feet of casino space, including seventy-one gaming tables, 2,400 slot machines, a 28,000-square-foot Coney Island arcade, a 1,000 seat theatre, and 2,000 hotel rooms. Once inside, only the changes in the carpet colour announce the dividing lines between the nine supposed 'buildings'.

This monstrous confection has received an astonishing response from customers, attracting 200,000 visitors a day in the first three days it was open. The reactions of

9

8 JON JERDE,
Fremont Street
Experience, Las
Vegas, 1995

9 GASKIN AND
BEZANSKI WITH
YATES AND
SILVERMAN,
New York, New York
Casino Complex,
Las Vegas, 1997

those seeing it for the first time have ranged from awe expressed at the level of detail used, to criticism over omissions; for example: Chinatown, an Automat, Jewish *knishes*, and muggings. The standing joke about New York, New York is that the bandits there have just one arm, and only the slot machines will mug you. These criticisms are a fascinating indication of the public's ability and willingness to buy into the fantasy, collectively suspending disbelief while happily paying twice the average market price for a regular cup of black coffee. New York, New York clearly shows how theming has been accurately identified by entrepreneurs as a welcome anaesthetic that numbs the senses, encourages sales, and awakens old memories that are as marketable as any of the physical merchandise on offer.

The success of theming in Las Vegas can be gauged further by the number of new mega-projects that are

Despite the increasing academic interest in developing a theoretical discussion about the origins and development of populist, or themed, architecture, few serious architects have become involved in its construction, despite the tangible overlap with the work of the historic preservationists and the new urban traditionalists. It can be hard to draw the line between the reconstruction of chunks of America's historic cities, or the new towns built along traditionalist lines, such as Seaside, and the more blatant, commercially driven, and firmly developer-led, themed developments of Las Vegas and LA. However, among these developers the Disney Company has always professed a commitment to patronizing good architecture in its theme parks, and a number of high-profile international architects – notably those of a post-modernist bent – have undertaken major projects for them. Michael Graves has turned his post-modern classical style into a

blocks whose tumbling arrangements suggests nothing so much as Christmas presents under a tree. Robert A M Stern has designed the Walt Disney World Casting Centre at Lake Buena Vista, in Florida, 1987–9, and the Disney Animation Building in Burbank, completed in 1993, which houses over 500 animators whose job it is to produce Disney's trademark animated feature films. Stern's building is a characteristic piece, decked out in ice-cream-like colours, the one Disney flourish being the six-storey-high replica of the sorcerer's hat that Mickey Mouse wore in *Fantasia* which marks the entrance to the building and the office of Roy Disney, head of the animation division.

All of these architects have a previous track record of theming history in individual buildings, but Disney seems to think it has not only packaged world-class architecture for popular consumption, but that it has also taught its designers to change their values to suit the

14 MICHAEL GRAVES, Team Disney Corporate Headquarters, Burbank, California, 1986

15, 16 (Overleaf) FRANK GEHRY, Festival Disney, Disneyland, Paris, Marne-la-Vallée, 1989

15

wrapper for the Dolphin and Swan Hotels in Walt Disney World completed in 1987, a year after he recast the Seven Dwarfs as cartoon caryatids on the Team Disney Headquarters in Burbank (site of the Walt Disney Studios and original Disneyland), and has designed the Hotel New York at EuroDisney, in Marne-la-Vallée on the outskirts of Paris, which opened in 1989. Frank Gehry designed the shopping and dining concourse for Disneyland Paris, producing an abstract but playful Festival Disney, which eschews theming but adopts pop imagery and themes from 1950s Los Angeles to create a sense of magic and excitement that really only becomes apparent after dark. The Japanese architect Arata Isozaki has produced another Team Disney Building, this time for Walt Disney World in Florida, 1990, which snaps a pair of Mickey ears on to a playfully colourful post-modernist collage of gift-wrapped

market place; it is akin to hiring Giorgio Armani, then asking him to design a Mickey costume. Disney head, Michael Eisner, obviously enjoys this role and has gone so far as to say that, 'thanks to Disney it is now socially acceptable in America for business people, investors, and developers to invite an architect to dinner'.[6] More recently, the Miami-based practice Arquitectonica was commissioned to design the All-Star Sports and Music Resorts in Lake Buena Vista. The Resorts are a series of mid-budget motels for Disney visitors, decked out in eclectic pop-culture 'add-ons' which could have been acquired wholesale on the Vegas Strip. In the first completed resort, the sports theme is reinforced by larger-than-life surf-boards, basketballs, megaphones and referees' whistles, which conceal staircases or other functional essentials, creating a colourful scene whose influences lie somewhere

invaders, implies. Although there are increasing numbers of theme-parks in Europe, they simply do not aspire to the scale and cultural dominance of the American model.

By contrast, the theming concept has been extremely popular in Japan, and is becoming increasingly common in the Far East. The Jerde Partnership, for example, has completed Canal City Hakata which applies the lessons learned at Horton Plaza to a nine-acre development along-side the Naka River in Fukuoka. It provides a 700-foot-long pedestrian promenade along the banks of an artificial canal which arcs through the site, surrounded by hotels, a performing arts centre, offices, a cineplex, department stores and parking garages, all focused on a series of urban spaces — Star Court, Moon Walk, Sun Plaza, Earth Walk and Sea-Life Playground — which heave with pedestrians at most times of the day and into the evening. The overriding theme at work here — as the names of the public walks and plazas suggests — is the earth and nature. The buildings are striped to suggest geological striations, and their facades rise steeply from the water's edge, a reference to how a river, over time, erodes the earth to form a canyon.

At a different scale, and in another city, Tokyo Disneyland is a highly successful enterprise, perhaps reflecting an established tradition in the Japanese culture and economy of importing commodities and concepts from abroad — particularly the West — and copying and adapting them for their own use. A new virtual reality park in Japan represents a celebration of national predominance in technological development, while a Tang Dynasty park in Singapore emphasizes the cultural legitimacy of a Chinese ethnic minority within a racially diverse city-state. Similarly, Sun City in South Africa suggests the possibility of a lost white race through the 'lost paradise' theme promoted by Circus Circus in Las Vegas. The enormous park is surrounded by ashlar limestone walls decorated with life-sized elephant heads and vine-covered friezes of monkeys and baboons that rise up out of the dense jungle cover as a literal, as well as symbolic, defence against the far-reaching social changes taking place in the nation beyond its walls. Inside, visitors can pretend that the myth of racial superiority is real, and inequality and poverty do not exist. The 'Lost World' of Sun City pushes the aphasia promoted in most theme parks to the extreme, but the financial purpose is the same, tapping into popular fears and insecurity about the future, offering reassurance through some collective vision bolstered by images of the past to encourage the public to spend. Special interest groups are also beginning to realize the potential of the theme park to promote their own agendas and the list of impending ideologically-orientated parks is extensive. There is ample evidence of the continuing growth and expansion of this phenomenon, which holds huge implications for the direction of architecture in the future. Architects should beware; the populists are on the march.

26 JON JERDE,
Canal City
Hakata, Fukuoka,
1996

The legendary Chicago architect and skyscraper pioneer, Louis Sullivan, declared that a skyscraper must be 'lofty', and that 'the glory and pride of exaltation must be in it', making it 'a proud and soaring thing'. This became the guiding principle for skyscraper designers for nearly a century. During the late 1970s, however, an invisible line was crossed and it became clear that commercial and corporate exultation in high-rise office buildings had taken over from the purely architectural ideal. The challenge to architects was to seek new forms of expression for what had become a rapidly evolving and expanding building type. At the end of the century, these evolving 'megastructures' are back in the forefront of design for architecture's most innovative players.

This process of evolution, from skyscraper to megastructure, has gone through what could roughly be seen as four stages since the end of the Second World War. The first phase was marked by the application of International Style Modernism to the office tower – the prime examples of this being Lever House in Park Avenue in New York of 1952, designed by Gordon Bunshaft of Skidmore Owings and Merrill (SOM) – who were to remain key figures in the early developments of the type – and the Seagram Building, also in Manhattan, designed in 1958 by the émigré Ludwig Mies van der Rohe along with Philip Johnson, who was then still an orthodox modernist.

The second phase, from the late 1950s to the mid-1970s, was a refinement of the first, with architects taking advantage of new technologies – such as high-speed elevators, high-strength steel, fusion welding and computer software – all of which allowed them to explore new structural systems which could extend the possibilities of the corporate high-rise type. Perhaps ironically, the high-rise structures of this period are largely excluded from architectural history books and have become seen as a separate strand of commercial architecture, no longer part of the avant-garde but maintaining a form of corporate Modernism and structural advance now outside wider architectural concerns. Incidentally, these early phases of skyscraper design are also seen as clearly distinct from the various high-rise housing developments – both luxury apartments and social housing – which developed in parallel with the office tower. There are examples of housing which have been highly significant in the development of the type, most notably Mies van der Rohe's Lakeshore Drive apartments in Chicago of 1948–51 – one of the most influential monuments of post-war high rise – or Charles Correa's Kanchanjunga apartment block in Bombay of 1980, with its two-storey verandahs, which represents an early example of the adoption of local living patterns and environmental principles to the high-rise type. But high-rise living is complicated by many other issues, and has been largely excluded from this chapter, which deals almost exclusively with the development of the skyscraper for commercial or corporate use.

The third phase in the evolution of the high-rise office tower can be seen to result from an attempt to win back a public which had become disaffected with tall face-less boxes sheathed in glass. This was mainly achieved through the use of post-modernist forms of expression, which had evolved in smaller building types, but which were widely adopted for commercial buildings as Post-Modernism established itself as the favoured commercial style of the 1980s. In effect, this phase was a return to the anthropomorphism of memorable Art Deco skyscrapers of the past such as the Chrysler Building by William van Alen, 1930, or the Empire State Building by Shreve, Lamb and Harmon, 1931. This can perhaps be characterized as the 'base, middle and top phase' of post-war skyscraper design.

The fourth phase is marked by the end-of-the-century supertower explosion, which has occurred primarily in Asia, but can be seen more widely as the architectural expression of a global economy that is transforming cities around the world. These new megastructures are monumental icons of this economy, representing the nodes of international electronic finance in which supertowers are replacing superpowers. Alongside these economic imperatives, this phase also marks the rising importance of wider architectural issues such as context, environmental and social interaction – as well as their conceptual expression – in the development of a building type which had hitherto tended to be dominated by issues of form, structure, detailing and servicing.

Lever House, the building which could be said to have sparked this rapid evolution, looks rather prosaic today. Indeed, it was only recently saved from destruction by a last-ditch effort to have it declared a national historical monument. The Lever Brothers Company, buoyed by sales of domestic detergents and various soaps, commissioned Skidmore Owings and Merrill to provide the architectural equivalent of their sanitary image, and SOM partner Gordon Bunshaft was the ideal choice as designer. He had toured Europe before the Second World War and visited many of the new buildings by Modernists such as Walter Gropius, Mies van der Rohe and Le Corbusier, which most American architects had not yet seen. Lever House was simply a twenty-four-storey tower on a broader, two-storey plinth base, rendered in an approximation of the International Style. However, it showed developers and architects how to build a skyscraper in a commercially viable way, and in the process it translated the pure ideology of Modernism into the language of high finance. Bunschaft and SOM remained as key players in the early developments of the office tower type.

The transformation that Lever House heralded had been prefigured by the design of Mies van der Rohe's Lakeshore Drive apartment blocks – in which two identical freestanding twenty-six-storey buildings are set at right angles to each other on a low podium – and as an office type it was later to be nationalized and authenticated by Mies. In 1958, in partnership with Philip Johnson,

3

1 (Previous page)
I M PEI, Bank of China, Hong Kong, 1990

2 SKIDMORE, OWINGS AND MERRILL, DESIGNER BRUCE GRAHAM, John Hancock Center, Chicago, 1965-70

3 SKIDMORE, OWINGS AND MERRILL, DESIGNER GORDON BUNSHAFT, Lever House, New York, 1952

Mies truly converted the skyscraper into a soaring 'cathedral of commerce' in his famous Seagram Building on Park Avenue. Louis Kahn described the building as 'a beautiful lady in a tight corset' because of its carefully controlled structural solution, in which a service core containing lifts, stairs and toilets is placed at the back of the 525-foot-high rectangular tower — both to increase wind resistance and to make the tower's forward profile thinner and the detailing more elegant. The thoroughness of that detailing is legendary. Because strict building codes required that the inner steel structure be sheathed in fire protection, smaller cast-bronze I-beams run vertically up the sides to suggest the inner 'steel-ness' of the tower. The project also made an unprecedented civic gesture — a plaza created by setting the tower back 100 feet from the site

upon it as a model without understanding or adopting its rigorous design principles.

The John Hancock Center in Chicago, designed by SOM in 1965–70, is the Seagram Building with its corset off, honestly expressing the importance of wind bracing. In engineering terms, the skyscraper can be thought of as a vertical tube, anchored to the ground at one end and cantilevered into space. As it rises from its base, it undergoes deflection from lateral forces such as wind, which can reach speeds in excess of 100 miles per hour, as well as punishing variations in air pressure. When a tower rises higher than seventy storeys, it is best to concentrate a majority of the structure on the exterior in order to present the maximum resistance to these forces. The John Hancock Center, which is just less than a 1,000 feet high and includes some 700 apartments as well as offices, shops and car parking, deals with the problem of wind bracing by adopting an exterior X-braced frame which absorbs wind load in the building's outer structure, and gains its integral strength through continuous connections from face to face. The tower's tapering form also combats the increase in the overturning force of wind pressure as the building rises. In the simplicity of its approach, the John Hancock Center is an undeniable scion of the Seagram Building; it advanced the structural argument that Mies began on Park Avenue considerably by turning windbracing and structure into an expressive part of the building form, and thereby helped to set the stage for the megastructures that we see at the end of the century.

At 1,368- and 1,362-feet high respectively, the World Trade Center Towers by the Japanese-American architect Minoru Yamasaki in New York City, of 1972–3, show how fully Miesian reductivism had permeated corporate consciousness in little more than a decade since the completion of the Seagram Building. The World Trade Center project actually began much earlier; David Rockefeller initiated the scheme in 1960 as a way of extending commercial activity to the tip of Manhattan, and the Port Authority of New York and New Jersey acquired the property in 1962. Structurally, the exterior refines the Hancock model of a braced tube, reducing the bracing in scale to form a steel lattice. Closely spaced external columns and their cross members act as a continuous truss bracing the building. This lattice, sheathed in aluminium, reads like a fine mesh and the token arcade at the base of each tower is not sufficient to offset the uniform, vertical visual field that prevails over the entire surface of the two buildings.

4

boundary on Park Avenue. This plaza set a new standard for corporate urban largesse, and has proven to be a popular lunch spot for New Yorkers frustrated by the city's general lack of public space. Its completion also led to the adoption of a 1961 zoning regulation requiring more open spaces around New York City skyscrapers, instead of the traditional practice of building up to the site line and using incremental setbacks to allow light to reach the street. Mies, the leading American proponent of the International Style, considered the Seagram Building to be the culmination of his career. However, the severity of Mies' detailing, which reflected the building's conceptual purity, was unfortunately read by lesser talents as a different kind of simplicity, and eager copyists seized

Skidmore Owings and Merrill extended the structural principles of the John Hancock Center to the extreme in the design of the Sears Tower in Chicago, which was completed two years after the World Trade Center, in 1974, and was for two decades the tallest building in the world until it was superseded by Cesar Pelli's twin Petronas Towers in Kuala Lumpur in 1996. Continuing SOM's involvement in the evolution of the skyscraper type, the

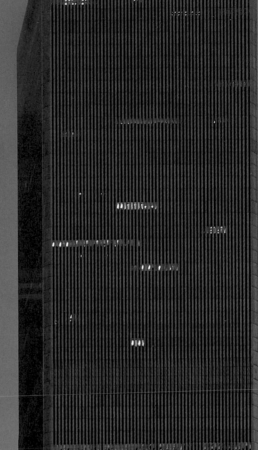

enclosing the corner cores, support eight-storey vieren-
deel beams, which in turn support clear-span office floors.
Thus, not only are there no columns within the offices, but
the vierendeels also enable the gardens — which echo
Yeang's 'sky courts' — to be free of structure as well.

Foster and Yeang's important experiments aside,
Cesar Pelli's Petronas Towers mark the firm establishment
of the megastructure as the final phase of skyscraper
development. The way towards it was paved by a number
of firms, such as Pei Cobb Freed and Partners, Kenzo Tange
Associates, SOM and Murphy Jahn. Their redefinitions of
the new typology have primarily, but not exclusively been
in Asia, echoing the 'many players' predicted earlier by
Martin Jacques.

Since the Hancock Tower, Pei Cobb Freed's most
convincing breakthroughs into the megastructure phase
of skyscraper design have been the First Interstate World
Center in Los Angeles and the Bank of China in Hong Kong,
completed in 1989 and 1990, respectively. Each of these
towers ranks among the top twenty tallest buildings in the
world. The First Interstate Center extends the now familiar base-middle-top division into four distinct parts,
owing to its greater height, the fourth being a feather-like
Art Deco head-dress that is very appropriate for downtown Los Angeles where original examples of this style
still exist. Unlike the Hancock Tower, the First Interstate
tower is plugged in to its surroundings at ground level.
Now that Los Angeles has assumed the title of 'capital' of
the West Coast, a suitably vertical profile of skyscrapers is
considered to be of the utmost importance for the downtown area, which is becoming increasingly prominent as a
cultural and financial focus. Not only is it composed
of powerful corporate interests, but it forms an industrial
base that employs more than 60,000 people and
generates upwards of $12 billion annually.

The First Interstate's plan form is derived from a
matrix of two overlapping and concentric geometries to
produce, in effect, a squared circle. The matrix helps to
organize the site and shape the building to respond to its
specific requirements. The square makes for optimum
usable floor plates and the circle, for an urbane and neigh-
bourly stance. The combination creates a visual richness
and an architectural character intended to distinguish the
tower as a special place both from nearby on the city
streets and from afar at high speed on the freeway. Across
the street, an original Art Deco masterpiece, the Los
Angeles Central Library of 1920, by Bertram Goodhue, has
literally been revived by the First Interstate Center's construction rather than threatened, since the seventy-three
storey 1,018-foot high building was only made
possible when the developer acquired the library's air
rights and transferred them to the tower's site. The money
gained by the city in the process was used to restore the
library to its former glory. The First Interstate represents a
determined attempt to weave the tower into the local
topography, particularly with the Bunker Hill Steps by

19

perceived need for a vertical marker to identify the Messe's location. After a triangular foundation that copes with an awkward site (created by the split in the railway at ground level) the H-shaped tower begins 80 feet above ground level. Purchasing, supply, public relations, social services and other offices related to the Messe are located in the foundation which supports a glass slab block encased in a stone wrapper. To accentuate this impression of layering, Ungers uses red sandstone and green mirror glass, opening up a large square section of the red wrapper to let the slim glass slab block shine through; it pops up out of the top of the tower, like a crystalline piece of toast out of a stone toaster.

The rising stakes of the urban power game in Frankfurt have prompted towers of ever greater height. Kohn Pedersen Fox's fifty-two storey, 650-foot DG Bank Headquarters tower, completed in 1993, is among the most striking of these new arrivals. It occupies a city block along Mainzer Landstrasse, a commercial strip which will eventually accommodate a series of high-rises linking the banking district to the railway station. In addition to accommodating the DG Bank, it provides low-rise rental offices, a wintergarden and fifteen apartments. It is an angular and slightly awkward composition – formed from a number of blocks collaged together – topped with a radiating crown perhaps all too tellingly suggestive of the Statue of Liberty's headgear. It is, unfortunately, an obvious American interloper in this predominantly low-rise city despite its architects' sensitive efforts to weave it seamlessly into its site at ground level.

Assertive on the skyline as it may be, the DG Bank tower is easily beaten in the height stakes by the Messe Turm, completed in 1991, which was one of Frankfurt's first high-rise landmarks. Designed by *Turm Meister* Helmut Jahn, at seventy storeys and 830-feet high it too is a loser to Foster's Commerzbank, but it is nonetheless almost twice as high as the Messe Gate House and provides 660,000 square feet of rentable office space. The desire for a 'real' skyscraper prompted the city authorities to commission Jahn's predictably tripartite design which conceptually is a glass cylinder rising out of a stone wrapper all topped with a pyramidal glass cap. This *parti* is familiar, having also been used by Jahn at 750 Lexington Avenue in New York City in 1989, where the wrapper changes from a rectangle at the base to a pair of polygons bracketing the cylinder in the middle, with a stepped and illuminated nose cone at the top. In Frankfurt, however, the slim profile was determined by German building codes which rule that no employee in an office building should be more than 25 feet from a window to optimize their exposure to natural light and air. Elsewhere in the world, this arrangement is not enforced by law but is encouraged by the high energy costs involved in lighting deep-plan buildings. Jahn faced strong environmental opposition to his Frankfurt tower from a vociferous local Green Party, but for all its apparent lack of subtlety, the tower relates well

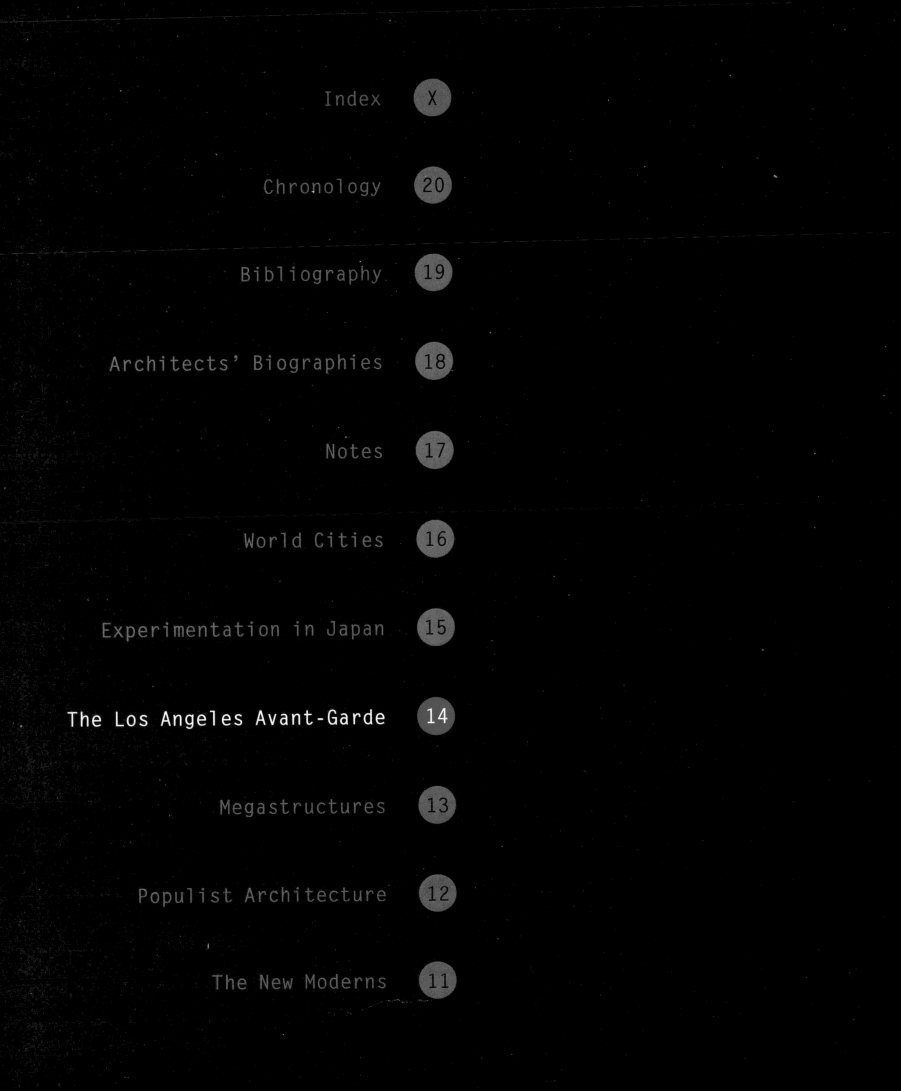

2

Los Angeles is a singular place. There is a growing consensus that, in terms of both its architecture and the way of life that underpins it, it represents the urban typology of the future. A city of complex dangers but almost limitless potential, it might be thought of as an urban metaphor for sex: titillating when viewed voyeuristically from afar, initially exciting and potentially intimidating when experienced, and likely to cause conflicting emotions with the passage of time.

Los Angeles is also distinctive not only for its particular architectural sensibility, but because it is a truly revolutionary civic experiment, without parallel anywhere else in the world. The mere fact that America still attracts millions of people who wish to live there is proof that it is not in decline, and Los Angeles is a premonition of this new nation as it evolves. This is an absolutely new phenomenon. There is no previous example of a civilization simultaneously created by so many races, nationalities and cultures. But whether this revolutionary model will be constructive or destructive has yet to be determined. Los Angeles architecture is singular because it reflects the present, it does not refer to history, of which the Modern Movement itself is now a part. This may be tied to the city's paradigmatic position as the ultimate consumer culture, but it goes beyond that, to a belief in the power of the present; to a trust in the efficacy of *now*.

The subversive tension that polyculturalism and the pressure to read and reread the present have caused, has been picked up by several architects whose work has continued to draw international attention and court controversy. Each of these architects can be seen as seismographic delineators of these underlying currents as they run through the city; and each interprets them in his or her own way. There have been numerous attempts to find a stylistic or a regional continuity in all of this. A group of architects, variously called the Los Angeles or the Santa Monica School, has been detected; and in that school, Frank Gehry is usually identified as the principal figure. Gehry has dominated the architectural scene in Los Angeles since the early 1970s, developing an idiosyncratic personal style which first came together in the design of his own house extension in Santa Monica in 1978, and continued to evolve through many residential designs to larger civic and commercial projects in the mid-1980s. Gehry's early style leaned heavily on a wide range of external influences. His house presents a collage of ordinary materials — chain-link fencing, corrugated iron and plywood shuttering board — which are collaged together after the dada assemblages of Marcel Duchamp. One can also detect the iconoclastic compositions of Kurt Schwitters, and the didactic institutionalization of revolutionary propaganda in the Constructivist movement in Russia in the 1930s. This early style changed markedly, however, when the scale of Gehry's projects, as well as his office, began to increase in the late 1980s.

4

5

In the 1960s, when Gehry was beginning his career, Walter Hopps had begun the Syndell Studio in Brentwood, which was as much a salon as a gallery to show the work of avant-garde artists in Los Angeles. As Hopps recalls: 'It's hard today to make somebody understand what the cultural milieu there was like in the early fifties. People don't remember the degree to which the new art was not shown, was not sold, was not written about, was not taught. Around 1952, the Los Angeles County Museum had to take down a painting by Picasso and one by Magritte because the city council said they were Communist artists'. Much of the new art was found-object assemblage by Wallace Berman, Ed Kienholz and George Herms. Ed Kienholz had his first show at the Syndell Studio, which began to take on the aura of a revolutionary coven in the public eye. In 1956 Kienholz and Hopps opened the Ferus Gallery on La Cienega Boulevard, named after a specimen Hopps had encountered in an anthropology course at UCLA called *Ferus Humanus*, or wild man. 'They were described', Hopps explains, 'as being very hardy, dangerous beings and I thought that was an apt description of the artists I was involved with.' The current art scene in Los Angeles, centred around the LA Louver Gallery in Venice, which frequently shows new work by artists of the calibre of North Hollywood resident David Hockney, is a far cry from this pioneering effort which is, however, put in clearer historical perspective by noting that Hockney did not move to Los Angeles until 1979.

Gehry's identification with the artistic trends in Los Angeles in the late 1960s centred around the Ferus Gallery and artists like Ed Moses and Ed Kienholtz. The ideas generated in the debates in which he participated there were layered over constructivist themes which allowed him to bring his own contemporary transformations into register with these earlier manifestations, and to translate them into architecture. Gehry has always closely identified with artists and has made a determined effort to bridge the gap between art and architecture that elsewhere has widened.

The story of Gehry's stylistic development in Los Angeles can be charted in a number of his most significant buildings there, beginning with his own house extension in Santa Monica which caused a sensation when Gehry first remodelled it, and still produced a critical frisson when he reworked it again in 1994. It has been the subject of extensive critical analysis. Most commentators agree that it is an important event in late-twentieth-century architecture but disagree about its meaning. The house is less daunting to the architect himself who simply sees it as his family's home and a place to experiment on spatial notions; a work in progress. The critic Gavin Macrae-Gibson interprets the shifting planes of the house as indicative of the seismographic paranoia that is a given in LA, and as the tectonic realization of the continental edge where ocean, sky and mountains collide, while Fredric

Jameson has detected a more post-modern agenda in the deliberate selection of cheap, as-found materials. By employing downmarket materials in this way, Jameson claims that Gehry is sending up the social emphasis on commodification, which minimalists reject out of hand. Gehry himself has hinted that his use of exposed wooden studs and cheap materials is a social critique, a commentary on the backward nature of the American construction industry that perpetuates archaic practices, such as the custom-cut stick and nail house building techniques, which are favoured by trade unions because the high levels of time and energy they rely on keep wages high.

Los Angeles is an unheralded battleground in the war against such labour-intensive tactics. The modernizers suffered a setback in the 1960s when the Case Study House programme fizzled out. The programme, initiated by John Entenza, advocated employing industrial materials and methods to bring the United States' construction industry into line with the level of technology prevailing in other sectors. It specifically targeted modularization and pre-fabrication which would have increased precision-building and reduced construction time. However, the initiative failed to generate national support and was instead viewed, at worst, suspiciously, or at best, as a local curiosity, by members of the power base that could have effected change.

In his early, revolutionary phase, which his house prefigured, until his success in the Disney Concert Hall Competition in 1989, Gehry may be characterized as a skirmisher attempting to instigate a new battle over the same issue. By mockingly glorifying archaic construction methods, he paradoxically shows his admiration for their materiality and handicraft while also literally exposing the incredible inefficiency involved in them.

Given his artistic affiliations, it is not surprising that Gehry has had several clients in Venice, a beach community of Los Angeles which historically has attracted artists because of its Bohemian atmosphere. Gehry's Spiller House, 1980, continues the dialogue begun in his own house. It is a two-part residence, with a forward, tower-like segment for its artist owner and a rental unit at the rear of a rectangular lot, separated by an open central courtyard. The Spiller House, clad in corrugated, galvanized metal sheet, is visually anonymous because of its ugly-duckling wrapper, and fits seamlessly into the semi-industrial texture of that part of town. The Norton House, 1984, located further south along the coast, uses a similar two-part formula. The owner in this instance mentioned his nostalgia for his youthful days as a lifeguard, and Gehry responded with an abstraction of a lifeguard tower perched high above the beach just a few feet away. In contrast to the Spiller house, the wrapper here is more colourful, tiles in tints of buff, green and blue answering to sea, sun and sand, as well as the parade of people that march past on summer weekends.

Much has been made of Gehry's iconoclastic skill in this phase of his career, using unlikely juxtapositions,

6

7 FRANK GEHRY,
California
Aerospace Museum,
Exposition Park,
Los Angeles, 1982

eccentric compositions and materials not normally used in the way, or for the purposes, he chooses. Much less has been said about his abilities as topographic interpreter, concerned with the literal definition of *topos* as the nature of place, and the way that these sensitive interpretations can conversely be utilized to understand various aspects of the complex city he first chose to examine. If his own house and the Spiller and Norton houses show the remarkable range available in the city, from cataclysmically unstable but arguably diverse geology, through post-industrial peripheral grime, to festive beach-side confection, the Schnabel House, 1990, which is Gehry's best residential design in Los Angeles, resonates with the craving for fantasy that pervades the city. As the final realization of an idea that Gehry has evolved through several, less eloquent iterations, the Schnabel House is a self-contained compound, an abstracted community, here metaphorically based on a New England village, with a few Los Angeles landmarks and a Finnish lake thrown in for good measure. The landmarks are Frank Lloyd Wright's Barnsdall House, and the Griffith Observatory; the former contributing its Wrightian grid and olive groves, the latter its easily identifiable dome. These respectively guide, and are grafted into, a generative 'village square', complete with 'church', 'factory' and 'port', the latter containing a 'ship' in full sail.

Gehry continued this hyper-serious playfulness in the public realm in the design of the California Aerospace Museum, 1982. Prompted by the prospect of the Summer Olympics, which were to be held in Exposition Park in 1984, the Aerospace Museum was commissioned to serve as an extension of the California Museum of Science and Industry. The concentration of aerospace industries in Southern California was seen as a good reason for locating such a museum in Los Angeles. Its large-scale sculptural forms, as well as the soaring interiors that Gehry has produced, provide a dramatic backdrop for the exhibits, with high seriousness leavened by wit, through a series of colliding volumes that manage to be contextual without seeming to be institutional. The overall effect is one of visual disjunction. The museum was intended to contribute to the evolving definition and enclosure of Exposition Park and to the community of museums that is growing there.

However, Gehry made what would prove to be a negative strategic decision to orientate his hall towards a central pedestrian spine which would link it with the strand of existing exhibition spaces in order to focus social interaction along the museum's entry route. The move was consistent with his reading of Los Angeles as an inhospitable urban wasteland that makes it necessary to 'circle the wagons' in protection against the city's constant dangers; but the consequence of denying the real city just outside the invisible perimeter of Exposition Park, in an attempt to fabricate an imitation one within, was to leave the way open for an interloper, willing to risk a broader civic reading, who might intervene along the boundary. Just such an eventuality was to transpire. An

8 FRANK GEHRY,
Chiat Day
Headquarters,
Venice, 1989

9 FRANK GEHRY,
'Fred and Ginger'
Building, Prague,
1995

earthquake which destabilized the brick pre-First World War Armory next to the Aerospace Museum made it necessary to close off the main entrance to Gehry's hall, short-circuiting the internal visual concept and main circulation system which had both been predicated upon it. The possibility of the removal of the Armory made it even more feasible for a building to occupy the corner of the site at the intersection of Exposition Boulevard and Figueroa Avenue, and a competition for a new United District High School held in 1992 to stretch from the corner to the Aerospace Museum was won by Morphosis, another high-profile Los Angeles firm. So, whether the Armory is removed or not, the internal workings of the Aerospace Museum have been seriously compromised. In spite of this, the museum represents an important marker in Gehry's move away from smaller projects; it was the largest building he had designed up to that point and is a treasure trove of spatial dynamics, signs and symbols of the architect's fragmented, collage-like technique.

Gehry's Edgemar Complex in Santa Monica, 1987, and his Chiat Day Headquarters along Main Street in nearby Venice, 1989, continue these themes of disjointed juxtaposition. At the same time they make a declaration of a territorial imperative and phantasmagorical allusion, since Edgemar and Chiat Day are basically a habitable sculpture and movie set, respectively. The cruciform light monitors that unmistakably establish constructivist connections on the Aerospace Museum roof convert to enlarged, distorted cages as the roofscape of Edgemar, reminders of the agitprop assemblages, propaganda art and stage sets of pre-Revolutionary Russia.

In contrast, the Chiat Day Headquarters, built for an international advertising company, is a collaboration between Gehry and the artists Claes Oldenburg and Coosje van Bruggen, who provided the giant binoculars which dominate the facade. Gehry wanted to prove that such a collaboration could work. However, Claes Oldenburg's binoculars have tended to inhibit commentary on the 'boat' and 'trees' that flank them on the left and right respectively, which have far more substantial connections to the city. With its curved outline, white metallic skin and Corbusian pipe railings, the staff offices have a yacht-like appearance reminiscent of both the glory days of Hollywood and the LA beach community, with harbours such as Marina del Rey nearby. The branch-like forms of the executive offices, on the other hand, evoke the forests that once grew here, running up to the sea. As in many of Gehry's public, commercial or institutional buildings, this capricious mask conceals an ultra-pragmatic interior. The architect started his practice by working with commercial developers and gained a reputation as a nuts-and-bolts professional who brought jobs in on time and on budget and provided efficient floor plans that worked. The basis of this reputation is evident in the Chiat Day office floors, which foster creativity and spontaneity through ergonomic layouts

rather than the free-form internal landscapes designed by some other members of the LA School.

The Disney Concert Hall has been another benchmark for Gehry in several ways, marking the beginning of a new phase in his career. Generated out of a competition to find a new home for the Los Angeles Philharmonic Orchestra, Gehry's design for the hall began as an intimate space in the round, based on Hans Scharoun's Berlin Philharmonie. Gehry intended it to be an urban building that would extend the music centre out into California Plaza, making it accessible, rather than placing it on a podium in the manner of the existing Dorothy Chandler concert pavilion. As its chief patrons, the Disney family wanted the hall to reflect Walt Disney's love of people, and Walt's wife, Lillian Disney, responded positively to the idea of an extraordinary object placed in a garden, open to all. However, a new acoustician whom Gehry consulted after he won the competition, recommended a change to a 'shoe box' configuration which was shown in computer simulation to produce the most uniform sound patterns within the hall. This profile produced a narrower, much more conventional 'room', and Gehry sought to mitigate this more rigid, fixed 'box' by wrapping the exterior of the building in undulating forms to soften its profile, and by putting the seating in what he called a 'boat' inside the hall, a gentle conceit to free his imagination from the constraints forced on him by the discipline of acoustics. Reflexively, the 'boat' began to inform the outside shell, which became its 'waves', and as the programme clarified, the box was rotated through ninety degrees to take advantage of a better aspect from the intersection of First Street and Grand Avenue. Parts of the box that could be removed without compromising acoustic performance were stripped away in order to open up the interior to the street.

At the height of Gehry's design activity the project team numbered countless people, but accurately documenting his quickly changing, fluid forms eluded them. They could not accurately transfer Gehry's study models, of large bits of cardboard and paper pasted onto a real shoebox base, on to paper. They tried using a primitive projection method, unchanged since the Renaissance, in which weights tied to pieces of string were suspended from different points along the outward curve of each sheet of paper, with the actual shoe box replaced with a glass substitute to help improve the sighting of coordinates. They were constantly disappointed, however, by the incongruities between the modelled and graphic versions, in spite of their efforts. In their frustration, and facing an impending presentation of the design at the Venice Biennale, they turned to a more technological solution using a computer program developed for the aerospace industry. The methodology of this system relies on a mechanical-arm probe which traces coordinates on the model's smooth surfaces and conic shapes and transfers them to a wire-frame computer model. Using this system, the team members were able to digitize and rationalize the

9

randomness of the cardboard models. They went further still and created a full-scale mock-up of the building's external wall, which is clad in Italian limestone, to prove its constructability and show its remarkable fluidity.

The repercussions of this technological transfer continue. The decision to clad the building in limestone, rather than the counter-culture heavy metal palette of corrugated chain link and galvanized metal sheet found on Gehry's earlier smaller projects, led to detailing, documentation and fabrication problems, in spite of initial optimism about the possibility of developing a computer program that would guide the stonecutters' sawblades. Similar efficiencies, in textile design and weaving, in which artists' designs on disc instruct the looms, had not yet been perfected in such detail, and at this scale in stone. Construction estimates began to rise alarmingly, making it look as if Los Angeles might end up with its own 'Sydney Opera House', with all the financial over-runs and time delays that that implies.

In the meantime, the computer-probe technology has been enthusiastically adopted to develop other projects in the Gehry office, which now has the appearance of an automobile assembly line rather than a large draughting room. After each initial sketch or rough model is produced, a design production team is assigned to a project, working on it primarily in large model form in a long narrow hall in which the computers and their probes are located. An obvious irony in this change is that Gehry, who has become as closely identified with Los Angeles as the automobile culture which created it, is finally producing buildings in the same way that designers produce cars. The paradox of technology prevails here too; the technology that was initially adapted to assist in the production process now guides it and the designs have altered to fit the technology. The trade-off caused by the paradox has been a discernable change in style. Suspending value-judgements on whether or not it is for the best, it is unquestionably different, yielding more homogeneous results such as the Guggenheim Museum in Bilbao, 1997, or the notorious 'Fred and Ginger' building in Prague, 1995.

The rancorous controversy caused by the Disney débâcle, with fingers pointed in all directions, but no blame firmly fixed, as well as a growing listing of impressive international commissions have prompted Gehry, in print, to suggest that he may leave Los Angeles, leaving the school, if it even existed at all, without a leader.

The untimely tragic death, in 1996, of Franklin D Israel, who was an acknowledged Gehry follower, has been another blow to the possibility of a united philosophical or stylistic front in the city. Israel brought a refined sensibility to Gehry's selection of rough materials, overlayed with a stagecrafter's eye. He had apprenticed as a Hollywood set designer, which is somehow appropriate for an architect hoping to make a visual impact in a city that is seduced by superficial images and is predicated on packaging them for global consumption. Israel's Art

11, 12 **Franklin D Israel**, Art Pavilion, Beverly Hills, 1991

13 **Franklin D Israel**, Drager House, Berkeley, 1995

14 (Overleaf) **Eric Owen Moss**, Paramount-Lindblade-Gary Group Complex, Culver City, 1987-90

11

12

Pavilion in Beverly Hills, 1991, is an adjunct to a private house belonging to an avid art collector. Designed to contain a gallery for the client's large art collection, this pavilion also contains two floors of studio space. The 8-acre site on which it is located slopes down to a stream and a dense eucalyptus grove, which the architect has made into a terraced sculpture garden. The pavilion has been conceived as a piece of art in this garden, rising up like a great Ark containing a precious cargo of Abstract Expressionist paintings. Grand stairways and an outdoor loggia, as well as large corner windows, establish a direct connection with the site. It demonstrates Israel's skill as an assimilator of regional influences and themes, as do a series of private homes that also reverberate with historical references to the distinguished history of early Modernism in California, particularly the work of the architects Rudolf Schindler and Richard Neutra. The Drager House in Berkeley, 1995, which was one of Israel's final projects, is a carefully controlled exercise in formal experiment and historical reference that is typical in his work; it is highly individual and identifiable with countless subtle connections to a wider regional dialogue.

Another member of this school, Eric Owen Moss, adamantly denies the existence of any such affiliation, characterizing this apparent fallacy as the 'Snow White and Seven Dwarfs' theory of Los Angeles architecture. His long established collaboration with the developer Frederick Smith in Culver City has allowed him the freedom to explore many ideas and get them built as long as he is able to negotiate the fine line between architectural outrageousness and solid commercial return. This collaboration began in the mid-1980s, almost ten years after Moss arrived in Los Angeles from the East Coast. After renting studio space in a building belonging to Smith where Moss' Paramount-Lindblade-Gary Group Complex now stands, Moss and Smith struck up a friendship based on long discussions about art, literature and philosophy which revealed many similar beliefs and tastes. Smith had inherited large tracts of land in this area west of the Los Angeles County line, which was once a motion picture production centre. Largely due to the publicity surrounding the buildings that have resulted from the Moss–Smith collaboration, several corporations such as MGM and Sony have been confident enough to return to Culver City, although efficient city administration and relatively low land values have also contributed to the local renaissance. Moss' Paramount-Lindblade-Gary Group Complex, 1987–90, set the pattern for later developments: generic steel-stud dry wall and plaster offices, interspersed with the occasional light well, courtyard or internal sculptural feature, are laid out behind an attention-grabbing wrapper that helps attract business as well as announce artistic individuality. There are intriguing parallels, and contrasts, between this cumulative complex and the Piazza della Signoria in Florence, even though such a comparison may initially seem to be somewhat

13

29 KATE DIAMOND,
Control Tower,
Los Angeles
International
Airport, 1993

30 CRAIG HODGETTS
AND MING FUNG,
Temporary Powell
Library, UCLA,
1992

The transfer of large-scale immigration to Los Angeles from New York — with its Statue of Liberty standing as an inspiring symbol of freedom for the tired, poor and huddled masses that passed her in steerage on their way to Ellis Island — is best represented in architectural terms by the West Coast Gateway, an unrealized project designed by Studio Asymptote in 1988. Combining most of the key elements of the Los Angeles car culture, the gateway was designed to span one of the largest intersections of the freeway system. Its upper pedestrian bridge led to shops and cafes faced with a huge electronic billboard intended to send out feel-good messages to the automobile-armoured throngs racing underneath. The freeway is arguably the most public space in a city with eight centres, since it is shared by people from all of them. Surveys show that Los Angeles drivers spend more time commuting than people in any other American city, and since the freeway system has not been substantially upgraded to accommodate the new masses using it, tailbacks are bound to increase. A popular radio station recently announced a contest, offering a prize for the 'most outrageous thing' that anyone had seen while driving on the freeway, expecting mainly sexual incidents. While those were well represented, there were also many stories of people doing things normally associated with the privacy of home, such as a woman waxing her armpits while at the wheel. The point is, of course, that the freeway *is* a home away from home for many Angelenos. Homeless immigrants from other countries and other states sometimes resort to living in their cars when they first arrive, but after finding housing, continue to live in their car whilst driving on the freeway for two or three hours a day. The West Coast Gateway was one of the first realizations of the opportunities that this captive audience represents. Contrary to the wishes of most planners and architects, suburban flight, which began in earnest after the Second World War, has not diminished. Rather, it has accelerated, now becoming 'exurban flight' as the information age settles down in earnest. Urban planners Peter Gordon and Harry Richardson at the University of Southern California, report relatively *faster* commutes outside the urban area in spite of an increase in trip length, indicating that living further out of Los Angeles County may be more time-efficient than living in the inner ring.

The growing architectural diversity in Los Angeles, which continues in spite of the fact that architects contribute very little to the built environment there in relative terms, is also evident on the fringes of the avant-garde, inhabited by those architects who have not yet enrolled in, or who are ineligible for admission to, the Los Angeles School. The Temporary Powell Library, 1992, on the UCLA Campus was intended as an inexpensive, stop-gap measure for relocating library books and services while the permanent Powell Library was undergoing post-earthquake repairs. The tensile steel and fabric structure has proven to be so popular, however, that it has now become a

30

Contemporary Japanese architecture is typically regarded by Western critics as either an indecipherable anomaly in the world scene or a skilled refinement of International Modernism, with little intrinsic reference to Japan's local or traditional culture. Only recently has a consensus begun to emerge on the singular importance of Japanese architecture, and penetrating analysis has begun to reveal a surprising reliance on rapidly vanishing national traditions. To begin to place the current architectural activity in Japan in context, it is important to stress several critical factors which have contributed to the evolution of a unique Japanese style.

The first of these is the country's size. Japan covers an area of approximately 140 thousand square miles, making it roughly the same size as the state of California. This landmass is distributed across five islands, each dominated by mountain ranges which limit the amount of land that can be comfortably inhabited or cultivated to only a third of the total geographic area. This means that land is a scarce commodity, and helps to explain why Shinto, a religion which originated in Japan, is based on the sacredness of nature and land. Another formative factor is climate. Japan has a climatic range that varies quite noticeably from the northern-most island in the archipelago to the southern-most, and four distinct seasons that are generally characterized by extremely cold winters with snow, hot humid summers and frequent, heavy rains. Added to this is a third element: Japan's long history of cultural isolation, which has led to a highly developed island mentality and a keen sense of ethnic identity. That isolation has slowly been broken, beginning with the introduction of Buddhism from India, through China, in the sixth century, and continuing with the opening up of trading ports by Admiral Perry in the eighteenth century; but the most significant influence, by far, was the country's traumatic occupation by American forces which followed the Japanese surrender that ended the war in the Pacific in 1945. This social upheaval affected every aspect of Japanese society, having particular impact on its religious, political and industrial traditions. Reliance on the rule of the emperor was replaced by the imposition of a democratic model, and a predominantly agrarian country was rapidly converted to an urbanized, industrialized society; its traditional relationship to nature was radically and abruptly disrupted in the process.

Kenzo Tange is possibly the best known of what might be called the first generation of Japanese architects whose careers grew along with this spectacular development. He continued a connection with Bauhaus design principles and the influence of Le Corbusier that began in Japan before the Second World War and, indeed, is evident as early as the beginning of the 1920s. By reinforcing and expanding on this previously established link, Tange projected an image of the Japanese architect as one dependent on modern Western forms, which has remained intact ever since. While he is recognized

2

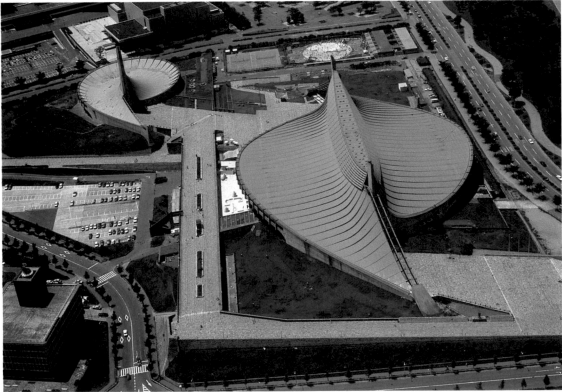

3

primarily for his gymnasium complex for the 1964 Tokyo Olympic Games, earlier buildings, such as his Peace Memorial and Museum in Hiroshima, 1949–55, and St Mary's Cathedral, Tokyo, 1961–4, show marked relationships to European paradigms, and can be seen as a frank imitation of the modernist style. His gymnasium complex, however, opened up that dialogue in a more metaphorical direction. Some critics have detected intentional historical references, such as the profile of a Samurai helmet in the building's sleekly curved, sweeping metal roof. Others, with a more structurally disciplined eye, find only a logical form derived from the engineering solution of cables suspended from towering masts to achieve the clear span that Tange had chosen. The creative energy and planning skill evident in this Olympic complex, however, were not generally sustained in his later work.

The Yokohama Museum of Art, 1983–9, located near the waterfront in Yokohama's Minato Mirai 21 district, broke the pattern of rather predictable production that had come out of the super-corporate Tange office since the late 1970s. A linear scheme that extends from Yokohama Station to Sakuragi-cho Station, it is a bare-knuckled urbanistic project with a symmetrical, Beaux-Arts *parti*, that glorifies in rejecting its harsh surroundings by providing a serene interior alternative to them. Reminiscent in some ways of a similar achievement by Gae Aulenti at the Musée d'Orsay in Paris, 1986, which is a skilled remodelling of a historic station, this is a brand new attempt at providing a public meeting place in the centre of Yokohama. The heart of the scheme is the grand gallery, a two-storey high, sky-lit spine that links all the galleries that are attached to it, both permanent and temporary. Monumental stairs at each end, flanked by escalators, provide a dignified connection between the levels as well as platforms for sculpture. An observation gallery is located at the top of a drum-like administrative tower overlooking Yokohama harbour. Tange's creative vision and power which inspired, and served as a model for, an entire generation of architects that followed him is evident once again in this project, in spite of his superficial stylistic references which may quickly be considered *passé*.

Fumihiko Maki, born in 1928, is one of the first of this next generation of architects. Educated at Harvard and tutored by Walter Gropius, he was exposed to Bauhaus doctrine from the source itself and this early influence has been consistently evident throughout his long career. Over time, however, there has been in his work a discernible interjection of traditional Japanese references alongside his typically spare modernist aesthetic. Rather harshly, perhaps, the architect and theorist Kisho Kurokawa has summarized Maki's work as: 'finely tuned craftsmanship applied to the simple spaces of modern architecture', adding that, 'he does not clearly advocate any direction for the new age, nor does he succeed in bringing a new meaning to space', only in using, 'technology as decoration, producing romanticism akin to expressionism. Maki was

1 (Previous page)
SHIN TAKAMATSU,
Kirin Plaza
Building, Osaka,
1987

2 KENZO TANGE,
Yokohama Museum
of Art, 1983–9

3 KENZO TANGE,
National
Gymnasium for
Tokyo Olympic
Games, Tokyo,
1964

4 KENZO TANGE,
Peace Memorial
and Museum,
Hiroshima,
1949–55

4

5 KENZO TANGE,
St Mary's
Cathedral,
Tokyo, 1961–4

educated in a system aimed at producing Western intellectuals. His credo is one of conscience, moderation and rationality; he is not a confrontational architect.'

Notwithstanding such summary judgement, Maki continues to surprise and delight an appreciative international following with work that is consistently accomplished and fresh and increasingly indicative of key issues in contemporary Japanese architecture. Two of his largest projects, the Makuhari Messe Exhibition Centre, 1986–9, and the Spiral Building, 1985, both in Tokyo, are good illustrations of his thoughtful interpretation of both Eastern and Western models.

The Makuhari Messe was the winning scheme in a national competition held among seven invited firms in August 1986. This immense complex, totalling approximately a million square feet, was designed in one year and constructed in two. The building is located on flat reclaimed land facing Tokyo Bay in Chiba Prefecture, a strategic location halfway between Tokyo International Airport and the city centre. It is the focus for a newly emergent business and residential centre called Makuhari New Town. The building extends into bridges that connect to a hotel to the east, parking to the west, office buildings to the north, and a seaside park to the south. This complex was the first of its kind in Japan, a comprehensive convention centre with exhibition hall, event hall, and international conference centre, housed in independent buildings. The exhibition hall has eight large identical bays located under a single sweeping arched roof. This space can either be arranged as eight independent halls, or used in its entirety. A linear mall on the building's upper level physically connects the individual halls where visitors may enjoy views down on to exhibits and events through glass screens before descending to the floor of the hall. To control natural light, the walls of the exhibition halls are solid, finished in white panels of glass wool board and there are only a limited number of strategically-placed openings along the perimeter. The exterior is finished in glass panels, through which one can see the white panels behind; these tend to reflect the sky giving the building an added impression of lightness. The large roof has been sheathed in stainless steel sheets, creating an image reminiscent of Tange's Olympic complex, but rendered as an updated and more intentionally metaphorical exercise.

The event hall can seat nine thousand people. It accommodates sporting events and is equipped with electronic and theatrical devices capable of serving a wide range of events and activities. When the Makuhari Messe hosts a large convention, the event hall can also provide space as an additional exhibition hall. The curvilinear roof of the distended form of the hall is again finished in stainless-steel sheets that form a smooth continuous envelope. The international conference centre at the northeast corner of the site has an independent entrance and porte-cochere. Within, are the banqueting hall to seat two thousand, an international conference room, meeting

rooms, a restaurant, and the administrative offices for the entire complex. The banqueting hall, event hall and international conference centre have all been placed in the foreground of the giant arch of the exhibition hall. Metaphorically, the exhibition hall abstracts the image of a natural Japanese landscape of hills and mountains, while the silhouette formed by the juxtaposition of these natural and geometric elements creates an abstracted image of the city. The three buildings form an informal plaza at the centre of the site which in turn contains steps, ramps and escalators leading to the entrance of the exhibition and event halls.

In order to minimize on-site labour, construction time and the use of industrial processes of systemizing and prefabricating materials, Maki employed industrialized components extensively. However, all the details that assemble these elements were designed specifically for the project. This combination of pre-fabricated products with site-intensive and hand-crafted pieces gives the Makuhari Messe a distinctive quality of its own.

The Spiral Building, one of Maki's best works, was designed to accommodate the cultural programme of the Wacoal Corporation. The ground floor, including the entrance lobby, is used for temporary exhibitions. It is a semi-cylindrical multi-storey atrium flooded by natural light from a clerestory at the rear of the building. A ramp following the curving atrium wall leads up to craft shops, while a monumental stair opens up on to an esplanade positioned to provide a view back over Hoyama Boulevard. This viewing gallery continues up on to the second floor, which also acts as a foyer for a three-hundred-seat theatre. There are video studios on the fourth floor, and a restaurant and terraced garden on the fifth. From this floor upwards there are private entertainment spaces and clubs, as well as a two-storey hall which Maki refers to as 'The Acropolis', which is used for larger private parties. There are few buildings as descriptive of the seemingly chaotic condition of Tokyo as Maki's Spiral, which can be read both as an anagram of the functions behind each of the monumental geometric forms on its street elevation, and as a commentary on the necessity of accepting a growing emphasis on the protected interior environment as an essential part of life in this urban chaos. The abstract signals of a conical hat over the fashion gallery, or piano-like curves in front of a bar, are obvious at a simple level once the building is understood either in plan or actuality, but its function as a protected enclave, or 'city within a city', is less apparent. Japanese apologists, such as Kisho Kurokawa, or Yoshinobu Ashihara in *The Hidden Order: Tokyo Through the Twentieth Century*, insist that there is actually a system of method behind the visible urban madness of Tokyo, while Maki seems to be saying, in this instance, that finding any such system is pointless and that only new, well-planned architecture can remedy matters.

The Kirishima International Concert Hall, 1994, represents a departure from a growing concentration on

6 FUMIHIKO MAKI,
Makuhari Messe
Exhibition
Centre, Tokyo,
1986–9

7 FUMIHIKO MAKI,
Spiral Building,
Tokyo, 1985

7

urban interaction that preoccupied Maki during the decade from the mid-1980s to the mid-1990s. It is prefigured by what he has termed his 'cloud' buildings, such as the Fujisawa Municipal Gymnasium in Tokyo, 1990, which are so called because of their distinctive billowing roofs; the concert hall also has a distinctive silhouette but obviously differs from these earlier models by virtue of its isolated mountainous setting. The ship metaphor that Maki has chosen offers tempting comparisons with the ongoing modernist fascination with the 'ark', or the image of the 'machine in the garden': Le Corbusier's Villa Savoye and Richard Meier's Atheneum in New Harmony immediately come to mind. Like these buildings, Maki's boat is also hermetically separated from its beautiful natural surroundings, the extended visual connections established by means of a carefully planned circulation path being the only links allowed. The metaphor of the building as an ark containing a precious cargo of culture is particularly

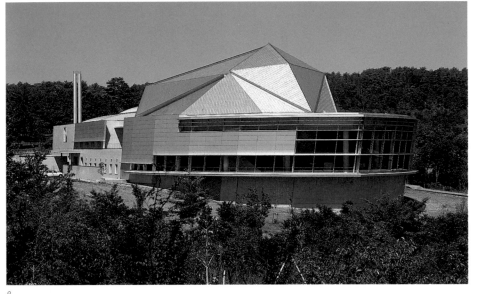

8

9

tempting here, since the active volcano of Sakurajima is visible in the Kirishima mountains nearby and represents nature in the raw. Maki personally disclaims such connections, however, admitting only to an attempt to find a form that would work in such an open landscape. The axiom that programmatic or topographical limits can actually help a good architect to produce a good design is proven here; Maki's Spiral emerged from a similar processional *parti*, and yet is far more powerful than this single, lonely ship adrift, like the *Marie Celeste*, in its sea of grass.

The question of a hidden order in Japanese city planning and architecture has even been attributed by some critics to the parallels in such fundamentals as language, in which there exists an 'a-coherence' or lack of importance given to syntax and grammatical rules. Given this premise, one might begin to understand the difference between urban landscapes such as those of Tokyo, where the new is juxtaposed with the old, and those of the West, where new and old cannot be conceived without a

10

compromise of formal harmony between them. Kisho Kurokawa has refined this concept of a hidden order into one of a hidden tradition very much apparent to a long-time resident of Tokyo but not visible to outsiders. He firmly believes that: 'the Japanese tradition is alive in Tokyo, in the lifestyle of its inhabitants, in their keen emotional sensitivity to natural changes, in their sense of order ... The Japanese are perfectly willing to incorporate new cultural elements, new technology, new forms and the symbols of modern cultures if they are certain they will be able to preserve their invisible tradition.'

While he is unable to say exactly how such invisible traditions are preserved in new technologies and foreign architectural styles, Kurokawa's work may itself provide an important clue. Metabolism, a movement he claims to have personally initiated in the 1960s, was the first architectural initiative to give Modernism a distinctly Japanese dimension by connecting it to the national passion for nature and the inevitability of perpetual or cyclical change that it represents; it also makes reference to the Buddhist belief in impermanence and reincarnation. In this cycle, which Kurokawa now calls 'symbiosis', he emphasizes life rather than death, calling the twenty-first century 'The Age of Life' in expectation of the greater appreciation of all living things that he sees as the consequence of an increasing environmental awareness among all sections of the population as the world moves towards a new millennium. There are also the more obvious continuities of respect for the innate qualities of materials, either natural or artificial, and attention to detail that have always characterized the best Japanese architecture.[1]

These themes are constantly evident in Kurokawa's work. The Museum of Contemporary Art in Hiroshima, 1988, for example, links participants and nature at every opportunity, and the galleries are organized like a small village spiralling out from a central plaza. This approach ensures that the museum remains in scale with the trees around it, and never becomes monumental. His City Art Museum in Nagoya, built in 1988, again demonstrates this evident sensitivity to the site, being partially buried to reduce the scale while still providing all the functions required in its extensive programme. Located in the middle of Shira Kawa Park, the museum is a hub of activity, and visitors are led inside from an open, transitional plaza along an undulating glass wall representing the symbiosis between nature and technology that Kurokawa believes can be achieved. It is dangerous to assume, however, that Kurokawa is entirely consistent in this regard. His Hotel Kyocera in Kagoshima, 1993–5, is a thirteen-storey elliptical monolith sited in view of the Kirishima Mountains and Kinko Bay; it dominates the landscape in an emphatic way, forming a highly visible landmark in this semi-industrialized landscape. At its centre is a spectacular atrium, extending the full height of the building. The hotel rooms surround this space giving

11

12

19 ᴀʀᴀᴛᴀ Iꜱᴏᴢᴀᴋɪ,
Nara Convention
Centre, 1992-5

20 ᴀʀᴀᴛᴀ Iꜱᴏᴢᴀᴋɪ,
Art Tower, Mito
Cultural Complex,
1990

19

phenomenology in very controlled hands. Rather than deferring to Western traditions, as it superficially seems to do, Tsukuba skilfully condemns them all as being as moribund, as the centre of this new town was also doomed to be. With the new high-speed bullet trains making the entire urban decentralization effort futile, Isozaki knew that Tokyo could not be successfully depopulated; satellite cities in Japan were doomed to suffer the same fate they have in many other countries and his sunken, empty and eroding version of the Campidoglio piazza is intended to send that message. 'My aim', he has explained, 'was to dismantle apparently integrated architectural styles and to fragment them so that at the moment they seem to be in ruins a schizophrenic state of suspension is created. The fragments lose their birthplaces.'

Isozaki's Cultural Complex in Mito, designed around a plaza, indicates a change of heart, however, perhaps because Mito had already been established for a century at the time of the building's completion in 1990. Unlike Tsukuba, the Mito Complex showcases Isozaki's return to a very personal formal curiosity, and its stunning Art Tower, appearing like a tortured campanile in this civic ensemble, is one of the most surprising and delightful geometric compositions that the architect has produced. Twisting upwards, the 100-metre-high tower looks like a three-dimensional metallic strip of celluloid, celebrating the theatre and concert hall grouped below it along the western edge of the plaza.

Isozaki's Nara Convention Centre, 1992–5, has once again reaffirmed his unparalleled ability to make an unexpected grand gesture, to follow the dictates of his own aesthetic rather than those promoted by others. By placing many of the same functions, such as theatres and a concert hall, inside a huge elliptical shell which serves as both roof and walls, Isozaki has returned to the pattern of function fitted within a form that he began with in the early 1970s, but at a far larger scale and to even greater effect. The technical difficulties involved in this decision were staggering, but it is very logical, considering the location. Because of its difficult position alongside several major highways in Nara, the hyperscale of the shell, appearing like some overturned mammoth ocean liner, commands attention in a way that a series of volumes of the kind used at Mito would not.

In a lecture delivered at the Royal Academy in London, 1995, Isozaki spoke poignantly about the beauty and venerability of Japanese culture as well as its mystique, especially among Western architects, who typically conclude that it is inscrutable to all except the Japanese themselves. Reversing Kurokawa's argument, which supports this theory in favour of the invisible tradition, Isozaki concluded that such sensibilities are being destroyed at the same rate that historical architecture itself is being dismantled, with the consequence that: 'The real essence of tradition in Japan is as distant from me as it is from you'. Rather than claiming privileged ethnic

21

22

knowledge of his own cultural past, Isozaki effectively said that the mass assimilation of Western values and commodities from television sets, computers and automobiles, to architecture, has destroyed his culture, even though all of these commodities have been combined into something that the rest of the world can identify as being uniquely Japanese.

Isozaki had characterized his own professional growth as a series of crises occurring almost concurrently with the start of each decade since 1960, when he worked for Kenzo Tange, through to 1970 when, 'ridding myself of a Modernism that pervaded my whole being was difficult since it was a tautological paradox to attempt to employ the modernist vocabulary, the only one I knew, in dismembering it'. Having decided that the device of Platonic solids as a classical compositional principle would be the basis of his new vocabulary, 'the mega-vocabulary of Architecture with a capital A!', as he calls it, Isozaki began the last decade of the century with an emphasis on what he has called 'wit'. After the irony expressed in the Tsukuba Civic Centre, which can be seen as symbolic of his attitude at the beginning of the 1980s, Isozaki's new reliance on wit and humour represents a lightening of touch. He explains: 'A sense of humour evokes what has vanished, paradox can be used to make what is invisible, visible. Not cynically, not desperately, but by dreaming of architecture as a pleasure machine.' Now in the most assured and least angst-ridden stage of his career, Isozaki is at the top of his form, producing memorable architecture unlike any other in Japan, or anywhere else in the world, for that matter.

Kisho Kurokawa and Arata Isozaki are perhaps the most prominent Japanese architects internationally. Yet their generation, born during the 1940s, also includes Minoru Takeyama, Hiroshi Hara, Kazuo Shinohara, Yoshio Taniguchi and Kan Izue. There has been little consistency among these architects who have had the advantage of developing their practices in parallel with a national economy that was also growing at a phenomenal rate. Minoru Takeyama went through a post-modern phase that roughly coincided with Isozaki's, before focusing primarily on commercial work. Hiroshi Hara, a professor at Tokyo University, has been extensively involved in research into Mediterranean vernacular architecture, finding basic elements in it that can be studied independently, then recombined. This has led him to transfer the idea of disassembly and reassembly to Japanese architecture, as related to the structural, three-part division of raised platform, framed centre and roof in the traditional Japanese house and temple. His Ida City Museum, 1988, in Nagano, dedicated to the paintings of the artist Shunso Hishida, stresses this idea, and while the historical connection is not clear at first sight, it becomes so when the architect's research interest and intentions are understood.

Hara's Yamato International Building in Tokyo, 1987, reveals the complex agenda evident in his work that nonetheless establishes it as an integral part of a wider Japanese national consciousness about nature, tradition and the incremental loss of both. Located in a warehouse district and facing a park, this headquarters for a textile company occupies a site that called for an overt metaphor for this gradual erosion of nature and tradition, and Hara provides it. He refers to five main ideas behind the linear complex: twelve vertical 'strata' symbolizing a city; an aluminium skin to literally reflect the environment; disjunction to ensure a non-uniform office landscape inside; uncertainty amplified by changes in materials; and circulation used like a path through nature. The result of such a heavily laden philosophical brief is surprisingly ordered and eloquent, clearly sending the message of urbanity encroaching on nature that the architect intends.

In the Umeda Sky Building in Shin Umeda City, Osaka, 1993, Hara updates this premise dramatically. Located near Osaka Station, the building comprises a pair of towers containing offices and a hotel which support a garden in the sky – an example of nature literally disconnected from the city far below. A connecting bridge allows escape from one tower to the other in case of retaliation by nature in the form of an earthquake and a slick curtain wall mirrors the sky, making the garden seem to levitate.

Like Hara, Kazuo Shinohara recognizes that Tokyo represents the antithesis of the Western urban model and seeks to combat the progressive anarchy he sees around him with an architectural *deus ex machina* that will effectively end the play. His Centennial Hall, Tokyo Institute of Technology, 1987, is just such a machine. It appears as a metallic cylinder, shining in the air and floating from place to place, a construct of pure and simple geometric forms, a metallic foil against the trees on the campus where it is sited. But a *deus ex machina* must land eventually, so Shinohara staked two vertical prismatic elements attached below the machine in order to land it and connect it to the ground. A rectangular podium is the ground station to which the legs of the machine are fixed. This 'zero-degree machine' is so named because Shinohara intended it to be the ultimate in technology as the F-14 is for fighter planes and the lunar module was at the time Apollo II dropped to the surface of the moon. Comparing Tokyo to the dark side of the moon doesn't seem far-fetched to Shinohara, nor does a protective sheath, emulating that of a war plane, seem excessive as a defence against it.

Shinohara's building is primarily a technological museum. The ground station is an exhibition hall with conference rooms; data research facilities and the director's room are located on the second floor directly above it, in a rather conventional bank of offices. It commemorates the one hundredth anniversary of the founding of the Institute, and the 'technology' in question is represented by actual machines and innovative hardware. Shinohara taught at the institute for nearly thirty years and has had a significant impact on the curriculum, as well as making this one of the most architecturally advanced educational facilities in Japan with the addition of this building.

21 HIROSHI HARA, Ida City Museum, Nagano, 1988

22 HIROSHI HARA, Yamato International Building, Tokyo, 1987

23 HIROSHI HARA, Umeda Sky Building, Shin Umeda City, Osaka, 1993

24 (Overleaf) KAZUO SHINOHARA, Centennial Hall, Tokyo Institute of Technology, 1987

23

31, 32 MINORU
TAKEYAMA, Tokyo
International
Port Terminal,
1991

33 KAZUHIRO ISHII,
San Juan Bautista
Museum, Ojika,
1996

which is hundreds of years old. The temple rose nine inches when its old tile roof was removed for replacement, the ancient wood beams lifting when the weight was removed. Feeling that this 'living' material symbolizes the essence of the Japanese love of nature, Ishii decided to make it as much a part of his design identity as concrete is of Ando's.

The San Juan Bautista Museum, 1996, commemorates the Keichou Delegation sent by Masamune Date in 1831 to counter Japan's growing isolation at that time. The one hundred and eighty member delegation, headed by Tsunenaga Hasekura, set sail for Europe from Tsukimoura on the *San Juan Bautista*. This has been built in replica as the centrepiece of Ishii's design, which wraps around its berth at Ojika like a glass necklace. Escalators and stairs lead up from the mooring to the main exhibition hall

32

33

carved into the hill above; this space has a long, arc-like glazed facade following the contours of the hill that allows a clear view of the ship below. The main hall houses items that were discovered on the expedition, the first of its kind from Japan, which explains its symbolic significance and treatment as far more than a historical curiosity.

In another project that reinforces Japan's traditional status as a sea-faring island nation, Minoru Takeyama's Tokyo International Port Terminal, 1991, is located on reclaimed land in Tokyo Bay. The architect has taken advantage of an edge condition between land and water to express the difference between the industrial and natural realms, turning again to this common theme in contemporary Japanese architecture. The terminal has been designed as a landmark to be clearly visible to those arriving by water. It is also symbolic as the point of departure

1 (Previous page)
VIEW OF SUNTEC
CITY, Singapore,
1995

2 VIEW OF LOS
ANGELES, 1996

Globalization is perhaps the most critical and least understood issue that we face at the end of this century. For those who are trying to grasp the effect that this complex phenomenon will have on cities and the built environment, it is salutary to note that by the year 2000, the United Nations predicts that the majority of people in the world will be living in cities and that almost all urban growth will occur in the developing world. Since 1950 the number of cities with a population of one million or more has increased from eighty-three to 280, and by 2015 that number will increase to 500. Of the fifteen largest of these, twelve will be in Asia, one will be in North America, and none will be in Europe.

Much of this shift is due to the economic recession in the West that was initiated by the oil crises of the mid-1970s, as well as rising interest rates in countries with established banking centres which were triggered in part by the inability of many developing nations to service foreign debt. With the exception of the dynamic Asian 'tiger' economies which kept growing during the 1980s, this was a lost decade for most developing countries, who were struggling to repay debt and were not channelling resources into the development of urban infrastructure, housing and services.[1] In that decade, the global economy also underwent a transformation, changing from one dominated by relatively closed national economies, or trading blocs, to one where most countries have more open economies and where production and service needs are increasingly integrated internationally.

An amplified worldwide concern for the environment (examined earlier in Chapter Ten) has also engendered the realization that runaway urban expansion has brought with it a harmful impact on nature, and that local regional and national agendas inevitably overlap in a complex global network. Ismaïl Serageldin, head of The World Bank division of Environmentally Sustainable Development, has described this as a dawning awareness that we are all 'downwind and upstream from one another'.

The combined effect of these economic and environmental changes is that each major city today does not exist in isolation but is a 'world city'. The response of each urban entity to rising rates of deteriorating housing stock, increasing pollution, homelessness, poverty, transportation problems and traffic congestion, and increasing density now have global implications. In the urban growth that will take place by the year 2000, percentage by total population in North America will be 77 versus 76 in Latin America, 75 in Europe, 37 in Africa and 38 in Asia. By 2025 these numbers will have increased dramatically to 85 per cent in North America, 84 in Latin America, 83 in Europe, 54 in Africa and 55 in Asia. The solutions that have emerged in each of these blocs have a common theme of increasingly aggressive and visionary strategies in the face of pervasive desperation and mounting odds; it is the specific differences of national flavour that provide the keenest

interest in the search for possible architectural prototypes for the future. Discussing each of these nations in North America, Latin America, Europe, Africa and Asia in turn would be a monumental undertaking, outside the scope of this chapter, but single examples in each category will serve to convey the breadth of solutions involved.

Los Angeles, as a North American prototype, is such an unfailing harbinger of future trends that an entire chapter is dedicated to it in this book; it has a new Downtown Strategic Plan that has been predicated on 'catalytic projects'. These include Pershing Square, Frank Gehry's promised but increasingly unlikely Disney Concert Hall, and the rejuvenation of Broadway, which is now a very successful, Hispanic open market that does not comply with certain 'dry-cleaned' images of gentrified urbanity. In spite of the good intentions that underlie these projects, they are not all socially inclusive and have not yet proven to restore life in the city. In some cases, they have actually excluded a large proportion of the population. The Downtown Strategic Plan is part of an important new initiative by the new urbanists who have a manifesto signed by the founding members, Andres Duany, Elizabeth Plater-Zyberk, Stefanos Polyzoides, Elizabeth Moule, Daniel Soloman and Peter Calthorpe. The New Urbanism is broadly based on the modernist mandate to improve public life as well as the emerging ethos of sustainable architecture, which is also discussed in a separate chapter here.

The New Urbanism, as a strategy for reviving Los Angeles specifically, and the city in general, focuses on communities and how pedestrian activity can be increased at the expense of the automobile, as well as on how energy can be conserved through the compactness of the overall development footprint, made possible by encouraging mixed uses that allow higher densities. The new urbanists advocate a return to traditional models, established before the fragmentation of our cities caused by the domination of car travel, and the tyranny of the freeway. The communities they propose are ordinance driven, and they are fighting to change institutional regulations of land-use planning, lot size, material and building height regulations, and street widths. The new developments they propose are intended as frameworks for others to follow. Significantly, they also appeal for teamwork and a multiplicity of designers and stylistic intentions — which strikes dread into the hearts of more conventional planners — and rather than being single-minded the New Urbanism has been conspicuously a co-operative effort.

The most visible example of this today is Playa Vista, a new residential and business district located near Marina Del Rey; it is one of the largest new towns in America currently in development. Playa Vista is based on New Urbanist planning guidelines and, in addition to providing more human-scaled open spaces than are customary in this city, it is one of the first instances of mixed use in the Los Angeles region. These innovative steps required

complex and costly legal challenges to existing legal ordi-nances, setting a precedent that others are now beginning to follow. Playa Vista is being promoted as being self-sufficient, and the majority of those who will live there will also work in the community. Significantly, much is being made of its 'green' credentials: it is being built on the edge of a protected wetland that the developers have had to restore in consideration for their permit, and renew-able materials are being used in the construction of its pri-marily low-scaled buildings.

In spite of their impressive advances, the ideas that the new urbanists have put forward remain contro-versial. Many planners continue to question whether their approach towards compact communities is realistic, given the present trends of growing urban flight and increased automobile use. Critics point to the rising rate of urban dispersion and note that in the United States, for example, there is dramatic growth in the previously deserted, rural hinterland, which they characterize as 'exurbia'. Hide-

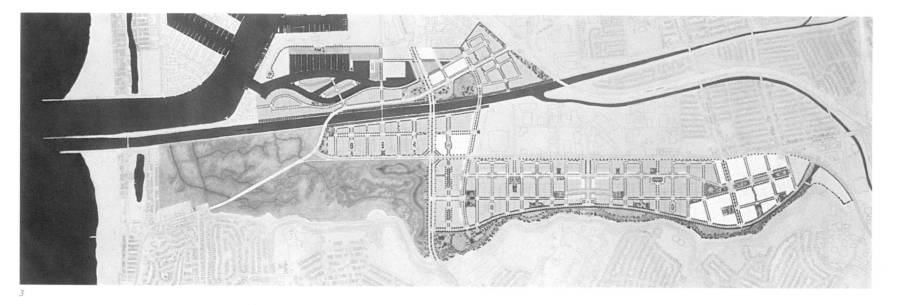

3

bound commentators claim – perhaps hopefully – that the concept of the home-office has become a reality, fed by advances in telecommunications. If this hypothesis is true, it is significant that one cycle begun by industrializa-tion has now been completed. The transition from cottage industry to factory that occurred during the Industrial Revolution has returned to the cottage once again. As 'outsourcing' continues to increase, this trend is expected to accelerate, creating an electronically literate class of working people, connected only by modem and telephone to their most recent contractor.

The computer has undoubtedly speeded up tradi-tional working practices, but an unexpected outcome has been that, because it has exponentially increased the amount of information available, the length of the working day has actually increased. The long-proclaimed advent of increased leisure time that the computer was supposed to make possible has not happened, largely due to this unforeseen circumstance. This has resulted in electronically skilled families of workers joined together in temporary, collective isolation, in secure internal cities. Rather than the exurban vision that some planners promote, such collectives are the result of the undeniable productive synergy that results from people working together. Employers recognize this, and are also reluctant to give up the control that comes from being able to see their employees in person.

The European city was once the centre of creativity and civilization, with walls built around it to protect those inside. In North America, however, the city is becoming an increasingly empty shell, the only walls being those put up by people who live in 'gated communities' to protect themselves from the threat of a growing urban underclass. Paradoxically, as large areas of established cities decline and become derelict, a third reality — as opposed to the New Urbanism and creeping 'exurbia' — is becoming evident as entrepreneurs attempt to reclaim these abandoned districts, driven by the low cost of land and buildings in a depressed market. In Culver City, Los Angeles, for example, an internal, electronic city designed by the architect Eric Owen Moss is springing up, composed of individual, hermetically sealed buildings, connected only by computers and asphalt. This growing conurbation, alternatively called the 'Palindrome' or 'Connected Points' by its developer, Frederick Smith, has now reached such a critical mass that an emerging urban framework of sorts can be determined; but it is completely unlike any previous models of city form. 'Connected Points' is based entirely on a commercial premise. Its employee inhabitants rarely leave their respective interiors due to the pressures of time, and the fact that no public amenities have been provided for them. Another key assumption of this urban vision is that the automobile will continue to be the primary means of transport far into the future. While electric power may replace the internal combustion engine, the planners of the Palindrome feel that nothing can replace the freedom that the automobile offers.

The new urbanist efforts, which have focused on undoing the damage caused in America by post-war planning, and reversing the deterioration of the public realm, have attracted media attention because they are apparently picturesque and novel; the product of the first movement to issue a manifesto since the 1933 CIAM conference that is anathema to them. Their insistence on rules, however, is just as doctrinaire in some ways as the CIAM manifesto; the emphasis on rediscovering the 'lost art of making a city block' has a familiar ring, as does the mantra of pedestrian movement. All of this is fascinating as an attempt to recover the small-town prototype that resonates so sharply in the American subconscious, but it tends to overshadow the sobering statistic that more than 70 per cent of the public housing built between 1929 and 1996 — with approximately one trillion dollars in government subsidies — has now been demolished, and that an

4

5

6

7

acute shortage of housing stock now exists in the United States. The effects of this rate of demolition on the ability of the new service-wage classes to find affordable housing has been exacerbated by gentrification of the kind fostered by the new urbanist initiatives. The US government defines shelter as 'affordable' if rent and utilities are no higher than 30 per cent of household income, and using that definition, fifteen million American households now spend more than they can afford.[2] Those spending half to three quarters of their income on housing now include working families, in addition to those on welfare and the elderly and disabled who have hitherto occupied this category. This housing crisis — of falling incomes and rising rents — and the disappearance of critically important housing stock at a time when the number of needy families has increased exponentially, has also come at a time when the government has severely cut its housing programme; and the term 'subsidized housing' has now taken on an extremely negative connotation.

The United Nations Conference on Human Settlements, or Habitat II, held in Istanbul in June 1996, broadcast the message that the housing crisis is not an isolated problem. At least one billion people lack adequate housing all over the world, 100 million have none at all, and Wally N'Dow, the Secretary General of the Conference, reiterated the United Nations' official line that the world's cities are the key to an environmentally compatible solution to this housing crisis, asserting that: 'No country can be a success if its cities are failures'. He believes that cities 'hold the promise for human development and the protection of the world's natural resources through their ability to support large numbers of people while limiting their impact on the natural environment'.[3]

In North America, optimistic architects see the destruction of a wide swathe of public housing as an unparalleled opportunity to find alternatives to the much maligned 'high rise in the park' model. Unwilling to wait for government leadership, architects in Seattle, Atlanta, Boston and St Louis, among others, are working directly with community groups on duplexes, low-rises and two-storey town-house typologies which include low-income housing in urban contexts. With most of the global population predicted to live in cities by 2005, and two-thirds by 2025, with a majority in the developing world, such initiatives take on increased urgency as part of what is perhaps the most underrated architectural issue today.

Questions about the emerging role and physical character of the world's cities have contributed to the confusion surrounding the urban future. As the global financial marketplace becomes increasingly digitized, the idea of the workplace has been radically altered. Cities, which vie with each other to become centres of corporate capital, are being transformed in the process, becoming spatial circuits for the transfer of international finance; this hyper-mobility has tended to make traditional notions of 'place' irrelevant. The global economy which dominates the market today does not exist in one or several cities as much as in the interstices between nations and has generated an incipient denationalism in its wake.[4] World cities will increasingly come to assume the full implications of that title as corporate power is further reduced to a momentary and simultaneous flash of data on computer screens in any number of locations around the globe.

In Latin America, Rio de Janeiro is as much of a predictor of the urban future as Los Angeles is in the North; and like that city, it is remarkable for its host of urban problems. In 1991, Rio was home to 9.6 million residents in seventeen municipalities. It also boasted fifty miles of recreational beach front on a coastline, in the State of Rio de Janeiro, that is ten times as long. Industrial inlets at Guanabara and Sepetiba bays make Los Angeles' Santa Monica Bay look pristine by comparison. Nearly ten thousand industries — including oil refineries, chemical manufacturers and metallurgy, ship transport and repair facilities — produce toxic and hazardous wastes, heavy metals and chemical spills which are dumped into the bays, or pumped into the atmosphere, leading to appalling levels of industrial air pollution. In the metropolitan region of Rio de Janeiro itself, urban settlements continue to grow uncontrollably over open and peripheral land, creating what have been termed 'official' and 'unofficial' cities, which makes it impossible for local government to provide basic services. Housing shortages have been exacerbated by land speculation which has frozen possible housing sites from availability, accelerating the growth of illegal settlements in environmentally sensitive areas.[5] The size of these settlements, as well as the disruption to natural drainage patterns that they have caused, has meant that only 40 per cent of the sewage in the metropolitan area is treated, resulting in dangerous levels of ground water and surface water contamination. The first *favela* — or squatter settlement — appeared in Rio in 1888; by the end of the Second World War this had increased to more than a hundred, with over 140,000 inhabitants. The relocation of these squatters into low-income housing between 1962 and 1974, however, proved to be too little, too late and the *favela* trend, fuelled by rural-urban migration, continued at an annual rate of about 5 per cent. There are now more than 500 *favelas* in the municipality of Rio and another 900 'irregular' settlements, including 17 per cent of the population squatting on public and private land.[6] In addition to water contamination, these settlements, as well as general population growth, have abetted deforestation, which has accelerated land erosion, leading to an increasing incidence of mud slides.

The Municipality of Rio de Janeiro Environmental Master Plan, enacted in 1990, was an attempt to overcome the lack of coordination between federal, state and local agencies in combating such conditions; focusing on the high concentration of population in the city and its municipal borders, and the number of urban plots without legal title, to better systematize the city's infrastructure. It introduced the concept of *suelo credo* — or 'built-up land' — building codes and ordinances which have established an index of building occupancy, to assist in levying taxes, all with the aim of providing better services. It studied the extent and reason for deforestation and contamination of water sources, and divided the municipality into several main hydrological basins. The plan primarily attempts to use building and subdivision regulations in restricted areas as a device to promote more sustainable development patterns. It has also, for the first time, identified areas of historical interest, environmental sensitivity and degradation, areas prone to dangerous mud slides or flooding, and poor or nonexistent services. Many would argue that this is the equivalent of sticking a band aid on a cancer patient — just bureaucratic business as usual — but there has been progress, and knowledge is the first important step towards change.

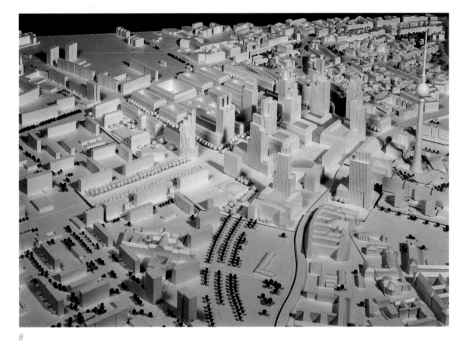

8

In Europe, one of the most graphic illustrations of a collective search for typologies and codified forms of development is the Internationale Bauausstellung (IBA) in Berlin, which sprang from an attempt to make that city the 'shop-window city of Europe'. As the instrument organized to assemble a full-scale exhibition of solutions for the urban reconstruction of Berlin — which has such close ties to the founders of the Modern Movement and, by implication, to the civic devastation caused by their ideology when it fell into the hands of less talented functionaries in public agencies — the IBA sought to establish strict planning guidelines for new construction. Among its key considerations were recovering the urban imprint lost beneath the destruction and demolition that took place during and after the war; an emphasis on architectural expressiveness; and recovering the traditional 'flavour' of the city. These goals were codified for systematic application, into guidelines for an international team of

9

10

architects who were either invited to contribute projects, or received them through competitions or commissions. Many architects took this opportunity to experiment with ideas considered to be too radical — or too conservative — in their own milieu, and to explore the possibilities of collaborating in a pre-determined urban framework. The IBA projects, (specific examples of which are discussed in Chapters Two and Five) are restricted to the extreme limits of West Berlin before the Wall was removed, which now comprises the greater part of the city centre. The IBA has been criticized as being as much a showpiece of the past as the Weissenhofsiedlung in Stuttgart of 1929 was a vision of the future, with equally mixed results, but reliant on a far less cohesive language.

Private development has also continued to thrive in Berlin, as projects such as the newly developed Potsdamerplatz (1994), by Richard Rogers, indicates. In 1993 Daimler Benz AG appointed Rogers to design two office blocks and one residential block as part of a master plan by Renzo Piano and Christoph Kohlbecker. The main entrance to the scheme faces Linkstrassen Park, and the basic form of each building is roughly based on the traditional Berlin block — as are the IBA projects — with a central courtyard located at the heart of each structure. The key objective of the project was to form a new European standard for the integration of a low-energy design approach to architecture in a dense urban environment, employing passive solar strategies, natural ventilation and lighting. This was facilitated by using the courtyards to maximize daylighting and winter solar gain within the buildings, and using a central atrium as a solar buffer and a means of natural ventilation. The design of the buildings' fine-tuned facades was also a key factor in minimizing conflicts between natural light and solar gain, and allowing the most efficient natural ventilation. Computer modelling and physical models were both used extensively to achieve optimum results, in a 'kit of parts' approach (that has been characterized in Chapter Three). Rogers maintains that the view into green areas through open porticos was the generating idea that has remained intact, and that while the city hates the idea that he has broken up their blocks he has managed to give everyone a view, even the people in the back of the building. To do otherwise would have created one facade looking at the park while the rest looked at the road. By scooping out the centres of the blocks everyone can look outwards and enjoy the view.

While Berlin has had the impetus of a booming economy, along with a recent epic political shift and governmental reorganization to spur new construction — which has led in the process to a search for a unified national style — London is still nursing a hangover from the rhetorically stimulated, over-inflated, economy of the 1980s, and the construction boom that took place as a result. More than any other northern post-industrial city that has been affected by the power shift from an

industrial to an information and service economy that has taken place over the last twenty years, London can be seen as a case study of the fundamental change in the nature of cities that has occurred in the developed world during that time. Once the repository of culture and civilization, as well as concentrated social and trading exchange, the traditional city represented the physical manifestation of the collective aspiration of its citizens who identified closely with it. Today, the free market has replaced institutions as the dominating force for urban viability and health; when it is active, a city thrives, and when it is not, a city declines. Consumers have replaced citizens and the city centre is now almost entirely a commercial entity rather than being driven by a cultural base. Over the last two decades, the annual earnings of the top 20 per cent in Britain increased by a tenth while the lowest 10 per cent have dropped by a quarter, reflecting a growing polarization that is also taking place in the United States and elsewhere in the Western World. This growing rift has exacerbated the sense of personal alienation which has come to characterize urban life at the end of the century, breaking the pattern of social interaction, however tense, that had hitherto been its prime attribute.

The impressive, if rather one-dimensional, commercial boom that took place in London in the 1980s has left a legacy of over-building, particularly in commercial office space, at the expense of neglected, decrepit housing stock, failing transportation systems and crumbling highways. Whereas other cities, such as Berlin, have recognized the importance of city-wide planning processes and the renewal of infrastructure in making valid future growth possible, London has moved towards privatization, with disastrous results. Following the legislated demise of the London County Council in 1986, no coordinating governmental body now exists to press for wide-ranging, positive change in the capital. Richard Rogers, as a highly visible and powerful voice for reinstituting such a central body, has consistently advocated a more forward-looking policy, to consolidate the best of recent gains, and to re-establish the historic 'covenant' between the city and its citizens. Not surprisingly, he believes that this may best be accomplished through architecture: 'now that computer and communications technology is beginning to break down monolithic corporations and encourage lighter and more flexible ways of working, we need fewer monumental buildings; and those we have can be colonized by a host of different organizations and activities, giving city centres a finer grain of use and occupation making them more accessible and ultimately more democratic. The city at its best is all about communication, the exchange of ideas, it fails if people feel they are isolated or have nothing to contribute.'

The key to finding a solution to London's problems, it seems, is a finer balance between free-market choice and enlightened planning control that addresses institutional as well as commercial issues. This must

12, 13 ORIOL
BOHIGAS AND
LLUIS DOMENECH,
Olympic Village,
Barcelona, 1992

address the heart and the soul as well as the wallet, moving beyond function to questions of identity, pride and human fulfilment. It may be that the delicate network that enlivened the city in the past has been irreparably destroyed and that no such balance can ever be established again. The commercially based proliferation of obvious cultural symbols such as museums and theatres — or the empty rhetoric of such proposals as the Millennium Dome, destined for a site on the River Thames at Greenwich — and the dearth of meaningful new art and performance to give them fresh legitimacy is a worrying symptom of current sterility. There are no new Manets, Mozarts or Beethovens to interpret the richness of urban life into art, since homogeneous contemporary life, fast approaching an international common denominator of mass culture, does not produce them. Perhaps Rogers, and those who share his hopes for the future of the city, is beating a dead horse, or at least a moribund civic animal whose configuration and potential have changed utterly. Despite this bleak prognosis, however, optimism springs eternal, especially among architects and planners. Studies of the kind launched by the Government Office for London in 1994 — and implemented by Rogers — for examining the Thames between Hampton Court and the Royal Naval College in Greenwich, with the aim of increasing views, pedestrian use and landscaping, and protecting buildings of historical value, to enhance environmental quality and improve access to the river, demonstrate this optimism at its best.

Elsewhere in Europe, cities such as Barcelona have used expositions or other world events, in this case the 1992 Olympic Games, as highly effective pretexts for urban renewal, providing an inspirational model for change in the process. Because of its resistance to the Franco regime, Barcelona was deliberately excluded from development funds distributed from Madrid after the War. For nearly thirty years, until the dictator died in 1975, city politics became inextricably aligned with architectural selection and preference, and building became a polemical response to the repressive tactics being used by the central government. The Socialist platform advanced by Narcis Serra and his architect Oriol Bohigas, designated when Serra was elected mayor of Barcelona in 1977, focused on public works and communal space and for five years there was a flurry of construction activity as parks and monuments sprang up in and around the city. These were strategically placed, to galvanize action and generate a sense of civic pride, dispersing outwards from the dense medieval core of the city to the suburbs as a connective device. Rather than attempting monumental gestures, this campaign deliberately specified manageable, small-scale projects implemented by dividing Barcelona into ten planning districts or neighbourhoods each of which has its own centre.

Barcelona's deliberate pursuit of the 1992 Olympics can be seen as the extension of a tradition of using international expositions to implement civic improvement that goes back to the late nineteenth century. It was an attempt by the city's leaders, mindful of the riches that could be gleaned from the European Economic Community to exploit the prestige of the Olympics, to raise billions for civic improvements as part of a considered move to elevate Barcelona's status in a new Europe where cities are increasingly vying with each other in the economic power game. In contrast to the typically superficial architectural activity that usually accommodates such events, Oriol Bohigas implemented four development zones carefully located in sections of the city that needed the most attention and where dislocation was least likely.

Every piece of the development that Bohigas and his co-director Lluis Domenech proposed was intended to

13

be self-sufficient after the Olympics closed; for example: rather than locating the Olympic Village outside the city, where it has usually been placed in past Games, the designers used it to replace a derelict industrial area that had previously separated the city centre from the waterfront; this new district now houses fifteen thousand people. Some people decry the loss of the old buildings in the area and wonder why they could not have been saved, but the overall strategy was visibility. Two towers by Inigo Ortiz Diez and Léon Gárcia and Bruce Graham of Skidmore Owings and Merrill serve as vertical markers between the village and the old port, now reconfigured into a park and promenade extending for five kilometres along the waterfront. The three other Olympic zones, of Vall d'Hebron, Montjuic and the Diagonal, in outlying areas of the city are connected to the centre by a ring road, intended as a

14

comprehensible boundary and covered in various segments to become a park-like terrace. The consensus of opinion on the success of the Barcelona Olympics seems to be that it represents one of the most extensive and important planning interventions in an existing city this century, but is ultimately a triumph of infrastructure over architecture. Many of the remaining buildings, eventually made considerably more modest by stringent cost considerations, are less impressive than the scope of the framework they delineate and this example of incremental or implied planning is the real model for the future that Barcelona represents.

In contrast to Barcelona's successes, the relative failure of Seville to capitalize on the opportunity presented by Expo '92 is salutary. Even though it involved the widest international participation of any world exposition, with 110 countries contributing ninety-five pavilions, the decision to locate them on a 530-acre island in the middle of the Guadalquivir River, in a grid-like plan intended to give each pavilion equal visual prominence, meant that the exposition has had little lasting impact on the city, or even more remarkably, on the riverfront. Spectacular new buildings, such as Nicholas Grimshaw's British Pavilion (see Chapter Ten, pages 283–5) or Imre Makowecz's Hungarian Pavilion (see Chapter Nine, page 276), which presented images of church spires and tree roots exposed beneath transparent floors to convey the sacred aspect that wood has for this architect, are not part of a continuing civic legacy. The new airport, designed by Rafael Moneo in anticipation of the Expo crowds, is the only substantial enduring architectural contribution to have resulted from the exercise.

Nothing could be further from this architectural set piece than Cairo, which shares Seville's Arab background and hot arid climate. While perhaps not the best example of the fourth, African zone now under scrutiny by urbanologists because it is so far north, it does exemplify most of the crushing burdens being experienced in major cities throughout the continent. All of the maladies that have been described as afflicting Rio de Janeiro are magnified here because of over-population — now fifteen million — fed by rural-urban migration. The lack of an effective tax collection mechanism of the kind developed in Rio also means that basic services, such as rubbish collection, are poor to non-existent; refuse in the medieval quarter is frequently simply stacked on rooftops to rot in the sun. This central area, where the city began in AD 969, is one of the most precious repositories of historical Islamic architecture in the world, with Fatamist, Mamluk and Ottoman masterpieces that few tourists ever see, but it is crumbling under the onslaught of relentlessly growing traffic, pollution and rising ground water contaminated by broken or non-existent sewers. Medieval Cairo is the staging area for those coming to the city from the countryside to seek their fortune, or at least to subsist. It is estimated that there is a new arrival in the city every ten

15

17 VIEW OF
SHENZAN ECONOMIC
AREA, Shanghai,
1996

18 VIEW OF PUDONG
NEW AREA,
Shanghai, 1997

17

18

seconds. Showpiece projects near the Nile, such as the new Opera House designed by Nikken Sekkei and completed in 1992, distract outside attention from the plight of many in the city, both in and outside the old quarter, who are barely managing to survive. The price to the world's historical heritage that is being paid to make that survival possible adds an additional, tragic layer to this example.

Asia, as the fifth most rapidly growing urban zone, contains three quarters of the world's rural population and nearly half of its urban dwellers, and has undergone a tripling of its urban population between 1955 and 1990. While these demographic statistics are heavily influenced by rapid growth in China and India, there has also been dramatic expansion in southeast Asia as well, and a first and second generation of 'tigers' have been responsible for economic changes that have produced some of the world's most visible architectural monuments to prosperity. After the republic of South Korea, which has had the highest per capita income growth of any country in the world, China has perhaps been the most spectacular example of the Asian miracle; Shanghai now rivals Hong Kong in construction activity. According to the latest United Nations global report on urbanization, the nations with the most rapid economic growth are Hong Kong, Singapore, Taiwan and China, with Japan, Indonesia, Malaysia and Thailand close behind. China's place in this list has been secured by the decision to declare Shanghai an 'economic zone' or open city in 1983. By 1990, many leaders from Shanghai had risen to top positions in the national government and were able to direct re-development projects to their city, and to generate a new, high-technology centre, or electronic city within the city east of the Huangpu river. Between the time it had been designated an open city and 1993, Shanghai's population increased from 6.27 million in the urban core, to 12.87 million including greater Shanghai as well, with a transient population of two million not included in this figure. This represents a doubling time of one decade, and the architectural result is chaotic, uncontrolled growth spreading out into the rural hinterland.

The new electronic city that is exploding into life across the river from the old neo-classical centre of Shanghai is known as Pudong. It is quite possibly the largest construction site the world has ever witnessed. Brooding over it all are the two red balls of the Oriental Pearl Television tower which hover on their steel tripod structure. Imagine Canary Wharf, downtown Manhattan and central Frankfurt distilled into a Chinese context and you have some idea of the scale of the enterprise; Pudong is intended to raise Shanghai's profile on the world financial stage so that it will rival Hong Kong and eventually Tokyo and New York as well. If the late 1980s was the era of the Asian 'tigers', the late 1990s must surely belong to China. Already the governing power in Hong Kong, it will soon enter the economic super league, seizing a place among the world's top five trading powers. Officials in

Shanghai boast further that by the turn of the century, the city will be home to at least a dozen conglomerates that will warrant a listing in the *Fortune* Top 500 Companies.

In cities with restricted land area, such as Hong Kong, Singapore and Kuala Lumpur, growth has been restrained by peripheral limits, and so new additions to the cityscape have been more carefully considered. These have been designed by local architects as well as by select members of the global diaspora of the internationally renowned such as Norman Foster, Richard Rogers, James Stirling and Michael Wilford, Cesar Pelli, Kisho Kurokawa and I M Pei, all of whom have added signature buildings to the skylines of southeast Asian cities. Foster's Hongkong & Shanghai Bank, of 1985, set a standard of excellence for others to follow, but his proposed design for the Millennium Tower, to be located near Tokyo Bay, comes closer to the spirit of competition that Japan introduced into Asia after the Second World War. As with the giant financial and manufacturing corporations there, which engage in a ritual code of 'competitive co-operation', the other rising economic giants in the region want their own high-rise statement in concrete, glass and steel to announce to the rest or the world that they have arrived; and in this context size matters. There is currently underway a race to have the tallest tower, with one national claimant soon supplanted by another. America has recently, and probably permanently, ceded superiority in skyscraper construction to Asia; the frenetic competition that once prompted a vertical, physical architectural expression in Manhattan and Chicago has now migrated to the Far East. In cities like Kuala Lumpur, skyscrapers such as Cesar Pelli's twin Petronas Towers project, completed in 1996 (see Chapter Thirteen, page 375), or the Menara Mesiniaga (see Chapter Thirteen, page 383) designed by the local architect Ken Yeang, highlight the fact that 60 to 80 per cent of gross national product (GNP) in the developing world is produced in its cities, but they tend to obscure the issue that a majority of the population survives barely above economic subsistence level.

Globalization also involves increased electronic communication, and Fordism, or the ethos of assembly-line production in a single manufacturing centre, has been replaced by 'flexism', in which different components for each product, such as a television set or automobile, are made in different countries to take advantage of the lowest labour cost and market conditions. The results are the same, however: huge profits increasingly made possible by rapid electronic communication remain mostly at the point of origin; the rich reap the benefit and the employees, from the very young to the old, remain poor.

The three decades following the Second World War and the subsequent collapse of colonialism in Asia, have been characterized by the establishment of independent nation states in the region. Countries with diverse social and ethnic frameworks have sought unity, leading to the establishment of centralized governments, and these in

19 (*Previous page*) TSAO AND MCKOWN, IMC Building, Kuala Lumpur, 1996

20 TSAO AND MCKOWN, Suntec City, Singapore, 1996

turn have portrayed themselves as agents of progressive change. Prior to the colonial era, government in Asia was determined by tribal traditions, monarchies, Confucianism or Islamic Sharia.[7] After the colonial era, such influences were repressed in the desire for a strong central government and national political frameworks. Local governments have consequently not developed, and have instead been seen as impediments to progress. As the demand for services has increased the need for local administration has grown, but the ability of local municipalities to deliver services, raise revenue and issue licences has been slow to develop because no workable precedents exist. As a United Nations report on Asian cities states: 'the weak institutional base of local government has meant that city planners and managers have been unable to cope with the rapid increase in urban population'.[8] Urban development corporations such as the Singapore Housing Development Board were formed in response to this need, with a capital

21

budget, quasi-governmental status and the ability to participate in the open market, to purchase and develop land, commission architects and contractors, and determine functional programmes and means of expression. These supra-local bodies look at urban growth from a regional rather than municipal viewpoint, managing the planning and development of entire metropolitan areas. Public sector intervention in urban housing in particular grew out of a realization, during the late 1960s and early 1970s, that central governments could not meet people's needs. Following the establishment of public housing agencies, housing programmes were established, slum clearance campaigns initiated, self-help movements organized, sites and services arrangements set up (in which government provided land and infrastructure and people built their house on it), and non-governmental organizations, to intervene on behalf of the poor, were formed as a familiar pattern throughout the region.

Singapore's Housing Development Board alone now accommodates 80 per cent of Singapore's 2.5 million people distributed among twenty new towns throughout the island. Ownership is financed by liberal government loans, while the construction activity generated by this programme also helps to fuel the economy; in combination with related services it currently comprises 5 per cent of the GNP. The Tampines Community is typical of these decentralized new towns which have populations ranging from seventy thousand to a quarter of a million, generally subdivided into neighbourhoods of 20,000 people which each have precincts of 2,500 to 5,000 residents. Commercial centres typically service these precincts, with a town centre usually located no more than a short walking distance from the furthest housing block. A local community centre, including child care, adult education and recreational facilities is typically included in this mix.

The Tampines North Community Centre (now renamed as the Pasir Ris South Community Club), by William Lim, completed in 1989, is an example of the attempt by such public authorities to find a balance between regimentation and private initiative. Lim has long been critical of the quality of architecture in this city-state but has been equally vocal in his support of social housing programmes. He has led the search, in the post-colonial period, for an architectural approach that will satisfy local as well as global influences, which is tricky in a situation in which culture is ephemeral and changing so rapidly. Two other important models for more expressive future development in Singapore, with critical implications for the rest of the region, contrast foreign and local responses to the direction growth should take. They highlight a distinct difference in approach. The master plan for Tamasek Polytechnic, 1991, by James Stirling, Michael Wilford and Associates, immediately raises the issue of varying cultural perceptions of public place. Located on a sprawling site between Tampines New Town and Bedok Reservoir, the Polytechnic has separate schools of Applied Science, Business, Design and Technology which together accommodate nearly 12,000 students, 1,000 academics and 500 support staff, in what has been referred to as a 'city of learning'. To humanize what they feared might otherwise become an anonymous architectural landscape, the architects have organized the four schools along a pedestrian concourse that emanates from a U-shaped administration building surrounding a raised entrance plaza, intended as a public forum for the campus. The promenade that it generates begins with shops, galleries and service facilities beneath the administration building and a 600-seat auditorium and 250-seat multi-purpose theatre under the plaza, before stretching out into a covered outdoor 'street' with lecture halls at concourse level and accommodation above. All facilities have been planned to be no more than a short walk from the centre, and breezeways have been strategically located to ensure as much natural air movement as possible along and

23 View of Seoul, 1988

24 View of Seoul showing the Olympic Games fencing gymnasium in the foreground, 1988

25 Akitek Tenggara II, Institute of Technical Education, Bishan, Singapore, 1993

23

24

across this pedestrian spine. Building orientation along the site has also been dictated by environmental factors. There are car parks to accommodate more than one hundred automobiles at the periphery, and landscaping has been used as a buffer between this zone and the central plaza and promenade.

The Institute of Technical Education (ITE) in Bishan, Singapore by Akitek Tenggara II, completed in 1993, demonstrates an alternative courtyard approach, with no real gesture towards public space except a large covered entrance that is accessible directly from the car park. Two 800-foot parallel blocks, delineating a 60-foot wide garden, curve along the site. Each four-storey block is covered by a deeply eaved curved roof and is cut open at regular intervals to allow the prevailing breeze to pass through. The naturally ventilated entrance atrium leads directly on to an auditorium that is open at its sides, and covered by a high, curved steel roof; this is the informal social hub of the school. Tay Kheng Soon, the founding principal of Akitek Tenggara II, describes the complex as resulting from 'an unlearning process', given the dominance of European architecture which has formed the basis of architectural training in Singapore for so long. There are several similarities between Tamasek and ITE, but it is the difference between them which defines that design process primarily in terms of an environmental understanding and the regional attitude towards public space, which in Asia is quite different from that in the West. The Tamasek scheme demonstrates the danger of trying to transport one set of cultural values into a foreign context; but this attempt at providing a European-inspired public realm in this region is not the first and surely won't be the last.

A similar conceit was used as a unifying device in Woo and Williams' design for the 1988 Olympic Village in Seoul, South Korea, which was converted into a new town for 25,000 residents after the games ended. In a similar way, but at a much smaller scale than the Barcelona initiative, this extensive residential development south of the city centre was selected in competition with thirty-nine other entrants because of its innovative organization of public and private spaces, which was intended as a prototype for future urban growth. The Chamsil district of Seoul, south of the Han river, was already a bustling commercial area, and the architects decided to focus this activity in a J-shaped hub next to a fork in the waterway. The project's architect, Kyu Sung Woo, used the occasion of the Olympics to rethink the nature of large-scale housing in Seoul, and exploited the irregularly shaped site to best advantage, organizing housing in a radial pattern related to the curving, branching river and a new commercial 'galleria'. As an alternative to the monolithic towers that are now endemic throughout the region, distinct precincts are formed with asymmetrical arrangements in blocks proportioned according to Manhattan grid dimensions, but dramatically reduced in scale, and cut through with pedestrian passageways in the best English Garden City tradition. Parking is mostly underground and vehicular access is restricted to enhance this image. The architects claim that the deliberate injection of green space into the radial plan represents a marriage of Western precedent and Korean tradition in garden design, with that tradition continued in the introspective courtyard typology used for the apartments and the communal play spaces in the wedge-shaped areas between the linear spokes. Along with the concept of public space used at Tamasek, this adds more fuel to the debate now underway about the possibility or appropriateness of blending diverse cultural precedents and sensibilities.

The breadth of the strategies described in each of the five geographical zones covered here — ranging from the delegation of power to parastatal agencies, or the devolution of government functions to sub-national entities, combined with privatization into non-governmental

25

organizations in the developing world, to infrastructural interventions on a massive scale in its post-industrial equivalent — indicate that it may be rather too soon to write the city off as a failed human institution. The rise of a new urban population in the low- and middle-income nations, which has been termed 'a peaceable revolution', has nonetheless been a painful upheaval, but government leaders recognize that the future lies in the cities, as well as the environmental health of the world. The scope and importance of such concerns puts any discussion about trends or style into clearer perspective: architects presently have very little impact on the built environment, particularly in the developing world where many of the most critical urban issues affecting the future are being played out. If they want to have more of a role, they will have to become more proactive and politically involved. Architects in the coming century, like cities, must learn to evolve if they are to succeed.

Notes

Chapter 1 The Modernist Legacy

1 William J Curtis, *Modern Architecture Since 1900*, London, 1996, p570.
2 Fiona MacCarthy, *William Morris*, London, 1994, p199.
3 C M Chipkin, 'Lutyens and Imperialism', *RIBA Journal*, 1969.
4 Kenneth Frampton and Yukio Futagawa, *Modern Architecture 1851–1945*, New York, 1983, p261.
5 Robert Wright, 'The Evolution of Despair', *Time*, 28 August 1995, pp34, 397.
6 Robert Venturi, 'Diversity, Relevance and Representation in Historicism, or plus ça change...plus a plea for pattern all over archi tecture...with a postscript on my mother's house', *Architectural Record*, June 1982, pp114–119.

Chapter 2 European Rationalism

1 From Quatremère de Quincy's *Dictionnaire* of 1832, quoted in Aldo Rossi, *The Architecture of the City*, Cambridge, MA, 1982, p40.
2 Alan Colquhoun, *Essays in Architectural Criticism*, Cambridge, MA, 1985, p46.

Chapter 3 High-Tech

1 Peter Buchanan, *Architectural Review*, July 1983, pp15–19.
2 Peter Davey, 'Courting Rights', *Architectural Review*, July 1995, p13.

Chapter 4 Minimalism

1 Francesco Dal Co (ed), *Tadao Ando: Complete Works*, London, 1995, p463.

Chapter 5 The Classical Revival

1 Michael Greenhalgh, 'The Classical Tradition', in *New Classicism*, edited by Andreas Papadakis and Harriet Watson, London, 1990, p29.
2 See Demetri Porphyrios, *Classical Architecture*, London, 1991.
3 Leon Krier, 'Classical Architecture and Vernacular Building', in *New Classicism*, op cit, p45.
4 Quinlan Terry, 'Seven Misunderstandings About Classical Architecture', *Quinlan Terry*, London, 1981. Also published in *Architects Anonymous*, Quinlan Terry, London, 1994.
5 See Demetri Porphyrios, *Classical Architecture*, op cit.
6 Andres Duany, 'The New Village of Windsor', in *Building Classical*, edited by Richard Economakis, London, 1993, p213–215.
7 Robert A M Stern, *What the Classical Can do for the Modern*, in *New Classicism*, op cit, p31.

Chapter 6 Post-Modernism

1 Robert Venturi, *Complexity and Contradiction in Architecture*, New York, 1966.
2 Charles Moore, 'You Have to Pay for Public Life', *Perspecta* No 9/10, 1965.
3 Michael Graves, 'A Case for Figurative Architecture', in *Michael Graves: Buildings and Projects 1966–81*, New York, 1982, edited by Karen Vogel Wheeler, Peter Arnell and Ted Bickford.
4 Fredric Jameson, *Postmodernism, or, The Cultural Logic of Late Capitalism*, London and New York, 1991, pp4–5.
5 Jean-François Lyotard, *The Postmodern Condition: A Report on Knowledge*, Minneapolis, 1984.
6 Paolo Portoghesi, *Postmodern: The Architecture of the Postindustrial Society*, New York, 1983.
7 Magali Sarfatti Larson, *Behind the Postmodern Facade: Architectural Change in Late Twentieth-Century America*, Los Angeles, 1993.
8 See Fredric Jameson, *Postmodernism, or, The Cultural Logic of Late Capitalism*, op cit.
9 See Robert Venturi, 'Diversity, Relevance and Representation in Historicism, or plus ça change...', op cit.

Chapter 7 Deconstructivism

1 Christopher Norris, *Derrida*, London. 1987, p. 13.
2 In Peter Brunette and David Wills, *Deconstruction and the Visual Arts*, Cambridge, 1994, p27.
3 Marshall Berman, *All That is Solid Melts Into Air: Experience of Modernity*, London, 1983.
4 See Herbert Muschamp, 'Eisenman's Spatial Extravaganza in Cincinnati', *New York Times*, 21 July 1996.
5 Martin Heidegger, 'Building, Dwelling, Thinking', in *Poetry, Language, Thought*, New York, 1971.
6 Jan A Wolff, *Contemporary Architects*, London, 1994, p406–7.

Chapter 8 Contemporary Vernacular

1 See E M Farrelly, *Three Houses by Glen Murcutt*, London, 1993.

Chapter 9 The New Expressionists

1 For more on this point see Colin St John Wilson *The Other Tradition of Modern Architecture, The Uncompleted Project*, London, 1995.

Wilson argues that 'resistance' was born at the CIAM meeting at LA Sarrez in June 1928, when 'an orthodoxy and its priesthood were es tablished with something of the fervour (not to forget ruthlessness) of the political seizures of power ...' and that this resistance is a critique that has 'been generated within the Modern Movement rather than outside its ranks'. Wilson identifies its first leaders as Hugo Häring and Alvar Aalto, pp6–7.
2 Kay Kaiser, 'Profile: Gunnar Birkerts', interview, in *World Architecture* No 36, p25.

Chapter 10 Ecological Architecture

1 United Nations World Commission on Environment and Development, *Our Common Future*, 1987.
2 Pragmatic and idealistic terms from conversations with Paul Ekins, senior lecturer in Environmental Policy, Department of Economics, Keele University, April 1996; in London.

Chapter 11 The New Moderns

1 *Five Architects*, George Wittenborn, New York, 1972.
2 Paul Goldberger, 'A Little Book that Led Five Men to Fame', *New York Times*, 11 February 1996, p38.
3 Ibid, p38.
4 Robert Maxwell, 'The Far Side of Modernity', *Architectural Review* No 12, 1992 p28.
5 Beatriz Colomina, 'On Adolf Loos and Josef Hoffman: Architecture in the Age of Mechanical Reproduction' in *Raumplan vs Plan Libre*, edited by Max Risselada, New York, 1987.
6 Michael J Crosbie, 'Raising Rock's Reliquary', *Progressive Architecture*, February 1995, p64.
7 Kenneth Frampton, 'Canberra's Shining Brow', *A+U* No 5, 1989, p18.
8 In Martin Meade, 'War Memorial', *Architectural Review*, 1992, p68.
9 See also Rem Koolhaas, 'Bigness or the Problem of Large', *Domus* No 764, October 1994.
10 Frederique Huygen, 'Dance to the Music of OMA', *Blueprint*, February 96, p35.

Chapter 12 Populist Architecture

1 John Allwood, *The Great Exhibitions*, London, 1977, p84.
2 Ibid, p26.
3 *Architectural Record*, April 1997.
4 Gianni Vattimo, *The End of Modernity: Nihilism and Hermeneutics in Postmodern Culture*, Cambridge, 1991.
5 Stanislaus von Moos, 'The Disney Syndrome', *Domus* No 787, November 1996, p88.
6 Dietmer Steiner, 'A Diary of Disney's Celebration', *Domus* No 787, op cit.
7 See, for example, his article 'Diversity, Relevance and Representation in Historicism, or plus ça change...', op cit.

Chapter 13 Megastructures

1 Judith Dupré, *Skyscrapers*, New York, 1996, p69.
2 Martin Jacques, 'Hunting Down the Asian Tigers', *The Independent*, 20 May 1996.

Chapter 14 Los Angeles Avant-Garde

1 See Chapter 4 of James Steele, *Los Angeles Architecture: The Contemporary Condition*, London, 1993.

Chapter 15 Experimentation in Japan

1 See Kisho Kurokawa, *The Philosophy of Symbiosis*, London, 1994.

Chapter 16 World Cities

1 *An Urbanizing World*, UN Centre for Human Settlements, 1996, p1.
2 Jason De Parle, 'Slamming the Door', *New York Times Magazine*, 20 October 1996, p52.
3 Alison Snyder, 'Adequate Shelter for All', *Metropolis*, January, February 1997, p66.
4 Saskia Sassen lecture on 'The Global City', International Association for the Study of Traditional Environments Conference, Berkeley, CA, 15 December 1996.
5 *Towards a Sustainable Urban Environment: The Rio de Janeiro Study*, A Kreimer, T Lobo, B Menezer, M Munasinghe, R Parker, World Bank, 1993, p5.
6 Ibid, p12.
7 Patrick Wakely and Adnan Aliani, 'Living in Asian Cities; the Impending Crisis', Report of the Second Asia, Pacific Urban Forum, United Nations, 1996, p4.
8 Ibid, p7.

Architects' Biographies

The brief biographies of the architects illustrated in this book given here are not intended to be complete. Their purpose is to offer the reader a guide to further research. Wherever possible each biography includes the following information: the architect's date of birth, nationality, education, select projects, select publications, select exhibitions and awards. In some cases, however, it has been impossible to find personal and other details of the architects illustrated in the book.

Robert Adam, b.1948
Nationality: British
Education: Regent Street Polytechnic, London
Projects: Aamdahl HQ, Dogmersfield Park, Hampshire (1985); Upton Park, Hampshire (1986); Paternoster Square development, London (1990); Fitzherbert House, Richmond (1991); Shepton Mallet Master Plan, Somerset (1991)
Publications: by Adam: 'In Defence of Historicism', *RIBA Journal*, 1981; 'Imitation and Innovation', *Architectural Design*, 1989; 'Invention, Modernity and the Classical Tradition', *Building Classical*, London, 1993
Exhibitions: RIBA, London (1990)

Akitek Tenggara II, comprising
Tay Kheng Soon (principal partner)
Nationality: Singaporean
Education: Singapore Polytechnic
Chung Meng Ker
Nationality: Singaporean
Education: Singapore Polytechnic
Patrick Chia
Nationality: Singaporean
Education: Singapore Polytechnic
Winston Yeh
Nationality: Singaporean
Education: Singapore Polytechnic, Harvard University
Projects: Chee Tong Temple, Singapore (1987); Institute of Technical Education, Bishan (1993); Kandang Kerbau Women's and Children's Hospital, Singapore (1997)
Publications: Robert Powell and Akitek Tenggara, *Line, Edge and Shade: The Search for a Design Language in Tropical Asia*, Singapore, 1997

Alsop and Störmer, comprising
William Alsop, b.1947
Nationality: British
Education: Architectural Association, London
Jan Störmer, b.1947
Nationality: German
Education: Ingenieruschule in Bremen; Planungstätigkeit in Bremen; Studium Hochschule für Bilende Künste, Hamburg
Projects: Hamburg Ferry Terminal (1988–91); Hôtel du Departement, Marseilles (1990–4); project for Trawsfynydd, North Wales (1994)
Publications: Mel Gooding, *William Alsop: Buildings and Projects*, London, 1992; Michael Spens, *Le Grand Bleu*, London, 1994
Exhibitions: Arc en Rêve Centre d'Architecture, Bordeaux (1991)
Awards: RIBA National Award for Architecture (1992)

Tadao Ando, b.1941
Nationality: Japanese
Education: self-taught in architecture
Projects: Azuma House, Sumiyoshi (1976); Koshino House, Kobe (1979–81); Nakayama House (1985); Kara-za Theatre (1987); Children's Museum, Himeji (1987–9); Church of Light, Osaka (1989); Chikatsu-Asuka Historical Museum, Minami-Kawachi, Osaka (1990–4); Water Temple, Awaji Island, Hyogo Prefecture (1990); Japan Pavilion, Seville Expo (1992); Naoshima Contemporary Art Museum, Kagawa Prefecture (1992); Meditation Space, Unesco, Paris (1995)
Publications: Francesco Dal Co, *Complete Works: Tadao Ando*, London, 1995 (includes articles by and on Ando); Richard Pare, *Tadao Ando: The Colours of Light*, London, 1996
Exhibitions: Institut Français d'Architecture, Paris (1982); touring exhibition, Japan (1983); Centre Georges Pompidou, Paris, and RIBA, London (1993)
Awards: Alvar Aalto Medal (1985); Gold Medal, French Academy of Architecture (1989); Pritzker Prize (1995); RIBA Gold Medal (1996)

Arquitectonica, comprising:
Bernardo Fort-Brescia
Nationality: American (born in Peru)
Education: Princeton University; Harvard University
Laurinda Hope Spear
Nationality: American
Education: Brown University; Columbia University
Projects: Babylon apartment complex, Miami (1978–81); Atlantis apartment complex, Miami (1980–2); Banco de Credito de Peru, Lima (1988); All Star Resorts, Walt Disney World, Lake Buena Vista (1995
Publications: Beth Dunlop, *Arquitectonica*, New York, 1991
Exhibitions: Center for Fine Arts, Miami (1984)

Studio Asymptote, comprising
Hani Rashid, b.1958
Nationality: Canadian
Education: Carleton University, Ottawa; Cranbrook Academy of Art, Michigan
Lise Anne Couture, b.1959
Nationality: Canadian
Education: Carleton University, Ottawa; Yale University
Projects: West Coast Gateway, Los Angeles (1988); Times Square Study, New York (1992); Multi-media Research Facility, Kyoto (1996)
Publications: Special issue of A+U, No 283, 1994; *Asymptote: Architecture at the Interval*, New York, 1995
Exhibitions: TZ Art Gallery, New York (1996) Kunsthalle, Vienna (1996)

Bernard Babka, see entry under Hammond, Beeby and Babka

Rasem J Badran, b.1945
Nationality: Jordanian
Education: Technical University of Darmstadt
Projects: Khoury House, Amman (1973); study and design of urban district in Sana'a, Yemen (1987); Qasr Al Hokm Justice Palace and Al Jame State Mosque, Riyadh (1992)
Publications: by Badran: 'Reconstruction of the Old City of Kuwait', *Architecture d'aujourd'hui*, 1973; on Badran: Udo Kulterman, *Architects of the Third World*, Cologne, 1980
Awards: Arab Town Organization Architect Award (1990); International Academy of Architecture Diploma and Medal (1991)

Shigeru Ban, b.1957
Nationality: Japanese
Education: University of Southern California, Los Angeles; Cooper Union School of Architecture, New York
Projects: Ban Building, Tokyo (1988); I House, Tokyo (1990); Curtain Wall House, Tokyo (1995); House of Paper, Kamanashi (1995); JR Tazawako Station (1997)
Publications: Shigeru Ban, GG Portfolio, Barcelona, 1997
Exhibitions: Gallery 91, New York (1984); INAX Gallery, Osaka (1995)
Awards: Mainichi Design Award (1995)

Luis Barragán, b.1902, d.1987
Nationality: Mexican
Education: Engineering, Dip.Ing (1925), self-taught as an architect; lived in Paris and attended Le Corbusier's lectures (1931–2)
Projects: El Pedregal, Mexico City (1945–50); Luis Barragán House, Mexico City (1947); Plaza y Fuente del Bebedero, Mexico City (1958–61); Egerstrom House, 'San Cristobal' stables and pool, Los Clubes, Mexico City (1968)
Publications: Paul Rispa (ed.), *Barragán: The Complete Works*, London, 1996; Antonio Riggen Martinez, *Luis Barragán: Mexico's Modern Master 1902–1988*, New York, 1996
Exhibitions: Museum of Modern Art, New York (1976); Architectural Association, London (1990)
Awards: Pritzker Prize (1980)

Geoffrey Manning Bawa, b.1919
Nationality: Sri Lankan
Education: Architectural Association, London
Projects: House and Studio, Colombo (1963); three Buddhist temples, Beira Lake, Colombo (1977); Triton Hotel, Ahungalla (1982); Parliament Building, Colombo (1983)
Publications: Brian Brace Taylor, *Geoffrey Bawa*, London, 1992
Exhibitions: RIBA, London (1986) and tour to New York, Boston, Colombo; Royal Australian Institute of Architects, Brisbane, Darwin, Sydney, Perth (1996)
Awards: Gold Medal, Sri Lanka Institute of Architects (1982)

Thomas Hall Beeby, see entry under Hammond, Beeby and Babka

Günter Behnisch, b.1922
Nationality: German
Education: Technische Hochschule, Stuttgart
Projects: Solar Research Institute, University of Stuttgart (1987); German
Post Office Museum, Frankfurt (1990); Parliament Building, Bonn (1992)
Publications: Christian Kandzial (ed) *Behnisch and Partner: Designs
1952–87*, Stuttgart, 1987
Exhibitions: Galerie der Stadt, Stuttgart (1992)
Awards: Grand Architecture Prize, Bund Deutscher Architekten (1972);
Germany Architecture Prize, Bundesarchitektenkammer (1977);
Gold Medal, Académie d'Architecture, Paris (1992)

Julian Bicknell, b.1945
Nationality: British
Education: Cambridge University
Projects: Henbury Rotunda, Cheshire (1984); Upton Viva,
Warwickshire (1990)
Publications: by Bicknell: *Rehabilitation and Conversion*, London, 1980

Gunnar Birkerts, b.1925
Nationality: American (born in Latvia)
Education: Technische Hochschule, Stuttgart
Projects: University of Michigan Library, Flint (1986); Central Library,
University of California at San Diego (1992); College of Law, Ohio State
University, Columbus (1993)
Publications: by Birkerts: *Subterranean Urban Systems*, Ann Arbor, 1974;
Buildings, Projects and Thoughts, 1960–1985, Ann Arbor, 1985; on
Birkerts: Kay Kaiser, *The Architecture of Gunnar Birkerts*, Washington
and Florence, 1989
Exhibitions: Bienal, São Paulo (1962); Museum of Modern Art, New York
(1971 and 1979); Triennale, Milan (1986); Triennial of World Architecture,
Belgrade (1991)
Awards: National Gold Medal in Architecture, Tau Sigma Delta (1971);
Arnold W Brunner Memorial Prize (1981); Award of Excellence, AIA and
American Library Association (1985)

Ricardo Bofill, b.1939
Nationality: Spanish
Education: Escuela Tecnica Superior de Arquitectura, Barcelona;
University of Geneva
Projects: Palais d'Abraxas, Marne-la-Vallée, Paris (1978–83); Hôtel de
Région, Montpellier (1990); Barcelona Airport (1992)
Publications: by Bofill: *L'Architecture d'un homme*, Paris, 1978; on Bofill:
Warren A. James (ed.), *Ricardo Bofill, Taller de Arquitectura: Buildings
and Projects 1960–1985*, New York, 1988
Exhibitions: Biennale, Venice (1976); Architectural Association, London
(1981); *Ricardo Bofill and Leon Krier: Architecture, Urbanism and
History*, Museum of Modern Art, New York (1985); Musée d'Ixelles,
Brussels, and tour to Barcelona, Paris and New York (1989)
Awards: Officier de l'Ordre des Arts et des Lettres, Ministère de Culture,
France (1984)

Oriol Bohigas, b.1925
Nationality: Spanish
Education: Escuela Tecnica Superior de Arquitectura, Barcelona
Projects: Olympic Village, Barcelona (1988–92)
Publications: Philip Drew, *Real Space: The Architecture of Martorell,
Bohigas, Mackay, Puig*, Berlin, 1993
Exhibitions: Bienal, São Paulo (1957); Biennale, Venice (1976); School of
Architecture, Lausanne (1979); Columbia University, New York, and tour
to US, Canada and Poland (1989–90)

Gottfried Böhm, b.1920
Nationality: German
Education: Technische Hochschule, Munich
Projects: University Library, Mannheim (1988)
Publications: S Raev (ed), *Gottfried Böhm: Bauten und Projekte 1950–1980*,
Cologne, 1982; Veronika Darius, *Der Architekt Gottfried Böhm: Bauten der
sechziger Jahre*, Düsseldorf, 1988; *Gottfried Böhm*, Stuttgart, 1988
Exhibitions: Kunsthalle, Bielefeld (1984–5); Graham Foundation,
Chicago, and Goethe House, New York (1986); RIBA, London (1987);
Rheinisches Landesmuseum, Bonn (1992)
Awards: Grand Prix, Bund Deutscher Architekten (1975); Gold Medal,
Académie d'Architecture, Paris (1983); Fritz Schumacher Prize (1985);
Pritzker Prize (1986)

Mario Botta, b.1943
Nationality: Italian
Education: Istituto Universitario di Architettura, Venice
Projects: Secondary School, Morbio Inferiore, Ticino (1972–7); house, Riva
San Vitale (1973); house, Ligornetto (1975–6); Casa Rotonda, Stabio,
Switzerland (1982); Evry Cathedral (1988–95); Museum of Modern Art, San
Francisco (1994); Lido Film Theatre, Venice (1990)
Publications: Perluigi Nicolin, *Mario Botta: Buildings and Projects 1961–1982*,
New York, 1984; Emilio Pizzi, *Mario Botta, The Complete Works*, vol. I,
1960–1985, Basle/Boston/Berlin, 1993; vol. 2, *1985–1990*, 1994
Exhibitions: Technische Universität, Vienna, and tour in Europe and US
(1977); Historisches Archiv, Cologne (1983); Museum of Modern Art, New
York (1986); Musée Rath, Geneva, and tour in Europe (1991)
Awards: CICA Award (1989, 1993); European Prize for Culture (1995)

Branson Coates, comprising:
Doug Branson, b.1951
Nationality: British
Education: Architectural Association, London
Nigel Coates, b.1949
Nationality: British
Education: Architectural Association, London
Projects: Bohemia Jazz Club, Tokyo (1986); Caffè Bongo, Tokyo (1986);
Nishi Azubu Wall, Tokyo (1990)
Publications: Rick Poynor, *Nigel Coates, The City in Motion*, London, 1989
Exhibitions: Architectural Association, London (1992)
Awards: Japan Inter-Design Award (1990)

Will Bruder, b.1946
Nationality: American
Education: University of Wisconsin, Milwaukee
Projects: Central Library, Phoenix (1988–95); Theuer Residence, Phoenix
(1992); Chart House Restaurant, La Jolla (1996)
Publications: in *Contemporary American Architects*, vol II, by P Jodidio,
Cologne, 1996
Awards: DuPont Benedictus Award (1996)

John Burgee, b.1933; partner with Philip Johnson, 1968–91
Nationality: American
Education: University of Notre Dame, Indiana
for projects and publications see entry under Philip Johnson

Santiago Calatrava, b.1951
Nationality: Spanish
Education: Escuela Tecnica Superior de Arquitectura, Valencia;
Eidgenössische Technische Hochschule, Zurich
Projects: Kuwaiti Pavilion, Seville Expo (1992); Alamillo Bridge, Seville
(1992); Lyon-Satolas TGV Station (1988–94)
Publications: Dennis Sharp, *Santiago Calatrava*, London, 1996
Exhibitions: Suomen Rakennustaiteen Museum, Helsinki (1991); RIBA,
London (1992); Deutsches Museum, Munich (1993), Ma Gallery, Tokyo
(1994); Navarra Museum, Pamplona (1995); Milwaukee Art Museum (1996)
Awards: Fritz Schumacher Prize for Urbanism (1988); Gold Medal,
Institution of Structural Engineers, London (1992)

Alberto Campo Baeza, b.1946
Nationality: Spanish
Education: Escuela Tecnica Superior de Arquitectura, Madrid
Projects: Fene Town Hall, La Coruña (1980); S. Fermin Public School,
Madrid (1985); Casa Turegano, Madrid (1989); Casa Garcia Marcos, Madrid
(1991); Casa Gaspar, Cadiz (1991); Public Library, Orihuela, Alicante (1992);
Public School, Cadiz (1992); CDER Offices, Mallorca (1996–7); Caja General
Bank Headquarters, Granada (1996–7)
Publications: K Frampton (introduction), *Alberto Campo Baeza*, Boston, 1996
Exhibitions: Accademia de Spagna, Rome, and Fundación Cultural Colegio
Oficial di Arquitectos, Madrid (1996)

David Chipperfield, b.1953, London
Nationality: British
Education: Architectural Association, London
Projects: Arnolfini Gallery, Bristol (1997); The Knight House, Richmond
(1989); office building, Okayama, Japan (1992); building in Kyoto (1992);
River and Rowing Museum, Henley-on-Thames (1996–7)
Publications: by Chipperfield: *Theoretical Practice*, London, 1994; on
Chipperfield: *David Chipperfield*, Barcelona, 1992

Cigolle & Coleman, comprising
Mark Cigolle, b.1949
Nationality: American
Education: Princeton University; Graduate School of Design, Harvard
University
Kim Coleman, b.1955
Nationality: American
Education: University of Virginia, Charlottesville
Projects: Alaia Retail Store, Beverly Hills (1992); Canyon House, Santa
Monica (1993); Sky Ranch House, Carmel Valley (1995)
Publications: in *40 Under 40*, by B Russell, Michigan (1995); in
Contemporary California Architecture, by P Jodidio, Cologne, 1995
Exhibitions: School of Architecture, University of Southern California,
Los Angeles (1984); Parsons School of Design, New York (1995)

Henri Ciriani, b.1936
Nationality: French (born in Peru)
Education: Universidad Nacional de Ingenieria, Peru
Projects: competition for Evry (1972); Noisy II, Marne-la-Vallée
(1975–80); Cour d'angle, Saint-Denis (1978–83); Crèche, Saint-Denis
(1978–83); Noisy III (1979–81); Kitchen of Saint-Antoine Hospital, Paris
(1981–5); Historial de la Grande Guerre, Peronne (1987–92); Museum of
Archaeology, Arles (1984–92)
Publications: François Chaslin *et al.*, *Henri Ciriani*, Paris, 1984;
L Miotto, *Henri Ciriani: cesure urbane e spazi filanti*, Turin, 1996;
Henri Ciriani, foreword by Richard Meier, introduction by François
Chaslin, Rockport, 1997
Awards: Grand Prix National d'Architecture (1983)

Nigel Coates, see entry under Branson Coates

Jo Coenen, b.1949
Nationality: Dutch
Education: University of Technology, Eindhoven
Projects: Chamber of Commerce, Maastricht (1988); Delft University of
Technology Library (1992); The Netherlands Architecture Institute,
Rotterdam (1988–93)
Publications: S Umberto Barbieri, 'Recent Works of Jo Coenen', *A+U*,
Sept 1988; Hans Ibelings, 'Joe Coenen', *A+U*, Nov 1992

Coop Himmelblau, founding partners:
Wolf Prix, b. 1942
Nationality: Austrian
Education: Technische Universität, Vienna
Helmut Swiczinsky, b. 1944
Nationality: Austrian (born in Poland)
Education: Technische Universität, Vienna
Projects: rooftop conversion, Falkestrasse, Vienna (1983-8); Funder
Factory, Carinthia, Vienna (1988-9); Groningen Museum (1990-4); Office
and Research Centre, Seibersdorf, Austria (1996)
Publications: *Blaubox, Coop Himmelblau: Wolf D Prix, H Swiczinsky*,
London, 1988; *Coop Himmelblau: die Faszination der Stadt*, foreword by
Frank Werner, Darmstadt, 1988; *Coop Himmelb (l)au: From Cloud to
Cloud*, Klagenfurt, 1996
Exhibitions: Museum of Modern Art, New York (1975); Centre Georges
Pompidou, Paris (1992); Biennale, Venice (1996)
Awards: Special Award, League of Austrian Architects (1989); Constructa
Prize (1992)

Cooper Robertson and Partners, see entry under Jaquelin Taylor
Robertson

Charles Mark Correa, b.1930
Nationality: Indian
Education: University of Michigan; MIT
Projects: plans for New Bombay (1971–4); Kanchanjunga apartment
block, Bombay (1980); Bhopal State Assembly Building (1986); Madras
Rubber Factory (1992); British Council Headquarters and Library, New
Delhi (1992); Inter-University Centre for Astronomy and Astrophysics,
Pune (1992)
Publications: by Correa: *The New Landscape*, Bombay, 1985; on Correa:
Sherban Cantacuzino, *Charles Correa*, London and Singapore, 1984 (2nd
edn, 1987); Charles Correa and Kenneth Frampton, *Charles Correa*,
London, 1996
Exhibitions: Biennale, Venice (1982); British Council, India (1984);

Architectural Association, London (1993)
Awards: RIBA Gold Medal (1984); Gold Medal, Indian Institute of Architects (1987); UIA Gold Medal (1990)

CZWG, comprising:
Piers Gough, b.1946
Nationality: British
Education: Architectural Association, London
Nick Campbell, b.1947
Nationality: British
Education: Architectural Association, London
Rex Wilkinson, b.1947
Nationality: British
Education: Architectural Association, London
Projects: China Wharf, London Docklands (1982–8); Cascades, Isle of Dogs, London (1986–8); The Circle, London Docklands (1989)
Publications: Deyan Sudjic *et al.*, *English Extremists: The Architecture of Campbell Zogolovitch Wilkinson & Gough*, London, 1988
Exhibitions: RIBA, London (1988)

Odile Decq and Benoît Cornette, comprising
Odile Decq, b.1955
Nationality: French
Education: UP 6 School of Architecture, La Villette, Paris; Institute of Political Studies, Urbanism and Development, Paris
Benoit Cornette, b.1953
Nationality: French
Education: UP 6 School of Architecture, La Villette, Paris
Projects: Banque Populaire de l'Ouest, Rennes (1990); Social Housing, Paris (1992–5); Motorway Viaduct and Operations Centre, Nanterre (1993–6)
Publications: Clare Melhuish, *Odile Decq Benoît Cornette*, London, 1997

Denton Corker Marshall, comprising:
John Denton, b.1945
Nationality: Australian
Education: University of Melbourne
William S Corker, b.1945
Nationality: Australian
Education: University of Melbourne
Barrington C Marshall, b.1946
Nationality: Australian
Education: University of Melbourne
Projects: Melbourne Civic Square (1980); Australian Embassy, Beijing (1981); 101 Collins Street, Melbourne (1991); Australian Embassy, Tokyo (1991); Governor Philip Tower, Sydney (1993); Cowes House, Philip Island (1994); Museum of Victoria (1994–); Melbourne Exhibition Centre (1996)
Publications: by Denton/Corker/Marshall: *The Reconstruction of the Australian City*, Melbourne, 1987; on Denton/Corker/Marshall: Haig Beck and Jackie Cooper, *Australian Architects: Denton Corker Marshall*, Canberra, 1987
Awards: Royal Institute of Australian Architects Gold Medal (1996)

Katherine Diamond, b.1954
Nationality: dual citizenship American/Israeli
Education: The Technion, The Israel Institute of Technology; University of California at Los Angeles
Projects: (Partner in charge of design for Siegel Diamond Architects) University of California Irvine Student Services Addition (1987); LAX Air Traffic Control Tower (1993)
Publications: incl. in *Contemporary American Architects III* by Philip Jodidio, Cologne, 1997

Diener and Diener, comprising
Marcus Diener
Nationality: Swiss
Education: ETH (Federal Institute of Polytechnics), Zurich
Roger Diener, b.1950
Nationality: Swiss
Education: EPF (Federal Institute of Polytechnics), Lausanne
Projects: Housing Complex, Salzburg (1987); Gmurzynska Gallery, Cologne (1990); Apartment building, Paris (1996)
Publications: *Diener and Diener, Projects 1978–1990*, New York, 1992
Exhibitions: Architecture Foundation, London (1992); Aedes Gallery, Berlin (1995)

Günther Domenig, b.1934
Nationality: Austrian
Education: Technische Hochschule, Graz
Projects: Z-Bank, Vienna (1974–9); Steinhaus, Steindorf (1983–); industrial complex, Völkermarkt (1995)
Publications: Raffaele Raja, *Günther Domenig: Werkbuch*, Salzburg, 1991
Exhibitions: Centre d'Information de l'Architecture, Brussels
Awards: Grand Prix International d'Urbanisme et d'Architecture (1969); Prix Européen de la Construction Métallique (1975); Steiermark Architecture Prize (1982)

Balkrishna Vithaldas Doshi, b.1927
Nationality: Indian
Education: Fergusson College, Poona; J J School of Art, Bombay
Projects: senior designer with Le Corbusier for major buildings in Chandigarh and Ahmedabad (1951–7); Doshi House, Ahmedabad (1961); Ahmedabad Institute of Indology (1962); Indian Institute of Management, Ahmedabad (1962, with Louis I Kahn); Doshi Studio, Sangath, Ahmedabad(1979–81); Indian Institute of Management, Bangalore (1977–85); Hussain-Gufa Gallery, Ahmedabad (1993)
Publications: by Doshi: *Between Notion and Reality*, Washington, DC, 1986; on Doshi: William Curtis, *Balkrishna Doshi: An Architecture for India*, Ahmedabad, 1988
Awards: Grand Gold Medal for Architecture, Academy of Architecture, Paris (1988); G B Mhatre Gold Medal, Indian Institute of Architects (1988)

Andres Duany and Elizabeth Plater-Zyberk, comprising:
Andres Duany
Nationality: American
Education: Princeton University; Ecole Supérieure des Beaux-Arts, Paris; Yale University
Elizabeth Plater-Zyberk
Nationality: American
Education: Princeton University; Yale University
Projects: Master Plan for Seaside, Florida (1982–); Playa Vista Community, Los Angeles (1989–); Windsor, Florida (1989–)
Publications: D Mohney and K Easterling (eds), *Seaside: Making a New Town in America*, London, 1991
Exhibitions: Graduate School of Design, Harvard University (1990); World Triennial of Architecture, Sofia (1994); Habitat II, Istanbul (1996)
Awards: Thomas Jefferson Medal (1993); Brandeis Award for Architecture (1994)

Charles Eames, b.1907, d.1978
Nationality: American
Education: Washington School of Architecture
Projects: (Worked in partnership with wife Ray Eames, 1941–78) Eames House, Pacific Palisades, California (1940); chair designs including Molded Plywood Chair (with Eero Saarinen, 1940); Stacking Fibreglass Chair (1955); Lounge Chair and Ottoman (1956); La Fonda Chair (1960); Loose Cushion Chair (1971)
Publications: by Eames: *A Computer Perspective*, Cambridge, Mass, 1973; on Eames: James Steele, *Eames House: Charles and Ray Eames*, London, 1994; Pat Kirkham, *Charles and Ray Eames: Designers of the Twentieth Century*, Cambridge, Mass., 1995
Exhibitions: Museum of Modern Art, New York (1973); University of California (1976)
Awards: Gold Medal (1954) and Grand Prize (1957), Milan Triennale; RIBA Gold Medal (1979)

Peter Eisenman, b.1932
Nationality: American
Education: Cornell University; Columbia University, New York; Cambridge University
Projects: House I, Princeton (1967–8); House VI, Cornwall, Connecticut (1972); Social Housing, Check Point Charlie, Berlin (1978); Aronoff Center for Design and Art, University of Cincinnati (1986); Carnegie Mellon Research Institute, Pittsburgh (1987–8); Gardiola Weekend House, Santa Monica Del Mar, Cadiz (1988); Wexner Center for the Visual Arts, Ohio State University, Columbus (1989); Convention Center, Columbus, Ohio (1992); Max Reinhardt Haus, Berlin (1992)
Publications: by Eisenman: *Giuseppe Terragni*, Cambridge, Mass., 1985; *Houses of Cards*, with Rosalind Krauss and Manfredo Tafuri, Oxford, 1987; on Eisenman: *Wexner Center for the Visual Arts: The Ohio State University*, essays by Rafael Moneo and others, New York, 1989;

Jean-François Bedard (ed.), *Cities of Artificial Excavation: The Work of Peter Eisenman 1978–1988*, Montreal and New York, 1994; *Eisenman Architects: Selected and Current Works*, Mulgrave, 1995
Exhibitions: Architectural Association, London (1985, 1986); Biennale, Venice and Contemporary Arts Center, Cincinnati (1991–2)

Abdel Wahed El-Wakil, b.1943
Nationality: Egyptian
Education: Ain Shams University, Cairo
Projects: Halawa House, Agany, Egypt (1975); Hamdy House, Cairo (1978); Al Sulaiman Palace and Mosque, Saudi Arabia (1979); Corniche Mosque, Jeddah (1986); Island Mosque, Jeddah (1986); King Saud Mosque, Jeddah (1987); Al-Ruwais Mosque (1987–90); Al-Miquat Mosque, Medina (1991)
Publications: 'The Mosque: Architecture of El-Wakil', *Albenaa*, vol. 6, no. 34, 1987; James Steele and Ismaïl Serageldin (eds), *The Architecture of the Contemporary Mosque*, London, 1996
Awards: Aga Khan Award for Architecture (1980 and 1989); King Saud Award for Design in Research in Islamic Architecture (1988)

Ralph Erskine, b.1914
Nationality: British
Education: Regent Street Polytechnic, London; Royal Academy of Art, Stockholm
Projects: Byker Wall, Newcastle upon Tyne (1969–81); The Ark, Hammersmith, London (1991)
Publications: Peter Collymore, *The Architecture of Ralph Erskine*, London, 1982; Mats Egelius, *Ralph Erskine, Architect*, Stockholm, 1990
Exhibitions: The Building Centre, London (1985)
Awards: Litteris et Artibus Royal Gold Medal, Sweden (1980); Gold Medal, Royal Architectural Institute of Canada (1982); RIBA Gold Medal (1987)

Evans and Shalev, comprising:
Eldred Evans
Nationality: British
David Shalev
Nationality: Israeli
Projects: Truro Crown Courts (1985–8); Private Residential development, Coventry (1986–8); Tate Gallery, St Ives, Cornwall (1993)
Publications: *Evans and Shalev*, 9H Gallery, London, 1988
Exhibitions: 9H Gallery, London (1988)

Terry Farrell, b.1938
Nationality: British
Education: University of Newcastle; Durham University; University of Pennsylvania
Projects: TV AM Headquarters, Camden, London (1981–2); Charing Cross Development, London (1987–90); Vauxhall Cross Government HQ, London (1988); Kowloon Station, Hong Kong (1997–)
Publications: Marcus Binney, *Palace on the River*, London, 1991; Kenneth Powell, *Vauxhall Cross*, London, 1992; *Terry Farrell*, London, 1993; *Terry Farrell: Selected and Current Works*, Mulgrave, 1994
Exhibitions: RIBA, London (1995)
Awards: OBE (1978); CBE (1996)

Hassan Fathy, b.1900, d.1989
Nationality: Egyptian
Education: School of Engineering, Giza
Projects: New Gourna, near Luxor (1946–53); New Bariz project (1970); Hassan Fathy House, Sidi Krier (1971); founded International Institute for Appropriate Technology (1977); Mosque at Dar el Islam, Abiquiu, New Mexico (1981); Khaleel-Al-Talhooly House, Ghur Numren, Jordan (1988);
Publications: by Fathy: *Architecture for the Poor: An Experiment in Rural Egypt*, Chicago/London, 1973; *The Arab House in the Urban Setting: Past, Present and Future*, London, 1972; *Natural Energy and Vernacular Architecture*, Chicago, 1986; on Fathy: J M Richards, I Serageldin and D Rastorfer; *Hassan Fathy*, London, 1985; *Hassan Fathy*, London, 1988
Exhibitions: Technische Universität, Vienna (1980)
Awards: Chairman's Prize, Aga Khan Awards for Architecture (1980); UIA Gold Medal (1984)

Frederick Fisher, b.1949
Nationality: American
Education: University of Pennsylvania
Projects: Caplin House, Venice, California (1978); Vena -Mondt Studio, Los Angeles (1983); L A Louver Gallery, Venice (1994)
Publications: Frederick Fisher, Architect, New York, 1995
Exhibitions:American Craft Museum, New York (1986); California State University, Long Beach (1994)

Norman Foster (Sir), b.1935
Nationality: British
Education: Manchester University; Yale University
Projects: Sainsbury Centre for the Visual Arts, University of East Anglia (1974–8); Willis Faber Dumas Building, Ipswich (1975); Hongkong & Shanghai Bank, Hong Kong (1979–85); Stansted Airport (1980–91); Carré d'Art, Nimes (1985–93); Sackler Galleries, Royal Academy, London (1985–93); Century Tower, Tokyo (1987–91); Commerzbank, Frankfurt (1997); Millennium Tower proposals, London and Tokyo (1997)
Publications: Ian Lambot (ed.), *Norman Foster ... Buildings and Projects*, vol. 1, *1964–1973*, Godalming, 1991, vol. 2, *1971–1978*, Hong Kong, 1990, vol. 3, *1978–1985*, Hong Kong, 1990; Daniel Treiber, *Norman Foster*, English edn., London, 1995
Exhibitions: Colegio de Arquitectos, Barcelona (1976); Museum of Modern Art, New York (1979, 1983); RIBA, London (1982, 1993); Royal Academy, London (1983); Palazzo Vecchio, Florence (1987)
Awards: Japan Design Foundation Award (1987); Grosse Kunstpreis, Akademie der Kunst, Berlin (1989); Gold Medal, Académie d'Architecture, France (1991); Arnold W Brunner Memorial Prize (1992); AIA Gold Medal (1994)

James Ingo Freed, see entry under Pei Cobb Freed and Partners

Tony Fretton
Nationality: British
Education: Architectural Association, London
Projects: Lisson Gallery, London (1986) and extension (1992); Artsway Building (1996); Quay Arts Centre, Isle of Wight (1997); storage facility for Arts Council Collection of Sculpture, Halifax (1997)
Publications: *Tony Fretton*, introduction by David Turnbull, Barcelona, 1995 (text in Spanish and English)
Exhibitions: Architectural Association, London (1990); RIBA, London (1993)

Massimiliano Fuksas, b.1944
Nationality: Italian
Education: La Sapienza University, Rome
Projects: Entrance Pavilion, Niaux caves, France (1988–93); Montaigne University Art School, Bordeaux (1993–4)
Publications: Mario Pisani, *Massimiliano Fuksas Architetto*, Rome, 1988; *Massimiliano Fuksas: neue Bauten und Projekte*, Zurich and London, 1994; Ruggero Lenci, *Massimiliano Fuksas: oscillazioni e sconfinamenti*, Turin, 1996
Exhibitions: Institut Français d'Architecture, Paris (1992)

Future Systems, comprising:
Jan Kaplicky, b.1937
Nationality: Czech
Education: College of Applied Arts and Architecture, Prague
Amanda Levete, b.1955
Nationality: British
Education: Architectural Association, London
Projects: Bibliothèque Nationale, Paris (competition entry, 1989); Hauer-King House, London (1995); Zero Emission Development Research Programme (with the Martin Centre, Cambridge, 1995–)
Publications: by Future Systems: *For Inspiration Only*, London, 1996; on Future Systems: Martin Pawley, *Future Systems – Story of Tomorrow*, London, 1993
Exhibitions: RIBA, London (1982, 1991); Architectural Association, London (1987); Architecture Foundation, London (1996)

Gaïa Associates, comprising:
(now Paul Leech: GAIA Ecotecture)
Paul Leech, b.1950
Nationality: Irish
Education: NUI Dublin
Projects: Financial Services Offices, Navan (1988); Computer Software

Facility, Carlow (1985); Environmental Study for UNDP, North Korea (1991); Waterfall House, County Meath (1989–90); Eco House, County Cork (1995–6); Social Housing/Urban Regeneration, Dublin (1997)
Publications: in: David Pearson, *Earth to Spirit: In Search of Natural Architecture*, London, 1994; Sydney Baggs, *The Healthy House*, Sydney/London, 1996
Awards: Construction Excellence Award (1995)

Aurelio Galfetti, b.1936
Nationality: Swiss
Education: Eidgenössische Technische Hochschule, Zurich
Projects: Kindergarten, Riva San Vitale (1966); Swimming Pool, Tennis Club and Apartments, Bellinzona, Switzerland (1967–85)
Publications: *Aurelio Galfetti*, Barcelona, 1989
Exhibitions: Architektur Forum, Zurich (1989); Museo Vela, Ligornetto, and tour to Morcote and Varese (1994)

Frank O Gehry, b.1929
Nationality: American
Education: University of Southern California; Harvard University Graduate School
Projects: Spiller House, Venice, California (1980); California Aerospace Museum (1982); Norton House, Venice, California, (1984); Vitra Furniture Museum and Factory, Weil am Rhein, Germany (1987); Edgemar Complex, Santa Monica (1987); Chiat Day Headquarters, Venice, California (1989); Disney Concert Hall, Los Angeles (1989); Schnabel House, Los Angeles (1990); 'Fred and Ginger' Building, Prague (1995); Guggenheim Museum, Bilbao (1997)
Publications: Peter Arnell *et al.*, *Frank Gehry: Buildings and Projects*, New York, 1985; *Frank O Gehry*, edited and photographed by Yukio Futagawa, Tokyo, 1993; Charles Jencks (ed.), *Frank O Gehry: Individual Imagination and Cultural Conservatism*, London, 1995
Exhibitions: Walker Arts Center, Minneapolis, and tour in the US (1986–7)
Awards: Arnold W Brunner Memorial Prize (1983); Pritzker Prize (1989); Wolf Prize (1992); Praemium Imperiale, Japan (1992)

Teodoro González de Leôn, b.1926
Nationality: Mexican
Education: Universidad Nacional Autonoma, de Mexico, Mexico City
Projects: Colegio de Mexico, Mexico City (1975); Tamayo Museum, Chapultepec Park, Mexico City (1981); Supreme Court, Mexico City (1987–92); State Auditorium, Guanajuato, Mexico (1991)
Publications: by González de Leôn: *Barra de Navidad: Survey of an Area*, Mexico City, 1958; *Housing in Mexico City*, Mexico City, 1960; *Research on Housing in Eleven Mexican Cities*, Mexico City, 1966; on González de Leôn: Paul Heyer, *Mexican Architecture: The Work of Abraham Zabludovsky and Teodoro González de Leôn*, New York, 1978
Exhibitions: Museo de Arte Contemporaneo Internacional Rufino Tamayo, Mexico City (1996–7)

Giorgio Grassi, b.1935
Nationality: Italian
Education: Milan Polytechnic
Projects: student housing, Chieti (1976); Municipal Library, Gröningen (1989); School, Santiago di Compostela (1992)
Publications: by Grassi: *La costruzione logica dell'architettura*, Milan, 1967; *Architettura: lingua morta*, Milan, 1988; on Grassi: Francesco Moschini (ed.), *Giorgio Grassi: Progetti 1960–1980* (Milan, 1984); Simona Pierini (ed.), *Giorgio Grassi: progetti per la città antica*, Milan, 1995
Exhibitions: Galleria AAM, Rome, and tour to Maastricht, Pescara and Berlin (1981); Istituto Italiano di Cultura, Buenos Aires (1983); Architecture Gallery, Munich (1986); Fondazione Masieri, Venice (1990)

Michael Graves, b.1934
Nationality: American
Education: University of Cincinnati; Harvard University; The American Academy in Rome
Projects: Hanselmann House, Indiana (1967); Benacerraf House, Princeton, New Jersey (1969); Snyderman House, Fort Wayne, Indiana (1972); Plocek House, New Jersey (1982); Portland Building, Oregon (1980–3); Humana Building, Louisville, Kentucky (1983–6); Whitney Museum of American Art, New York (addition, 1985); Walt Disney World Dolphin and Swan Hotels, Florida (1987); Hotel New York, Euro Disney, France (1989); Denver Central Library, Colorado (1990)
Publications: *Michael Graves: Building and Projects 1966–1981*,

New York, 1983; *Michael Graves: Buildings and Projects 1982–1989*, New Haven/London, 1990, *Michael Graves; Buildings and Projects 1990–1994*, New York, 1995
Exhibitions: Columbia University, New York, and tour in US (1976)
Awards: Arnold W Brunner Memorial Prize (1980); AIA Award for Excellence (1992)

Allan Greenberg, b.1938
Nationality: American (born in South Africa)
Education: University of Witwatersrand, Johannesburg; Yale University
Projects: offices and reception rooms for the US Department of State, Washington, DC (1984); Paternoster Square development, London (1990); The News Building, Athens, Georgia (1992)
Publications: *Allan Greenberg, Selected Work*, London, 1995
Exhibitions: Biennale, Venice, and tour to Paris and San Francisco (1981–2)

Vittorio Gregotti, b.1927
Nationality: Italian
Education: Milan Polytechnic
Projects: Housing Development, Berlin (1984); University of Palermo Science Building, Sicily (1984); ENEA Research Centre, Rome (1985);
Publications: by Gregotti: *New Directions in Italian Architecture*, London, 1968; *La città visible*, Turin, 1993; on Gregotti: Manfredo Tafuri, *Vittorio Gregotti: progetti e architetture*, Milan and New York, 1982
Exhibitions: Triennale, Milan (1964)

Nicholas Grimshaw, b.1939
Nationality: British
Education: Edinburgh College of Art School of Architecture; Architectural Association, London
Projects: Camden Sainsbury's, London (1985–8); Financial Times Printing Plant, Docklands, London (1986–8); Waterloo International Terminal, London (1988–93); Igus GmbH, Cologne (1990–2); *Western Morning News* HQ, Plymouth (1990–3); Ludwig Erhard Haus, Stock Exchange and Communications Centre, Berlin (1991–4); British Pavilion, Seville Expo (1992); Waterloo International Terminal, London (1993); Eden Project, Cornwall (1997)
Publications: Rowan Moore (ed.), *Structure, Space and Skin, The Work of Nicholas Grimshaw & Partners*, London, 1993; *Architecture, Industry and Innovation: The Early Work of Nicholas Grimshaw and Partners*, introduction by Colin Amery, London, 1995
Exhibitions: RIBA, London (1987–8, 1993)
Awards: CBE (1993); Royal Academician (1994)

Gwathmey Siegel & Associates, comprising
Charles Gwathmey, b.1938
Nationality: American
Education: University of Pennsylvania, Philadelphia; Yale University
Robert Siegel
Nationality: American
Education: Pratt Institute; Harvard University
Projects: Gwathmey House and Studio, New York (1965); Library and Science Building, Westover School, Connecticut (1979); De Menil Residence (1986); three buildings, Cornell University (1991); addition to Fogg Museum, Harvard (1991); extension to Guggenheim Museum, New York (1992)
Publications: Peter Arnell and Ted Bickford (eds.), *Charles Gwathmey and Robert Siegel: Buildings and Projects, 1964–1984*, New York, 1984; *Gwathmey Siegel, Buildings and Projects 1982–1992*, New York, 1993; Oscar Riera Ojeda (ed.), *Ten Houses: Gwathmey Siegel*, Rockport, 1995
Awards: Arnold W Brunner Memorial Prize (1970); Medal of Honour, AIA New York Chapter (1983)

Zaha Hadid, b.1950
Nationality: Iraqi
Education: American University, Beirut; Architectural Association, London
Projects: Peak Club, Hong Kong (1982); Vitra Fire Station, Weil-am-Rhein (1990–3); Cardiff Opera House (1994)
Publications: Yukio Futagawa (ed), *Zaha Hadid*, Tokyo, 1986; *Zaha Hadid 1983–1991*, El Croquis monograph, Madrid, 1991
Exhibitions: Guggenheim Museum, New York (1978); GA Gallery, Tokyo (1985); Graduate School of Design, Harvard University (1995); Galerie Renate Kammer, Hamburg (1996)
Awards: British Architectural Awards Gold Medal (1982)

Hammond Beeby and Babka, Thomas Beeby, Principal and
Director of Design:
Thomas Hall Beeby, b.1941
Nationality: American
Education: Cornell University; Yale University
Projects: One Woodfield Place, Schaumburg, Illinois (1975); National
Bank, Ripon, Wisconsin (1976); Doane Observatory, Chicago (1978); Bank
of the North Shore, Northbrook, Illinois (1978); Paternoster Square
development, London (1990); Harold Washington Library Center,
Chicago (1991); Rice Building, Art Institute of Chicago (1991); Hole-in-the-
Wall Gang Camp, Ashford, Connecticut (1993)
Publications: in S Cohen, *Chicago Architects*, Chicago, 1976; R Jensen
and P Conway, *Ornamentalism*, New York, 1981
Awards: National Design Award (1984)

Hiroshi Hara, b.1936
Nationality: Japanese
Education: University of Tokyo
Projects: Niramu House, Tokyo (1978); Yamato International Building,
Tokyo (1987); Ida City Museum, Nagano (1988); Umeda Sky Building,
Osaka (1993)
Publications: Y. Futagawa (ed), and D. B. Stewart, *Hiroshi Hara*, Tokyo, 1993
Exhibitions: San Francisco Museum of Modern Art (1987)

Itsuko Hasegawa, b. 1941
Nationality: Japanese
Education: Kanto Gakuin University, Yokohama
Projects: Tokumara Children's Clinic, Matsuyama (1979); Shonandai Cultural
Centre, Fujisawa (1990); Sumida Culture and Education Centre, Tokyo (1994)
Publications: *Itsuko Hasegawa*, 1993; *Itsuko Hasegawa: Recent Buildings
and Projects*, Basle, 1997
Exhibitions: Institut Français d'Architecture, Paris (1997)

Zvi Hecker, b.1931
Nationality: Israeli (born in Poland)
Education: Cracow Polytechnic; Israel Institute of Technology, Haifa
Projects: Military Academy, Negev Desert (1963–7; 1969–71); Ramot Housing
Project, Jerusalem (1973–86); Heinz-Galinski School, Berlin (1990–3)
Publications: Kristin Feireiss (ed.), *Zvi Hecker: die Heinz-Galinski Schule
in Berlin*, Tübingen, 1996
Exhibitions: Cooper Union School of Architecture, New York (1986);
Biennale, Venice (1991); Architektur Galerie am Weissenhof, Stuttgart
(1996); Tel Aviv Museum of Art (1996)

John Hejduk, b.1929
Nationality: American
Education: Cooper Union School of Art and Architecture, New York;
University of Cincinnati; Graduate School of Design, Harvard University;
University of Rome School of Architecture
Projects: Skinner Duplex Apartments, Austin, Texas (project, 1954–63);
restoration of Foundation Building, Cooper Union, New York (1975);
Victims design and construction of elements for IBA project, Berlin
(1984); IBA Housing at Tegel and Kreuzberg, Berlin (1988); Lancaster/
Hanover Masque, Georgia Institute of Technology, Atlanta (1990)
Publications: by Hejduk: *Mask of Medusa: Works 1947–1983*, New York,
1985; *Vladivostok, Lake Baikal*, New York, 1989; *The Lancaster/Hanover
Masque*, London, 1992; *Soundings*, New York, 1993; *Adjusting
Foundations*, New York, 1995
Exhibitions: Le Corbusier Foundation, Paris (1972); Architectural Associa-
tion, London (1978); Eidgenössische Technische Hochschule, Zurich (1983);
Architectural Association, London (1986); Aedes Galerie, Berlin (1988)
Awards: Arnold W Brunner Memorial Prize (1986)

Herron Associates:
Ronald Herron, b.1930
Nationality: British
Education: Brixton School of Building, London; Regent Street
Polytechnic, London
Projects: Imagination Headquarters, London (1990); Daimon Kite
Museum/Bus Station, Toyoma (1993)
Publications: editor (with Peter Cook), *Archigram*, London, 1973;
Sutherland Lyall (ed), *Herron Notebooks: Buildings in Japan*, London,
1993; Reyner Banham, *The Visions of Ron Herron*, London, 1994
Exhibitions: Art Net Gallery, London and Institute for Architecture and
Urban Studies, New York (1977–8); RIBA, London (1989)
Awards: RIBA National Award for Architecture (1990)

Herzog & de Meuron, partnership comprising:
Jacques Herzog, b.1950
Nationality: Swiss
Education: Eidgenössische Technische Hochschule, Zurich
Pierre de Meuron, b.1950
Nationality: Swiss
Education: Eidgenössische Technische Hochschule, Zurich
Projects: Goetz Art Gallery, Munich (1989–92); The Signal Box, Basle
(1992–5); New Tate Gallery at Bankside, London (1995–);
Publications: Wilfried Wang, *Herzog & de Meuron, Projects and
Buildings 1982–1990*, New York, 1990; Wilfried Wang, *Herzog & de
Meuron*, Zürich, 1992; *Herzog & de Meuron, El Croquis* monograph no.
60, 1993; *Herzog & de Meuron, A+U* monograph, no. 300, 1995
Exhibitions: Architektur-museum, Basle (1988); Rijksmuseum Kröller-
Müller, Otterlo (1992); Centre Georges Pompidou, Paris, and Museum of
Modern Art, New York (1995)
Awards: European Prize for Industrial Architecture, Hanover (1996)

Hodgetts and Fung, comprising:
Craig Edward Hodgetts, b.1937
Nationality: American
Education: Oberlin College, Ohio; Yale University
Hsin-Ming Fung, b.1953
Nationality: American
Education: California State University; University of California at Los
Angeles
Projects: Design of Blueprints for Modern Living exhibition, Museum of
Contemporary Art, Los Angeles (1989); Powell Library, UCLA (1992);
Click and Flick Agency, Hollywood (1993)
Publications: *Hodgetts + Fung: Scenarios and Spaces*, introduction by
Kurt Foster, New York, 1997
Awards: Award of Excellence, AIA/American Library Association (1993);
Architecture Award, American Academy of Arts and Letters (1994)

Steven Holl, b.1947
Nationality: American
Education: University of Washington; Architectural Association, London
Projects: Housing, Fukuoka, Japan (1990); Stretto House, Dallas (1992);
Chapel of St Ignatius, Seattle (1997)
Publications: by Holl: *Intertwining*, New York, 1992; *Stretto House,
Steven Holl Architects*, New York, 1996; on Holl: 'Steven Holl', *GA
Document Extra*, 1996
Exhibitions: Venice, Biennale (1991, 1996); Museum of Modern Art, New
York (1995)
Awards: AIA National Honor Award (1989, 1991, 1992, 1993); Arnold W
Brunner Memorial Prize (1990)

Hans Hollein, b.1934
Nationality: Austrian
Education: Academy of Fine Arts, Vienna; Illinois Institute of
Technology, Chicago; University of California at Berkeley
Projects: Städtisches Museum, Mönchengladbach (1970–82); Austrian
Travel Bureau, Vienna (1976–8); Museum of Fine Art, Frankfurt
(1982–91); Haas House, Vienna (1987–90)
Publications: Christoph Mackler, *Hans Hollein*, Aachen, 1978;
Architekten Hans Hollein, Stuttgart, 1987; Giani Pettena, *Hans Hollein:
Works 1960–1988*, Milan, 1988
Exhibitions: Museum of Modern Art, New York (1967); Documenta 6,
Kassel (1977); Centre Georges Pompidou, Paris, and tour to Vienna and
Berlin (1987–8)
Awards: Grand Austrian State Award (1983); Pritzker Prize (1985)

Michael Hopkins (Sir), b.1935
Nationality: British
Education: Architectural Association, London
Projects: Hopkins House, Hampstead, London (1976); Schlumberger
Cambridge Research Centre (1982–5 and 1992); Mound Stand, Lord's
Cricket Ground, London (1987); David Mellor Cutlery Factory,
Hathersage, Derbyshire (1989); Bracken House, City of London (1992);
Glyndebourne Opera House, Sussex (1989–94); Inland Revenue Centre,
Nottingham (1992–4);Queen's Building, Emmanuel College, Cambridge
(1996); New Parliamentary Building, London (1997–)
Publications: Colin Davies, *Hopkins: The Work of Michael Hopkins and
Partners*, London, 1993
Awards: RIBA Gold Medal (1994)

Richard Horden, b.1944
Nationality: British
Education: Architectural Association, London
Projects: Queen's Stand, Epsom Racecourse (1989)
Publications: by Horden: *Light Tech: Towards a Light Architecture*,
Basle, 1995
Awards: RIBA National Award for Architecture (1993)

Kazuhiro Ishii, b. 1944
Nationality: Japanese
Education: University of Tokyo
Projects: '54 Windows', Soya Clinic and Residence, Hiratsuka, Kanagawa
(1975); Spinning House, Tokyo (1985); Sukiya Village, Okayama (1989);
San Juan Bautista Museum, Ojika (1996)
Publications: *Kazuhiro Ishii*, Tokyo, 1990

Arata Isozaki, b. 1931
Nationality: Japanese
Education: University of Tokyo
Projects: Gunma Prefectural Museum of Modern Art, Takasaki (1971–4);
Central Library, Kitakyushi (1973–5); Fujima Country Club (1974); Civic
Centre, Tsukuba (1978–83); Museum of Contemporary Art, Los Angeles
(1986); Cultural Complex, Mito (1990); Convention Centre, Nara
(1992–5); Museum, Coruna Spain (1993–5)
Publications: Philip Drew, *The Architecture of Arata Isozaki*, New York
and London, 1982; Brunilde Barattucci and Bianca di Russo, *Arata
Isozaki: Architecture 1959–1982*, Rome, 1983; *Arata Isozaki: Architecture
1960–1990*, preface by Richard Koshalek, essays by David B Stewart and
Hajime Yatsuka, New York, 1991; Yukio Futagawa (ed), criticism by
Kenneth Frampton, *Arata Isozaki, Vol. 1: 1959–1978*, Tokyo, 1991; *Arata
Isozaki: opere e progetti*, preface by Francesco Dal Co, essays by
Yoshitake Doi and Arata Isozaki, Milan, 1994
Exhibitions: *The Architecture of Fumihiko Maki and Arata Isozaki*, Japan
Society, New York, and tour in US (1985); Museum of Contemporary Art,
Los Angeles (1991); Aedes Gallery, Berlin (1993–4); RIBA, London (1995)
Awards: Architectural Institute of Japan, Annual Prize (1966, 1974); RIBA
Gold Medal (1986); Arnold W Brunner Memorial Prize (1988); AIA
National Honor Award (1992)

Franklin D Israel, b.1945, d.1996
Nationality: American
Education: University of Pennsylvania; Yale University Graduate School
of Art and Architecture; Columbia University, New York; American
Academy, Rome
Projects: Art Pavilion, Beverly Hills (1991); Virgin Records, Beverly Hills
(1991); Limelight Productions, Hollywood (1991); Goldberg Bean
Residence, Hollywood Hills (1992); Drager House, Berkeley (1995)
Publications: *Franklin D Israel, Buildings and Projects*, introduction by
Frank O Gehry, essays by Thomas S Hines and Franklin D Israel, New
York, 1992; Aaron Betsky, *Drager House*, London, 1996
Awards: AIA Gold Medal (1971); Academy Award in Architecture,
American Academy of Arts and Letters (1993); AIA National Honor
Award (1995)

Toyo Ito, b. 1941
Nationality: Japanese (born in North Korea)
Education: University of Tokyo
Projects: Silver Hut, Tokyo (1984); Tower of the Winds, Yokohama
(1986); Nomad Cafe, Roppongi (1986); Yatsushiro Municipal Museum,
Kumamoto (1991)
Publications: Sophie Roulet and Sophie Soulie, *Toyo Ito: l'architecture
de l'ephemère*, Paris, 1991; *Toyo Ito*, introduction by Charles Jencks,
London, 1995
Exhibitions: Institut Français d'Architecture, Paris (1991); Architectural
Association, London (1992)
Awards: Architectural Institute of Japan, Annual Prize (1986)

Helmut Jahn, b.1940
Nationality: German (resident in US)
Education: Technische Hochschule, Munich; Illinois Institute of
Technology, Chicago
Projects: State of Illinois Center, Chicago (1985); 750 Lexington Avenue,
New York (1989); Barnett Center, Jacksonville (1990); Messe Tower,
Frankfurt (1991)
Publications: Nory Miller, *Helmut Jahn*, New York, 1986; *Helmut Jahn
1982–1992*, Todyo, 1992; *Murphy/Jahn*, Master Series, Mulgrave, 1995

Exhibitions: Biennale, Venice, and tour to Paris and San Francisco (1980); Gallery MA, Tokyo (1986); Architekturgalerie, Munich (1987); Cupples Design Forum, Tokyo (1991)
Awards: Arnold W Brunner Memorial Prize (1982); Chevalier, Ordre des Arts et des Lettres, Paris (1988)

Jon Jerde, b.1940
Nationality: American
Education: University of Southern California, Los Angeles
Projects: Horton Plaza redevelopment, San Diego (1985); MCA City Walk, Universal Studios, Los Angeles (1994); Fremont Street Experience redevelopment, Las Vegas (1995); Canal City, Fukuoka (1996)
Publications: in: Hess, Alan (Foreword by R Venturi, D Scott Brown and S Izenour), *Viva Las Vegas: After Hours Architecture*, San Francisco, 1993; *Architecture After Modernism*, London, 1996; Anderton, Frances and John Chase, *Las Vegas: The Success of Excess*, London, 1997;
Awards: AIA Honor Award (1984, 1985)

Eva Jiricna, b.1939
Nationality: British (born in Czechoslovakia)
Education: University of Prague; Prague Academy of Fine Arts
Projects: staircase, Joseph Shop, Sloane Street, London (1989); extension, Ove Arup House, Highgate, London (1991)
Publications: *Eva Jiricna Designs*, London, 1987; Martin Pawley, *Eva Jiricna: Design in Exile*, London, 1990
Exhibitions: Architectural Association, London (1987)

Philip   Johnson, b.1906
Nationality: American
Education: Harvard School of Architecture
Projects: Founder and Director (1930–6 and 1946–54) of the New York Museum of Modern Art's Department of Architecture, mounted the landmark exhibition *The International Style* (with Henry-Russell Hitchcock, 1932); The Glass House, New Canaan (1949); Hodgson House, New Canaan (1951); Seagram Building (with Mies van der Rohe) (1958); Asia House, New York (1959); Sheldon Memorial Art Gallery, University of Nebraska (1963); Extension to Boston Public Library (1973); Pennzoil Place, Houston (1976); American Telephone and Telegraph Building, New York (1979); Republic Bank Center, Houston (1981–4); Pittsburgh Plate Glass Tower (1981)
Publications: by Johnson: *The International Style: Architecture since 1922* (with Henry-Russell Hitchcock, New York, 1932); *Mies van der Rohe*, New York, 1947; R. Stern (ed), *Philip Johnson: Writings*, New York, 1978; *Philip Johnson: A Portrait of the Architect in his own Words*, New York, 1994; on Johnson: John M. Jacobus, *Philip Johnson: Architecture*, New York, 1979; Carleton Knight, *Philip Johnson/John Burgee Architecture 1979–85*, New York, 1985; Franz Schulze, *Philip Johnson, Life and Work*, New York, 1994; Jeffrey Kipnis, *Philip Johnson: Recent Works*, London, 1996
Exhibitions: *New Directions in American Architecture*, New York (1977); *Philip Johnson: Processes*, New York (1978)
Awards: AIA Gold Medal (1978); Pritzker Prize (1979); Lifetime Achievement Award, New York Society of Architects (1993)

Louis I Kahn, b.1901, d.1974
Nationality: American
Education: Pennsylvania Academy of Fine Arts, Philadelphia
Projects: Richards Medical Research Building, Philadelphia (1957–64); US Consulate, Luanda (1959–61); dormitories, Bryn Mawr College (1960–4); Mikvah Israel College, Philadelphia (1961–72); National Assembly Building, Dacca (1962–74); Congress Hall, Venice (1968–74)
Publications: by Kahn: *Louis I Kahn: Talks with Students*, Houston, 1969; on Kahn: Vincent Scully, *Louis I Kahn*, New York, 1962; Heinz Ronner, Sharad Jhaveri and Alessandro Vesella, *Louis I Kahn: The Complete Works 1935–1974*, Boulder, 1977; David Brown and David Delong, *Louis I Kahn: In the Realm of Architecture*, New York, 1991; Urs Buttiker, *Louis I Kahn: Light and space*, Basle, 1993
Exhibitions: Museum of Modern Art, New York (1939, 1966); Swiss Federal Institute of Technology, and tour of Europe (1969); Museum of Art, Philadelphia, and tour of US, Paris and Gunma, Japan (1991–4)
Awards: Arnold W Brunner Memorial Prize (1960); AIA Gold Medal (1971); RIBA Gold Medal (1972); Gold Medal, National Institute of Arts and Letters (1973)

Ram Karmi, b.1931
Nationality: Israeli
Education: Technion: Israeli Institute of Technology, Haifa; Architectural Association, London
Projects: El-Al office building, Tel Aviv (with Dov Karmi, 1963); Department of Humanities, Hebrew University, Jerusalem (1978); Giloh Housing, near Jerusalem (1981); Supreme Court Building, Jerusalem (1987–93)
Publications: by Karmi: Yosef Sharon, *The Supreme Court Building, Jerusalem*, London, 1993
Exhibitions: RIBA, London (1994)
Awards: Rokach Prize, Tel Aviv (1965); Reinholds Prize, Tel Aviv (1969)

Josef Paul Kleihues, b.1933
Nationality: German
Education: Technische Universität, Stuttgart; Ecole des Beaux-Arts, Paris
Projects: German Steel Museum, Solingen (1982); Gerleve Monastery, extension, Coesfeld (1982); Museum of Contemporary Art, Chicago (1991)
Publications: John O'Regan, *Josef Paul Kleihues*, Dublin, 1983; Kim Shkapich (ed), *Josef P Kleihues, The Museum Projects*, New York, 1989; Andrea Mesecke and Thorsten Scheer (eds), *Josef Paul Kleihues: Themes and Projects*, Basle, 1996

Pierre Koenig, b.1925
Nationality: American
Education: University of Southern California, Los Angeles
Projects: Koenig House I, Glendale (1950); Case Study House numbers 21 and 22, Hollywood (1958–9 and 1960); Seidel House, Malibu (1960); Rolle House addition, Brentwood (1983); Schwartz House, Pacific Palisades, Los Angeles (1993)
Publications: by Koenig: *The Chemehuevi Project* (with P Rodemier and KH Grey), Los Angeles, 1971; *This is Our Land*, Los Angeles, 1974; on Koenig (forthcoming): James Steele, *Pierre Koenig*, London, 1998
Exhibitions: Bienal, São Paulo (1957); Museum of Contemporary Art, Los Angeles (1989–90)
Awards: São Paulo Bienal Exhibition Award, Brazil (1957); Los Angeles Grand Prix (1964); AIA 200/2000 Award (1983)

Kohn Pedersen Fox, comprising:
Eugene Kohn (partner in charge)
Nationality: American
Education: University of Pennsylvania, Philadelphia
William Pedersen (design partner)
Nationality: American
Education: University of Minnesota, Minneapolis; Massachusetts Institute of Technology, Cambridge; American Academy, Rome
William Louie (design partner)
Nationality: American
Education: City College of New York
Projects: 333 Wacker Drive, Chicago (1979–83); One Logan Square, Philadelphia (1983); DG Bank, Frankfurt (1993)
Publications: *Kohn Pedersen Fox: Buildings and Projects 1976–1986*, ed. Sonia R Chao and Trevor D Abramson, New York, 1987; *KPF: Kohn Pedersen Fox: Architecture and Urbanism 1986–1992*, ed. Warren A James, New York, 1993
Exhibitions: RIBA, London (1985)
Awards: AIA National Honor Award (1984); Arnold W Brunner Memorial Prize (Pedersen, 1985)

Hans Kollhoff and Helga Timmermann, comprising:
Hans Kollhoff, b.1946
Nationality: German
Education: University of Karlsruhe
Helga Timmermann, b.1953
Nationality: German
Education: University of Aachen
Projects: Alexanderplatz master plan, Berlin (1993); Housing development 'KNSM-Island', Amsterdam (1994); Landeszentralbank Leipzig, Administration building (1996); Office building, Daimler Benz AG, Berlin (1994–)
Publications: *Hans Kollhoff*, Barcelona, 1991; *Hans Kollhoff and Helga Timmermann: Projects for Berlin*, Antwerp, 1994
Exhibitions: Gallery de Singel, Antwerp (1994)
Awards: Merkelbach Prize, Amsterdam (1994)

Koning Eizenberg, comprising:
Hank Koning
Nationality: Australian
Education: University of Melbourne, University of California at Los Angeles
Julie Eizenberg
Nationality: Australian
Education: University of Melbourne, University of California at Los Angeles
Projects: Electric Art Block, Venice, California (1988); Tarzana House, Santa Monica (1992); 31st Street House, Venice, California (1993)
Publications: *Koning Eizenberg Buildings*, New York, 1996
Exhibitions: University of Technology, Sydney (1988); University of California, Los Angeles (1990); Wexner Center for the Arts (1994)
Awards: National AIA Award (1996)

Rem Koolhaas, b.1944
Nationality: Dutch
Education: Architectural Association, London
Projects: (working with Elia Zenghelis, Zoe Zenghelis and Madelon Vriesendorp as OMA since 1975) 'Delirious New York' (1972–6), a project also published as a book; De Koepel Prison Renovations, Arnheim (1979–80); competition entries for IBA housing projects, Berlin (1980); National Dance Theatre, The Hague (1984–7); Kuntshal, Rotterdam (1987–92); housing for Nexus World, Fukuoka, Japan (1990); Le Grand Palais, Euralille (1990–4)
Publications: by Koolhaas: *Delirious New York: A Retroactive Manifesto for Manhattan*, New York and London, 1978; *OMA Projects 1978–1981*, London, 1981; *S,M,L,XL*, Rotterdam, 1995; on Koolhaas: Patrice Goulet, *OMA, Rem Koolhaas: Six Projects*: Paris, 1990; Jacques Lucan, *OMA, Rem Koolhaas*, Milan and Paris, 1990
Exhibitions: Guggenheim Museum, New York (1978); Architectural Association, London (1981)

Leon Krier, b.1946
Nationality: Luxembourgan
Education: University of Stuttgart (8 months)
Projects: reconstruction of Pliny's Villa, Laurentium (1982); Krier-Wolff House, Seaside, Florida (1987); Poundbury Master plan, Dorset (1988–)
Publications: by Krier: *The Reconstruction of the European City*, Brussels, 1978; *Architecture: choix ou fatalité*, Paris, 1996; on Krier: Richard Economakis (ed.), *Leon Krier: Architecture and Urban Design 1967–1992*, London, 1992
Exhibitions: Museo di castelvecchio, Verona (1980); Walker Art Center, Minneapolis, and US tour (1980); ICA, London (1983); Deutsches Architekturmuseum, Frankfurt am main (1987–8)
Awards: Architecture Prize, Berlin (1975); Jefferson Memorial Medal (1985)

Rob Krier, b.1938
Nationality: Austrian (born in Luxembourg)
Education: Technische Universität, Munich
Projects: Social Housing, Ritterstrasse, Berlin-Kreuzberg (1977–80); Social Housing, Berlin-Spandau (1978–84); Social Housing, Berlin-Wilmersdorf (1980–4); IBA Housing, Rauchstraße, Berlin (1981–5)
Publications: by Krier: *Urban Space*, London, 1979; *Rob Krier on Architecture*, London, 1982; *Architectural Composition*, London, 1988; on Krier: Kenneth Frampton (ed.), *Rob Krier*, New York, 1982
Exhibitions: Vienna Secession (1984); Institut Français d'Architecture, Paris (1988); Biennale, Venice (1991)
Awards: Architecture Prize, City of Berlin (1975); Architecture Prize, City of Vienna (1982)

Shiro Kuramata, b.1934, d.1991
Nationality: Japanese
Education: Kuwazawa Design Institute
Projects: Issey Miyake stores, Paris (1983), New York (1984), Tokyo (1988)
Publications: *Shiro Kuramata 1967–1987*, Tokyo, 1988; *Shiro Kuramata*, 1996
Exhibitions: Itara Museum of Contemporary Art, Tokyo, Centro Cultural Arte Contemporaneo, Mexico City and San Francisco Museum of Modern Art (1996–7)
Awards: Japan Cultural Design prize (1981); Chevalier, ordre des Arts et des Lettres, France (1990)

Kisho Kurokawa, b.1934
Nationality: Japanese
Education: University of Kyoto; University of Tokyo
Projects: Sony Tower, Osaka (1976); Museum of Contemporary Art, Hiroshima (1988); Shirase Expedition Memorial Hall, Akita (1988–90);

Hotel Kyocera, Kagoshima (1993–5); Ehime Museum of Science (1994)
Publications: by Kurokawa: *Metabolism in Architecture*, London and
New York, 1977; *From Metabolism to Symbiosis*, London, 1992; *Each One
a Hero: The Philosophy of Symbiosis*, Tokyo and London, 1997; on
Kurokawa: *Kisho Kurokawa: architecture de la symbiose*, Paris, 1987;
Kisho Kurokawa: Selected and Current Works, Mulgrave, 1995; *Kisho
Kurokawa: Abstract Symbolism*, preface by Aldo Castellano,
introduction by Kisho Kurokawa, Milan, 1996
Exhibitions: *Kisho Kurokawa: Architecture of Symbiosis*, London, and
touring in Europe (1981–4); Museum of Architecture, Wroclaw, and
SARP, Warsaw (1986)
Awards: Richard Neutra Award (1988); Chevalier, Ordre des Arts et des
Lettres, Paris (1989); Architectural Institute of Japan, Annual Prize (1990)

John Lautner, b.1911, d.1996
Nationality: American
Education: Northern Michigan University, Marquette
Projects: Chemosphere House (now Kuhn House), Los Angeles (1960);
Silvertop, Micheltorena, Los Angeles (1963); Sheats/Goldstein
Residence, Beverly Hills (1963; 1989–96)
Publications: Pierluigi Bonvicini, *John Lautner: Architettura organico-
sperimentale*, Bari, 1981; Frank Escher (ed.), *John Lautner, Architect*,
London, 1994
Exhibitions: Hochschule für Angewandte Kunst, Vienna (1991); National
Institute of Architectural Education, New York (1992)

Ricardo Legorreta, b.1931
Nationality: Mexican
Education: Universidad Nacional Autonoma de Mexico, Mexico City
Projects: Camino Royal Hotels, Mexico City (1968), Cancun, Quintana
Roo (1975), Ixtapa, Guerrero (1981); IBM Offices, Solana, Texas (1988);
Renault Factory, Gómez Palacio Durango, Mexico (1985); Solana Village
Centre, Texas (1988); Playa Vista Community, Los Angeles (1989–);
Managua Metropolitan Cathedral, Nicaragua (1993); Pershing Square,
Los Angeles (1994)
Publications: Wayne Attoe, *The Architecture of Ricardo Legorreta*,
Austin, 1990; John V Mutlow (ed.), *The Architecture of Ricardo
Legorreta*, London, 1997
Exhibitions: Graduate School of Design, Harvard University (1991)
Awards: Architect of the Americas Award, Montevideo (1992)

Daniel Libeskind, b.1946
Nationality: American (born in Poland)
Education: Cooper Union, New York; University of Essex
Projects: Jewish Museum, Berlin (1989–); Boilerhouse extension,
Victoria and Albert Museum, London (1996)
Publications: by Libeskind: *Between Zero and Infinity*, New York, 1981;
Theatrum Mundi, New York, 1985; *Daniel Libeskind: Countersign*,
London, 1992; *Radix: Matrix: Works and Writings of Daniel Libeskind*,
New York, 1996
Exhibitions: Museum für Gestaltung, Zurich (1993); Art Institute of
Chicago and Jewish Museum, New York (1993)
Awards: Leone di Pietra Prize, Venice Biennale (1985); International
Bauausstellung Prize, Berlin (1987)

William Lim, b.1932
Nationality: Singaporean
Education: Architectural Association, London; Harvard University
Projects: Singapore Conference Hall (1964); Three Conservation Houses,
Singapore (1984); Tampines Community Centre, Singapore (1987); Adam
Place Development, Singapore (1992)
Publications: by Lim: *Cities for People*, Singapore, 1990; *Contemporary
Vernacular: Evoking Traditions in Asian Architecture*, Singapore, 1997
Exhibitions: Royal Melbourne Institute of Technology (1997)

Fumihiko Maki, b.1928
Nationality: Japanese
Education: University of Tokyo; Cranbrook Academy, Michigan;
Harvard University
Projects: Spiral Building, Tokyo (1985); Makuhari Messe Exhibition
Centre, Chiba (1986–9); Fujisawa Gymnasium, Tokyo (1990); Yerba
Buena Gardens, Center for the Arts, San Francisco (1993); Kirishima
International Concert Hall (1994)
Publications: by Maki: *Investigations in Collective Form*, St Louis, 1964;
on Maki: Serge Salat, *Fumihiko Maki, an Aesthetic of Fragmentation*,
New York, 1988; *Fumihiko Maki, Maki and Associates: Recent Major

Work, Japan Architect, 1990
Exhibitions: Japan Society, New York, and tour in the US (1985); IFA,
Paris, and tour in Italy, Switzerland, Germany, The Netherlands and
Denmark (1987–91)
Awards: Pritzker Prize (1993); AIA Gold Medal (1993)

Imre Makovecz, b.1935
Nationality: Hungarian
Education: Technical University of Budapest
Projects: Cultural Centre, Sárospatak (1974–83); Excursion Centre,
Restaurant and other projects, Visegrád (1978–); Community Hall,
Zalaszentlászló (1983); Community Centre, Bak (1985–8); Roman
Catholic Church, Paks (1989); Hungarian Pavilion, Seville Exposition
(1992)
Publications: Frank János, *Imre Makovecz*, Budapest, 1979; Edwin
Heathcote, *Imre Makovecz*, London, 1997
Exhibitions: Biennale, Venice (1973); Museum of Finnish Architecture,
Helsinki (1981); Matthew Architecture Gallery, Edinburgh (1992)

Thom Mayne, see entry under Morphosis

Mecanoo, see entry under Erick van Egeraat

Richard Meier, b.1934
Nationality: American
Education: Cornell University, Ithaca, New York
Projects: Smith House, Connecticut (1967); Douglas House, Michigan
(1973); High Museum of Art, Atlanta (1980–3); Museum für
Kunsthandwerk, Frankfurt (1984); Getty Center, Los Angeles (1984–97);
Barcelona Art Museum (1996)
Publications: by Meier: *Richard Meier, Architect: Buildings and Projects
1966–1976*, New York, 1976; *Richard Meier, Architect: 1964–1984*, New
York, 1984; on Meier: Philip Jodidio, *Richard Meier*, Cologne, 1995;
Werner Blaser, *Richard Meier Details*, Basle, 1996; Paul Goldberger and
Richard Rogers, *Richard Meier Houses*, London, 1996; Ingeborg Flaggel
(ed.), *Richard Meier in Europe*, Berlin, 1997
Exhibitions: Swiss Federal Institute of Technology, Zürich; Max Protech
Gallery, New York (1983); touring exhibition (1990)
Awards: Pritzker Prize (1984); RIBA Gold Medal (1996);
AIA Gold Medal (1997)

Scott Merrill, b.1956
Nationality: American
Education: University of Virginia; Yale University
Projects: Honeymoon Cottages, Seaside, Florida (1993); Molz/
Dionne/Atwell Residences, Windsor, Florida (1993); Giffin/Dominguez
Residences, Windsor, Florida (1994); Windsor Town Center, Florida
(1996); Windsor Town Hall (with Leon Krier, 1997)
Publications: in: *The New Urbanism*, New York, 1993; *A Vision of Europe,
Urban Renaissance*, 1996
Exhibitions: Fondations pour l'Architecture, Brussels (1991); University
of Bologna (1996)

Enric Miralles, b.1955
Nationality: Spanish
Education: Escuela Tecnica Superior de Arquitectura, Barcelona
Projects: Olympic Archery Range, Barcelona (1991); Takaoka Train
Station, Japan (1993); Eurythmics Centre, Alicante (1993); Sports Hall,
Huesca (1993); Igualada Park and Cemetery, Barcelona (1995)
Publications: Benedetta Tagliabue, *Enric Miralles: Opere e progetti*,
Milan, 1996; *Enric Miralles* ed. Benedetta Tagliabue, London, 1995;
Anatxu Zabalbeascoa, *Igualada Cemetery*, London, 1996
Exhibitions: Aedes Gallery, Berlin, and Graduate School of Design,
Harvard University (1993); Architekturforum, Zurich (1994); Rice
University, Houston, and Arizona University, Phoenix (1996)
Awards: First National Architectural Prize, Spain (1995); Golden Lion
Award, Venice Biennale (1996)

Mitchell/Giurgola, partnership comprising:
Romaldo Giurgola, b.1920
Nationality: American (born in Italy)
Education: School of Architecture, University of Rome; Columbia
University, New York
Ehrman Mitchell, b.1924
Nationality: American
Education: University of Pennsylvania, Philadelphia

Projects: Princeton University Art Museum, extension and renovation
(1988); Parliament House, Canberra (1988); Australian National
University, Institute of the Arts, extension (1992); Yerba Buena Gardens,
San Francisco (1993)
Publications: by Giurgola: *Louis I Kahn*, with Jaimini Mehta, Zürich and
Boulder, 1975; on Giurgola: *Mitchell/Giurgola Architects*, New York,
1983; Alan Fitzgerald, *Canberra and the New Parliament House*, Sydney,
1983; *Parliament House, Canberra: A Building for the Nation*, ed. Haig
Beck, Sydney, 1988
Exhibitions: Pennsylvania Academy of Fine Arts, Philadelphia (1975;)
Royal Australian Institute of Architects, Sydney (1988)
Awards: Sir Zelman Cowen Award, Royal Australian Institute of
Architects (1989)

Rafael Moneo, b.1937
Nationality: Spanish
Education: Escuela de Arquitectura, Madrid; Spanish Academy, Rome
Projects: Urumea Residential Building, San Sebastián (1968–71);
Bankinter Bank, Madrid (with Ramón Bescos, 1973–6); Town Hall, Logroño
(1973–6); National Museum of Roman Art, Mérida (1980–6); Offices for
La Previsión Espanol, Seville (1982–7); Seville Airport (1987–92);
Atocha Station, Madrid (1985–92); Thyssen-Bornemisza Gallery, Madrid
(conversion, 1989–92); St Vibiana Cathedral, Los Angeles (1996)
Publications: by Moneo: 'On Typology', *Oppositions*, 13, 1978; on Moneo:
Rafael Moneo, A & U, no.8, 1989; *Rafael Moneo 1990–1994, El Croquis*,
no. 64, 1994; *Rafael Moneo. Contra la indiferencia como norma*,
Santiago, 1995
Exhibitions: Akademie der Bildenden Künste, Vienna (1993);
Architekturmuseet, Basle (1993); Architekturmuseum, Stockholm (1993)
Awards: Gold Medal for Achievement in the Fine Arts, Spanish
Government (1992); Arnold W Brunner Memorial Prize (1993); Schock
Prize in the Visual Arts, Stockholm (1993); Pritzker Prize (1996); Gold
Medal, French Academy of Architecture (1996); UIA Gold Medal (1996)

Charles Moore, b.1925, d.1993
Nationality: American
Education: University of Michigan; Princeton University
Projects: (Principal of Moore Ruble Yudell since 1976)
Moore House, Orinda, California (1962); Sea Ranch, California (various
buildings 1964–90); Faculty Club, University of California at Santa
Barbara (1968); Kresge College, University of California at Santa Cruz
(1973); Piazza d'Italia, New Orleans (1975–9); Hood Museum of Art,
Dartmouth College, New Hampshire (1985); Beverly Hills Civic Center
(1985); Playa Vista, Los Angeles (1989–96)
Publications: by Moore: *The Place of Houses*, with G Allen and D
Lyndon, New York, 1974; *Body, Memory and Architecture*, with K C
Bloomer, New Haven, Conn., 1977; on Moore: *Charles W Moore:
Buildings and Projects, 1949–1986*, New York, 1986
Exhibitions: Biennale, Venice (1976); Williams College of Art,
Williamstown, Mass. (1986)
Awards: AIA Gold Medal (1991)

Morphosis: principal architect Thom Mayne, b.1944
Nationality: American
Education: University of Southern California; Harvard University
Projects: Kate Mantilini Restaurant, Beverly Hills (1986); Cedars-Sinai
Hospital, West Hollywood (1988); Salick Office Tower/8201 Beverly Blvd
(1990–1); Crawford House, Montecito (1990); Yuzen Vintage Car
Museum, Los Angeles (1991); Science Museum School, United School
District (in progress); Diamond Ranch High School, Pomona (in
progress); Blades Residence, Santa Barbara (in progress)
Publications: by Mayne: *Morphosis: Tangents and Outtakes*, London,
1993; *Connected Isolation*, London, 1993; on Mayne: Peter Cook and
George Rand, *Morphosis: Buildings and Projects*, New York, 1989;
Richard Weinstein, *Morphosis: Buildings and Projects II*, New York, 1994
Exhibitions: Aedes Gallery, Berlin (1990); Sadock & Uzzan Gallery, Paris
(1992); Form Zero, Culver City, CA, and tour in US (1995–6)
Awards: AIA National Honor Award (1986, 1988); Award in Architecture,
American Academy of Arts and Letters (1992)

Eric Owen Moss, b.1943
Nationality: American
Education: University of California at Berkeley; Harvard University
Projects: Petal House, Los Angeles (1984); Samitaur, Culver City
(1989–95); 8522 National Boulevard, Culver City (1988–90); Hayden
Tower, Culver City, Los Angeles (1992); Stealth, Culver City (1992–6);

Paramount-Lindblade-Gary Group Complex, Culver City (1987–90);
Lawson-Westen House, Los Angeles (1993); The Box, Culver City (1995)
Publications: *Eric Owen Moss, Buildings and Projects 1*, foreword by
Philip Johnson, introduction by Wolf Prix, New York, 1991; *Eric Owen
Moss*, London, 1993; *Eric Owen Moss, Buildings and Projects 2*,
introduction by Anthony Vidler, New York, 1996
Awards: AIA National Honor Award (1988, 1989); AIA National Interior
Design Award (1992, 1994)

Moule & Polyzoides, comprising
Elizabeth Moule, b.1960
Nationality: American
Education: Princeton University
Stefanos Polyzoides, b.1946
Nationality: American (born in Greece)
Education: Princeton University
Projects: Playa Vista Community, Strategic Plan, Los Angeles
(1989–present)
Publications: in J Steele, *Los Angeles Architecture*, London, 1993
Exhibitions: Biennale, Venice (1984); Los Angeles Museum of
Contemporary Art (1994)

Glenn Murcutt, b.1936
Nationality: Australian
Education: University of New South Wales
Projects: Laurie Short House, Sydney (1973); Marie Short House,
Crescent Head (1975); Local History Museum and Tourist Information
Centre, South Kempsey (1982); Ball-Eastaway House, Glenorie (1983);
Tom Magney House, Bingi Point (1984); Littlemore House, Woollahra
(1983–6); Magney House, Paddington (1987–90); Marmabura Marika
House, Yurkalla (1990–2); Kakadu Visitor Centre (1992)
Publications: Philip Drew, *Leaves of Iron: Glenn Murcutt, Pioneer of an
Australian Architectural Form*, Sydney, 1985; *Three Houses*, E M Farrelly,
London, 1993; Françoise Fromonot, *Glenn Murcutt: Works and Projects*,
London, 1995
Awards: Australian Institute of Architecture Gold Medal (1992);
Alvar Aalto Medal (1992)

Juan Navarro Baldeweg, b.1939
Nationality: Spanish
Education: Escuela Tecnica Superior de Arquitectura, Madrid
Projects: Congress and Exhibition Hall, Salamanca (1992); Municipal Public
Library, Madrid (1992); Villaneuva de la Cañada Cultural Centre, Spain (1996)
Publications: Juan José Lahverta, Angel González Garcia and Juan
Navarro Baldeweg, *Juan Navarro Baldeweg: opere progetti*, Milan, 1990;
2nd edn., 1996 (Spanish edn., Madrid, 1993) *Juan Navarro Baldeweg*, El
Croquis monograph no.73, Madrid, 1995
Exhibitions: Carpenter Center, Harvard University (1975); Biennale,
Venice (1978); Eidgenössische Technische Hochschule, Zurich and
Lausanne (1995); Graduate School of Design, Harvard University (1997)
Awards: Spanish National Prize for Fine Arts (1990)

Jean Nouvel, b.1945
Nationality: French
Education: Ecole des Beaux-Arts, Paris
Projects: Institut du Monde Arabe, Paris (1987); Nemausus Housing
Development, Nîmes (1985–7); Opera House, Lyons (1987–93);Fondation
Cartier, Paris (1991)
Publications: *Jean Nouvel: Ra obra reciente 1987–1990*, Barcelona,
1990; Patrice Goulet, *Jean Nouvel*, Paris, 1994; Olivier Boissière, *Jean
Nouvel*, Basle, 1996
Exhibitions: Institut Français d'Architecture, Paris (1987); Collegi
d'Arquitectes, Barcelona (1990); ICA, London, and Arc en Rêve Centre
d'Architecture, Bordeaux (1992–3)
Awards: Chevalier, Ordre du Mérite (1987); Aga Khan Award (1989);
Commandeur, Ordre des Arts et des Lettres (1997)

John Outram, b.1934
Nationality: British
Education: Regent Street Polytechnic, London; Architectural
Association, London
Projects: Storm Water Pumping Station, Isle of Dogs, London (1985–8);
Cambridge Management Centre (1991–5)
Publications: *British Architects Today: Six Protagonists*, Milan, 1991
Exhibitions: Biennale, Venice, 1991
Awards: Bayer Prize for Colour in Architecture (1990)

John Pawson, b.1949
Nationality: British
Education: Architectural Association, London
Projects: Neuendorf House, Majorca (with Claudio Silvestrin, 1989);
House, London (1995); Calvin Klein Store, New York (1995)
Publications: by Pawson: *Minimum*, London, 1996; on Pawson; *John
Pawson*, introduced by Bruce Chatwin and Deyan Sudjic, Barcelona, 1992

Ieoh Ming Pei, see entry under Pei Cobb Freed

Pei Cobb Freed and Partners, comprising:
Ieoh Ming Pei, b.1917
Nationality: American (born in China)
Education: Massachusetts Institute of Technology, Cambridge;
Graduate School of Design, Harvard University
Henry N. Cobb, b.1926
Nationality: American
Education: Harvard University
James Ingo Freed, b.1930
Nationality: American (born in Germany)
Education: Illinois Institute of Technology
Projects: Mile High Center, Denver, Colorado (1955); Place Ville Marie,
Montreal (with Ray Affleck, 1956–65); Kennedy Library, Boston
(1965–79); Des Moines Art Center addition (1968); Everson Museum of
Art, New York (1968); East Building, National Gallery of Art, Washington
(1968–78); Canadian Imperial Bank of Commerce, Toronto (1972);
Johnson Museum of Art, Cornell University (1973); Hancock Tower,
Boston (1973); Dallas Municipal Center (1977); extension at the Louvre,
Paris (1983–93); Holocaust Museum, Washington (1986–92); Bank of
China, Hong Kong (1989–90); First Interstate World Center, Los Angeles
(1990); First Interstate Bank, Dallas (1992); Rock and Roll Hall of Fame,
Cleveland, Ohio (1993–5)
Publications: Carter Wiseman, *The Architecture of I M Pei*, London,
1990; Michael Cannell, *IM Pei: Mandarin of Modernism*, New York, 1995
Awards: Arnold W Brunner Memorial Prize (1961); AIA Gold Medal (1979)
Gold Medal, Académie d'Architecture France (1981); Pritzker Prize (1983)

Gustav Peichl, b.1928
Nationality: Austrian
Education: Academy of Fine Arts, Vienna
Projects: Städel Museum extension, Frankfurt (1987–90); Federal Art
Gallery, Bonn (1986–92); Burg Theatre, rehearsal stage, Vienna (1991–3)
Publications: Franco Fonatti, *Gustav Peichl: Opere e projetti*, Milan,
1988; *Gustav Peichl: von der Skizze zum Bauwerk*, ed. Kristin Feireiss,
Berlin, 1992; *Gustav Peichl: Buildings and Projects*, Stuttgart, 1992;
Gustav Peichl: neue Projekte, Basle, 1996
Exhibitions: Biennale, Venice (1975, 1991); State Academy of Art,
Düsseldorf (1981); RIBA, London (1989); Art Institute of Chicago (1991)
Awards: Austrian State Award for Architecture (1971); Mies van der Rohe
Award (1986)

Cesar Pelli, b.1926
Nationality: American (born in Argentina)
Education: Universidad Nacional de Tucumán;
University of Illinois, Urbana
Projects: Pacific Design Center, Los Angeles (1971); World Financial
Center, New York (1981); Norwest Center, Minneapolis (1983–7); Canary
Wharf, London (1986–91); Petronas Towers, Kuala Lumpur (1992–7)
Publications: Paul Goldberger *et al.*, *Cesar Pelli: Buildings and Projects
1965–1990*, New York, 1990; Lee Edward Gray and David Walters,
Pattern and Context, Essays on Cesar Pelli, Charlotte, NC, 1992 ; Cesar
Pelli: *Selected and Current Works*, introduction by Michael J Crosbie,
Mulgrave, 1993
Exhibitions: Biennale, Venice (1976); Schindler House Gallery, Los
Angeles (1986); World Architecture Biennale, Sofia (1989); Delphi
Research Incorporated, Tokyo (1993)
Awards: Arnold W. Brunner Memorial Prize (1978); AIA Gold Medal
(1995); Award, Academia Nacional de Arquitectura/Sociedad de
Arquitectos Mexicanos, Mexico (1996)

Dominique Perrault, b.1953
Nationality: French
Education: Ecole Supérieure des Beaux-Arts, Paris; Ecole Supérieure
des Ponts et Chaussées, Paris; Ecole des Hautes Etudes en
Sciences Sociales, Paris
Projects: Higher School of Engineering (ESIEE), Marne-la-Vallée

(1984–7); Hôtel Industriel Jean-Baptiste Berlier, Paris (1986–90);
Bibliothèque Nationale, Paris (1989–96); Olympic Velodrome, Berlin
(1992); European Courts of Justice, Luxembourg (1995)
Publications: by Perrault; *Dominique Perrault*, London, 1994; on Perrault:
Michael Jacques (ed.), *La Bibliothèque Nationale de France*, Basle, 1995
Exhibitions: Institut Français d'Architecture, Paris (1992);
Biennale, Venice (1996)
Awards: Grand Prix National d'Architecture, France (1993)

Renzo Piano, b.1937
Nationality: Italian
Education: Polytechnic, Milan
Projects: Pompidou Centre, Paris (with Richard Rogers, 1971–7); Museum
for Menil Collection, Houston, Texas (1981–6); Kansai International
Airport, Osaka, Japan (1994); J M Tjibaou Cultural Centre, New
Caledonia (1997)
Publications: Paul Goldberger, *Renzo Piano and Building Workshop:
Buildings and Projects 1971–89*, New York, 1989; Peter Buchanan, *Renzo
Piano Building Workshop: Complete Works*, vols. 1–3, London, 1993–7
Exhibitions: Triennale, Milan (1967); Architectural Association, London
(1970); Centre Georges Pompidou, Paris (1987); Architectural League of
New York (1992)
Awards: Auguste Perret Prize, UIA (1978): RIBA Gold Medal (1989);
Praemium Imperiale, Japan (1995)

Demetri Porphyrios, b.1949
Nationality: Greek
Education: Princeton University
Projects: Belvedere Village, Ascot, Surrey (1989); Pitiousa Village,
Spetses, Greece (1990); New Longwall Quadrangle, Magdalen College,
Oxford (1991)
Publications: by Porphyrios: *Sources of Modern Eclecticism*, London, 1982;
Classicism is not a Style, London, 1982; *Classical Architecture*, London, 1991
Awards: Royal Fine Art Commission Award (1996)

John Portman, b.1924
Nationality: American
Education: Georgia Institute of Technology, Atlanta
Projects: Hyatt Regency Hotel, Atlanta (1967); Peachtree Harris Tower,
Peachtree Center, Atlanta (1976); office tower, One Peachtree Centre,
Atlanta (1992)
Publications: by Portman: *The Architect as Developer*, with Jonathan
Barrett, New York, 1976; *John Portman*, with Paola Riani and Paul
Goldberger, Milan, 1989; on Portman: Paul Goldberger, *GA57: John
Portman and Associates*, Tokyo, 1981
Awards: Design in Steel Award, American Iron and Steel Institute (1975);
Medal for Innovation in Hotel Design, AIA (1978)

Christian de Portzamparc, b.1944
Nationality: French
Education: Ecole Supérieure des Beaux-Arts, Paris
Projects: Paris Opera School, Nanterre (1983–7); Cité de la Musique,
Paris (1985–95); Crédit Lyonnais Tower, Lille (1996)
Publications: *Christian de Portzamparc, Institut Français d'Architecture*,
Paris, 1984; *Généalogie des formes, les designs de Christian de
Portzamparc*, Paris, 1996
Awards: Grand Prix National de l'Architecture, France (1993);
Pritzker Prize (1994)

Antoine Predock, b.1936
Nationality: American
Education: University of New Mexico, Albuquerque;
Columbia University, New York
Projects: United Blood Services Building, Albuquerque (1982); New
Mexico Heart Clinic, Albuquerque (1985); Fuller House, Scottsdale,
Arizona (1987); Mandell Weiss Forum, University of California, San
Diego campus (1987); Nelson Fine Arts Center, Arizona State University,
Tempe (1989); Zuber House, Paradise Valley, Arizona (1989); Institute of
American Indian Arts, Santa Fe (1989); Beach House, Venice, California
(1989); Las Vegas Library and Discovery Museum (1990)
Publications: Brad Collins and Juliette Robbins, *Antoine Predock
Architect*, New York, 1994; *Architectural Journeys – Antoine Predock*,
New York, 1995
Awards: AIA National Honor Award (1987, 1990)

Bart Prince, b.1947
Nationality: American
Education: Arizona State University, Tempe
Projects: Prince House, Albuquerque (1984); Spence House, Pasadena (1986); Shinenkan Pavilion, Los Angeles County Museum of Art (1988); Henry Whiting House, Sun Valley, Idaho (1989); Price House, Corona Del Mar (1989)
Publications: Christopher Mead, *Houses by Bart Prince*, Albuquerque, 1991

Wolf Prix, see entry under Coop Himmelblau

Raj Rewal, b.1934
Nationality: Indian
Education: School of Architecture, Delhi; Architectural Association, London; Brixton School of Building, London
Projects: (all New Delhi) Staff Quarters for the French Embassy (1967–9); Trade Fair Grounds (1970–4); State Trading Corporation (1976–89); SCOPE Housing Complex (1980–9); Asian Games Village (1980–2); Central Institute for Education Technology (1986–9); National Institute of Immunology (1990); World Bank Building (1993)
Publications: *Raj Rewal*, Paris, 1986; Brian Brace Taylor, *Raj Rewal*, London, 1992
Awards: Gold Medal, Indian Institute of Architects (1989); Robert Matthew Award, Commonwealth Association of Architects (1992)

Ian Ritchie, b.1947
Nationality: British
Education: Liverpool University; Polytechnic of Central London
Projects: B8 Block, Stockley Park, Heathrow, London (1988); New Leipzig Messe Central Glass Hall (1992–6)
Publications: by Ritchie: (*Well*) *Connected Architecture*, London and Berlin, 1994
Exhibitions: Grassi Museum, Leipzig (1993); Biennale, Venice (1996)
Awards: Iritecna Prize for Europe (1992); Eric Lyons Memorial Award for Housing in Europe (1992); Robert Matthew Award, Commonwealth Association of Architects (1994)

Jaquelin Taylor Robertson, b.1933
Nationality: American
Education: Yale University; Magdalen College, Oxford
Projects: (Principal of Cooper Robertson and Partners)
Henry Moore Sculpture Garden, Kansas City (1989); Ertegun Villa, Long Island (1990); New Albany Master Plan and Club House, Ohio (1992)
Publications: on Robertson: The City in Conflict, edited by C Johnson, London, 1985; by Robertson: contributor to (with R Weinstein) *Urban Design as Public Policy*, by J Barnett, New York, 1973.
Exhibitions: Institute of Architecture and Urban Studies, New York (1977)
Awards: AIA Honor Award (1988)

Richard Rogers (Lord Rogers of Riverside), b.1933
Nationality: British
Education: Architectural Association, London; Yale University
Projects: Reliance Controls Factory, Swindon (with Norman Foster, 1966); home for his parents, Wimbledon, London (1968–9); Pompidou Centre, Paris (with Renzo Piano, 1971–7); Lloyds Building, London (1978–86); Channel 4 HQ, London (1990–4); Daimler Benz offices, Potsdamerplatz, Berlin (1994); European Court of Human Rights, Strasbourg (1989–95); Master plan for Majorca (1994–)
Publications: Bryan Appleyard, *Richard Rogers, A Biography*, London, 1986; Richard Burdett, *Richard Rogers Partnership*, Milan, 1995
Exhibitions: Royal Academy, London (1986); Biennale, Venice (1991)
Awards: RIBA Gold Medal (1985); Chevalier, l'Ordre National de la Légion d'Honneur (1986); Knighthood (1991); Chevalier, l'Ordre des Arts et des Lettres (1995)

Aldo Rossi, b.1931, d. 1997
Nationality: Italian
Education: Milan Polytechnic
Projects: Gallaratese Housing, Milan (1970); San Cataldo Cemetery, Modena (1971–8); Carlo Felice Opera House, Genoa (1982); IBA Social Housing, Berlin (1989); Hotel Il Palazzo, Fukuoka, Japan (1989); Bonnefantin Museum, Maastricht (1994)
Publications: by Rossi, *L'architettura della città*, Padua, 1966; on Rossi, *Aldo Rossi: architetture 1959–1987*, ed. Alberto Ferlenga, Milan, 1987; *Aldo Rossi: The Complete Buildings and Projects 1981–1991*, London, 1992;

Aldo Rossi: architetture 1988–1992, ed. Alberto Ferlenga, Milan, 1993; *Aldo Rossi: Drawings and Projects*, ed. Morris Adjmi et al., New York, 1993; *Aldo Rossi: opera completa 1993–1996*, ed. Alberto Ferlenga, Milan, 1996
Exhibitions: Triennale, Milan (1960); Eidgenössische Technische Hochschule, Zurich (1973); Institute for Architecture and Urban Studies, New York (1976); ICA, London (1983); Palazzina dei Giardini, Modena, and Rocca Paolina, Perugia (1983)
Awards: Pritzker Prize (1990)

RoTo Architects, comprising
Michael Rotondi, b.1949
Nationality: American
Education: Southern California Institute of Architecture
Clark Stevens, b. 1963
Nationality: American
Education: University of Michigan; Harvard University Graduate School
Projects: (1976–91, Michael Rotondi in partnership with Thom Mayne in Morphosis, see entry under Morphosis for buildings from this period); (Principal of RoTo Architects) Carlson-Reges Residence, Los Angeles (1992–5); Nicola Restaurant, Los Angeles (1992–5)
Publications: *RoTo*, Michigan Architecture Papers I , Ann Arbor,. 1996
Awards: Award in Architecture, American Academy and Institute of Fine Arts (1992)

Joshua Schweitzer, b.1953
Nationality: American
Education: University of Kansas; Pitzer College, Claremont
Projects: Venue Restaurant, Los Angeles (1993); California Chicken Cafe, Los Angeles (1992); The Monument, Joshua Tree (1987–90)
Publications: in: *Architects House Themselves*, New York, 1994; P Jodidio, *Contemporary California Architects*, Cologne, 1995
Exhibitions: Pacific Design Center, Los Angeles (1994) ; Dansk Arkitektur Center – Gammel Dok, Copenhagen (1997)

Denise Scott Brown, see entry under Venturi, Scott Brown

Scogin Elam and Bray, comprising:
Mack Scogin, b.1943
Nationality: American
Education: Georgia Institute of Technology, Atlanta
Merrill Elam, b.1943
Nationality: American
Education: Georgia Institute of Technology, Atlanta
Lloyd Bray, b.1951
Nationality: American
Education: Tulane University, New Orleans
Projects: Chmar House, Atlanta (1989); Law Library, Arizona State University, Tempe (1993)
Publications: Mark Linder (ed.), *Scogin, Elam and Bray: Critical Architecture/Architectural Criticism*, New York, 1992
Exhibitions: High Museum, Atlanta (1990); GA Gallery, Tokyo (1994)
Awards: AIA National Honor Award (1988, 1989, 1992, 1993)

Kazuo Shinohara, b.1925
Nationality: Japanese
Education: Tokyo Institute of Technology
Projects: Cubic Forest House, Kawasaki (1971); House and Art Gallery, Karuizawa (1975); Tokyo Institute of Technology (1987); K2 Building, Osaka (1989–92)
Publications: *Kazuo Shinohara: architecte japonais – 30 maisons contemporaines*, Paris, 1980; *Kazuo Shinohara*, New York, 1981; *Kazuo Shinohara*, introduction by Irmtraud Schaarschmidt-Richtor, Berlin, 1994
Exhibitions: Société Française des Architectes, Paris (1979–80); Institute for Architecture and Urban Studies, New York, and tour in US and Canada (1981–3); Architectural Institute of Japan, Tokyo (1984); Columbia University, New York (1991)
Awards: Architectural Institute of Japan, Annual Prize (1972)

Short, Ford and Associates
(now Short and Associates)
Charles Alan Short, b.1955
Nationality: British
Education: Cambridge University; Harvard University Graduate School
Brian Ford, b.1949
Nationality: British
Education: Canterbury College of Art, School of Architecture, Kent;

Royal College of Art, London
Projects: New Farson's Brewery, Malta (1990); Gateway House, Leicester (1991); Sustainable city design including low-energy housing for Leicester City Council (1992–); Queen's Building, School of Engineering and Manufacture, De Montfort University, Leicester (1993)
Publications: in: Jeremy Myerson, *New Public Architecture*, London, 1996; Charles Jencks, *The Architecture of the Jumping Universe*, London, 1995

Claudio Silvestrin, b.1954
Nationality: Italian
Education: Architectural Association, London
Projects: Neuendorf House, Majorca (with John Pawson, 1989); Johan Menswear Shop, Graz (1992); White Cube Gallery, London (1993); Calvin Klein Collection Store, Paris (1997)

John Simpson
Nationality: British
Education: Bartlett School of Architecture, London University
Projects: Master plan for Paternoster Square, London (1990); London Bridge City, project, London (1990); Ashfold House, Sussex (1991); project for Market Hall, Poundbury (1991)
Publications: in *Paternoster Square, The Masterplan*, London (no date)

SITE see entry under James Wines

Alvaro Siza, b.1933
Nationality: Portuguese
Education: University of Porto
Projects: (all Portugal unless otherwise stated) Magalhaes House, Porto (1967–70); Caxinas Housing Estate, Villa do Con (1970–2); Pinto & Sotto Mayor Bank, Oliveira de Azemis (1971–4); Banco Borges e Irmao, Succursal de Villa do Conde (1982–6); Centro Galego de Arte Contemporaneo, Santiago de Compostela, Spain (1994)
Publications: by Siza: *Escrits*, Barcelona, 1994; on Siza: Adolf Max Vogt, *Alvaro Siza: Architektur 1940–1980*, Berlin, Frankfurt and Vienna, 1980; *Alvaro Siza: Works and Projects 1954–1992*, ed José Paulo dos Santos, Barcelona, 1993; Brigitte Fleck, *Alvaro Siza*, London, 1995; *Alvaro Siza 1986–1995*, ed. Luiz Trigueiros, Lisbon, 1995; *Alvaro Siza: opere e progetti*, ed Pedro de Llano and Carlos Castanheira, Milan, 1996
Exhibitions: Centre Georges Pompidou, Paris, and Galeria de Exposiciones del MOPU, Madrid (1990); RIBA, London (1991)
Awards: Portuguese Architects' Association Award (1987); Gold medal, Colegio de Architectos, Spain (1988); Gold Medal, Alvar Aalto Foundation (1988); Pritzker Prize (1992)

Skidmore, Owings and Merrill, comprising:
Louis Skidmore, b.1897, d.1962
Nationality: American
Education: Massachusetts Institute of Technology, Cambridge
Nathaniel Owings, b.1903, d.1984
Nationality: American
Education: University of Illinois; Cornell University
John Merrill, b.1896, d.1975
Nationality: American
Education: Massachusetts Institute of Technology, Cambridge
Gordon Bunshaft, b.1896, d.1990
Nationality: American
Education: Massachusetts Institute of Technology, Cambridge
Projects: Lever House, New York (Bunshaft, 1952); John Hancock Center, Chicago (1965–70); Sears Tower, Chicago (1974); Hajj Airport Terminal, Jeddah (1980); National Commercial Bank, Jeddah (Bunshaft, 1983); Gas Company Tower, Los Angeles (1992)
Publications: *Skidmore Owings & Merrill: Architecture and Urbanism 1973–1983*, introduction by Albert Bush-Brown, London, 1984; Carol Herselle Krinsky, *Gordon Bunshaft of Skidmore, Owings & Merrill*, Cambridge, Mass., and London, 1988; *Skidmore, Owings & Merrill: Selected and Current Works*, Mulgrave, 1995
Exhibitions: Museum of Modern Art, New York (1944, 1950, 1979)
Awards: Skidmore: AIA Gold Medal (1957); Owings: AIA Gold Medal (1983); Merrill: AIA Honor Award (1968); Bunshaft: Gold Medal, American Academy and Institute of Art and Letters (1982); Pritzker Prize (1988)

Thomas Gordon Smith, b.1948
Nationality: American
Education: University of California at Berkeley; American Academy in Rome
Projects: Vitruvian Villa, South Bend, Indiana (1989–90); House in Central Illinois (1993–)
Publications: by Smith: *Classical Architecture: Rule and Invention*, 1988
Exhibitions: Biennale, Venice (1980, 1982); Deutsches Architekturmuseum, Frankfurt (1984); IBM Gallery, New York (1987)

Luigi Snozzi, b. 1932
Nationality: Swiss
Education: Federal Polytechnic, Zurich
Projects: Casa Popolare, Locarno (1966); Library, Thun (1982); Bernasconi House, Carona, Switzerland (1989); Elementary School, Restoration of St Augustin convent, Monte Carasso (1993)
Publications: Pierre-Alain Croset, *Luigi Snozzi, 1957–1984*, Zurich, London and Milan, 1984; *Luigi Snozzi: costruzioni e progetti 1958–1993*, ed. Peter Disch, Lugano, 1994; Claude Lichtenstein, *Luigi Snozzi*, Basle, 1997
Exhibitions: Eidgenössische Technische Hochschule, Zurich (1975); 9H Gallery, London (1986); Suomen Rakennustaiteen Museo, Helsinki (1990)

Philippe Starck, b.1949
Nationality: French
Education: Ecole Nissim de Camondo, Paris
Projects: Café Costes interior, Paris (1984); Royalton Hotel interior, New York (1988); Paramount Hotel interior, New York (1990); Unhex Nani Nani Building, Tokyo (1989); Asahi Beer Azumabashi Hall, Tokyo (1989)
Publications: *Philippe Starck*, Cologne, 1991; *Philippe Starck, Interior Design*, USA, March 1991 (special supplement)
Exhibitions: National Museum of Modern Art, Kyoto (1986); Seibu Museum of Art, Tokyo (1987); Design Museum, London (1993)
Awards: Chevalier de l'Ordre des Arts et des Lettres, France (1985)

Robert A M Stern, b.1939
Nationality: American
Education: Columbia University, New York; Yale University
Projects: House in Chilmark, Martha's Vineyard, Mass. (1979–83); Observatory Hill Dining Hall, University of Virginia, Charlottesville (1984); The Hamptons housing development, Lexington (1987); Walt Disney World Casting Center, Lake Buena Vista (1989); Banana Republic Store, Chicago (1991); Golf Resort, Tochigi Prefecture, Japan (1990–)
Publications: by Stern: *New Directions in American Architecture*, New York, 1969; on Stern: Elizabeth Kraft (ed.), *Robert A M Stern: Buildings and Projects 1987–92*, New York, 1992; *Robert A M Stern: Buildings*, New York, 1996
Exhibitions: Biennale, Venice (1976, 1980, 1996); Newberger Museum, State University of New York, Purchase (1982)
Awards: AIA National Honor award (1980, 1985, 1990, 1991)

James Stirling Michael Wilford and Associates
(Michael Wilford and Partners from 1993) comprising
James Frazer Stirling, b.1926, d.1992
Nationality: British
Education: Liverpool University; School of Town Planning and Regional Research, London
Michael Wilford
Nationality: British
Education: Kingston Technical School; Northern Polytechnic School of Architecture, London; Regent Street Polytechnic, London
Projects: Engineering Faculty, University of Leicester (1959–63) with James Gowan; History Faculty, Cambridge University (1964–7); Andrew Melville Hall, University of St Andrews (1964–8); Low-cost Housing, Runcorn New Town (1967–76); Darby City Centre (plan) (1970); Olivetti Headquarters, Milton Keynes (1971); Neue Staatsgalerie, Stuttgart (1977–84); Tate Gallery, Liverpool (1984–8); Clore Gallery at the Tate, London (1985–6); Transport Interchange, Bilbao (1985); Music School and Theatre Academy, Stuttgart (1986–95); Temasek Polytechnic, Singapore (1991); Braun Research and Production HQ, Melsungen, Germany (1992)
Publications: by Stirling: *James Stirling*, with Robert Maxwell, New York, 1983; on Stirling: *James Stirling: Buildings and Projects 1950–1980*, ed. Peter Arnell and Ted Bickford, New York, 1984; *James Stirling and Michael Wilford*, London, 1994
Exhibitions: Galleria Comunale d'Arte Moderna, Bologna (1990)
Awards: Alvar Aalto Medal, Finland (1978); RIBA Gold Medal (1980); Pritzker Prize (1981); Thomas Jefferson Medal (1986)

Hugh Stubbins, b.1912
Nationality: American
Education: Georgia Institute of Technology, Atlanta; Harvard University
Projects: Citicorp Center, New York (1976–8); MM21, Yokohama, Japan (1988–93)
Publications: by Stubbins: *The Design Experience*, New York, 1976; on Stubbins: Diane M. Ludman, *Hugh Stubbins and his Associates: the First Fifty Years*, Cambridge, Mass., 1986
Exhibitions: Museum of Modern Art, New York (1946); Harvard School of Design (1988)
Awards: AIA National Honor Award (1979); Thomas Jefferson Medal (1979)

Helmut Swiczinsky, see entry under Coop Himmelblau

Shin Takamatsu, b.1948
Nationality: Japanese
Education: Kyoto University
Projects: Origin I and III, Kyoto (1981-2); Kirin Plaza Building, Osaka (1987); Syntax, Kyoto (1988-90)
Publications: Xavier Guillot, *Shin Takamatsu*, Paris, 1989; *Shin Takamatsu: Architecture and Nothingness*, Milan, 1996
Exhibitions: Biennale, Venice (1985, 1991); Aedes Gallery, Berlin (1991); San Francisco Museum of Modern Art, and tour to Osaka and Tokyo (1993); Tokyo Station Gallery and Kyoto Municipal Museum of Art (1995)
Awards: Annual Prize, Architectural Institute of Japan (1989)

Takasaki Masaharu, b.1953
Nationality: Japanese
Education: Meijo University
Projects: Crystal Light Building, Tokyo (1987); Zero Cosmology Building, Kagoshima, Kyushi (1989-91)
Publications : *Takasaki Masaharu: An Architecture of Cosmology*, Princeton, 1997
Exhibitions: Sydney Institute of Technology (1988); Plaza Gallery, Tokyo (1995)
Awards: Japan Institute of Architects 'Best Young Architect' (1996)

Minoru Takeyama, b.1934
Nationality: Japanese
Education: Waseda University, Tokyo; Harvard University
Projects: Ichiban-Kan, Tokyo (1969); Hotel Beverley Tom, Hokkaido (1972-4); Nakamura Hospital, Sapporo (1979-81); Tokyo International Port Terminal (1991)
Publications: *Minoru Takeyama*, London, 1995
Exhibitions: Bienal, São Paulo (1957); The Work of Minoru Takeyama, toured US (1989-90)
Awards: Grand Prix, São Paulo Bienal (1957); Special Prize, World Biennale of Architecture, Sofia (1981)

Kenzo Tange, b.1913
Nationality: Japanese
Education: University of Tokyo
Projects: Peace Memorial and Museum, Hiroshima (1949–55); Prefectural Government Office, Kagawa (1955–8); St Mary's Cathedral, Tokyo (1961–4); gymnasium complex for Tokyo Olympics (1961–4); Yamanashi Press and Radio Centre, Kofu (1961–7); Yokohama Museum of Art, Kanagawa (1983–9); Tokyo City Hall (1991)
Publications: by Tange: *Katsura – Tradition and Creation in Japanese Architecture*, Tokyo and New Haven, 1960; *A Plan for Tokyo*, Tokyo, 1961; *Ise – Prototype of Japanese Architecture*, 1962, English edn., Cambridge, Mass., 1965; on Tange: R. Boyd, *Kenzo Tange*, New York and London, 1962; Udo Kultermann (ed.), *Kenzo Tange 1946–1969: Architecture and Urban Design*, Zurich and London, 1970; *Kenzo Tange: 40 ans d'urbanisme et d'architecture*, Tokyo, 1987; Udo Kultermann, *Kenzo Tange* Barcelona, 1989
Exhibitions: Ecole des Beaux-Arts, Paris (1986)
Awards: Special Prize, Architectural Institute of Japan (1965, 1970); RIBA Gold Medal (1965); AIA Gold Medal (1966); Légion d'Honneur, France (1966); Gold Medal, Académie d'Architecture, France (1973)

Yoshio Taniguchi, b.1937
Nationality: Japanese
Education: Keio University; Harvard University
Projects: Kanazawa Municipal Library (1978); Ken Domon Museum of Photography (1983); Tokyo Sea Life Park (1989); Municipal Museum of Art, Toyota, Aichi Prefecture (1995)
Publications: Yohio Taniguchi, *The Architecture of Yoshio Taniguchi*, Kyoto, 1996; Special issue of *Japan Architect*, No 21, 1996
Awards: Japan Academy of Arts (1987); Togo Murano Memorial Prize (1994)

Quinlan Terry, b.1937 (partner with Raymond Erith (d. 1973), Erith and Terry Architects)
Nationality: British
Education: Architectural Association, London; British Academy in Rome
Projects: Richmond Riverside, Surrey (1985–7); Ionic Villa (1988), Veneto Villa (1989), Gothick Villa (1989), Regent's Park, London; Howard Building, Downing College, Cambridge (1989)
Publications: by Terry: *Architects Anonymous*; London, 1994; on Terry: Clive Aslet, *Quinlan Terry: The Revival of Architecture*, London, 1986

Tsao and McKown, comprising:
Calvin Tsao, b.1952
Nationality: British
Education: University of California at Berkeley; Harvard University
Zack McKown, b.1952
Nationality: American
Education: University of South Carolina; Harvard University
Projects: Ai-Jian Da Lou residential tower, Shanghai (1988); IMC Building, Kuala Lumpur (1994); Habitat II, Singapore (1995); Suntec City, Singapore (in progress)
Publications: in: Jonathan Glancey and Richard Bryant, *The New Moderns*, New York, 1990; Herausgegeben von Angelika Taschen, *New York Interiors*, Cologne, 1997

Bernard Tschumi, b.1944
Nationality: French-Swiss
Education: Federal Institute of Technology, Zurich
Projects: Master Plan, Parc de la Villette, Paris (1984-90); Glass Video Gallery, Groningen (1990)
Publications: by Tschumi: *Architecture and Disjunction: Collected Essays 1975–90*, Cambridge, Mass., and London, 1994; on Tschumi: *A+U*, special issue, March 1994
Exhibitions: Architectural Association, London (1979); Internazionale Bauausstellung, Berlin (1984); Museum of Modern Art, New York (1994)
Awards: Grand Prix National d'Architecture, France (1996)

Oswald Mathias Ungers, b.1926
Nationality: German
Education: Technische Hochschule, Karlsruhe
Projects: Architecture Museum, Frankfurt (1979–84); Messe Gate House, Frankfurt (1984); German Embassy, Washington DC (1995)
Publications: Heinrich Klotz, *O. M. Ungers, 1951–1984, Bauten und Projekte*, Brauschweig and Wiesbaden, 1985
Exhibitions: Bienal, São Paulo (1957); Biennale, Venice (1976, 1991), Documenta 8, Kassel (1987); International Architecture Exhibition, Tokyo (1988)
Awards: Grand Prize, Bund Deutscher Architekten (1987); Rhenan Prize, Strasbourg (1989)

Ushida Findlay, comprising:
Eisaku Ushida
Nationality: Japanese
Education: University of Tokyo
Kathryn Findlay
Nationality: Scottish
Education: Architectural Association, London; University of Tokyo
Projects: Echo Chamber, Tokyo (1989); Chiaroscuro House, Tokyo (1993); Truss Wall House, Tokyo (1993); Soft and Hairy House, Tsukuba (1994); Kaizankyo, Wakayama (1994); '1009 Footpath', Adelaide Festival (1996)
Publications: Special issue of *Kenchiku Bunka*, 1994; *Parallel Landscapes*, Tokyo, 1996; Leon van Schaik and Paul Carter (eds), *Ushida Findlay – 2G Monograph*, Barcelona (forthcoming, 1998)
Exhibitions: Architecture Foundation, London (1994); Gallery MA, Tokyo (1996)
Awards: Architectural Design Commendation, Architectural Institute of Japan (1996)

Jørn Utzon, b.1918
Nationality: Danish
Education: Royal Academy of Arts, Copenhagen
Projects: Sydney Opera House (1957–73); National Assembly Building,
Kuwait (1972); Bagsvaerd Church, Copenhagen (1976)
Publications: by Utzon: *Sydney Opera House*, Sydney, 1962; *Church at
Bagsvaerd*, Tokyo, 1971; on Utzon: *Jørn Utzon, Houses in Fredensborg*,
Berlin, 1991; *Sydney Opera House*, London, 1995
Exhibitions: Museum of Modern Art, New York (1979)
Awards: Gold Medal, Royal Academy of Arts, Copenhagen (1945); Gold
Medal, Royal Australian Institute of Architects (1973); RIBA Gold Medal
(1978); Alvar Aalto Medal (1982)

Ben van Berkel, b.1957
Nationality: Dutch
Education: Rietveld Academie, Amsterdam, Architectural
Association, London
Projects: Karbouw Office and Workshops, Amersfoort (1992);
Erasmus Bridge, near Rotterdam (1996)
Publications: Ben van Berkel: Mobile Forces, Berlin, 1994
Exhibitions: Gallery Aedes, Berlin (1993); Puntgaaf Gallery,
Groningen (1994)

Erick Van Egeraat, b.1956
Nationality: Dutch
Education: Technical University, Delft
Projects: Boompjes Pavilion, Rotterdam (with Mecanoo, 1990);
Nationale Nederlanden and ING Bank, Budapest (1992–4)
Publications: in *Contemporary European Architects*, by P Jodidio,
Cologne, 1996
Exhibitions: Biennale, Venice (1991); Colegio Oficial de Arquitectos de
Madrid (1992)

Venturi, Scott Brown and Associates, comprising:
Robert Venturi, b.1925
Nationality: American
Education: Princeton University; American Academy in Rome
Denise Scott Brown, b.1931
Nationality: American (born in Zambia)
Education: University of Witwatersrand, Johannesburg; University of
Pennsylvania, Philadelphia
Projects: North Pennsylvania Visiting Nurses Association Headquarters,
Ambler (1960); Guild House, Philadelphia (1960); Vanna Venturi House,
Philadelphia (1963); Franklin Court, Philadelphia (1976); Brant House,
Bermuda (1977); Gordon Wu Hall, Princeton University (1983); Seattle
Art Museum (1985); Sainsbury Wing, National Gallery, London (1986);
Children's Museum of Houston (1991–) Reedy Creek Emergency Services
HQ, Orlando, Florida (1992);
Publications: by Venturi: *Complexity and Contradiction in Architecture*,
New York, 1966; *Learning from Las Vegas*, with Denise Scott Brown and
Steven Izenour, Cambridge, Mass., 1972; *A View from the Campidoglio:
Selected Essays 1953–84*, with Denise Scott Brown, New York, 1984;
*Iconography and Electronics Upon a Generic Architecture: A View from
the Drafting Room*, Cambridge, Mass., 1996; on Venturi: Stanislaus von
Moos, *Venturi Rauch and Scott Brown: Buildings and Projects*, New
York, 1987; *Venturi Rauch and Scott Brown Associates, on Houses and
Housing*, London, 1992
Exhibitions: Pennsylvania Academy of Fine Arts, Philadelphia (1975);
University of Illinois, Urbana, and tour in US (1984)
Awards: Arnold W. Brunner Memorial Prize (1973); AIA Honor Award and
Medal (1977, 1978); Pritzker Architecture Prize (1991); National Medal of
Arts, US Presidential Award (1992)

Rafael Viñoly
Nationality: Argentinian
Education: University of Buenos Aires
Projects: John Jay College of Criminal Justice (phase I), New York (1988);
Lehman College, Physical Education Facility, New York (1994);
Tokyo International Forum (1990–6)
Publications: in *SD*, March 1997, *Rafael Viñoly Selected Projects*,
New York, no date
Awards: AIA New York Chapter Medal of Honor (1995)

Von Gerkan, Marg and Partners, comprising:
Meinhard von Gerkan, b.1935
Nationality: German
Education: University of Berlin; Technical University of Brunswick
Volkwin Marg, b.1936
Nationality: German
Education: University of Berlin; Technical University of Brunswick
Projects: Desert settlements, Taima and Sulayyll, Saudi Arabia (1980); Low
energy house, IBA Berlin (1984); Glass roof, Museum of Hamburg History
(1989); Buildings for Premier TV channel, Hamburg (1994); New Trade Fair,
Leipzig (1996)
Publications: *Von Gerkan, Marg & Partners*, London, 1993; Volkwin Marg,
Neue Messe Leipzig/New Trade Fair Leipzig, Basle, 1997
Exhibitions: Berlinische Galerie, Berlin (1995); Venice Biennale (1996)
Awards: USITT Architectural Honour Award

Michael Wilford, see entry under James Stirling Michael Wilford
and Associates

Colin St John Wilson, b.1922
Nationality: British
Education: University of Cambridge; Bartlett School of Architecture,
University of London
Projects: Coventry Cathedral competition design (with Peter Carter, 1951);
Housing Estate, Bentham Road, Hackney, London (1954); annex to the School
of Architecture, Cambridge (with Alex Hardy, 1957–9); Harvey Court,
Gonville and Caius College, Cambridge (with Sir Leslie Martin, 1957–62); 3
libraries, Manor Road, Oxford University (with Sir Leslie Martin, 1959–64);
British Library, St Pancras, London (1963–present)
Publications: by Wilson: *Architectural Reflections*, London, 1992; *The
Other Tradition in Modern Architecture*, London, 1995
Exhibitions: Architectural Association, London (1951, 1954); Royal
Academy, London (1984); RIBA, London (1997)

James Wines, b.1932
Nationality: American
Education: Syracuse University, New York
Projects: (founded SITE in 1969, in partnership with Emilio Sousa, Alison
Sky and Michelle Stone since 1973) Best Products Showrooms various
locations (1972–84); Ghost Parking Lot, Hampden, Conn. (1978); Avenue
Five, Seville Expo (1992); Tennessee Aquatorium, Chattanooga (1993);
Trawsfynydd, North Wales (1994)
Publications: by Wines: *De-Architecture*, New York, 1987; *SITE*, with
Herbert Muschamp, New York, 1989; on Wines: Pierre Restany and Bruno
Zevi, *SITE: Architecture as Art*, London and New York, 1980
Exhibitions: Biennale, Venice (1975) Museum of Modern Art, New York
(1975, 1979); Virginia Museum of Art, Richmond (1980–1); Galerie Cour de
Mai, Paris, and tour to Fiesole and Lyons (1988–9)

Minoru Yamasaki, b.1912
Nationality: American
Education: University of Washington, Seattle; New York University
Projects: Pruitt Igoe housing, St Louis (1954); Michigan Consolidated Gas
Company building, Detroit (1963); World Trade Center, New York (1972–3);
World Trade Centre, Bangkok (1988)
Publications: by Yamasaki: *A Life in Architecture*, Tokyo and New York, 1979;
on Yamasaki: Lamia Doumato, *Minoru Yamasaki*, Monticello, 1986
Exhibitions: World's Fair, Brussels (1958); Architectural League of New
York, and tour to Indianapolis, Honolulu and San Francisco (1959–60);
Oakland University, Rochester, Michigan (1974)
Awards: Architectural Institute of Japan Award (1957)

Ken Yeang, b.1948
Nationality: Malaysian
Education: Cambridge University; Architectural Association, London
Projects: (with Tengku Robert Hamzah as TR Hamzah & Yeang Sendirian
Berhad) MBF Tower, Penang (1990–3); Menara Mesiniaga tower (1992);
Tokyo-Nara Tower, Japan (1997–)
Publications: by Yeang: *Tropical Urban Regionalism: Building in a South-
East Asian City*, Singapore, 1987; *Designing with Nature*, New York, 1995;
The Skyscraper Bioclimatically Considered, London, 1996; on Yeang:
Robert Powell, *Ken Yeang: Rethinking the Environmental Filter*,
Singapore, 1989; *Bioclimatic Skyscrapers/Ken Yeang*, essays by Alan
Balfour and Ivor Richards, London, 1994
Awards: International Award, Royal Australian Institute of Architecture
(1995); Aga Khan Award (1996)

Acknowledgements

Illustration Acknowledgements

Photographs courtesy of the architects unless otherwise stated. Figures below refer to page numbers:
Acme Photo: 310; AKG/Dieter E. Hoppe: 13; J.Apicella: 375; Arcaid/Alex Bartel: 72-3; Arcaid/Reiner Blunck: 319; Arcaid/Richard Bryant: 23(r), 27(r), 33, 67, 74, 77, 94, 95, 130, 132, 184, 185, 186-7, 188, 189(t), 194-5, 211, 225, 234-5, 285, 304, 312, 314-5, 373, 390-1, 460(b), 464, 474, 481, 482-3 , 485; Arcaid/Niall Clutton: 152-3; Arcaid/Jeremy Cockayne: 274; Arcaid/Richard Einzig: 18(b), 70,71; Arcaid/Gisela Erlachet: 281, Arcaid/Mark Fiennes: 84-5, 141; Arcaid/Dennis Gilbert: 324; Arcaid/Martine Hamilton-Knight: 288(l); Arcaid/Hiroshi Hara: 450(b); Arcaid/Ben Johnson: 90(t), 284(b), 476; Arcaid/Nicholas Kane: 275(b); Arcaid/Ian Lambot: 12(b), 368, 478-9; Arcaid/John Linden: 278-9, 325,477; Arcaid/John Utson: 276; Arcaid/Richard Waite: 90(b); Archipress/Frank Eustache: 100, 270, 271(l); Bastin & Evrard: 226(t); Tom Bernard: 148, 174(t); D. Biggi: 60(t); Fundacion del Museo Guggenheim Bilbao: 7; Helen Binet/Black Dog Publishing Limited: 280(l); Hedrich-Blessing: 62, 63, 378(r); Hedrich-Blessing/Nick Merrick: 384; Tom Bonner: 256-7, 410-11, 412, 413, 415(r), 416-7, 418, 419, 469; Bitta Bredt: 214; Stefania Bretta: 56; Judith Bromley: 164-5; Steven Brooke: 351; Fondation pour l'architecture, Brussels: 169; Richard Bryant: 190(t); Tim Buchman: 162,163; Robert Canfield: 53,54,55; Center for Regenerative Studies: 301; Ken Champlin:29(m); Martin Charles: 75,88; Richard Cheek: 161; Peter Cook: 20(m), 30(t), 91; Mark Cohn: 173; Commerell: 222; S. Couturier: 101; Whitney Cox: 168; Hayes Davidson: 472(b); Hayes Davidson/Chorley Handford: 472(t); Hayes Davidson/Tom Miller: 389(b); Richard Davies; 29(r), 81(t), 82(b), 83(r),96,97; J.P Delagarde: 98(b); M. Denancé: 135(l), 291; Tod Eberle: 20(b), 120; Esto Photographics/Peter Aaron: 17(b), 29(l), 167, 243, 328, 356-7,360,362-3; Esto Photographics/Ezra Stoller: 308-9,316,372; Esto Photographics/Jeff Goldberg: 23(r), 136-7, 202, 204-5, 206, 207, 311(r), 352-3,354; Esto Photographics/Tim Griffith: 405; Esto Photographics/Peter Mauss: 183, 361; Georges Fessy: 134,135(r); Mark Fiennes/Duchy of Cornwall: 147; Dick Frank: 10, 203; Katsuaki Furudate 32(l), 267(l), 458, 459 (r); Gaston: 98(t); Fred George Photography: 379; Dennis Gilbert: 25(t), 81(b), 82(t), 255, 285-6, 389(t); Gilman Paper Company: 19(l); Richard Glover: 131(t); John Gollings: 320; Gmurzynska Gallery: 307(l); Enea Gregotti: 57; Paul Hester: 120-3; Hiroyki Hirai: 124,456; Kanji Hiwatashi:104; Wolfgang Hoyt: 382; Franz Hubmann: 192; Eduard Hueber: 61,423; Tim Hursley: 41(r), 121, 122, 123, 128, 1749b), 175,176, 197,220, 221, 258, 259, 262, 264-5, 318, 324, 336, 337, 340, 343-4, 347, 348, 349, 350, 402-3, 424, 427; Yasuhiro Ishimoto: 358, 359, 445, 449; Aga Kahn Trust for Culture: 226(b), 228, 229, 231, 244; Barbara Karant: 378(l); Christoph Kichener: 131(b); Ken Kirkwood: 78,79; Toshiharu Kitajima: 436,437, 438(r); Balthazar Korab: 18(m); Ian Lambot: 26(l), 386, 387,388,473; Lourdes Legorreta: 238; Dieter Leistner: 65; Jane Lidz: 385; Janne Linders: 327; Duccio Malagamba: 58,59; Antonio Martinelli: 267(r); Mitsuo Matsuoka 110, 114(l); Norman McGrath: 22(r), 171, 179, 196, 376, 381(r); Jean Marie Monthiers: 321, 322-3; James H. Morris: 80; Grant Mudford: 404, 408, 409, 410(b), 420(b), 425; Osamu Murai: 31, 394-5, 432, 433, 434-5; Pino Musi: 52,550-1; Grazia Neri: 40(r); Nacsa & Partners: 430, 461; Tomio Ohashi: 440, 441, 442-3, 444, 446-7; Eamon OMohany: 296(b); Shigeo Ogawa: 329(r); Taisuke Ogawa/Shinkenchiku-Sha: 439; Paschall/Taylor:180,181; Richard Payne: 377, 380; Erhard Pfeiffer: 426; Mark Portman: 374(l); Salas Portugal: 128, 240-1; Paul Raftery: 266; Uwe Rau: 471; Jo Reid & John Peck: 89, 92-3, 268; Retoria: 460(t); Christian Richters: 25(b),34, 35, 43, 44-5, 213, 252, 277, 330; Simo Rista: 17(t); Rocky Mountain Institute: 300; Jordi Sarra: 269; Hans Sauter: 462; Mikio Sekita: 125; Masao Arai, Shinkenchiku-Sha: 452-3; Shinkenchiku-Sha: 105, 106-7, 126-7, 272-3, 275(t), 450(t), 451, 463; Julius Shulman: 27(l); Jim Simmons/Annette del Zoppo: 338; Stephen Simpson: 344; Margherita Spiluttini: 138(b),139, 218-9; Tim Street-Porter: 20(t), 68, 30(b), 262, 396, 401; Morley Von Sternberg: 76; The Stock Market: jacket; Studio Hollein/Arch. Sina Baniahmad: 193; Hisao Suzuki: 326; Sygma/C. Carrion: 470; Sygma/G. Giasanti: 486; Sygma/Daniel Giry: 480(t); Sygma/van Hasselt: 480(b); Sygma/Derek Hudson: 475; Victoria & Albert Museum: 215; View/Peter Cook: 15(t), 133, 292, 293, 406-7, 467; View/Dennis Gilbert: 86, 154; Collection Viollet: 10; Ingrid Voth-Awslinger 60(b); Paul Warchol: 332, 333; Matt Wargo: 22(m), 198, 199, 364; Alan Weintraub: 260-1; Hans Welermann: 329; Alfred Wolf: 317; Shuji Yamada: 457; Nigel Young: 189(b), 190(b); Alo Zanetta: 46(b), 47, 49; Gerald Zugmann: 201, 216, 217; Kim Zwarts: 420(t), 421.

Author's Acknowledgements

Good editors are rare these days and I have been fortunate to have had several on this project. David Jenkins, Editorial Director at Phaidon, has made a substantial contribution, suggesting timely examples to make chapters more comprehensive, helping to clarify each of the arguments, giving the book a central focus. Working through a laborious, but extremely constructive process of rewrites, each of the sixteen chapters was honed to achieve the proper balance between historical background, theory, and the teasing out of the legible expression of each in appropriate examples. Senior Editor Vivian Constantinopoulos assisted in the process, particularly with the chapters on Post-Modernism and Deconstructivism. I am grateful to both David and Vivian for their perseverance. The large number of examples that have been used over the broad spectrum of issues that comprise the book, required extensive research and I wish to thank Eleanor Mercado for her invaluable assistance and thoroughness in this task. Jemima Rellie, at Phaidon, has also been exceptionally resourceful in picture research, tracking down hard-to-find photographs that contribute to a better understanding of the text. Stuart Smith, who designed and laid out the book, worked painstakingly to ensure that text and image worked together, and brought the whole thing to life.Finally, the architects and office archivists who have contributed material are too numerous to mention here, but they all have my gratitude for their cooperation.

The publishers would also like to thank Kenneth Powell and Clare Melhuish for reading the manuscript and offering their advice and editorial input during the course of its preparation.

Author's Note

This book started as a series of lectures entitled 'Contemporary Issues in Architecture' at King Faisal University in Saudi Arabia, begun in 1980, given in similar format at several institutions over 37 consecutive terms ever since. The popularity of the course and the lack of a suitable comprehensive text, as well as the staggering amounts of information generated by the rapid pace of change in the past 17 years, caused the subject matter and the sources used in the course to increase accordingly, prompting the idea of a single volume source. David Jenkins, Editorial Director at Phaidon, with his breadth of knowledge of the contemporary scene recommended additions to an already substantial body of material, helping to further refine the arguments, bringing the examples up to date and tightening the thread between the various lectures to focus them into various facets of a single narrative.

512

Phaidon Press Limited
Regent's Wharf
All Saints Street
London N1 9PA

First published 1997

© 1997 Phaidon Press Limited

ISBN 0 7148 3617 6

A CIP catalogue record for this book is
available from the British Library

Jacket illustration: Composite panoramic
view of Las Vegas

Printed in Italy